UNDERGROUND PASSAGES

ANARCHIST RESISTANCE CULTURE,
1848–2011

Underground Passages: Anarchist Resistance Culture, 1848–2011
© 2014 Jesse Cohn.

This edition © 2014 AK Press (Oakland, Edinburgh, Baltimore).
ISBN: 978-1-84935-201-7 | E-ISBN: 978-1-84935-202-4
Library of Congress Control Number: 2014940772

AK Press	AK Press
674-A 23rd Street	PO Box 12766
Oakland, CA 94612	Edinburgh EH8 9YE
USA	Scotland
www.akpress.org	www.akuk.com
akpress@akpress.org	ak@akedin.demon.co.uk

The above addresses would be delighted to provide you with the latest AK Press distribution catalog, which features the several thousand books, pamphlets, zines, audio and video products, and stylish apparel published and/or distributed by AK Press. Alternatively, visit our websites for the complete catalog, latest news, and secure ordering.

Cover design by Kate Khatib | manifestor.org/design
Printed in the USA on acid-free paper.

Previous page: illustration by "Seth" for *A Voz do Trabalhador*, May 1, 1913.

The production of this book was made possible in part by a generous donation from the Anarchist Archives Project.

UNDERGROUND PASSAGES
ANARCHIST RESISTANCE CULTURE, 1848–2011

JESSE COHN

AK
PRESS
EDINBURGH · OAKLAND · BALTIMORE

CONTENTS

Part I   Resistance and Culture

Introduction: Of Tunnels and Theaters 1
1. The Reader in the Factory 27

Part II   Speaking to Others: Anarchist Poetry, Song, and Public Voice

1. The Poet's Feet 67
2. The Devil's Best Tunes 91
3. Two Crises of Language 105
4. "A Need Without A Hope" 121
5. Fight or Flight? 133

Part III   "Out of the Bind of the Eternal Present": Anarchist Narrative

1. White Rooms 151
2. Varieties of Estrangement 161
3. Outcast Narratives 177
4. From Cretinolândia to Common-Sense Country 193
5. Stronger Loving Worlds 209
6. From *Terre Libre* to *Temps de Crises* 221
7. Barbarizing Visions 233
8. A Social Spectacle? 245
9. The Mirror Stage 269

Part IV   Breaking the Frame: Anarchist Images

1. Virile Bodies 283
2. "He Peddles Signs": Words and Images 301
3. "Evolution Is Not Over Yet": Visual Narrative 317
4. The Stuttering Image: Anarchist Cinema 343

Conclusion: Lines of Flight 379
Index 395

ACKNOWLEDGMENTS

Too, too many people gave me support and encouragement while I worked on this book. Among them, I need especially to recognize, in addition to my lovely family, James Birmingham, Andy Hoyt, Nathan Jun, Barry Pateman, Daniel Cairns, Jorell Meléndez Badillo, Rubén Hidalgo Pérez, Montse Feu, Jamie Heckert, Andy Cornell, Javier Parada, and Beth Parada. Amy Gorelick prompted me to start thinking about this book ten years ago and stuck with me while I worked at it; Kenyon Zimmer and Kirwin Shaffer read early drafts of the manuscript and kindled me with compliments. The compañerxs of Archivo-BAEL (Biblioteca Archivo de Estudios Libertarios)/ FLA (Federación Libertaria Argentina) helped me to track down archival sources, as did Nildo Avelino, Marcolino Jeremias (NU-ELCA—Núcleo de Estudos Libertários Carlo Aldegheri, Guarujá, São Paulo, Brazil), and Lily Litvak. K.R. Johnson, Susie Anderson, and April Milam patiently fed my outlandish requests into the interlibrary loan system. Gavin Grindon, Marcella Bencivenni, Francis Shor, Adrienne Hurley, and Dongyoun Hwang graciously fielded impossible questions. Artists Clifford Harper and Paul Glover were generous with their works. More materials were made available to me by Richard Prost, Mo Karnage, Teun de Reijke and Monique van der Pal at the IISH (International Institute of Social History), Sarah Carrier at Duke University's Rubenstein collection, M. Lourdes Prades i Artigas of the Universitat de Barcelona, Miriam Intrator at Ohio University, and Patrick Jules Dupuis, Valerie Mayman, and Sarah Severson of McGill University. Thanks go to my colleague Agripina Monsivais, Lucía Secco of *Semanario Brecha* in Uruguay, and the indefatigable Montse Feu for trying to help me track down the Photo That Got Away. Everyone should be so lucky as to have Charles Weigl for an impresario.

My special gratitude for the labor of the unknown multitudes of archivists who have allowed me the illusion of traveling everywhere and everywhen.

Innumerable other helping hands are being forgotten here, as always, and I hope they will forgive me. (All belongs to all).

This book is dedicated to my all, my unforgettable, Darlene.

PART I

RESISTANCE AND CULTURE

The adverse decision of the Board of Pardons terminates all hope of release by legal means.... The authorities are determined that I should remain in the prison, confident that it will prove my tomb. Realizing this fires my defiance, and all the stubborn resistance of my being. There is no hope of surviving my term. At best, even with the full benefit of the commutation time—which will hardly be granted me, in view of the attitude of the prison management—I still have over nine years to serve. But existence is becoming increasingly more unbearable; long confinement and the solitary have drained my vitality. To endure the nine years is almost a physical impossibility. I must therefore concentrate all my energy and efforts upon escape.

—Alexander Berkman, "Chapter XXXIII: The Tunnel," *Prison Memoirs of an Anarchist.*

What strikes me .... is how after ten years in a maximum-security prison, as soon as there was a tiny possibility of escape, the spirit and prose style of Alexander Berkman sprang alive as if he had not been dehumanized at all.

—Paul Goodman, *New Reformation.*

INTRODUCTION: OF TUNNELS AND THEATERS

IT is true: there is a tony mall there now. In Montevideo, Uruguay, the very walls that once formed El Penal de Punta Carretas, where, for decades, political prisoners were held without trial and executed, now harbor Punta Carretas Shopping, featuring a Nike Shop, a Swarovski, an Adidas, a Burger King, and, apparently, a women's clothing shop called "Tits." Eighty years ago, across the street at 2529 Calle Solano García, there stood a zinc-roofed warehouse that a small family of Italian immigrants—Gino Gatti, Primina Romano, and their child—had turned into a coal-dealer's shop in the spring of 1929, hanging up a sign: "Carbonería El Buen Trato" (fig. 1). It is from the back of this

Fig. 1: The "Buen Trato" charcoal shop.

shop that a fifty-meter-long tunnel was dug, over the course of a year
and a half, into the prison bathroom, enabling a number of anarchist
prisoners to escape from Punta Carretas in August 1931 (fig. 2). The
policemen who discovered the tunnel later on could not help but admire its construction: no crude crawlway, it had a vaulted ceiling that
could accommodate a standing adult of average height. It was well ven-
tilated, electrically lit, and rigged with a system of alarm bells.

At a certain point along the route of this tunnel, it intersects with
another tunnel that also runs under the floors of Punta Carretas, this
one dating from 1971, when over one hundred Tupamaro guerrillas
made their prison break. When they broke through into the old tunnel, they recognized it for what it was—they had read the accounts.
"My eyes will never forget," one of the escapees later wrote, "the clearly
visible traces of their tools crossed with ours at the summit of the vault."
In a small ceremony, they planted a sign there: "AQUÍ SE CRUZAN
DOS GENERACIONES, DOS IDEOLOGÍAS Y UN MISMO

Fig. 2: Gino Gatti's tunnel.

2

DESTINO: LA LIBERTAD [At this place there was a crossing of two generations, two ideologies, and one destiny: freedom]."[1] This crossing of ways and *destinos* does indeed invite contrasts as well as comparisons, and not only contrasts of generation and ideology. Whereas the first prison break was accomplished from the outside, the second was dug from within.[2] The Tupamaros, who called their movement one of "national liberation," were overwhelmingly Uruguayan in origin, while the anarchists were of diverse national origins—Italian, Catalan, Argentinean, German. Their movement, a "vast rhizomal network," was in no small part the byproduct of an age of expansion, a creature of the telegraph line, the railway, and the steamship, carried by flows of immigration.[3] Arriving always before (or after) its time, in the words of Sandra Jeppesen, it had "no real permanent space of its own"; it subsisted in a state of perpetual motion. The Gatti family participated in this circulation on many different levels: not only were they multiple immigrants (Gino, for instance, first emigrated to Argentina in 1923 before making his way to Uruguay), they also seem to have been engaged in illegal border-crossing almost as a kind of profession. Archival records testify to governments' ever-frustrated, ever-renewed attempts to *locate* and *fix* the address of this family, tracking it from one address to another, from one name to another. The Italian embassy in Buenos Aires reported to Rome that Gino, later dubbed "El Ingeniero [The Engineer]" for his tunneling prowess, had "a small motor boat that ... provides for the transfer of their fellow anarchists as well as for smuggling operations."[4]

Tunnels belong to this theme of mobility. A tunnel is a means of escape to *la libertad*—transitory, not a home, not a *destino*. But El Ingeniero built his tunnel as if it were meant to last. Was this not a little more than merely practical? Gatti may have been a logistical

---

1 Movimiento de Liberación Nacional (Uruguay), *Actas Tupamaras* (Rosario, Argentina: Cucaña Ediciones, 2003), 252.

2 Victoria Ruetalo, "From Penal Institution to Shopping Mecca: The Economics of Memory and the Case of Punta Carretas," *Cultural Critique* 68 (Winter 2008): 51.

3 Benedict Anderson, *Under Three Flags: Anarchism and the Anti-Colonial Imagination* (London: Verso, 2005), 3–4.

4 Osvaldo Bayer, *Severino di Giovanni: el idealista de la violencia* (Buenos Aires : Editorial Legasa, 1989), 387n26 (note: all translations are mine unless otherwise noted).

genius, but he seems to have had a lyrical streak; he described his friend's very life as "a true epic poem." What kind of space, then, was his tunnel: logistical or lyrical?

The very being of a tunnel, to a sufficiently lyrical eye, could seem to be a paradox, a contradiction in terms: a subterranean structure erected by destruction, built by sheer subtraction, the negation of solidity itself. Mikhail Bakunin used the figure of the tunnel to evoke the manner in which radical "spirit" survives underneath the world's crushing weight: "the spirit of revolution is not subdued, it has only sunk into itself in order soon to reveal itself again as an affirmative, creative principle, and right now it is burrowing—if I may avail myself of this expression of Hegel's—like a mole under the earth." Well said, old Bakunin.[5] To live mole-wise, to live tunneling, is to make the very means of escape one's home.

If you can imagine living this way, then you can imagine what this book is about: anarchist resistance culture. My intention, in this book, is to examine the ways in which anarchist politics have historically found aesthetic expression in the form of a "culture of resistance," is to some extent unique. It is hardly unheard of, in my corner of the academic world, to utter the word "resistance" in such close connection

---

5   Mikhail Bakunin, *Bakunin on Anarchism*, trans. and ed. Sam Dolgoff (Montréal: Black Rose Books, 1980), 56. This is a double allusion, and it begs for some context. Bakunin is alluding to Hegel, who was alluding to Shakespeare's Hamlet, Act I, Scene V: "Spirit often seems to have forgotten and lost itself, but inwardly opposed to itself, it is inwardly working ever forward (as when Hamlet says of the ghost of his father, 'Well said, old mole! canst work i' the ground so fast?'), until grown strong in itself it bursts asunder the crust of earth which divided it from the sun, its Notion, so that the earth crumbles away" (Hegel, *Lectures on the History of Philosophy*, vol III, trans. Elizabeth Sanderson Haldane and Frances H. Simson [London: K. Paul, Trench, Trübner, & Co, 1896], 546–547). Marx, of course, uses the same image in his *Eighteenth Brumaire*: describing the "purgatory" of the 1848 revolution in France and the rise to power of Louis Bonaparte, he imagined that this, too, might be a preliminary to a final burst of "destruction": "When the revolution shall have accomplished this second part of its preliminary programme, Europe will jump up from her seat to exclaim: 'Well hast thou grubbed, old mole!'" (*The Eighteenth Brumaire of Louis Bonaparte,* trans. Daniel De Leon [Chicago: C.H. Kerr, 1913], 141–142). Commentators generally miss the fact that Bakunin's allusion to Hegel's "mole in the earth," appearing in his 1842 essay, "Die Reaktion in Deutschland," precedes Marx's by almost a decade.

with the word "culture"; for some, the two terms have become synonymous, so that instances of "culture" as innocuous as playing a video game or wearing a T-shirt can be taken to be instances of "resistant" behavior, making the phrase "resistance culture" almost redundant. Furthermore, what if the word *resistance*, modifying *culture*, implies that only some forms of culture, and not others, are authentically subversive or threatening to the established order of things, i.e., "resistant"? This *is* what I mean; I am interested in what makes the difference between innocuous or conservative moments in culture and those that potentially or actually defy, disturb, and challenge the given.

Though I am not the first to speak of a "culture of resistance" or "resistance culture," the currency of these terms hasn't fixed their meanings. Some of the ambiguity probably derives from the ambiguity of the word "culture" itself, which, as Raymond Williams points out, has come to mean both the special kinds of "works and practices," supposedly distinct and separate from everyday life, that we call "art and learning," and the more amorphous notion of "a particular way of life."[6] Thus, for instance, Vivian Schelling speaks of "cultures of resistance" in the plural, defining these as "more subtle and everyday practices of opposition to domination" by contrast with "systematic and confrontational forms of struggle."[7] James C. Scott, similarly, describes a "culture of resistance" as the sharing of the "risk" entailed in individual acts of resistance by an entire community aligned against an external source of oppression.[8] For Robert M. Press, a "culture of resistance" is "greater than the sum of the acts of resistance": it "involves a change of thinking ... a decision to no longer accept authoritarian rule in daily life, not just at the top ... but at all levels."[9] Writers from Stanley Aronowitz to Dinesh D'Souza use the term "culture of resistance" or "resistance culture" to refer to an informal climate of

6   Raymond Williams, *Keywords: A Vocabulary of Culture and Society* (New York: Oxford University Press, 1985), 90.

7   Vivian Schelling, "'The People's Radio' of Vila Nossa Senhora Aparecida: Alternative Communication and Cultures of Resistance in Brazil," in *Culture and Global Change*, eds. Tracey Skelton and Tim Allen (London: Routledge, 1999), 171.

8   James C. Scott, *Weapons of the Weak: Everyday Forms of Peasant Resistance* (New Haven: Yale University Press, 1985), 35.

9   Robert M. Press, *Peaceful Resistance: Advancing Human Rights and Democratic Freedoms* (Aldershot, UK: Ashgate, 2006), 35.

recalcitrance and opposition created by marginalized people unable to revolt openly—slaves in the fields, working-class students in the classroom, workers in fast-food restaurants.[10] In odd cases, it serves to describe the behavior of rather privileged subjects, e.g., doctors or businessmen, defending their group interests against external imperatives; usually, however, it is used to characterize the behavior of poor, especially black people, either to appreciate their creativity and agency in the face of overwhelming institutional forces or to decry their stubborn refusal to respond to the well-meant interventions of teachers, social workers, and other supposed agents of change.[11]

In all of these formulations, the word "culture" serves to qualify the concept of "resistance," to indicate forms of resistance that are, on the one hand, relatively atmospheric, even vaporous—not formalized or embodied in any visible institutions, perhaps not even conscious or coherent—and on the other hand, not merely sporadic or fleeting but generalized, communal, habitual, and entrenched. In any case, the sense of the word "culture" that is evoked is that of "a way of life" rather than specific "works and practices." Occasionally, however, one encounters references to "resistance culture" in something more like the artifactual sense: American hip-hop, a particularly subversive film, "an alternative news network" are given as instances. The last of these is specifically described as "a tool for changing attitudes, raising public awareness and relaying the views of the movement to a wider public ... to mobilize concerned citizens not normally involved in action

10 Stanley Aronowitz, "Introduction," in Paul E. Willis, *Learning to Labor: How Working Class Kids Get Working Class Jobs* (New York: Columbia University Press, 1981), XII; Dinesh D'Souza, *The End of Racism: Principles for a Multiracial Society* (New York: Free Press, 1995), 99; Jennifer Parker Talwar, *Fast Food, Fast Track: Immigrants, Big Business, and the American Dream* (Boulder: Westview Press, 2004), 116.

11 Francis T. Cullen, review of *Prescription For Profit: How Doctors Defraud Medicaid*, in *Contemporary Sociology* 23.3 (May 1994): 419; Eugene Bardach and Robert A. Kagan, *Going by the Book: The Problem of Regulatory Unreasonableness* (New Brunswick: Transaction Publishers, 2002), 114; Margaret Washington Creel, *A Peculiar People: Slave Religion and Community-Culture Among the Gullahs* (New York: New York University Press, 1988), 10; Phil Frances Carspecken, "The Hidden History of Praxis Theory Within Critical Ethnography and the Criticalism/Postmodernism Problematic," in *Ethnography and Schools: Qualitative Approaches to the Study of Education*, eds. Yali Zou and Enrique T. Trueba (Lanham, MD: Rowman & Littlefield Publishers, 2002), 66.

protests."[12] During South Africa's transition to postapartheid, the term "resistance culture" is used synonymously with "*écriture engagée*" or "protest" theater, the kind of cultural artifact produced specifically and consciously as the expression of an organized resistance *movement* (in the words of Albie Sachs, "art ... seen as an instrument of struggle").[13] This is far closer to the sense I intend, with two crucial differences.

First, the anarchist conception of "resistance" is—with all due respect to the astounding trials undergone by the South African anti-apartheid movement—something different and broader, aimed not only at one particular oppressive regime but at all forms of domination and hierarchy, whether these are constituted through the formal institutions of violence and property or the infinity of informal power relations through which we form our sense of ourselves and our world. Anarchist "resistance," declares Georges Yvetot (1868–1942), encompasses

all the popular movements, all the ambitions of the people to revolt against tyrannies, *whatever their source*, against all the tyrannies and all the entities in the names of which they are exercised: God, Truth, Homeland, Honor, Universal Suffrage, Labor, Property, Church, State, Law, Dictatorship, Justice, General Interest, Peace, Law, Culture, Humanity, Progress, etc.... Resistance must be a way of understanding our role in an *entire society* based on social inequality.[14]

---

12 Geneva Smitherman, "'The Chain Remain the Same': Communicative Practices in the Hip Hop Nation," *Journal of Black Studies* 28.1 (Sept. 1997): 7; Paul Routledge, "The Imagineering of Resistance: Pollok Free State and the Practice of Postmodern Politics," *Transactions of the Institute of British Geographers* 22.3 (1997): 363; Tracey Skelton, "Jamaican Yardies on British Television: Dominant Representations, Spaces for Resistance?" in *Entanglements of Power: Geographies of Domination/Resistance*, ed. Joanne P. Sharp (London: Routledge, 2000), 196.

13 Rob Nixon, "Aftermaths," *Transition* 72 (1996): 64; Ian Steadman, "Theater beyond Apartheid," *Research in African Literatures* 22.3 (Autumn 1991): 77; Zoë Wicomb, "Culture Beyond Color?" *Transition* 60 (1993): 29; Albie Sachs, "Preparing Ourselves for Freedom," in *Writing South Africa: Literature, Apartheid, and Democracy 1970–1995*, eds. Derek Attridge and Rosemary Jane Jolly (Cambridge: Cambridge University Press, 1998), 239.

14 Georges Yvetot, "Résistance," in *Encyclopédie anarchiste*, ed. Sébastien Faure (Paris: Librairie internationale, 1934), 2344, emphases mine.

7

To be an anarchist, in a place and time that is like any part of the world in the twentieth century, is to deny the legitimacy of almost every feature of that world: its nation-states, its religions, its pretense of representational government, its organization of production and consumption, its patriarchal customs, its warped ideals—*etc., etc.*: there is almost no end to the things one is "against," to the point that one continually risks slipping into an entirely negative and reactive self-definition (anti-capitalist, anti-statist, anti-clerical, anti-imperialist, anti-racist, anti-authoritarian, anti-sexist...).[15] When an "entire society," i.e., *almost everything around you*, seemingly to the smallest detail, reflects assumptions contrary to your most deeply held convictions about what the world is and can be—namely, the assumption that hierarchy, domination, violence, and injustice are the natural, necessary, and permanent characters of existence—then merely to persevere in imagining and acting on the assumption of the possibility of another kind of world is in itself a monumental and continual effort of resistance.

At one end of the tunnel is a prison (or a mall). At the other end is a little theater in which a humble spectacle is staged for the benefit of the public: a simulation of law-abiding commerce (*El Buen Trato*—literally, "The Good Deal"!) and normal family life (the "Gatti Family"). A farce, perhaps? In light of such theatricality, it might come as no surprise to learn from certain websites dedicated to anarchist history that the famed playwright, Armand Gatti, was the child of this couple.[16] It makes a further kind of perverse sense that Gatti *fils* should become known, decades later, for his experimental work with prisoners. An ex-prisoner himself—having been arrested and thrown into a Nazi labor camp as a young French Resistance fighter—he, like Gatti *père*, had learned to escape. Like his father before him, Armand Gatti became an anarchist.[17]

The themes of imprisonment and escape are, indeed, of fundamental importance in Armand Gatti's works, including his screenplay

---

15 Daniel Colson, *Petit lexique philosophique de l'anarchisme de Proudhon à Deleuze* (Paris: Librairie Générale Française, 2001), 33.

16 Cathy Ytak and Eric Coulaud, "26 janvier," *Ephéméride Anarchiste,* http:// ytak.club.fr/janvier26.html#gattia and "18 mars," http://ytak.club.fr/ mars18.html#evasion; David Brown, "January 26," *The Daily Bleed,* 1997, http://www.eskimo.com/~recall/bleed/0126.htm.

17 Dorothy Knowles, "Armand Gatti's Two Theatres: 'Théâtre Institutionnel' and 'Théâtre d'Intervention,'" *French Studies* 49.1 (1995): 52.

for the film *L'Enclos* (1961) and the plays *L'Enfant-Rat* (1960), *Le deuxième existence du camp de Tatenberg* (1962), *Chant public devant deux chaises éléctriques* (1964), *Chroniques d'une planète provisoire* (1967), *Le labyrinthe* (1981), *Ulrike Meinhof* (1986), *Les 7 possibilités du train 713 en partance d'Auschwitz* (1987), *Le Combat du jour et de la nuit dans la maison d'arrêt de Fleury-Mérogis* (1989), and *Le chant d'amour des alphabets d'Auschwitz* (1989). One of the experiences that first marked out this thematic trajectory took place in the courtyard of the labor camp in which the young Gatti was interned. There, one day, he saw another prisoner, who had been subjected to three months solitary confinement, emerge into the courtyard for the first time, dancing strangely and singing the alphabet. Gatti immediately understood this *"danse alphabétique,"* later written into one of his theatrical pieces, as a means of mental survival and escape: "That day ... the war had been won."[18] Gatti resisted his jailers and torturers by writing poems in his head and reciting in lieu of answering questions—"buil[ding] up a defensive linguistic barrier around himself," as his biographer Dorothy Knowles observes.[19]

In dramaturgical workshops with prisoners, Gatti puts this hard-earned knowledge to use, leading them through exercises designed to trace the histories that have imprisoned them and to allow them to reimagine themselves as something other than prisoners.[20] The aim of Armand Gatti's theater, "becoming conscious of what one is, of one's own possibilities, to the profoundest measure," is quite continuous with the aim of Gino Gatti's engineering.

There is only one problem with this analogy-via-genealogy between the two Gattis: if the analogy is true, the genealogy is false. The father of the playwright born Dante Sauveur Armand Gatti in 1924 was indeed an Italian immigrant anarchist, but in 1929–1931, he was not in Montevideo but in Monaco, having previously sought

---

18 Jean-Jacques Van Vlasselaer, "Music, Memory, and the Holocaust: Viktor Ullmann, the Ultimate Witness," in *Building History: The Shoah in Art, Memory, and Myth*, ed. Peter M. Daly (New York: P. Lang, 2001), 180; Armand Gatti, *Œuvres théâtrales*, ed. Michel Séonnet (Lagrasse: Verdier, 1991), 1174.

19 Dorothy Knowles, *Armand Gatti in the Theatre: Wild Duck against the Wind* (London: Athlone Press, 1989), 5–6.

20 Dorothy Knowles, "Armand Gatti's Theatre of Social Experiment, 1989–1991," *New Theatre Quarterly* 8.30 (1992): 124–125.

work in Chicago; named Auguste Gatti, he was a street sweeper, not an engineer, and his wife, Letizia Luzana, gave birth to her son, the future playwright, in Monaco,[21] half the world away from Gino Gatti, Primina Romano, and their *daughter*. In fact, "Gino Gatti" was merely the *nom de guerre* of a man identified by Argentine police as "José Baldi"—in Italian, Giuseppe.[22]

Given the spurious nature of the paternity claim *in re Gatti*, we might ask: what is the meaning of this misidentification? It seems a particularly odd mistake, after all, given the general indifference toward questions of pedigree in the anarchist tradition.[23] If it has any occult or unconscious significance, perhaps it is in the fact of the peculiar *affinity* between these two persons, falsely linked by a name, truly linked by the *analogy* between their actions.[24] There is, in short, a strange kind of family resemblance, an affinity or analogy.

What makes the tunnel of Punta Carretas such an apt analogue for this culture is the nature of the fundamental problem to which the culture constitutes a strategic response. Let me explain this by way of another brief anecdote. In his memoirs, Abraham Frumkin

---

21 Knowles, *Armand Gatti in the Theatre*, 2.

22 Osvaldo Bayer, *Los anarquistas expropiadores, Simón Radowitzky, y otros ensayos* (Coyhaique, Argentina: Sombraysén Editores, 2008), 387n26.

23 This indifference could be said to derive from the very nature of the anarchist tradition qua tradition. For all the diversity of Marxist thinkers and parties, all claim a theoretical pedigree with Marx and Engels at its head. Anarchism, on the contrary, enjoys a plurality of origins—a source of scorn for its critics, for whom it appears as a "political illegitimate," in the words of a popular turn-of-the-century tract on the Anarchist Peril: "there appear to be several 'fathers'.... Some cast the blame on Proudhon; others on Max Stirner; a third section makes Josiah Warren responsible; while yet others lay the crime at the door of Bakounine ... [or] Kropotkin" (W.C. Hart, *Confessions of an Anarchist* [London: E. Grant Richards, 1906], 171n). More vexing yet, since even Proudhon, in coining the word "anarchist" in its positive sense, was only appropriating an existing word (heretofore merely an epithet used to bastardize one's political opponents), and since the content given to this word came from already-existing workers' movements (such as the Mutuellistes of Lyon, after whom Proudhon spoke of "mutualism" as the economic system proper to anarchism) and social tendencies (Kropotkin traces anarchist practices of "mutual aid" back to human prehistory and prehuman natural history), even these "fathers" cannot be said to be the absolute originators of anything. We wear our bastardy with pride.

24 On the importance of the concepts of "affinity" and "analogy" to anarchist thought, see Colson, *Petit lexique*, 20–21 and 24–26.

(1872–1946) recounts how a fellow Yiddish-speaking anarchist, Moshe, once asked the Russian gentile anarchist Kropotkin the rather rabbinical question: "*Tsi meg an anarkhist hobn a bank-bikhl* [Can one be an anarchist and save money in the bank at the same time]?"). There is one easy way to interpret this anecdote. For Karen Rosenberg, it merely serves as one more demonstration that "anarchism is a sect," i.e., "a religious ... cult of self-sacrifice."[25] Here is one of the most tediously repeated commonplaces about anarchism: i.e., that the counter-cultures or "counter-communities" formed by anarchists bear a strong resemblance to religious communities, e.g., the sixteenth-century Anabaptists or the medieval Cathars (the more exotic, the better; few think to compare them to the church down the block from us).[26] While this claim is regularly made by writers hostile towards anarchism, with the assumption that such a resemblance is either proof of anarchism's backwardness ("religion" standing here for all that is antithetical to rational modernity) or incoherence (since anarchists most often claim to be opposed to religion), it is also frequently abetted by anarchists themselves, who are not slow to admit a kinship with history's heretics, prophets, and iconoclasts.[27] Among

25 Karen Rosenberg, "The Cult of Self-Sacrifice in Yiddish Anarchism and Saul Yanovsky's *The First Years of Jewish Libertarian Socialism*," in *Yiddish and the Left*, eds. Gennady Estraïkh and Mikhail Krutikov (Oxford: European Humanities Research Centre, 2001), 179, 181.

26 I borrow the term from Sharif Gemie, "Counter-Community: An Aspect of Anarchist Political Culture," *Journal of Contemporary History* 29 (April 1994): 349–367.

27 For classic examples of the anarchism-as-quasi-religious-atavism argument, see Eric J. Hobsbawm, *Primitive Rebels* (New York: W.W. Norton, 1965), 74–92, or Karl Mannheim, *Ideology and Utopia: An Introduction to the Sociology of Knowledge* (New York: Harcourt, Brace, 1936), 225. For classic anarchist denunciations of religion, see Bakunin's *God and the State* (New York: Dover, 1970) or Peggy Kornegger's "The Spirituality Ripoff," in *The Second Wave* 4.3 (1975): 12–18. For an acknowledgment of affinities with religious antecedents on the part of atheist anarchists, see, for instance, Gustav Landauer's paean to medieval Christianity in *Die Revolution* (*Revolution and Other Writings* [Oakland, CA: PM Press, 2010], 127–137), or Peter Kropotkin's nod to several centuries' worth of heresies and millenialist movements in *Ethics*, trans. Louis S. Friedland and Joseph R. Piroshnikoff (New York, London: The Dial Press, 1924), 133–134. Paul-François Tremlett's "On the Formation and Function of the Category 'Religion' In Anarchist Writing," in *Culture and Religion* 5.3 (2004): 367–381, provides what may be the best analysis of these discrepancies in the treatment. Demetrio

the Yiddish-speaking (and atheist) anarchists of turn-of-the-century London, for instance, the German gentile anarchist Rudolf Rocker was jokingly referred to as "our rabbi." (In a more pointed spirit, Paris anarchists of the *fin-de-siècle* referred to Jean Grave as "the Pope of the Rue Mouffetard.")[28]

It would be easy to make a Jewish joke out of poor Moshe, but the laugh would not be worth enough to put in a *bank-bikhl*. What this episode indicates, I would argue, is not the emptiness of Moshe's pretensions to revolutionary modernity (see, he's just another superstitious old Jew, afraid of breaking a commandment!) or the incoherence of his will to break with an authoritarian world (see, the would-be anarchist craves authority!), but the deep affinity between the anarchist experience and the Jewish experience of diaspora as *galut* (exile). In exile, continual pressure to assimilate, alternating with cycles of persecution forcing Jews to publicly abjure their religion, confronted Jews with the horror of self-estrangement. It is to this experience of alienation that Joseph S. Bloch traced the origins of the *Kol Nidrei*—the eerie, wailing *niggun* sung each year on the Day of Atonement pleading with God to pardon us for breaking our own strongest vows, fragmenting our very selves.[29] For an anarchist to simply continue to *exist* in a radically false world, a world that requires participation in a violent and unequal economy of money and power—this, too, is a profound experience of self-exile.

Blaine McKinley speaks of this experience in terms of a "dilemma of vocation." Since "an anarchist could not live a consistent life

Castro Alfín ("Anarquismo y protestantismo: Reflexiones sobre un viejo argumento," *Studia historica: Historia contemporánea* 16 [1998]: 197–220) reconsiders this old historiographic chestnut in the Spanish context.

28 Sam Dreen qtd. in W.J. Fishman, *East End Jewish Radicals, 1875–1914* (London: Duckworth, in association with the Acton Society Trust, 1975), 254; Jean Maitron, *Le Mouvement Anarchiste En France* (Paris: F. Maspero, 1975), 1.145.

29 Isaac Klein, *A Guide to Jewish Religious Practice* (New York: Jewish Theological Seminary of America, 1979), 213. Bloch's hypothesis is disputed, since the *Kol Nidrei* seems to predate Bloch's history, but whatever its origins, the significance of the song in Jewish life was certainly cemented by experiences of persecution, all the more so after Bloch's 1917 interpretation, in the wake of the Shoah. See also Margaret Olin, "Graven Images on Video?," in *Complex Identities: Jewish Consciousness and Modern Art*, eds. Matthew Baigell and Milly Heyd (New Brunswick, NJ: Rutgers University Press, 2001), 47.

in America" or anywhere else where conditions of statism and capitalism prevailed, and insofar as the hallmark of anarchist ethics is the refusal to distinguish between ends and means or principles and practices, to be an anarchist is almost always to live in an intolerable moral bind.[30] As the anarcho-communist Luigi Galleani (1861–1931) put it: "By accepting a wage, by paying rent for a house, we, with all our proclaimed revolutionary and anarchist aspirations, recognize and legitimate capital ... in the most tangible and painful way."[31] The individualist anarchist Albert Libertad (1875–1908) perhaps stated the problem most forcefully in his declaration that "Every day we commit suicide partially":

> I commit suicide when I devote, to hours of absorbing work, an amount of energy which I am not able to recapture, or when I engage in work which I know to be useless....
>
> I commit suicide whenever I consent to obey oppressive men or measures.
>
> I commit suicide whenever I convey to another individual, by the act of voting, the *right* to govern me for four years....
>
> Complete suicide is nothing but the final act of total inability to react against the environment.
>
> These acts, of which I have spoken of as partial suicides, are not therefore less truly suicidal. It is because I lack the power to react against society, that I inhabit a place without light and air, that I do not eat in accordance with my hunger or my taste, that I am a soldier or a voter, that I subject my love to laws or to compulsion.[32]

---

30 Blaine McKinley, "'The Quagmires of Necessity': American Anarchists and Dilemmas of Vocation," *American Quarterly* 34.5 (Winter 1982): 507.

31 Luigi Galleani, *The Principle of Organization*, trans. Wolfi Landstreicher (Cascadia: Pirate Press Portland, 2006), 4. In a contemporary echo, Laura Portwood-Stacer observes that among anarchists today, "everyone can be called out at some point for not living up to anarchist principles," since— no less than 1925—"to live in contemporary society is to be complicit with capitalism and other forms of exploitation" (130).

32 Albert Libertad, "The Joy of Life," in *Man! An Anthology of Anarchist Ideas, Essays, Poetry and Commentaries*, ed. Marcus Graham (London: Cienfuegos Press, 1974), 355–356. Cf. Alexandra Myrial (a.k.a. Alexandra David-Néel, 1868–1969), in *Pour la Vie* (1901): "Obedience is death. Each instant man submits to an alien will is an instant cut off from his life" (13).

At every turn, the anarchist is compelled to endorse a universe of values that is the antithesis of her own, to cancel herself out—a kind of ongoing moral suicide.

Anarchists and Jews are of course not the only people to suffer such alienation, which is to some extent the common fate of all who are marked as marginal or radical. What is unique about our case is not only the *extent* of our disagreement with the world as it is given to us (defining our being by way of a longer list of things-to-be-against) but its unmediated *intensity*. For a Marxist, for instance, the desire for another world, however palpable, is supposed to be subject to the dialectic of history: capitalism will die of its own contradictions. No such consolation is available for anarchists—not even, as is often asserted, the consolation of a pure "human nature" that is bound to shine forth again once the dross of history is washed away.[33] On the contrary, this romantic myth is vigorously denied by every major statement of anarchist theory, beginning with the excoriation of Rousseau by Proudhon and Bakunin alike.[34] It is no more a question of substituting biology for history than it is of substituting history for morality. The moral question—how to *live?*—is left quite bare, and confronts us in all its force.

The main body of the cultural production to emerge from the anarchist movements of the nineteenth and twentieth centuries, I contend, can best be understood as a response to this question—not quite a "solution" or an "answer" so much as a way of living with the

---

33 The notion that anarchists were anarchists because they believed in the existence of a good human nature, repressed by social institutions such as the State, that merely awaited expression, is really a durable misreading that survives in spite of many concerted attempts to puncture it, perpetuated by political scientists, philosophers, and historians alike. See, for instance, Dave Morland's "Anarchism, Human Nature and History: Lessons for the Future" (in *Twenty-First Century Anarchism*, eds. Jon Purkis and James Bowen [UK: Cassell, 1997], 8–23), David Hartley's "Communitarian Anarchism and Human Nature" (in *Anarchist Studies* 3.2 [1995]: 145–164), and my own *Anarchism and the Crisis of Representation: Hermeneutics, Aesthetics, Politics* (Selinsgrove, PA: Susquehanna University Press, 2006), 56–60.

34 See, for instance, the ridicule heaped by Proudhon on Rousseau's notion that *"Man is born good ... but society ... depraves him"* (*System of Economic Contradictions: or, the Philosophy of Misery*, trans. Benjamin R. Tucker [Boston: Benjamin R. Tucker, 1888], 404), or Bakunin's contempt for Rousseau's conception of "primitive men enjoying absolute liberty only in isolation" (*Bakunin on Anarchism*, 128).

problem for as long as it lasts, a means of inhabiting history until it stops hurting. Anarchists practice culture as *a means of mental and moral survival* in a world from which they are *fundamentally alienated*. Stated positively—well, it is hard to do better than the anarchist poet Kaneko Mitsuharu (1895–1975): "To oppose is to live. / To oppose is to get a grip on the very self."[35]

This immediately risks being mistaken for some other kind of theory about the relation between anarchist politics and anarchist culture. One of these is the notion of cultural rebellion as a substitute for the political kind. David Weir, for instance, argues that we can read the history of anarchism as follows: whereas anarchists were on the losing side of every revolution from 1871 to 1939, their politics translated nicely into the aesthetic realm, where it came to mean a kind of individualist stance, a willful refusal to make sense to a mass audience—in other words, what came to be known simply as "modernism." In short, Weir suggests, "anarchism succeeded culturally where it failed politically."[36] Of course, the same half-full glass might look completely empty if viewed from a slightly more politically engaged perspective than Weir's. Even if anarchist impulses might be said to have migrated successfully into the domain of art, and even if they produced there practices that resisted the capitalist imperative to produce mass-market cultural commodities, this still amounted to a kind of capitalism-by-other-means, a contest for the "accumulation of symbolic capital," which could later be traded in for the economic variety, making modern art into a kind of luxury good that would testify to the owner's social status.[37] Whether or not these modernist works eschewed symbolism entirely—even an ultra-abstractionist work such as Kasimir Malevich's *Black Square* became a kind of symbol of the artist's supreme will not to symbolize—they also ran the risk of becoming privatized surrogates for political refusal, something one turned to in place of collective action, a "compensation and

---

35 Kaneko Mitsuharu, "Opposition," trans. Geoffrey Bownas and Anthony Thwaite, in *99 Poems in Translation: An Anthology*, ed. Harold Pinter et al. (New York: Grove Press, 1994), 54–55.

36 David Weir, *Anarchy and Culture: The Aesthetic Politics of Modernism* (Massachusetts: University of Massachusetts, 1997), 5.

37 Pierre Bourdieu, *The Field of Cultural Production: Essays on Art and Literature*, trans. Randal Johnson (New York: Columbia University Press, 1993), 75.

palliative," as John Zerzan (b. 1943) bluntly puts it, for what cannot be realized in "life."[38]

This is all as may be. However, the kind of anarchist-inspired cultural production that formed the kernel of modernism—the Cubist abstractions of a Pablo Picasso or the conceptual music of a John Cage, for instance—was never very deeply embedded in any real community of anarchists. It was never firmly connected to an anarcho-syndicalist organization such as the Confederación Nacional de Trabajo (CNT) or the revolutionary syndicalist Industrial Workers of the World (IWW),[39] for instance, which sponsored and produced very different forms of art, e.g., the strikingly symbolic mass poster art of Manuel Monleón Burgos (1904–1976) or the satirical folk songs of Joe Hill (1879–1915). The modernist aesthetic studied by Weir and others, in its rejection of representation and narrative, actually has little in common with the aesthetics favored by most anarchists. The demands made on art by the residents of a bohemia, however politicized they may have been at times, were not quite the same as those made by the broader constituencies of what was, at its height, an international working-class movement.[40]

What anarchists *did* demand from art, by and large, was what they demanded from all the forms and moments of their political lives: i.e., that it should, as much as possible, embody the idea in

---

38 John Zerzan, *Elements of Refusal* (Seattle: Left Bank Books, 1988), 56.

39 The term "revolutionary syndicalism" refers to the radical movement emerging in the 1890s, eclectic as to ideology but firmly internationalist and anti-statist (and harboring a substantial faction of self-defined anarchists), that saw direct action and self-organization through unions (in French, *syndicats*) as the means proper to workers' emancipation. The origins of the term "anarcho-syndicalism" (and its cognates) are somewhat cloudy, but it appears to have come into use in the early 1920s, first as an epithet hurled by Communist Party members at syndicalists who resisted the assimilation of their movement, then as a self-description adopted by some of those same syndicalists (David Berry, *A History of the French Anarchist Movement, 1917–1945* (Oakland, CA: AK Press, 2009), 152; Mintz,"Guión provisional sobre el anarcosindicalismo," *El Solidario* 14 [Fall 2008]: xii–xiii). Anarcho-syndicalists specifically defined the emancipatory goal of revolutionary syndicalism as anarchy (or, in the formulation of the CNT, "libertarian communism").

40 For a somewhat contrary view, see Allan Antliff's *Anarchist Modernism: Art, Politics, and the First American Avant-Garde* (Chicago: University of Chicago Press, 2001).

the act, the principle in the practice, the end in the means. If anarchism is "prefigurative politics," striving to make the desired future visible in and through one's actions in the present, then anarchist resistance culture had to somehow *prefigure* a world of freedom and equality.

The sociologist Howard J. Ehrlich offers us what could be a helpful handle on this notion of anarchist culture as prefigurative when he speaks of a "revolutionary transfer culture," i.e., "that agglomeration of ideas and practices that guide people in making the trip from the society here to the good society there in the future."[41] The metaphor of "transfer" is misleading, however, if it makes us imagine this process as something too easy; in the age of globalization, after all, a "trip" is inevitably only a matter of hours at most. Particularly during periods of intense repression, committed anarchists were not always convinced that rapid change was imminent: "Not for a hundred, not for five hundred years, perhaps, will the principles of anarchy triumph," Emma Goldman (1869–1940) surmised.[42] Nor was the revolution she wanted only a matter of overthrowing the State or abolishing Capital; a "transvaluation not only of social, but also of human values," encompassing "*every phase* of life,—individual, as well as the collective; the internal, as well as the external phases," was not necessarily to be imagined on the Jacobin model of a single, swift transformation.[43] Traveling, movement, mobility are all appropriate images, except insofar as they foreground the endpoint, the *destino*. While anarchists generally think of their aspirations in terms of "revolution," the journey—"walk[ing]

---

41 Howard J. Ehrlich, "How to Get from Here to There: Building Revolutionary Transfer Culture," in *Reinventing Anarchy, Again*, ed. Howard J. Ehrlich (Edinburgh: AK Press, 1996), 329.

42 Qtd. in Michelson "A Character Study of Emma Goldman," *Emma Goldman: A Documentary History of the American Years*, Vol. 1, ed. Candace Falk (Berkeley: University of California Press, 2003), 441.

43 Emma Goldman, *My Disillusionment in Russia* (Mineola, NY: Dover Publications, 2003), 259; and *Anarchism and Other Essays* (New York: Mother Earth Publishing Association, 1910), 56. Similarly, Ruth Kinna has argued that recent poststructuralist interpreters of the anarchist tradition misread Kropotkin's conception of revolution: "It was not a matter of going to sleep in a statist system one night and waking up in utopia the next morning. Kropotkin believed that revolution was necessary, but it was work in progress as much as a cataclysmic event" (82).

toward anarchy," as Errico Malatesta (1853–1932) put it—is at least as important as the goal.[44] How could anarchists maintain such a pitch of activity, such an optimism of the will, in the face of such pessimism of the intellect? As prefigurative politics, anarchism can entail a paradoxically pessimistic attitude toward the possibility of arriving at a revolutionary *moment*: a certain historical *amor fati* or "anarcho-fatalism." Francis Dupuis-Déri notes precisely such an indifference toward "the revolution" as event among contemporary anarchist activists. Instead of deferring desires into a utopian future seen as imminent, anarchist activists seek to make their desires as immanent as possible—to demand more from their relationships, from the process of political activity, from their everyday lives.[45] While Dupuis-Déri attributes contemporary anarcho-fatalism in part to a realistic reckoning of the poor prospects for a classical "revolution" in the relatively affluent and stable global North, such an orientation is hardly a recent phenomenon; we find it clearly and forcefully theorized in the writings of Gustav Landauer (1870–1919), anarchist martyr of the abortive German revolution of 1919.

In *Die Revolution*, written in 1911 and reissued on the eve of the actual event itself, Landauer took up Proudhon's suggestion that "there is a permanent revolution in history," reinterpreting history in terms of a continuity of revolutionary energies—sometimes forced "underground," at other times erupting into the open air.[46] In this interpretation, revolution becomes not a historically and geographically isolated event but a more nebulous process that only occasionally condenses into decisive moments—"evolution preceding revolution," as Elisée Reclus put it, "and revolution preceding a new evolution, which is in turn the mother of future revolutions."[47]

44 Errico Malatesta, "Towards Anarchism," in *Anarchism: A Documentary History of Libertarian Ideas, Vol. 1*, ed. Robert Graham (Montréal: Black Rose Books, 2005), 506.

45 Francis Dupuis-Déri, "En deuil de révolution? Pensées et pratiques anarcho-fatalistes." *Réfractions* 13 (Automne 2004): 139–150.

46 Proudhon, *Oeuvres complètes 17* (Paris: Librairie Internationale, 1868), 142; Landauer, *Revolution*, 116, 154.

47 Elisée Reclus, "Evolution, Revolution, and the Anarchist Ideal," in *Anarchy, Geography, Modernity: The Radical Social Thought of Elisée Reclus*, eds. and trans. John Clark and Camille Martin (Lanham, MD: Lexington Books, 2004), 153.

This takes the logic of revolution far from the scientific pretensions of historical materialism. Indeed, where Marx rebuked Bakunin for looking to "*willpower*" and not "economic conditions" as the source of revolution, for Landauer, it is precisely will and desire, social emotions, that are the primary revolutionary forces: revolution is "possible at all times, if enough people want it":[48]

> Little is to be expected from external conditions, and people think too much about the environment, the future, the others, separating means and ends too much, as if an end could be attained in this way. Too often you think that if the end is glorious, dubious means must also be justified. But only the moment exists for us; do not sacrifice the reality to the chimera! If you seek the right life, live it now; you make it difficult by seeking it outside yourselves, in the future, and for the sake of this beautiful future you fill your present with ugliness.... If the glory and the kingdom of God on earth should ever come for the world, for the masses, for people and nations, can it come in any way other than by the fact that one immediately begins to do what is right?[49]

If we can await nothing from "external conditions," we must demand everything from ourselves, from within. This inward turn, however, is not to be understood as a subjective substitute for social action (like one of the "revolutions from within" peddled by pop psychologists); it is a fully social and material attempt to come to grips with the world. Like Gatti's tunnel, it is a "line of flight"—"not a leap into another realm," Todd May explains, but "a production within the realm of that from which it takes flight."[50] In short, this is a matter of resistance, of finding ways, "at every instant," to "*withdraw* from injustice."[51] In the words of Landauer's essay, "Durch Absonderung zur Gemeinschaft [Through Separation to Community]," it is out of a profound sense

---

48 Karl Marx and Frederick Engels, *Collected Works Vol. 24: Marx and Engels, 1874–83* (London: Lawrence & Wishart, 1989), 518; Gustav Landauer, *For Socialism*, trans. David J. Parent (St. Louis, MO: Telos Press, 1978), 74.

49 Gustav Landauer, *Der Werdende Mensch: Aufsätze über Leben und Schrifttum*, ed. Martin Buber (Potsdam: G. Kiepenheuer, 1921), 228.

50 Todd May, *Gilles Deleuze: An Introduction* (Cambridge: Cambridge University Press, 2005), 128.

51 Landauer, *Der Werdende Mensch*, 228, trans. and emphasis mine.

of responsibility to others that anarchists seek "to leave these people," to keep "our own company and our own lives"; "Away from the state, as far as we can get! Away from goods and commerce! Away from the philistines! Let us ... form a small community in joy and activity."[52] Landauer's conception of anarchism as exodus, striving toward "community" precisely *through* separation," illuminates the purpose of anarchist resistance culture: to enable us, *while remaining within the world of domination and hierarchy, to escape from it.*

Something like Ehrlich's "transfer culture" or Landauer's "community through separation" is carried by the Italian Autonomists' concept of "exodus." Exodus, a process of *"engaged withdrawal"* from authoritarian institutions, which is at the same time the "founding" of a new community, was partly inspired by observations of U.S. black nationalism, which used the image of the passage out of Egypt "to change circumstances without [anyone] shifting one millimetre in space."[53] Indeed, from the perspective of exodus, the question of whether the emancipated future is imminent or remote is beside the point:

> The motivating force of the sticking together and the unity—
> the "being together"—of that group that was on its way ("in
> movement") toward the Promised Land, toward the collective
> dimension of its own emancipation, was probably more the uni-
> dimensionality of the desert, its immobility and immutability,
> than any hopes for the approach of some eventual future goal.[54]

---

52 Landauer, *Revolution*, 94–108.

53 Paolo Virno, "Virtuosity and Revolution: The Political Theory of Exodus," trans. Ed Emory, in *Radical Thought in Italy: A Potential Politics*, eds.
Michael Hardt and Paolo Virno (Minneapolis: University of Minnesota
Press, 1996), 196; Andrea Colombo qtd. in Steve Wright, "Confronting
the Crisis of 'Fordism': Italian Debates Around Social Transition," http://
www.arpnet.it/chaos/steve.htm.

54 Marco Revelli, "Worker Identity in the Factory Desert," trans. Ed Emory,
in *Radical Thought in Italy*, 118–119. This also recalls Walter Benjamin's
concluding remarks in "Theses on the Philosophy of History": "We know
that the Jews were prohibited from investigating the future.... This does
not imply, however, that for the Jews the future turned into homogeneous,
empty time. For every second of time was the strait gate through which
the Messiah might enter" (Walter Benjamin, *Illuminations: Essays and Reflections*, trans. Harry Zohn and ed. Hannah Arendt [New York: Schocken
Books, 1969], 264).

Anarchist resistance culture is a way of living in transit *through* this desert. The resistance culture of the anti-apartheid movement had not only a specific target but a *destino*, a Promised Land, an end. Anarchist resistance is not mainly defined by its end; it is a middle, a means. It is a tunnel.

I have constructed this book as an exploration of anarchist cultural resistance work in just some of the genres or media that have been historically most important to the movement. It may be that in doing so, I am paying too much respect to an artifactual conception of "culture." The goal cannot be to secure equal bragging rights (Armand Gatti is the anarchist Brecht![55]); in any case, such boasting would be ill considered, as competing for symbolic capital in the cultural marketplace is not in keeping with the anarchist spirit. Instead, I hope to make these artifacts speak of the ways of being in the world that they have helped to construct.

The organizing device of genre or medium allows us (dangerously) extravagant scope for comparison. The best studies of anarchist cultural resistance have been fairly narrowly bounded by place and period, reflecting the assumption that these will be the dimensions most salient to interpretation.[56] While there is much to be said for this kind of attention to the local conditions and contexts within and against which acts of cultural production take on meaning, it may also simply reflect the biases built into academic publishing, which increasingly pays lip service to "interdisciplinary" research without ever ceasing

---

55 Among those who have thought that Armand Gatti might be the anarchist Brecht, apparently, was Gilles Deleuze ("How Do We Recognize Structuralism?" trans. Melissa McMahon and Charles J. Stivale, in *The Two-Fold Thought of Deleuze and Guattari*, ed. Charles J. Stivale [New York: Guilford Press, 1998], 264). Erwin Piscator thought Gatti might be the anarchist Piscator (Knowles, "Armand Gatti's Two Theatres," 52). Martin Esslin thinks that the anarchist Brecht is none other than the early Bertolt Brecht (*Brecht: A Choice of Evils* [London: Eyre Methuen, 1980], 151).

56 See, for instance, Kirwin Shaffer's *Anarchism and Countercultural Politics in Early-Twentieth-Century Cuba* (Gainesville, FL: University Press of Florida, 2005); Tom Goyens's *Beer and Revolution: The German Anarchist Movement in New York City, 1880–1914* (Urbana, IL: University of Illinois Press, 2007); Caroline Granier's *Les briseurs de formules: les écrivains anarchistes en France à la fin du XIXe siècle* (Coeuvres-et-Valsery: Ressouvenances, 2008); or George McKay's anthology, *DiY Culture: Party & Protest in Nineties Britain* (New York: Verso, 1998).

to impose disciplinary categories. As a massively transnational, migratory phenomenon, the anarchist movement fails to comply with the compartmentalization of knowledge; it is at least worth asking whether, as anarchist ideas traveled from France to China, from China to Korea, from Russia to Brazil, from Germany to the U.S., and so on, anything *did* remain constant. Given the variety of historical and cultural conditions in which anarchists made their homes, whatever elements of anarchist culture might have been carried from city to city or from generation to generation, anarchist works of culture might have tended to take on the colors of each time and place. Given the fundamental situation in which anarchists of every place and time have found themselves—the empire of State and Capital, the universal prison-house, the changeless desert—anarchist works of culture might have converged substantially in their evolution.

Here, then, are the primary questions animating this book: How has anarchist resistance, global both in its aspirations and in its movements, been *translated* into the local vernacular of particular cultures and historical situations, *adapted* to the constraints of the genres and media available? Is there anything uniquely or consistently *anarchist* about the variety of cultural forms that some seven generations of anarchist men and women have happened to create?

I could stop there if I wanted to preserve the illusion of scholarly detachment, but it is really too late for that; I must be counted among the many researchers who have gotten too close to the material. I came of age in the suburban and semi-rural U.S. after the fall of the Berlin Wall, in the heyday of TINA (There Is No Alternative), when, after more than half a century of consolidation, the dominant model of life—roughly speaking, the one I was surrounded by, like a 360° diorama—had come to seem all but inescapable. It has been breathtaking and disorienting to witness, over the past decade, the reemergence of something like concerted opposition to that model, an opposition that has worn many names—"anticapitalism," "horizontalism," "Zapatismo," "altermondialisme," "alternative globalization movement," "autonomous movement," "movement of movements"— and occasionally, that of "the new anarchism."[57] From the perspective

---

57 See Milstein, "Something *Did* Start in Quebec City," in *Confronting Capitalism: Dispatches From a Global Movement*, ed. Daniel Burton-Rose et al. (New York: Soft Skull Press, 2004), 126–133; Barbara Epstein, "An-

of these new times, in which those reigning structures seem to have once again entered a real crisis, I want to seek the intersection of new lines of flight with old ones.[58] Where might our tunnels intersect and diverge? In other words: what lessons, if any, can be taken from this history for any future anarchist cultural resistance?

A quick note, before we go on, about the nomenclature of anarchist history: many historiographers are wont to distinguish between what they call "classical anarchism" (vaguely after the title of George Crowder's *Classical Anarchism: The Political Thought of Godwin, Proudhon, Bakunin, and Kropotkin* (1991), and the "new anarchism" that is said to have emerged, as if sprung fully grown from a god's head, in the period after the end of the Cold War, making its real public debut in Seattle in 1999. Classical anarchism, supposedly founded on the thought of this handful of philosopher-founders, has been the subject of many philosophical critiques (e.g., Saul Newman's *From Bakunin to Lacan*), which suffer from many kinds of reductionism, not least that of reducing anarchism to the history of a few thinkers' thoughts, but also making a fairly reductive representation of those thoughts, and all but completely ignoring developments taking place after the end of the Spanish Civil War. More cannily, the late John Moore suggested that we should distinguish between "first-wave" and "second-wave" anarchisms, the second wave appearing only after the Second World War, with its finest moment being defined by the May '68 events; the intellectual stars of this constellation would include the situationist and post-situationist thinkers, and perhaps also the autonomous movements of Italy and Germany, as well as the new Zapatismo. Daniel Colson has suggested a three-part model:

> The first period is that of its appearance as a current in political philosophy.... During this period—from the beginning of the 1840s to the creation, twenty-five years later, of the International Workingmens' Association/Association Internationale

---

archism and the Anti-Globalization Movement," *Monthly Review* 53.4 (2001): 1–14; David Graeber, "For a New Anarchism," *New Left Review* 13 (2002): 61–74 and "Occupy and Anarchism's Gift of Democracy," *Guardian* (November 15, 2011).

58 I'm borrowing the concept of "lines of flight" very loosely from Gilles Deleuze and Félix Guattari, who use it to speak of attempts to flee from imprisoning spaces and systems, particularly by the creation of something new.

Fig. 3: Cover for Ricardo Flores Magón's play, "Tierra y Libertad" (1917).

des Travailleurs (IWA/AIT)—anarchism does not exist as an effective political current, identifiable in organizations, groups, or symbols in public demonstrations.

This first period, then, can be thought of as a period of ideological gestation, a process fomented by some—but not all—of the founding figures of "classical anarchism" (Proudhon and Bakunin, but not Godwin or Kropotkin; Colson also cites Joseph Déjacque [1821–1864], Max Stirner [1806–1856], and Ernest Coeuderoy [1825–1862]). Yet even without organizations adequate to its ambitions, anarchism is not thinkable without relation to "the transformations and the explosive situation of Europe in the middle of the 19th century, and more particularly to the events and the revolutionary movements of 1848." Moreover, while "its reality is mainly philosophical and journalistic," these are "thoroughly blended into the theoretical and political ferment of the time as to the material and social upheavals which Europe was experiencing"—e.g., Proudhon's ties to the Lyons *mutuellistes*, Bakunin's experience of the uprising in Berlin.

Colson's second period elaborates upon "this practical dimension of the anarchist idea":

> It crystallizes in London, in 1864, with the creation of the First International, and disappears rather precisely in Barcelona, in May 1937, when ... the republican State and the Communist

International put an end to the Spanish and Catalan revolutionary movements. It is of considerable duration, lasting a little more than seven decades—involving around five or six generations of workers—and it comprises a great number of specific moments or modes of being.

Here, we encounter not only individual thinkers like Kropotkin but a host of tinkerers not counted in the ranks of political philosophers. Their experiments and experiences range from

the anti-authoritarian First International of 1871 to 1881, the *attentats* and attempts at insurrectionary "propaganda by the deed" at the end of the 19th and beginning of the 20th centuries, French "revolutionary syndicalism," illegalism, Argentinian "forism," Spanish "anarcho-syndicalism," etc.

Also present in this period but absent from the register of philosophy are the great anarchist rhetors, from Pietro Gori to Emma Goldman, whose cultural work, as Nathan Jun and Kathy Ferguson have convincingly argued, has been denied a fair reckoning by academic histories for which practice is the reading-off of theories first thought by thinkers.

Colson imagines anarchism's "third period"—somewhat inaccurately, I will argue—as emerging after a near total eclipse, a historical blackout stretching from the beginning of the Second World War to the opening of the Sixties. The return of anti-authoritarian thought and practice carries an "eruptive force" proportional to the optimism of that historical moment, but is marked by some discontinuity with the traditions and organizations established in the second period, together with the new predominance of Marxist, Freudian, and Nietzschean thought. The result: a revival of anarchism in several guises, from the Dutch Provos and Kabouters to the French Situationists and Italian Autonomists, from poststructuralism to eco-anarchism and anarcha-feminism. In every case, the new anarchism presented an idea which "was not new, but which, having been forgotten, then appeared as an astounding innovation."[59] And here it is, then, that

59 Daniel Colson, *Trois Essais de Philosophie Anarchiste: Islam, Histoire, Monadologie* (Paris: Léo Scheer, 2004), 9–29, trans. mine.

we find an astonishing and unforeseen crossing between generations, ideologies, and destinies. Well dug, old mole—well dug indeed.

A final note about limitations: inevitably, this book suffers from them. Because it relies so heavily on original translations of previously untranslated literary and scholarly works (victims of the general oblivion to which anarchist history has been consigned), it reflects the uneven distribution of my linguistic skills: I am capable enough as a reader of French, able to muddle through Spanish and Portuguese, far worse in other European languages, and barely capable of deciphering anything else. This means that while I can do some justice to the anarchist cultures of Western Europe and the Americas, I can offer only a glimpse of the anarchist cultures of Eastern Europe and Asia (and a blurry picture of the terrifically important Yiddish and Italian contributions). Sometimes, as in chapters 3–5 of Part II ("Speaking to Others: Anarchist Poetry, Song, and Public Voice"), although I am describing a global phenomenon (anarchist poets' shift away from public, rhetorical modes of address), my attention is focused on one or two particular cases (mainly those of the United States and Britain). Despite my comparative ambitions, I have given more attention to the second period than to either the first or third. Even if scholarly coverage of punk vastly exceeds that given to Pouget or the Cinéma du Peuple, it has received unforgivably short shrift here. Important thinkers, movements, and events have gone unmentioned. So much for the panoptical promise. Mainly, what I hope to show, however incompletely and indirectly, is what I have been astonished to discover: *how much more there is to be seen.*

There is a McDonalds, a Lancôme, an Urban Outfitters. One and a half thousand employees go to work at the building formerly known as El Penal de Punta Carretas; a million consumers flow through every month.[60] Where is their tunnel for escape?

---

60 Silvana Nicola, "Los consumidores iluminan el camino," *El País Digital* (June 23, 2006), http://200.40.120.165/Suple/Empresario/06/06/23/elempre_223059.asp.

1. THE READER IN THE FACTORY

IN an influential survey, *The Radical Novel in the United States 1900–1954: Some Interrelations of Literature and Society*, Walter B. Rideout takes just two pages to consider the literary production of anarchists, pondering "why the movement should have produced no novels": perhaps, he speculates, this was due to "absorption in labor struggles and the task of propagandizing, the lack of an amenable publisher ... or the Anarchist 'temperament,' which expended itself more readily in personal reminiscence, critical analyses, short poems, and long arguments." In any case, the question is only of interest in that "the nonexistence of such novels emphasizes by contrast the domination of radical fiction at that time by the Socialist writers."[1] Subsequent scholars have allowed this judgment to stand, even as they have sought to overturn almost every other aspect of the midcentury critical establishment. Alan M. Wald, in *Writing From the Left: New Essays on Radical Culture and Politics* agrees: "No one ... has as yet been successful in making the argument for a substantial achievement in fiction, poetry, or literary criticism on the part of social democrats and anarchists, or other types of radicals in the 1930s or thereafter."[2] Rideout's book was republished in 1992, and a more recent survey, Barbara Foley's *Radical Representations: Politics and Form in U.S. Proletarian Fiction 1929–1941*, mentions—purely in passing—only a single anarchist novel.[3]

---

1   Walter B. Rideout, *The Radical Novel in America, 1900–1954: Some Interrelations of Literature and Society* (NY: Hill & Wang, 1956), 90–91.
2   Alan M. Wald, *Writing from the Left: New Essays on Radical Culture and Politics* (London: Verso, 1994), 19.
3   Barbara Foley, *Radical Representations: Politics and Form in U.S. Proletar-

This failure to find any "substantial achievement" by anarchists in the field of literature doesn't just mean that there are not enough anarchist books to talk about; this is not just a quantitative but a qualitative judgment, one we find repeated even in scholarship focusing on anarchist cultural production. In fact, scholars who give the matter any attention often call attention to the sheer volume of anarchist cultural production (fig. 1): "During the two years 1922 and 1923," remarks Arif Dirlik, "more than seventy anarchist publications appeared inside and outside China." Marcello Zane remarks on the bulk of column space given to poetry in Spanish anarchist newspapers (nearly two hundred poems published in twenty-one papers between 1882 and 1910), while Serge Salaün catalogs some 8,500 anarchist poems (by around 3,400 poets) published during the Spanish Civil War alone, and María-Luisa Siguán remarks on the "rather high" print runs (10,000–50,000 copies apiece) of the six hundred popular fiction titles in the *Novela Ideal* series issued by the anarchist journal *La Revista Blanca*.[4] These observations are almost always followed, however, by variously disparaging or apologetic accounts of the "weak" quality of the product—"more of a brief cry of anguish than an argued essay," as Peter Zarrow puts it, describing a typical entry in the journal *Tianyi Bao* (*Natural Justice*, 1907–1908).[5] Anarchist cultural productions are generally described as a matter of "propaganda" rather than literature, "maudlin and bombastic" in tone, "didactic" in intent, permeated by a simplistic "moral dualism" or "angry naïveté"—in short, as Siguán concludes, "quite similar to 'party literature,'" of historical interest at best.[6] Only if it

---

ian Fiction, 1929–1941 (Durham: Duke University Press, 1993), 89, 96.

4 Arif Dirlik, *Anarchism in the Chinese Revolution* (Berkeley: University of California Press, 1993), 154; Marcello Zane, "Vivir entre las nubes," *Belphégor* 6.2 (June 2007); Salaün cited in Joseph Steinbeiß, "'Meine Verse sollen Bomben sein…'," *grazwurzelrevolution* 265 (Jan. 2002); María-Luisa Siguán, "'La Novela Ideal'," *Anuario de filologia* 4 (1978): 419. Likewise, Gonzalo Santonja notes the volume and vigor of the *Novela Proletaria* series, which sustained print runs of 30,000 copies apiece (17).

5 Gonzalo Santonja, *La Novela proletaria (1932–1933)* (Madrid: Ayuso, 1979), 17; Peter G. Zarrow, "He Zhen and Anarcho-Feminism in China," *The Journal of Asian Studies* 47.4 (Nov. 1988): 807.

6 Brigitte Magnien, "La novela del pueblo: analyses d'une collection de nouvelles publiée sous la dictature de Primo de Rivera," in *L'Infra-littérature en Espagne au XIXe et XXe siècles*, ed. Victor Carrillo (Grenoble: PUG,

Fig. 1: A sampling of the worldwide anarchist press, ca. 1930 (Foto-Semo; image courtesy of International Institute of Social History).

is considered strictly from the standpoint of "a sociological phenomenon" can this "boring and banal manipulation of the literary code" be worthy of our interest, for Maria Eugenia Boaventura; considered in itself, all this literature presents is "a shopworn language, full of clichés"—ironically, a "conservative, moralistic and even authoritarian" discourse.[7] All of this underscores what is, for David Weir, the "unfortunate but poignant paradox: that innovative, progressive art is no guarantee of social progress"—and vice versa, as Zane puts it, that revolutionary content is "unable to find really innovative words and structures."[8] In other words: if it's anarchist (in content), it ain't literary (in form), and if it's literature, it can't possibly be anarchist.

1977), 250, 256; Serge Salaün, *Romancero libertario* (Paris: Ruedo Ibérico, 1971), 35–36; Zarrow, "He Zhen," 802; Siguán, "La novela Ideal," 419.

7   Maria Eugenia Boaventura, "A Ficção Anarquista Classe Média," *Remate de Males* 1.4 (Jan. 1983): 80–81, 92. Ana Lozano de la Pola calls this rhetorical maneuver, after Patricia V. Greene, "the ethico-aesthetic paradox": how can a truly radical content be conveyed by a conservative form? The presupposition, Lozano de la Pola notes, is that we can neatly distinguish, in advance, between "radical genres" and "conservative genres," as if *all* the ideological consequences were *already* spelled out *at that level*, regardless of how particular authors set those inherited materials to work, regardless of how particular readers encounter it, in what contexts, etc. See Ana Lozano de la Pola "Re-visitando a Federica Montseny. Una lectura de *La Victoria* y sus lecturas," *Arbor: ciencia, pensamiento, y cultura* 182.719 (May–June 2006): 399–400.

8   Weir, *Anarchy and Culture*, 1; Zane, "Vivir entre las nubes."

Sometimes—in the apologetic version of this judgment—the supposed incompatibility of anarchist content and literary form is confined to the domain of *writing*. Weir, for one, asserts that "the kind of culture that practicing anarchists preferred"—lectures, performances, songs—"was insistently oral in character," noting, for instance, "Emma Goldman's interest in modern drama as an important cultural medium for anarchist ideology." He goes so far as to argue that "the form of the novel itself" militates against anarchism:

> The argument is often made that the novel is the cultural form par excellence for the expression of day-to-day experience in the capitalist nation-state, and it very well may be that the ideological influences that have shaped the novel into its traditional realist form make it an inappropriate medium for the cultural expression of anarchism.... The tradition of the nineteenth-century novel ... requires a formal mode of narrative discourse that cannot accommodate the largely oral culture of anarchism.[9]

It is interesting to contrast this with Goldman's own assessment, in her introduction to the most widely read collection of her writings, *Anarchism and Other Essays* (1910):

> My great faith in the wonder worker, the spoken word, is no more. I have realized its inadequacy to awaken thought, or even emotion.... Oral propaganda is at best but a means of shaking people from their lethargy: it leaves no lasting impression. The very fact that most people attend meetings only if aroused by newspaper sensations, or because they expect to be amused, is proof that they really have no inner urge to learn. It is altogether different with the written mode of human expression. No one, unless intensely interested in progressive ideas, will bother with serious books.[10]

Here, Goldman appeals to the traditional association of the spoken word with ephemerality, as opposed to the permanence of the written word, in a way that would not surprise literary scholars who

9 Weir, *Anarchy and Culture*, 87–88.
10 Goldman, *Anarchism and Other Essays*, 47–48.

have been trained to suss out the prejudices associated with "the illusion of full and present speech."[11] This illusion, we are told, dates back to the arch-authoritarian Plato, who has Socrates inveigh against the art of writing. Relying on the oral process of dialogue as a means to discover truth, Socrates finds all written texts—presumably including those of his disciple Plato, which claim to present records of his spoken words—to be inadequate simulations of living speech.[12] Writing introduces a gap between author and reader, a spatial and temporal void in which the original meaning can be lost, so that when Shelley's "Traveler from an antique land" shows up to read King Ozymandias's words—"look on my works, ye Mighty, and despair!"—they have been reversed, undone, rendered irremediably ironic by the sheer passage of time ("Round the decay / Of that Colossal Wreck, boundless and bare, / The lone and level sands stretch far away").[13] In the absence of the author, the author-ity of the written word is ruined.

We might expect, as Weir imagines, that Goldman would condemn the written word as lifeless and abstract in comparison with the immediacy of living speech; no one worries about the effects of *writing* "fire" in a crowded theater. Orality does take on a certain importance in anarchist resistance culture, as we shall see—partly, as Weir suggests, because it "gets round the problem of illiteracy that many anarchists faced (especially in Spain)." But this, too, is used to disqualify anarchism, once again depicted as a politics of "primitive rebels," in Eric Hobsbawm's phrase—a vestige of the premodern world, without a future.[14]

It is true that Goldman was a public speaker, a specialist in incendiary speech; perhaps the better part of her militant life was spent in free speech fights, in physical confrontations with hecklers and police

11 Jacques Derrida, *Of Grammatology*, trans. Gayatri Chakravorty Spivak (Baltimore: Johns Hopkins University Press, 1997), 140.
12 Plato, *Phaedrus*, in *Dialogues*, trans. Benjamin Jowett (New York: C. Scribner, 1911), 581.
13 Percy Bysshe Shelley, "Ozymandias, " *The Complete Poetry of Percy Bysshe Shelley*, eds. Donald H. Reiman and Neil Fraistat (Baltimore: Johns Hopkins University Press, 2000), 1.
14 Weir, *Anarchy and Culture*, 88; Hobsbawm, *Primitive Rebels*; see also Karl Mannheim's equation of anarchism with "chiliasm" (*Ideology and Utopia*, 196). For a bracing critique of these and similar historiographic strategies, see Davide Turcato, *Making Sense of Anarchism: Errico Malatesta's Experiments with Revolution, 1889–1900* (Basingstoke: Palgrave Macmillan, 2012).

over the right to a public audience for subversion, sex, solidarity, and sedition. And yet her brief, in this introduction to her own essays, is for reading, not for hearing:

> In meetings the audience is distracted by a thousand nonessentials. The speaker, though ever so eloquent, cannot escape the restlessness of the crowd, with the inevitable result that he will fail to strike root. In all probability he will not even do justice to himself.
>
> The relation between the writer and the reader is more intimate. True, books are only what we want them to be; rather, what we read into them. That we can do so demonstrates the importance of written as against oral expression....
>
> I am not sanguine enough to hope that my readers will be as numerous as those who have heard me. But I prefer to reach the few who really want to learn, rather than the many who come to be amused.[15]

Goldman was not alone in this conception of the possibilities of writing. A writer for Barcelona's *Tierra Libre*, for example, argues that anarchist newspapers are "the strongest, most universal, most effective action for propaganda" precisely *because* of this "intimate" quality:

> The printed word works more and better within the consciousness of the individual; it suggests his own thoughts to him, intimate commentaries that increase the value of the concepts he reads about, and in this periodic *conversation* between him and the printed page, expanded concepts and new horizons emerge. The suggestion exerted by the press goes so far as to overcome the reader's indifference or prejudice; then sooner or later, the newspaper becomes his inseparable companion, whom he soon presents to his friends of the workshop, the factory, or the soil, and with whom he identifies like the flesh of his flesh.[16]

---

15 Goldman, *Anarchism and Other Essays*, 48–49.
16 Qtd. in Lily Litvak, *La Mirada Roja: Estética y arte del anarquismo español (1880–1913)* (Barcelona: Ediciones del Serbal, 1988), 55–56, trans. mine.

It is important to note the difference, here, between these aspirations and those of, say, Lenin's conception of vanguard leadership. While Lenin, too, speaks of the desirability of the revolutionary leaders and the led "becom[ing] intimate," it is only this leadership that occupies the epistemological high ground of "correct revolutionary *theory*";[17] in effect, it stands out over against the proletariat, surveying it as if from above and outside. The masses cannot see themselves accurately (at best, they can achieve "trade-union consciousness"); they do not possess theoretical truth.[18] Like empty vessels waiting to be filled, they must receive this theory from the vanguard. By contrast, the desire to suggest the reader's own thoughts, to constitute an "intimate commentary," is a desire not to instruct, to direct, to lead from above, but to form an *internal* bond. To read, on this account, is, as Daniel Colson puts it, a matter of writers and readers "establishing relations from the *interior* of that which constitutes them," of "*finding oneself* in the other and finding the other within oneself as *already there*."[19]

This appeal to the "intimate," to a kind of identification and active partnership with the reader, is, according to Caroline Granier, precisely what the variety of novels written by anarchists have in common: they "try to establish a particular relationship with the reader, a relation that is not founded on authority."[20] Goldman's hope for this non-authoritarian, personal relationship with the reader is great enough to override her fear that her written words, too, will be misunderstood, that they will not penetrate the veil of received ideas and prejudices mediating between the reader and the page. She is all too aware of the "disheartening tendency common among readers ... to tear out one sentence from a work, as a criterion of the writer's ideas or personality." Specifically, she anticipates that she will be vilified both by socialists and by communist anarchists for excoriating, in the essay "Minorities versus Majorities," the alleged passivity and conformity of the "mass," endorsing instead the heroic individualism

---

17 V.I. Lenin, *"Left-Wing" Communism: An Infantile Disorder* (Detroit: Marxian Educational Society, 1921), 17.

18 V.I. Lenin, *What Is to Be Done?*, trans. Robert Service (London: Penguin Books: 1988), 98.

19 Colson, *Petit lexique*, 71 and *Trois essais*, 42–43, trans. mine, italics mine.

20 Caroline Granier, *"Nous sommes des briseurs de formules": Les écrivains anarchistes en France à la fin du dix-neuvième siècle* (Diss., Université Paris-VIII, 2003), 1.2.3.

of Nietzsche and Stirner. The popular perception of these thinkers as antisocial elitists, which she regards as the work of "shallow interpreters," obscures the "social possibilities" she takes to be implicit within their individualism. "No doubt," she laments, despite these efforts to forestall or blunt these misreadings—efforts that were, as she foresaw, not entirely successful[21]—"I shall be excommunicated as an enemy of the people"; nonetheless, she is determined to stake her wager on the power of writing: "For the rest, my book must speak for itself."[22] As for *this* book, it will attempt not only to demonstrate that a written anarchist literature exists, but to treat its supposed paradoxes or impossibilities as questions to be investigated.

In his famous study, *The Lonely Voice*, Frank O'Connor divorces the modern fiction of Maupassant, Hemingway, and Joyce from its folkloric antecedent, the oral tale. Where the folktale was told in the presence of hearers with a shared experience, within a community,

> Almost from its beginnings the short story, like the novel, abandoned the devices of a public art in which the storyteller assumed the mass assent of an audience to his wildest improvisations—"and a queer thing happened him late one night." It began, and continues to function, as a private art intended to satisfy the standards of the individual, solitary, critical reader.

To both of these images of reading—"public" or "private," "mass" or "solitary"—we could contrast another: that of the workers in a cigar factory, say, in Florida, Puerto Rico, or Cuba, sometime around the turn of the twentieth century, listening to *el lector*—or, in some cases, *la lectora*—reading aloud from a raised platform called *la tribuna*. The selection—on the previous shift, a novel by Zola in Spanish translation; on this shift, a selection from Elisée Reclus's scientific tract, the *Nueva Geografía Universal*; next time, the new edition of the anarchist newspaper *La Voz del Esclavo*—has been made, after deliberation, by a vote of the workers on the shop floor; they have chipped in perhaps a quarter each to pay for this performance, which is indeed something

---

21 See Laura Greenwood, "Goldman's Nietzschean Anarchism: A Greimasian Reading of 'Minorities Versus Majorities,'" *Theory in Action* 4.4 (October 2011): 90–105.

22 Goldman, *Anarchism and Other Essays*, 50–51.

of a dramatic act (it is no easy thing to project one's voice with enough amplitude to carry over the noise of three hundred workers in a single room, and it demands a certain stage presence).[23] Is this a form of mass entertainment? A project of collective self-improvement? Propaganda? Popular education? It is all of the above; and it is simultaneously oral and literate, communal and modern.

One of these *lectores*, Luisa Capetillo (1879–1922), who became an important anarchist labor organizer and propagandist for women's equality, author of numerous essays and manifestos, also wrote poems and plays. Her three-act drama, *La Influencia de las Ideas Modernas* (1907), in fact, opens on a scene of reading: a young woman, Angelina, daughter of the patrón, Don Juan, is reading Tolstoy's *The Slavery of Our Times*. At the beginning of the second act, Don Juan nervously observes her reading Zola's *Fecundity* ("I already read *Truth*," she tells him), and a few scenes later, he has been converted by her to Tolstoy's gospel: "Yes, now I see that you have won me over," he sighs, giving in to the strikers' demands. Her friends Ernestina and Marieta are tougher to reach, as their devout mother only lets them read Christian tracts; "Don't either of you read Malato or Kropotkin or Zola?" Angelina hectors them. "Do not buy finery or jewels, because books are worth more than they are," she admonishes them, quoting from one of her books; "Adorn your understanding with their precious ideas, because there is no luxury that dazzles like the luxury of science."[24] Even if Capetillo, a dabbler in spiritism, has more

---

23 Araceli Tinajero, *El Lector: A History of the Cigar Factory Reader* (Austin: University of Texas Press, 2010), 124; Abelardo Gutiérrez Díaz qtd. in Louis A. Pérez, *Essays on Cuban History: Historiography and Research* (Gainesville, FL: University Press of Florida, 1995), 76–77. By no means were such customs confined to a Caribbean context; they also appeared, for instance, in Spain (where the out-loud readers were called "*recitadores*"), as well as in Argentina (Javier Navarro Navarro, *A la revolución por la cultura: prácticas culturales y sociabilidad libertarias en el País Valenciano (1931–1939)* [Valencia: Univ. de Valencia, 2004], 154–155; Eva Golluscio de Montoya, *Teatro y folletines libertarios rioplatenses (1895–1910)* [Ottawa: Girol Books, 1996], 37).

24 Luisa Capetillo, "La Influencia de las Ideas Modernas," in *Absolute Equality*, ed. and trans. Laura Walker (Houston: Arte Público Press, 2009), 26, 16, 12, 13. Interestingly, Angelina seems to find the house servants hardest to subvert: at Angelina's cry of "Long live the revolution!" the butler, Ramón, can at first manage only a "Long live... a...ahem..." (27). Even he, though, cannot long resist her anarchist arguments.

optimism about the efficacy of reading than do her more materialist comrades, her fervor for reading, the urgency she lends to practices of self-education, are unmistakably anarchist traits. And if Javier Navarro Navarro is right, this faith was not entirely misplaced: a highly typical "life trajectory" for anarchists *did* begin with "a fellow worker, a relative, or an acquaintance lend[ing] a book, pamphlet, newspaper or magazine to a child or adolescent."[25] A recent study suggests that more continue to arrive at anarchism via the written word—albeit now often in electronic form—than orally (e.g., via social contacts or song lyrics). A surprisingly typical response: "Emma Goldman set me on fire."[26]

Anarchists don't regard ideas as pale reflections of material life; "the idea," for Paul Brousse (1844–1912), can and should go "in flesh and blood."[27] Sometimes this is put into practice rather literally by anarchist authors such as Alberto Ghiraldo (1875–1946), José de Maturana (1884–1917) and Florencio Sánchez (1875–1910), who would actually go to read their *own* works aloud to worker audiences.[28] At other times, the embodiment of ideas takes on an inward dimension: Alexander Berkman wrote rapturously of imaginings in which, "in transports of ecstasy, we kissed the image of the Social Revolution," and Emma Goldman spoke of "my Ideal" as her "one Great Love."[29] Daniel Colson clarifies: "The anarchist Idea ... is neither an *ideal*, nor a *utopia*, nor an abstraction; neither a program, nor a catalogue of regulations or prohibitions"; rather, "it is a living force ... which, under certain circumstances, takes us outside of ourselves."[30] Accordingly, anarchists conceive of reading as an active, *embodied* practice, as Gustav Landauer describes it:

25 Navarro Navarro, *A la revolución por la cultura*, 147–148.
26 Stefanie Knoll and Aragorn Eloff, "2010 Anarchist Survey Report" (August 2010).
27 Paul Brousse, "Propaganda by the Deed," trans. Paul Sharkey, *Anarchism: A Documentary History of Libertarian Ideas, Vol. 1*, 151.
28 Golluscio de Montoya, *Teatro y folletines libertarios rioplatenses*, 37.
29 Berkman and Goldman qtd. in Don Herzog, "Romantic Anarchism and Pedestrian Liberalism," *Political Theory* 35.3 (2007): 329; however, for a significant feminist critique of Herzog, see also Lori Marso, "The Perversions of Bored Liberals: Response to Herzog," *Political Theory* 36.1 (2008): 123–128.
30 Colson, *Petit lexique*, 152, trans. mine.

We think of the total effect that Goethe has had: we sit in peaceful composure of the body, a transfigured beauty and serenity appears on our faces, our muscles relax and our widened eyes gaze out over the land. We think of Ibsen: our foreheads wrinkle, our eyes look sharper and as if in evil doubt, our mouths twitch, our heads sway in uncertainty, and we touch our noses with one finger. But those who have beheld this wild man Tolstoy become his completely: we swing our arms forcefully, throw them up and back, thrust our heads and necks forward; the agitation of our soul has turned into turmoil, into an inability to stand still, a trembling, a rearing up, and a striding forth.[31]

When reading, then, an anarchist is not (only) engaged in abstract, silent, immobile cognition; reading becomes something concrete, physical, bodily, kinetic. The relation of reader to author is also imagined in terms of a kind of visceral, immediate presence that resists the anomie and isolation O'Connor identifies as the defining features of modern, urban, industrial life.

Anarchist readers, even when they are not really listeners to a *lector* or *lectora*, sometimes seem to be trying to create or recreate communal conditions through the practice of reading, in part *because* they are so often "geographically, economically, and intellectually marginalized," as Joanne Ellen Passet puts it.[32]

Geographically, first: they are often prisoners, deportees, immigrants, hobos, refugees, and other people in transit: displaced Andalusian peasants in Barcelona; Catalans in the Brazilian port city of Santos; Puerto Ricans and Germans in New York; Jews and Italians in Buenos Aires or Rosario; Spanish exiles in London or Mexicans in St. Louis; Koreans in China; Chinese in Tokyo or Paris; and so on.

Economically, in the second place: anarchist readers are generally working-class, often in precarious positions; many are (or, having been displaced, were) artisans, practicing trades threatened by the advance of industrial capitalism (e.g., shoemakers, weavers, tanners,

31 Landauer, "Lew Nikolajewitsch Tolstoi," in *Der werdende Mensch*, trans. Siegfried Bernhauser and Birgit Wörishofer, 199.
32 Joanne Ellen Passet, *Sex Radicals and the Quest for Women's Equality* (Urbana, IL: University of Illinois Press, 2003), 121.

cabinetmakers), although many, particularly with the rise of revolutionary syndicalism, are also to be found among the industrial working class (e.g., miners, garment workers, longshoremen, sailors); before the Second World War, a minority are middle-class professionals (e.g., journalists, educators, doctors, artists, engineers) or economically marginalized (tramps, migrant laborers, prostitutes, etc.).[33] In the late-twentieth century, with the ethnic assimilation of immigrants, the recuperation of workers' movements and the emergence of oppositional youth subcultures, young people living in semi-voluntary poverty reinvent drop-out culture. Half the respondents to a recent global survey of anarchists were aged sixteen to twenty-five, and almost two-thirds reported coming from middle-class backgrounds.[34]

Last, intellectually: many anarchists, particularly in the periods before the First World War, if they are not illiterate, lack a formal education, excluded from the institutions that produce, consecrate, and circulate knowledge (especially before the advent of compulsory public schooling, which arrived especially late in Spain, for instance). Driven by what Lily Litvak describes as an "enormous thirst for knowledge, encompassing all fields of culture and science," they frequently become autodidacts.[35]

It is not at all surprising that such "unstable, marginal, and heterogeneous reader[s]" set about constituting counter-communities.[36] What is striking is the extent to which it was "the printed word," as Kenyon Zimmer observes, that "created an imagined, text-based transnational community of anarchists, and transmitted the movement's ideology across space while sustaining collective identities across time."[37] This took place partly through

---

33 Alain Pessin, *La Rêverie anarchiste, 1848–1914* (Paris: Librairie des Méridiens, 1982), 43–49; see also Jean Maitron, "Un 'anar', qu'est-ce que c'est?," *Le mouvement social* 83 (April–June 1973): 23–45.

34 Knoll and Eloff, "2010 Anarchist Survey Report."

35 David Ortiz, "Redefining Public Education: Contestation, the Press, and Education in Regency Spain, 1885–1902," *Journal of Social History* 35.1 (Fall 2011): 75; Lily Litvak, "La buena nueva," *Revista de Occidente* 304 (September 2006): 8.

36 Hugo R. Mancuso, "Horizonte epistemológico del relato social moderno," *AdVersuS: Revista de Semiótica* 2.4 (December 2005).

37 Kenyon Zimmer, "*The Whole World is Our Country*": Immigration and Anarchism in the United States, 1885–1940 (Diss., University of Pittsburgh, 2010), 12.

the establishment of an ongoing conversation in anarchist periodicals among the readers and writers—who were and are often the same people.

Pick up a typical anarchist zine, circa the last thirty years, the great era of low-budget printing—it might be on a rack at a local infoshop, on a table at a punk show or an anarchist book fair, or handed around at a protest[38]—and notice the design characteristics, the look and feel of it, the whole *gestalt*. Chances are, it's got what Sandra Jeppesen kindly calls "a DIY or cut-and-paste aesthetic."[39] Apart from a relative few professional-looking, mass-printed publications (e.g., the German *graswurzelrevolution* ca. 2000–present, with a circulation of 3,500–5,000; U.S.-based *Anarchy: A Journal of Desire Armed* ca. 1990–present, at 6,000-plus circulation; or the French *Le Monde Libertaire*, with a print run of 15,000),[40] most anarchist periodicals look like this (fig. 2). Sloppy layout, misspellings, smudgy drawings, contempt for bourgeois journalistic standards: the zine typically advertises its own amateurishness as a way of signaling not only its authenticity (this is not capitalist media!) but the identity of sender and receiver, writers and readers—in keeping with the principles of an anarchist economy, in which production and consumption are to be fused together as much as possible.[41]

Turn the dial of history back to the dawn of the twentieth century, and you will find anarchist newspapers that *look* immediately very, very different (figs. 3). Look closer, though, and you will find a similar dynamic at work, reducing the distance between the poles. Here is an 1883 issue of *La Autonomía*, a newspaper published by *compañeros* in Seville. On page 4, we see contributions of poems written by a peasant and a cork-maker, accompanied by letters apologizing for "these poorly drawn lines," respectfully requesting that the editors correct any

---

38 Or, as Anna Poletti writes, "left in public places: on trains, in cafés and pubs, and slipped between the pages of slick magazines in newsagents" ("Self-Publishing in the Global and Local," *Biography* 28.1 [2005]:185).

39 Sandra Jeppesen, *Guerrilla Texts and Textual Self-Production* (Diss., York University, 2006), 135.

40 *Anarchy: A Journal of Desire Armed* 37 (Summer 1993); John D. H. Downing, ed., *Encyclopedia of Social Movement Media* (Los Angeles: Sage Publications, 2011), 38, 44.

41 Paul Goodman and Percival Goodman, *Communitas: Means of Livelihood and Ways of Life* (New York: Vintage Books, 1960), 153.

Fig. 2: Anarchist aesthetic, ca. 2011 (artist unknown).

spelling mistakes.[42] Pick up an issue of *O Baluarte* (*The Bulwark*), organ of the anarchist hatmakers' union in Rio de Janeiro (1907–1912), and alongside the writings of anarchists as illustrious as Anselmo Lorenzo, you can read stories signed by an "anonymous hatter [*chapeleiro anônimo*]," just as, in the pages of *Nuestra Tribuna* (1922–1925), directed by the gifted autodidact Juana Rouco Buela (1889–1969), essays, poetry, and fiction written by ordinary women subscribers scattered across Argentina appeared alongside a virtual Who's Who of international anarchist women: Louise Michel and Madeleine Vernet from France; Lucy Parsons and Luisa Capetillo from the U.S. and its conquests; Teresa Claramunt and Federica Montseny from Spain; Maria Lacerda de Moura from Brazil; Virgilia d'Andrea from Italy.[43]

---

42 Lily Litvak, *El cuento anarquista (1880–1911): Antología* (Madrid: Taurus, 1982), 17.

43 chapeleiro anônimo, "Um sonho," in *Contos Anarquistas: Antologia da prosa libertária no Brasil (1901–1935)*, eds. Arnoni Prado, Antonio and Francisco Foot Hardman (São Paulo: Editorial Brasiliense, 1985), 107–110; Elsa Calzetta, "Juana Rouco Buela, una mujer anarquista,"

Fig. 3a: Anarchist design aesthetic ca. 1908–1914: cover for *Die Freie Generation* 2.12 (June 1908)...

A great deal of anarchist poetry published in the newspapers of the Spanish CNT was signed pseudonymously or anonymously, as if to answer Michel Foucault's famous question, "What Is An Author?" with a resounding "who cares?"[44] In short, decades before terms like "zinester" and "DIY" came into use, anarchist publications were challenging the distinctions between authors and readers, constituting anarchist discourse as an open-ended dialogue (a "periodic conversation," as the writer for *Tierra Libre* put it) rather than a monologue.

---

in *Nuestra Tribuna: Hojita del sentir anárquico femenino (1922–1925)* (Bahia Blanca, Argentina: Editorial de la Universidad Nacional del Sur, 2005), 21, 25.

44 Salaün, "Introducción," *Romancero libertario*, 23–25.

Fig. 3b: Fermín Sagristá, cover for the *Almanaque de Tierra y Libertad* for 1912...

Active and critical readership also turned the publication of literary writing in anarchist periodicals into a dissensual, reflexive "conversation." For instance, in 1913, as Sakai Toshihiko's translation of
George Bernard Shaw's *Man and Superman* unfolded in serialized installments on the pages of *Kindai shisō* (*Modern Thought*), anarchist
readers vigorously debated its politico-literary merits (was Shaw's satire as effective as Ibsen's harsh social critique?) as well as its implications for gender relations.[45] In the anarchist free-love journal *Lucifer,*

---

45 Mutsuko Motoyama, *Shaw and Japanese Drama* (Diss., University of
   Washington, 1975), 136, 181.

Fig. 3c: and Ludovico Caminita, illustration for first page of Regeneración 4.192 (June 13, 1914).

the Light-Bearer, the "tragic ending" of a short story by May Huntley (a.k.a. Lizzie M. Holmes, 1850–1926), "Nature and the Law" (Apr. 6–13, 1901), kicked off a months-long discussion among readers, editors, and contributors, men and women alike, on the ethics of love and romance.[46] Following a similarly lengthy and involved dispute over the literary merits of the writer Vargas Vila (April 1924–March 1925) Federica Montseny's novel *La Victoria* (billed as a "story of the

---

46 These included Moses Harman, "Love Dies—Why Should Love Die?" *Lucifer* 864 (May 11, 1901); Helen Webster, "Why Should Love Die?" *Lucifer* 867 (June 1, 1901); Mabel M'Coy Irwin, "Why Does Love Die?—A Suggestion," *Lucifer* 873 (July 13, 1901); Elsie Cole Wilcox, "Some Reasons Why Love Should Die," *Lucifer* 876 (Aug. 3, 1901); and Voltairine de Cleyre, "The Death of Love," *Lucifer* 883 (Sept. 21, 1901). See Ernesto A. Longa, *Anarchist Periodicals in English Published in the United States (1833–1995)* (Lanham, MD: Scarecrow Press, 2010), 160.

Fig. 4: A poster for the Mujeres Libres' cultural campaign: "The book you read must affirm your ideological position, enrich your intelligence, and improve your sensibility."

moral problems faced by a woman of modern ideas") sparked a heated debate in the pages of *La Revista Blanca*, with male readers such as Cirilo Viñolas complaining of the seemingly anti-romantic decision taken by the romantic heroine, Clara Delval: was it in keeping with the expectations of the genre? With her character? With femininity? Other anarchist women writers weighed in with reasoned and impassioned "Defense[s] of Clara."[47]

---

47 For the Vargas Vila controversy, see Federica Montseny, "Comentando a un hombre," *La Revista Blanca* 2.22 (Apr. 15, 1924); Montseny, "La Obra de los mediocres," *La Revista Blanca* 2.30 (Aug. 15, 1924); Montseny, "Alrededor de Vargas Vila," *La Revista Blanca* 2.35 (Nov. 1, 1924); J. Serret, "Vargas

Periodicals played a key role in sustaining this global print culture, to be sure, but so did books. Works of popular science by anarchists, such as Peter Kropotkin's *Mutual Aid: A Factor of Evolution* (1902), Elisée Reclus's *L'Homme et la Terre* (1905–1908), and Fernando Tarrida del Mármol's *Problemas Transcendentales: Estudios de Sociología y Ciencia Moderna* (1908) helped to establish a sense of the entire universe as seen from an anarchist perspective—a view codified and monumentalized by Sébastien Faure's four-volume *Encyclopédie anarchiste* (1934); so did literary works published in book form such as Adrián del Valle's *Fin de la Fiesta: Cuadro Dramático* (1898), Charles Erskine Scott Wood's *The Poet in the Desert* (1915), Miyajima Sukeo's *The Miner* (*Kōfu*, 1916), and Federica Montseny's *El Hijo de Clara* (1927).

Anarchist book culture and the world of libertarian periodicals overlapped considerably and worked to reinforce one another. Frequently, book-length plays and novels would be reviewed, advertised, and serialized in the anarchist newspapers and magazines, then discussed and debated in the same pages. In this sense, as we shall see further, the anarchist universe of reading forms an extension of anarchist pedagogy. During the Spanish Civil War, pamphlets created by the anarchist women's association, the Agrupación Mujeres Libres, advised women against "buy[ing] just 'any old books' ... The book you read must affirm your ideological position, enrich your intelligence, and improve your sensibility" (fig. 4); another anarchist propaganda poster illustrated by the artist Cimine urged passersby to "Read anarchist books and become a man."[48] In spite of Cimine's masculinist tone, both

Vila (I)," *La Revista Blanca* 2.40 (Jan. 15, 1925); Serret, "Vargas Vila (II)," *La Revista Blanca* 2.41 (Feb. 1, 1925); Montseny, "Sobre Vargas Vila," *La Revista Blanca* 2.42 (Feb. 15, 1925); Ignacio Cornejo, "Sobre Vargas Vila y sus obras," *La Revista Blanca* 2.43 (Mar. 1, 1925); Montseny, "Las mujeres y Vargas Vila," *La Revista Blanca* 57 (Sept. 1, 1925); Julia Acosta and Matilde Mota, "Las Mujeres y Vargas Vila," *La Revista Blanca* 2.56 (Sept. 15, 1925). For the "Clara" controversy, see Montseny, "En defensa de Clara (I)," *La Revista Blanca* 2.46 (Apr. 15, 1925); Montseny, "En defensa de Clara (II)," *La Revista Blanca* 2.47 (May 1, 1925); Montseny, "En defensa de Clara (III)," *La Revista Blanca* 2.48 (May 15, 1925); Isabel Hortensia Pereyra, "En Defensa de Clara: Mi Humilde Opinion," *La Revista Blanca* 3.51 (Jul. 1, 1925); and Antonia Maymón, "En Defensa de Clara," *La Revista Blanca* 3.53 (Aug. 1, 1925).
48 Mujeres Libres qtd. in Laura Ruiz Eugenio and Gregori Siles Molina "Aportaciones de Mujeres Libres (1936–1939) desde la educación para la

campaigns were invested with the same hope and the same anxiety: if the right books could fortify you for the fight against fascism, then this implied that there were also such things as the *wrong* books—what Domingos Ribeiro Filho (1875–1942), author of several anarchist novels, called "literary poison."[49] Indeed, as early as the very first period of the development of anarchism, we find Proudhonian militants such as Henri Tolain (1828–1897), writing in *La Tribune Ouvrière* (1865), fretting about the taste of newly literate workers for *romans-feuilletons*, serialized novels, featuring lurid crime stories (featuring "at least two corpses per episode") and—worse!—stories that took the police for their heroes or invited workers to live vicariously in the "elegant and delicate world" of the trysting aristocrats who still populate romance novels.[50] Around the same time, the journalist Jules Vallès (1832–1885), writing for *Le Figaro* (1862), bemoans the "influence" of popular novels such as *Robinson Crusoe, Last of the Mohicans*, or *Ivanhoe*, escapist fantasies that set up false ideals of romance or heroism for us to compare ourselves with.[51] Well into the second period, Tolain's arguments are reiterated by anarchists such as Liu Shifu (1884–1915), attacking the popular fiction of the late Qing as "inducive to wantonness," "cater[ing] to the tastes of the times," or E. Statio, writing in *Le Libertaire* under the title "L'Art et le Peuple" (1905):

> Melodramas with grand, sentimental, tearjerking tirades, sputterings of artifice, the Eiffel Tower, fountains of light, this is what suits and distracts the people. As long as they laugh or cry, they

inclusión de las mujeres obreras y campesinas," in *El largo camino hacia una educación inclusiva, Vol. 2*, eds. María Reyes Berruezo Albéniz and Susana Conejero López (Pamplona, Spain: Universidad Pública de Navarra, 2009): 343; Cimine, *Lee libros anarquistas y serás un hombre* (1936–1938).

49 Domingos Ribeiro Filho, "O veneno literário," *Renascença: arte e pensamento* 1.3 (Apr. 1923): 8. Interestingly, Ribeiro Filho's anxiety is focused on female readers—he is writing in the pages of Maria Lacerda de Moura's journal—who are especially imperiled by reading novels that "extol the beauties of the shop window and the sentiments of the seraglio." The identification of consumerism at once with lasciviousness and femininity is not alien to this line of anarchist argument.

50 Georges Duveau, *La vie ouvrière en France, sous le second empire* (Paris: Gallimard, 1946), 471. It must be said that Tolain also fulminates a good deal against the moral "depravity" supposedly taught by these novels.

51 Jules Vallès, "Les Victimes du Livre," *Les Réfractaires* (Paris: G. Charpentier, 1881), 160, 162–163, 171–172.

do not think. [This is] the morphine that anesthetizes minds and numbs intellects. The serial novel, in which characters whose emotional faculties know no expression short of paroxysm go through endless convulsions, is an excellent educator, very conducive to making the People stupid.... [Popular novelists such as] Montépin, Ponson du Terrail, Sardou, Ennery, Richebourg, Déroulède, Sarcey, etc., are true pillars of society.[52]

Some sixty years later, we still find militants like Charles Hotz (a.k.a. Edouard Rothen, 1874–1937) denouncing, in a pamphlet titled, once again, *L'Art et le Peuple* (1924), the "merchants of evil literature" who peddle "the worst adventure stories, police stories, crime stories, the exploits of the most unlikely romantic heroes," while Shin Chae-ho (a.k.a. Tanjae, 1880–1936) attacks "pretty operas and novels" focused on the lives of "the rich privileged class" (1925), and Camillo Berneri (1897–1937) concludes that "the readership of the serial novel is conservative," preferring dated "clichés" to the complexities of modern life (1928).[53] And if contemporary anarchists reserve their scorn for mass-market movies and TV,[54] it is still possible to find Peter Lamborn Wilson attacking popular novelists such as Stephen King for their "saliromaniac" fiction, a symptom, if not a cause, of "decadence" (1991).[55]

Nor is the mistrust of anarchists reserved for mass literature and the "low" culture manufactured by capitalism. Stuart Christie writes of growing up alienated from the "imperialist culture of the

---

52 Liu Shifu qtd. in P. Chan, *Liu Shifu*, 64, trans. Chan's; Statio qtd. in Vittorio Frigerio, "La Vérité par la fiction," *Belphégor* 9.1 (February 2010).

53 Charles Hotz, *L'Art et le Peuple* (Paris: Groupe de propagande par la brochure, 1924), 22; Shin Chae-ho qtd. in Song Chae-So, "The Changes of Tanjae's Thought Seen in 'The Dream Sky' and 'The War of the Dragons,'" *Korea Journal* 20.12 (December 1980): 20; Camillo Berneri, "La novela de folletón," *Almanaque de la Novela Ideal* (Barcelona: Publicaciones de "La Revista Blanca," 1928), 83–84.

54 See, for instance, Paul Goodman's 1963 essay "Television: The Continuing Disaster," in *Drawing the Line: The Political Essays of Paul Goodman* (New York: Free Life Editions, 1977), 99–103; or George Bradford's (a.k.a. David Watson's) 1984 piece, "Media: Capital's Global Village," in *Reinventing Anarchy, Again*, 258–271.

55 Peter Lamborn Wilson, "Amoral Responsibility," *Science Fiction EYE* 8 (Winter 1991): 55.

victor" represented, for him, by Shakespeare.[56] This sentiment is often echoed by East Asian anarchists, for whom a fixed body of literary "classics" is often associated with the dead hand of tradition and hierarchy; thus, Shin Chae-ho names "literature" and "the fine arts," along with "religion," "customs," and "public morals," as one of the means by which "servile cultural thoughts" are perpetuated among the people.[57] This classical literary culture formed the foundation for the French educational system parodied by Vallès in his quasi-autobiographical "Jacques Vingtras" trilogy—a system designed to teach respect for and rote imitation of the official canon of "Great Writers."[58] The class composition of these canons also renders them suspect in the eyes of anarchists: thus, in his entry on "Literature" for the *Encyclopédie anarchiste*, Rothen regards the rise of a body of erudite writing by and for the ruling classes, increasingly detached from the wellsprings of popular creativity, as a real loss for culture.[59] Many anarchists cottoned to Tolstoy's argument, in *What Is Art?*, that literature should be "accessible to all."[60]

At the same time, anarchists often see the corpus of "high" literature as part of a wider cultural patrimony that properly belongs to the people, and therefore as something to which access must be demanded and obtained. Indeed, we can find among anarchists a surprising reverence for "great" works. Gustav Landauer authors an entire book's worth of lectures on Shakespeare, while Bernard Lazare praises Dante and Rabelais as models for modern practitioners of *l'art social*.[61] "On the advice of Longinus," Paul Goodman remarked, "I 'write it for Homer, for Demosthenes,' and other pleasant company who somehow

56 Stuart Christie, *My Granny Made Me an Anarchist: The Cultural and Political Formation of a West Scotland "Baby Boomer"* (Hastings, UK: Christie Books, 2002), 85.

57 Shin Chae-ho, "Declaration of the Korean Revolution," trans. Dongyoun Hwang, in *Anarchism: A Documentary History of Libertarian Ideas, Vol. 1*, 375.

58 Ali Nematollahy, "Jules Vallès and the Anarchist Novel," *Nineteenth-Century French Studies* 35.3–4 (Spring–Summer 2007): 575.

59 Edouard Rothen, "Littérature," in *L'Encyclopédie anarchiste*, 1295.

60 Peter Kropotkin, *Ideals and Realities in Russian Literature* (New York: A.A. Knopf, 1915), 298–299.

61 Gustav Landauer, *Shakespeare: Dargestellt in Vorträgen* (Frankfurt am Main: Rütten & Loening, 1920); Bernard Lazare, *L'Écrivain et l'Art Social* (Béarn: Bibliothèque de l'Art Social, 1896), 13–14.

are more alive to me than most of my contemporaries."[62] Unlike the ephemeral clamor produced by a bomb, Pierre Quillard observes, a great poem can constitute a "permanent" disruption of the mediocre order: "the terrible irony flies across the centuries, and it will strike all the governors, the pharisees, the money-changers, today, tomorrow, and forever." Thus, "just as infallibly as the braver anarchist comrades, Shakespeare and Aeschylus pave the way to the collapse of the old world."[63] A 1937 editorial in the Spanish antifascist journal *Documentos Históricos* voices a very similar sentiment, this time in reaction to the famous Nazi quip, "Whenever I hear the word 'culture,' I reach for my revolver": "When we hear culture spoken badly of, we have to reach, not for the revolver—because we think that the pistol has a very limited physical field of action in relation to the infinite domain of the spirit—but for our force of persuasion, to convince the vacillating that doing cultural labor and working for a dignified and humanist culture means performing a revolutionary task for the cause of the working class."[64] Neither was this attitude confined to intellectuals from privileged backgrounds such as Quillard, a product of the élite Lycée Fontanes and habitué of the Symbolist circles, or the correspondent for *Documentos Históricos* (about whom we shall hear more later); Emma Goldman, for instance, treasured literature in Russian, English, and especially German, which she regarded as languages of high culture, rather than the demotic Yiddish of her upbringing, which she associated with religious strictures and parochialism, and spent a surprising amount of time on the stump speaking on topics such as "Russian Literature—The Voice of Revolt" and "Walt Whitman, the Liberator of Sex."[65]

What we can see at work, in the global anarchist movements of the late-nineteenth and early-twentieth centuries, is the formation

62 Paul Goodman, "The Present Plight of a Man of Letters," in *Criticism and Culture: Papers of the Midwest Modern Language Association 2*, ed. Sherman Paul (Iowa City: Midwest Modern Language Association, 1972), 6.

63 Pierre Quillard, *L'Anarchie par la littérature* (Paris: Édicions du Fourneau, 1993), 11, 13–14.

64 Félix Martí-Ibañez, "La Cultura en el nuevo orden revolucionario," *Documentos Históricos* 1.1 (October 1937): 12.

65 Candace Falk, "Forging Her Place: An Introduction," *Emma Goldman: A Documentary History of the American Years, Vol. 1: Made for America, 1890–1901* (Berkeley: University of California Press, 2003), 46.

of something like an anarchist canon of non-anarchist writers. This is not to be confused with what is often referred to as "literary anarchism"—i.e., the broad swathe of avant-garde writers, from Apollinaire to Artaud, influenced by and expressing sympathies for anarchism.[66] With a few exceptions, these names almost never appear in the anarchist press during the period of their ascendancy (a couple of decades on either side of 1910, that year Virginia Woolf arbitrarily selects as the one in which "everything changed")—except as occasional objects of derision. However, a survey of the world-wide anarchist press during the same period would find the names of a number of non-anarchist literary figures repeated disproportionately: especially Henrik Ibsen, Leo Tolstoy, and Émile Zola, but also Leonid Andreyev, Anatole France, Maxim Gorky, Gerhart Hauptmann, Heinrich Heine, Victor Hugo, William Morris, Ada Negri, Friedrich Nietzsche, Romain Rolland, Percy Bysshe Shelley, August Strindberg, Walt Whitman, and Oscar Wilde. What do these writers have in common? Obviously, all but one are male, though this is not unlike other canonical selections then or since.[67] Some are classified as Naturalists (Hauptmann, Zola; and more problematically, Ibsen, Strindberg, and Rolland), or as representatives of some brand of Realism (Andreyev, France, Gorky, Negri, Tolstoy); others are in the line of Romanticism (Heine, Hugo, Morris, Poe, Shelley, Whitman)

---

66 Clara E. Lida, for instance, distinguishes between what she calls "*anarquismo literario*" (with the emphasis on the "literary") and "*literatura anarquista*" (with the emphasis on the "anarchist"). See Lida, "Literatura anarquista y anarquismo literario," *Nueva Revista de Filología Hispánica* 19.2 (1970): 360–381.

67 If Vittorio Frigerio is right to say that this "appropriation and use of texts and writers from outside the movement" constituted a kind of "diver[-sion] of the symbolic capital of official literature and science for its own purposes" ("La Vérité par la fiction"), then the sexist values inherent in the evaluations forming such a list might reflect that formation of symbolic capital—already massively skewed towards male writers—as much as the (by no means inconsiderable) residual sexism in the anarchist movement and its media apparatuses. It also presents a striking contrast to the gender balance among ordinary militants who wrote for anarchist publications: here, women's participation is notable. Indeed, Lida asserts that "the presence of women who contributed to the anarchist press was much higher than that of other socialist movements of the time" ("Discurso e imaginario en la literatura anarquista," *Filología* 29.1–2 [1996]: 123).

or Aestheticism (Nietzsche, Wilde)—tendencies commonly seen as diametrically opposite to one another. Indeed, this embrace of opposites signals something important about anarchist tastes in literature, as we shall see. We might further observe that each of these writers is valued by anarchist critics for qualities usually associated with writers in the opposite camp: e.g., Zola for his ability to stir passion, Wilde for the concrete protest of his *Song of Reading Gaol*. In any case, the works of all of these writers have been, to some extent, adopted, appropriated, or, to borrow Sandra Jeppesen's terms, "consecrated" as anarchist, despite their refusal of anarchist commitments, by repeated inclusion in anarchist "spaces."[68]

A similar process of "consecration" takes place in Asia, where translations of many of the same Euro-American writers take the same place, but where there are also efforts to develop a native corpus of classics untainted by the authoritarian aura. We can see such a project under way in the curriculum developed by anarchist educator Sun Lianggong (1894–1962) for a course at the National Labor University in Shanghai (1927–1932) in "Labor Literature"—"a kind of proletarian-populist literature," as Ming K. Chan and Arif Dirlik describe it, "with a major aim of reflecting and revealing social realities, especially the authors' grievances and criticism of social ills."[69] In other words, it constituted something like what Japanese anarchist critic Akiyama Kiyoshi called *anakizumu bungaku* (a "literature *of* anarchism" or "literature of opposition") as distinct from *anakisuto no bungaku* ("literature written *by* anarchists").[70]

In addition, then, to works consecrated by inclusion in anarchist spaces, written by

a) *committed writers from the middle classes* (Octave Mirbeau, Bernard Lazare, Florencio Sánchez, Avelino Fóscolo, etc.) and

---

68 Some of these writers made more or less equivocal gestures toward anarchism; Wilde went so far as to declare his political preference for anarchism in response to Jules Huret's famous survey. However, none were integrated into any anarchist organization or movement *per se*.

69 Ming K. Chan and Arif Dirlik, *Schools into Fields and Factories: Anarchists, the Guomindang, and the National Labor University in Shanghai, 1927–1932* (Durham: Duke University Press, 1991), 87.

70 Stephen Filler, *Chaos From Order: Anarchy and Anarchism in Modern Japanese Fiction, 1900–1930* (Diss., Ohio State University, 2004), 4, 216–217.

b) *non-committed writers adopted or appropriated by anarchists* (Émile Zola, Leo Tolstoy, Walt Whitman, Henrik Ibsen, etc.), we find circulating in the same media

c) *works written by working-class anarchist militants without literary training or credentials* (e.g, Luisa Capetillo or Gigi Damiani, but especially anonymous works, often signed in ways that signal this identity—e.g., "anonymous hatter").

We might further distinguish between anarchist works directed partially or primarily at *non-militants* and those written *by and for* militants—a truly self-directed literature. Of the works produced for non-militant audiences, there is often a palpable difference between those intended for working-class readers (urban and rural manual workers) and those intended for a middle-class readership (urban intellectual workers). This difference is sometimes manifested in terms of genre: thus, the forms of the dialogue story and the serial novel may have more often been directed toward manual workers, while the novel written for publication in book form, as Flávio Luizetto notes, was often meant "to attract followers to the anarchist cause among public servants, journalists, lawyers, writers, teachers and students—people who form part of what are called, for lack of a more precise term, the urban middle classes."[71] It is possible that these genres were at times also gendered: in a study of the anticlerical journal *A Lanterna*, Walter da Silva Oliveira suggests that "there was, in the period studied [1909–1916], a strong link between short stories and novels [published in its pages] and an audience of female readers," whom the

---

71 Marcella Bencivenni, *Italian American Radical Culture in New York City: The Politics and Arts of the Sovversivi, 1890–1940* (Diss., City University of New York, 2003), 121; Flávio Luizetto, "O recurso da ficção: um capítulo da história do anarquismo no Brasil," in *Libertários no Brasil: Memória, Lutas, Cultura*, ed. Antônio Arnoni Prado (São Paulo: Editora Brasilense, 1986), 131; Boaventura, "A Ficção Anarquista," 79–92. Boaventura further notes that the subjects shifted depending on the audience: the novels of Brazilian anarchists such as Fábio Luz and Domingos Ribeiro Filho concerned "the life of the Brazilian middle class at the turn of the century," with the intention of "denounc[ing] the frivolity and corruption of that world, suggesting alternative ways of life," whereas short stories and serial novels in anarchist journals more often featured working-class protagonists, locating the sources of oppression in the workplace (84).

editors considered to be those most harmed by religious discourse.[72]

Michel Ragon reminds us, too, that there are differences between, on the one hand, an "anarchist literature" written in a spirit of commitment by credentialed intellectuals, and on the other hand, "proletarian literature" without a clearly signaled sectarian identity as anarchist, destined *for* working-class readers without further qualification, written *by* workers without any credentials (e.g., Henri Poulaille [1896–1980] or Albert Soulilou [1905–1967]):

> The worker-writers are often possessed of a libertarian spirit; some are even anarchist militants. But anarchist literature *per se* merits its own study. If its themes are frequently evoked in the course of these pages, it nonetheless expresses a particular vision of the world that is not always of a proletarian spirit. It is more philosophical than descriptive, more rebellious than constructive. It counts in its ranks more essayists than novelists, more journalists than poets.[73]

Works of pure "proletarian literature," too, are to be found in the anarchist world, from Japan (where *puroretaria bungaku* was one of the more lasting legacies of an anarchist movement largely crushed in the 1920s) to France (where Poulaille becomes one of its first champions).

To all of these complications in the authorship and readership of anarchist literature, we must add another: at several points in the history of anarchism, conditions are hostile enough to incur serious censorship and reprisal against anarchist writers and publications. In these situations—e.g., in Spain following the infamous political trials at Montjuich (1897), or under the dictatorship of Primo de Rivera (1923–1930)—it became impossible to openly publish and distribute works directly advocating anarchism. One of the ways in which anarchists adapted to this was to further "culturalize" their media, to camouflage politics under the guise of social science and aesthetics. Thus, as David Ortiz notes, anarchist journals benefited from "avoiding use of the words 'anarchism' and 'anarchist,'" taking on oblique, politically

---

72 Walter da Silva Oliveira, *Narrativas à luz d'A "Lanterna": Anticlericalismo, anarquismo e representações* (Diss., Pontifícia Universidade Católica de São Paulo, 2008), 13–14, 83.

73 Michel Ragon, *Histoire de la littérature prolétarienne en France* (Paris: A. Michel, 1974), 145.

"blank" titles such as *Revista Blanca* (1898–1905, 1923–1936) *Ciencia Social* (1895–1896), or *Natura* (1903–1905), presenting anarchist texts under the lofty, academically consecrated rubrics of "sociology," "history," "letters," "art," "science," and so on. Taking another direction, the wildly popular "Novela Libre" and "Novela Ideal" book series issued by *Revista Blanca* disseminated anarchist ideas in the form of *novelas rosas*, i.e., paperback romances. Other popular novel series authored by anarchists adopted different genre identities, all while gesturing discreetly, in the words of an advertisement for the anarcho-syndicalist "Novela del Pueblo" series, toward "criticism ... of some aspect of modern society" and certain "hints and anticipations of a better human society."[74]

The use of established genres of "culture"—both high and low, erudite and popular—as protective coloration for the continuation of political propaganda under repressive conditions poses some possibilities and some problems. On the one hand, softening the sectarian political content, presented as either edification or entertainment, might reach audiences otherwise beyond the range of anarchist ideological messages (say, middle-class intellectual workers interested in cultural trends, or depoliticized manual workers seeking distraction and relaxation). On the other hand, stripping away the symbols that distinguish anarchism, that establish it as a political identity, might allow readers to walk away unchanged—or worse, to appropriate the text for some other ideological purpose. The contents of *La Revista Blanca* might leave no room for such misunderstanding, but what about the paperback melodramas? The relative openness to interpretation that makes for the "literary" might work against the anarchists' radical agenda. If a text is always, as Umberto Eco has it, "a lazy machine that appeals to the reader to do some of its work," literary texts might be said to elicit even more activity on the reader's part, an imagining, projecting, fantasizing activity that could erase or overwrite the anarchist content of anarchist literature, producing a depoliticized text—or worse, a politically co-opted text.[75]

This danger, the ineliminable possibility that what you've written or painted or sung can take on a life of its own or be turned

---

74 Qtd. in J. Rafael Macan, "Prologo," *Narraciones anarco-sindicalistas de los años veinte* (Barcelona: Icaria, 1978), 22–23, trans. mine.

75 Umberto Eco, *Six Walks in the Fictional Woods* (Cambridge, MA: Harvard University Press, 1994), 49.

against itself, is the condition of all art. Nonetheless, it is a special risk for anarchists just because the Idea is almost universally perceived as so terrifically threatening that it is all but literally unthinkable. "Someone whose legs had been bound from birth but had managed nevertheless to walk as best he could," Malatesta wrote, "might attribute his ability to move to those very bonds.... That man would ferociously defend his bonds and consider as his enemy anyone who tried to remove them."[76] Thus with anarchists' proposals to remove the bonds of Capital, State, and Church. Readers can resist, and the popular audience for anarchist messages resists "ferociously." And anarchists are all too familiar with popular distortions of the Idea—the notion that anarchy means "chaos," that anyone who is destructive or disregarding of others is an anarchist, and so on. In effect, these symbolic uses of "anarchy" are co-optations of anarchist themes for capitalist uses, promoting the kind of hedonistic individualism that moves product (and providing the police and the priests with a handy folk-devil). An anarchist writer can expect to be misread in many directions at once.

At the same time, there is also the danger of making anarchism into—again, in the words of Malatesta (apropos of his Russian colleagues' attempt to formalize anarchist beliefs and methods into a "Platform")—"a government and a church":[77] that is, anarchist militants could attempt to so tightly control meanings as to choke off any alternative readings, reintroducing authoritarianism into the heart of anti-authoritarian thought and practice. Here, I think of Roland Barthes's speculation that a certain authoritarian element would always inhere in *"the very fact"* of speaking: *"All speech is on the side of the Law,"* he gloomily surmised, suggesting that to teach as an anti-authoritarian, the best one could do would be to somehow soften one's speech, "'presenting' a discourse without imposing it."[78] This might indeed be taken as a model of anarchist pedagogy: the teacher presents but does not impose. "Teaching," Ricardo Mella insists,

76 Errico Malatesta, *Anarchy*, trans. Vernon Richards (London: Freedom Press, 2001), 15–16.
77 Errico Malatesta, *The Anarchist Revolution*, ed. and trans. Vernon Richards (London: Freedom Press, 1995), 98.
78 Roland Barthes, *Image-Music-Text*, ed. Stephen Hill (New York: Hill and Wang, 1977), 191–192; *A Barthes Reader*, ed. Susan Sontag (New York: Hill and Wang, 1982), 476.

"neither can nor must be propaganda."[79] And yet it is not the model of pedagogy most widely adopted by actual anarchists; that would be Francisco Ferrer y Guardia's (1859–1909) *Escuela Moderna*, which dispensed with most of the disciplinary apparatus of conventional schools but retained for the teacher a considerable role as an active propagator of values:

> This does not mean that we will leave the child, at the very outset of its education, to form its own ideas.... The very constitution of the mind, at the commencement of its development, demands that at this stage the child shall be receptive. The teacher must implant the germs of ideas.[80]

To merely leave the pupil to think alone, for Ferrer, is to surrender to capitalist ideology, popular prejudices, Church hegemony, and a thousand other authoritarian influences already in place. Accordingly, many anarchists have accepted the notion of anarchist culture as a form of propaganda, in the root sense of seed-sowing ("implant[ing] the germs of ideas"): Peter Lamborn Wilson suggests that fiction should function as "*propaganda for life*," while Derrick Jensen (b. 1960) flatly declares that "all writing is propaganda."[81]

How can an anarchist text make propaganda without treating its readers as a passive mass to be led? How can it overcome the resistance of its readers without thereby exercising a tyrannical power over them? Here we might turn Socrates's problem around: rather than seeing the text as a helpless victim of mischievous readers, unable to defend or "speak for" itself, we could see it as a little dictator, a voice that can't and won't "shut up." If texts are inherently incapable of *listening* to their readers' responses, how can they ever be anything

---

79 Ricardo Mella, *IdearIo* (Gijón, Spain: Impr. "La Victoria," 1926), 242.

80 Francisco Ferrer y Guardia, *The Origin and Ideals of the Modern School*, trans. Joseph MacCabe (New York and London: G.P. Putnam's Sons, 1913), 28.

81 Wilson, "Amoral Responsibility," 56–57; Jensen, interview in Margaret Killjoy, *Mythmakers & Lawbreakers: Anarchist Writers on Fiction* (Oakland, CA: AK Press, 2009), 22. While many anarchists read Jensen (who does not self-identify as anarchist), they have criticized his recent attacks on transgendered people. Wilson, too, is highly controversial among anarchists for his defense of pedophilia.

but monologues, forms of "speech" more unilateral than any partici-pant in ordinary dialogue could ever claim? On the other hand, how can anarchist readers defend themselves against the author's authori-ty without simply squeezing the life out of the texts they read, "read-ing into them" the pre-formed contents of their prejudices, closing off possible interpretations?

For a long time, the *Revista Blanca* bore on its cover a peculiar message, written in a cursive font: "*Lector: cuanto veas en ésta revis-ta contrario a tus opiniones en ella misma puedes refutarlo* [Reader, if you see anything in this journal contrary to your own opinions, you may refute it]." If this sounds like a kind of haughty challenge in En-glish, it does not appear to have the same connotative force in Span-ish; Antonio Elorza parses this as a kind of editorial policy, a way of signaling "total acceptance of the principle of dissent regarding their positions."[82] And as we have seen, the solicitation of dissent was evi-dently successful, as *La Revista Blanca* regularly drew vigorous, con-testatory correspondence from readers.

Inviting reply, questioning, participation, and engagement, an-archist periodicals turn readers into writers, recipients into senders, consumers into producers. Thus, readers of Rosa Graul's utopian nov-el, *Hilda's Home: A Story of Woman's Emancipation*, first published by installments in *Lucifer* in 1897, turned the pages of the journal into a months-long forum on "Where to Practicalize Hilda's Home": i.e., what would be the best site on which to found a real colony on the principles proposed by the novel.[83] Rather than distinguishing the fictional from the factual, the distant, cognitive sphere of utopian dreaming from the immediate, embodied realm of "practical" action, these readers freely appropriated Graul's story for their own purpos-es. This, too, demonstrates a convergence of the roles of writer and reader within anarchist literary discourse, as both claim and exercise the right to create.

This constitution of the reader as active agent is mirrored by an emphasis on what the Mujeres Libres called *capacitación* (at once "training," "preparation," and, more literally, "empowerment") as

---

82 Antonio Elorza, *La utopía anarquista bajo la segunda república* (Madrid: Editorial Ayuso, 1973), 370.

83 Carol Farley Kessler, *Daring to Dream: Utopian Fiction by United States Women Before 1950* (Syracuse, NY: Syracuse University Press, 1995), 112.

distinct from *captación* ("capture" or successful proselytization).[84] In this spirit of *capacitación*, Errico Malatesta recommended that propagandists working among depoliticized people "[make] an effort not to appear to be expounding and forcing on them a well-known and universally accepted truth," favoring a problem-posing method that would "stimulate them to think, to take the initiative and gain confidence in themselves." Such propaganda would aim, in fact, not so much at teaching "unconscious" masses what to believe as at "making people who are accustomed to obedience and passivity consciously aware of their real power and capabilities."[85] This is, indeed, one of the themes we will see running throughout anarchist culture—in imaginations and performances of rebellion (Part III), as well as in lyrical (Part II) and visual (Part IV) images of powerful bodies breaking their bonds (fig. 5). Resistance culture, for anarchists, meant nothing less than the *cultivation* of resistant bodies and souls.

Another way in which anarchists conceived of readers' empowerment entailed learning "the habit of *reading* twice, or at least with a *double* intent" recommended by Voltairine de Cleyre: i.e., an empathetic or recollective reading that allows the reader "to feel what the writer felt" and a skeptical reading that places the text at a distance from the reader.[86] This weaving back and forth between what one might identify as a Romantic *hermeneutics of recollection* (aimed at reconstructing a perspective that is historically or culturally distant from one's own) and a *hermeneutics of suspicion* with roots in the Enlightenment tradition (looking at the text as an instrument of power, as called into being by certain "interests" that might be distinct from or antagonistic to one's own), we can both resist the force of "Dominant Ideas" transmitted by texts and, at the same time, allow texts to educate us out of the dogmas, prejudices, and fixed ideas we've

---

84 Martha A. Ackelsberg, *Free Women of Spain: Anarchism and the Struggle for the Emancipation of Women* (Oakland, CA: AK Press, 2005); see also Mujeres Libres, "Salvemos a las mujeres de la dictadura de la mediocridad. Labor cultural y constructiva para ganar la guerra y hacer la Revolución," in *Mujeres Libres: España 1936–1939*, ed. Mary Nash (Barcelona: Tusquets Editor, 1977), 93–95.

85 Errico Malatesta, *Life and Ideas*, ed. Richard Vernon (London: Freedom Press, 1965), 179.

86 Voltairine de Cleyre, *Selected Works of Voltairine de Cleyre*, ed. Alexander Berkman (New York: Mother Earth Publishing Association, 1914), 379.

Fig. 5: From the Brazilian anarchist journal *A Guerra Social* 1.2 (July 16, 1911): the "Libertarian Ideal" is restrained by the clergy, the bourgeoisie, etc.: "All strive to stifle him, but he is developing, preparing … the day will come when, breaking all bonds, he will triumph, driving away all tyrants."

already absorbed.[87] Gustav Landauer, Rudolf Rocker, B. Rivkin, Ethel Mannin, Herbert Read, George Woodcock, Paul Goodman, and a host of other anarchist literary critics offer demonstrations of these resistant, ethically engaged modes of reading. Casting their critical gaze not only "*on* the page" but "*behind* the work," as de Cleyre put it,

87 Ibid., 79.

they gauge not only its adequacy as a representation of life, but its value for living; not only how it reflects the way of life it emerges from, but what modes of living it demonstrates and proposes.[88]

Nor was criticism reserved for critics. Rather, according to Ramón Flecha, anarchist educational practices aimed "to make every worker an intellectual."[89] This was pursued by establishing dialogues among working-class adult readers, not only through the mediation of print, important as that was, but face to face. Among the institutions created for this purpose were the *círculos culturales* and *centros de estudios* in Argentina, the *universités populaires* in France and Brazil, and in Spain, the storefront *ateneos* (workers' atheneums) and *tertulias*.[90]

Tertulias, literally "gatherings," began as an entirely informal practice of socializing among friends in cafés, but acquired a more formal dimension in the 1880s, as certain regular gatherings started to give themselves names like "Avant [Forward]," "Los Afines [The Like-Minded]," or "Ni Rey, Ni Patria [Neither King Nor Country]."[91] Emerging during the period of propaganda by the deed, these more formalized *tertulias* at first functioned as places where *grupitos* ("little groups," later known as *grupos de afinidad* or "affinity groups") formed for the purposes of action rather than education, planning

88 See, for example, de Cleyre's "Literature the Mirror of Man" in *Selected Works*, 359–380; Gustav Landauer's *Ein Weg deutschen Geistes* (München: Forum-Verlag, 1916) and "Fragment über Georg Kaiser" in *Der werdende Mensch*, 349–355; Rudolf Rocker, *Artistas y Rebeldes: escritos literarios y sociales* (Buenos Aires: Argonauta, 1922); B. Rivkin, *Di Grunt Tendentsin fun Yiddishe Literatur* (New York: Ikuf, 1947); Ethel Mannin, *Bread and Roses: An Utopian Survey and Blue-Print* (London: Macdonald, 1944); Herbert Read, *Icon and Idea: The Function of Art in the Development of Human Consciousness* (Cambridge, MA: Harvard University Press, 1955); George Woodcock, *The Writer and Politics* (London: Porcupine Press, 1948); Paul Goodman, *Speaking and Language: Defence of Poetry* (New York: Random House, 1972).

89 Flecha qtd. in Ruiz Eugenio and Siles Molina, "Aportaciones de Mujeres Libres," 344.

90 Juan Suriano, *Anarquistas: Cultura y política libertaria en Buenos Aires, 1890–1910* (Buenos Aires: Manantial, 2001), 39.

91 George Richard Esenwein, *Anarchist Ideology and the Working-Class Movement in Spain, 1868–1898* (Berkeley: University of California Press, 1989)132–133; Gerald Brenan, *The Spanish Labyrinth: An Account of the Social and Political Background of the Civil War* (Cambridge: Cambridge University Press, 1950), 163; Murray Bookchin, *The Spanish Anarchists: The Heroic Years, 1868–1936* (San Francisco: AK Press, 1998), 105.

violent strikes against the régime; by staging prolonged, focused conversations about anarchist texts and ideas, the *tertulia* could produce a collective with strong ideological agreement, capable of acting in a concerted, harmonious fashion.[92] However, that very ability to sustain continuous, open conversation among equals turned out to be valuable beyond the waning of the *attentat* as a tactic; it proved ideally suited for an egalitarian mode of education, the *tertulia literaria*.

Pepita Carpeña, a member of the Mujeres Libres during the Spanish Civil War, recollects the *tertulias literarias* promoted by the group:

> We all would read the same book, and then you cannot imagine the change of views that takes place in a general meeting ... maybe what you haven't perceived before, you realize when you say it to someone else, and the other person realizes what you have perceived. It was a great education. It taught me a lot; this is all the education I have, I have no more. I left school at age 11 and that was it.[93]

This kind of open-ended, critical dialogue is well-situated to evoke what Pierre-Joseph Proudhon called "collective reason": allowing each individual ego, each one a little "absolute" unto itself, both to express itself and to modify itself with the aid of all the other absolutes, in order to produce a new thought that is neither the average nor the sum of all the participants.[94]

Another form of collective reason is perhaps at work in another common anarchist practice: the practice of rereading through rewriting. This goes for songwriting, too—anarchist poets and

---

92 Parallel forms developed among anarchists elsewhere. In France, for instance, "groupes" gave themselves names like "Les Enfants de la Nature [The Children of Nature]," "Les Gonzes Poilus du Point-du-Jour [The Hairy Guys of Point-du-Jour]," "Les Indomptables [The Uncontrollables]," "Les Niveleurs [The Levellers]," "Les Insoumises [Disobedient Women]," or "Les Revoltées [Women In Revolt]" (Félix Dubois, *Le péril anarchiste: l'organisation secrète du parti anarchiste* [Paris: E. Flammarion, 1894], 43; David Berry, *History of the French Anarchist Movement*, 314).

93 Carpeña qtd. in Ruiz Eugenio and Siles Molina, "Aportaciones de Mujeres Libres," 343.

94 Pierre-Joseph Proudhon, *Selected Writings of P.-J. Proudhon*, ed. Stewart Edwards, trans. Elizabeth Fraser (Garden City, NY: Anchor Books, 1969), 121–122.

songwriters, as we shall see in Part II, freely rewrite hymns and anthems to suit their own purposes—and even for images, which anarchist artists subject to caricature, deformation, and *détournement* (Part IV). But it is perhaps most notable in the field of writing. B. Traven rewrites tales from the Brothers Grimm ("Macario") and the folk legend of the men who went hunting for Death (*Treasure of the Sierra Madre*); in his strange, unclassifiable book *Die Sechs* (1928; translated as *The Six*, 1938), Rudolf Rocker rewrites the stories of Faust, Don Juan, Hamlet, and Don Quixote; Federico Urales serializes his own versions of Don Quixote (*El Último Don Quijote*, 1925) and Don Juan (*Mi Don Juan*, 1935–1936); Bernard Lazare also rewrites the story of Don Juan ("La Confession de Don Juan"), as well as that of Shakespeare's Prospero ("La Fuite de Prospero"), Bluebeard ("Barbe-Bleu"), Moses ("L'Illusion"), Samson and Delilah ("Dalila"), Ahasuerus ("L'Attente Éternelle")...

At this point, I seem to hear the voice of Karl Marx thundering against "the tradition of all the dead generations [that] weighs heavy on the brains of the living": after all, wasn't the reproduction of antique Roman forms and symbols a sign of the French Revolution's inability to bring forth the "poetry of the future"? Could all these obsessive-seeming rewritings, on the part of the anarchists, constitute evidence of a slavish lack of originality—or, on the contrary, of a juvenile impulse to tear everything down by cheap parody? Either way, anarchists would seem to be disqualified once again from entry into the study of *literature*, that consecrated space inhabited only by an élite of "isolate[d] individual[s]," "strong misreader[s]" who anxiously disguise their Oedipal obligations to their "precursors," as Harold Bloom tells us, giving their creations what Walter Benjamin might call the "unique aura," the appearance of special value.[95] But *originality* per se is a propertarian concern, whereas *spontaneity*—the surprises that emerge when old signs are encountered in new contexts, which is a feature of their *repetition*[96]—is an anarchist concern, and while many anarchist works parody conventional or traditional texts in a

95 Harold Bloom, *Agon: Towards a Theory of Revisionism* (New York: Oxford University Press, 1982), 21; Benjamin, *Illuminations*, 231. For comparison, see Jonathan Lethem, "The Ecstasy of Influence: A Plagiarism," *Harper's* 314 (February 2007): 59–71.

96 See the entries for "Éternel retour" and "Répétition" in Daniel Colson's *Petit lexique*, 99–108 and 279–281.

spirit of hostile criticism, this is by no means always the case (Don Quixote, for instance, is a figure sincerely beloved by anarchists, who recognize this knight as one of our own).[97] Rather, anarchist revision, the delight in turning consumption into production and readers into writers, "repeats the meaning and revives the spirit of past makings, so they are not a dead weight," as Paul Goodman says—having written his own *Don Juan: Or, the Continuum of the Libido* (1942)—"by using them again in a making that is occurring now."[98]

This is the spirit in which anarchists read.

---

97 See, for instance, Peter Kropotkin's citation of Turguenev's unfavorable comparison of the hung-up intellectual Hamlet, who knows a hawk from a handsaw, to Don Quixote, "the man of action" who knows that windmills are giants—and more importantly, that "the witches, the giants," i.e., "the forces hostile to mankind" that must be fought against, are "the oppressors" (*Ideals and Realities*, 110–112).

98 Goodman, *Speaking and Language*, 160; Taylor Stoehr, "Introduction," in Paul Goodman, *The Facts of Life: Stories, 1940–1949*, ed. Taylor Stoehr (Santa Barbara: Black Sparrow Press, 1979), 9.

PART II

He returns. From the white ship
He looks upon the deep blue austerity...
....
Palpitating with fever and tension,

With daring escapes, with audacious leaps,
With hopes and magical futures ...

  —Virgilia d'Andrea, "Il Ritorno Dell'Esule [The Exile's Return]."

This ocean, humiliating in its disguises
Tougher than anything.
No one listens to poetry. The ocean
Does not mean to be listened to....
....
                ... Aimlessly
It pounds the shore. White and aimless signals. No
One listens to poetry.

  —Jack Spicer, "This Ocean, Humiliating In Its Disguises."

1: THE POET'S FEET

THE quintessential anarchist poetry might be the deliberately obscure verse of Stéphane Mallarmé or the entirely indecipherable "sound-poetry" of Hugo Ball. Significantly, both of these are marked by a certain contact with political anarchism: Mallarmé welcomed some anarchists to his circle, spoke publicly in their defense, and occasionally adopted their imagery to describe his own poetic enterprise, while Ball was an assiduous reader of Bakunin.[1] An analogy between anarchist politics and avant-garde poetics as "individualist politics," on the one hand, and "individualist aesthetics" on the other, has been argued for.[2]

Much attention has been lavished on these traces of anarchism in the experiences and experiments of the avant-gardes. However, it may be objected that their poetic revolt is not so analogous to political revolt as it is to other generational "swerves" of poets from their precursors. If, as Harold Bloom suggests, "strong" poets are always engaged in a struggle, this struggle may always be, on some level, a struggle against the elder poets from whom they have learned, a systematic attempt to cover up the extent to which they are subject to the "influence" of their

---

1   Mallarmé qtd. in Richard Sonn, *Anarchism and Cultural Politics in Fin De Siècle France* (Lincoln: University of Nebraska Press, 1989), 225, 332n28, 255; Ibid., 22; Rosemary Lloyd, *Mallarmé: The Poet and His Circle* (Ithaca, NY: Cornell University Press, 2005), 207, 212. See also Mallarmé's response to Jules Huret's political questions in his *Enquête sur l'évolution littéraire* (Paris: n.p., 1891), 61–62; and Hugo Ball, *Flight Out of Time: A Dada Diary*, ed. John Elderfield (Berkeley: University of California Press, 1996), 10, 12, 24–25, etc.

2   Weir, *Anarchy and Culture*, 4.

literary forebears.[3] Thus, by 1933, Lucía Sánchez Saornil (1895–1970), subsequently one of the founders of the anarchist-feminist Mujeres Libres, came to repudiate her early participation in the avant-garde Ultraísmo movement as a futile exercise in "snobbery," declaring, in a tone of wry exasperation: "The avant-gardists were 'sons of the bourgeoisie.'" Not in spite of, but because of the avant-garde's constitutive hostility to "bourgeois" philistinism: "New and old, bourgeois and anti-bourgeois, are properly, eminently bourgeois terms."[4] This kind of opposition is all too closely tied to what it opposes. Avant-garde "Revolutions of the Word" might fall into the very pattern that anarchism sought to break, whereby revolutionaries come to mimic and identify with the authorities they overthrow, becoming the new bearers of authority—"the re-writing of the father," as Bloom puts it.[5]

Accounts of the avant-gardes that seek to write them into the history of anarchism face another embarrassment: their engagement with anarchism rarely amounted to participation in or "commitment" to the anarchist movement.[6] Mallarmé maintained a gingerly distance from anarchist action, and Ball flatly declared, "I am not an anarchist."[7] Moreover, the anarchist movement, which refused to nullify social commitments in the name of the autonomous individual, was not, on the whole, welcoming toward these experimenters, whose work they often saw as willfully obscure at best, more suited to

---

3   Harold Bloom, *The Anxiety of Influence: A Theory of Poetry* (New York: Oxford University Press, 1997).

4   Lucía Sánchez Saornil qtd. in *Poetas del Novecientos: entre el Modernismo y la Vanguardia, Tomo I: De Fernando Fortún a Rafael Porlán*, ed. José Luis García Martín (Madrid: Fundación BSCH, Fundación Santander Central Hispano, 2001), 159.

5   Harold Bloom, *A Map of Misreading* (New York: Oxford University Press, 2003), 19.

6   For an extended argument on this point, see Hubert van den Berg, "Anarchismus, Ästhetik und Avantgarde," in *Anarchismus und Utopie in der Literatur um 1900*, ed. Jaap Grave et al. (Würzburg: Königshausen & Neumann, 2005), 22–45, and "Anarchismus für oder gegen Moderne und Avant-garde?," *Avant-Garde* 3 (1989): 86–97.

7   Julia Kristeva, *Revolution in Poetic Language*, trans. Margaret Waller (New York: Columbia University Press, 1984), 195; Catherine Coquio, "Le soir et l'aube: Décadence et anarchisme," *Revue d'histoire littéraire de la France* 99.3 (mai–juin 1999): 454; Uri Eisenzweig, "Poétique de l'attentat: anarchisme et littérature fin-de-siècle," *Revue d'histoire littéraire de la France* 99.3 (1999): 443; Ball, *Flight Out of Time*, 19.

ANARCHISTES !!! — DILETTANTE
ANARCHISTEN !!! — DILETTANTE

— Oui, ma chère, ce Monsieur est anarchiste!
— Ja, lieve, die Heer is anarchist!

Fig. 1: Portrait of the avant-garde artist as anarcho-poseur (or mere "dilettante"): "Yes, my dear, this gentleman is an anarchist!" (*Le Communiste: Organe du propagande libertaire* 1.9 [Feb 29, 1908])

the narcissistic enjoyment of a self-appointed élite than to the needs of working-class people in struggle (fig. 1).[8] As Georges Poinsot and Mafféo-Charles Normandy bluntly conclude, in their review of the "social poets," with regard to the Symbolists: "They are not social."[9] If

8   E.g., Lazare, *L'Écrivain et l'art social*, 23–25; Fernand Pelloutier, "L'Art et la révolte," in *Fernand Pelloutier et les origines du syndicalisme d'action directe*, ed. Jacques Julliard (Paris: Éditions du Seuil, 1971), 507; Luigi Fabbri, *Bourgeois Influences on Anarchism*, trans. Chaz Bufe (Tuscon, AZ: See Sharp Press, 2001), 8.

9   Georges Poinsot and Mafféo-Charles Normandy, *Les Poètes Sociaux* (Paris: Louis Michaud, 1909), xxv. This judgment might have to be considerably complicated by a consideration of the Korean case. During the period of anti-Japanese resistance, poets such as Hwang Seok-Woo (1895–1959)

Fig. 2: Front page of an Italian anarchist journal, *Il Piccone* (May 1, 1905), with Olindo Guerrini's poem, "Aurora." Note the central placement of the poem.

the avant-garde poetics of the early-twentieth century were less quietistic and more confrontational than their Symbolist forebears, they were no more inclined to position themselves as speakers in a public arena of discourse: faced with a "crowd," as André Breton famously put it in 1929, "the simplest Surrealist act consists of dashing down

and Kwon Ku-hyeon (1898–1938), while concretely engaged with anarchist projects and organizations like the Heukdo Hoe (Black Wave Society), sometimes drew on Symbolist resources to articulate a utopian vision. Moreover, Symbolist coterie poetry journals like *Jangmichon* (*Rose Village*) often blurred the lines between poetry and political militancy. However, in the 1920s and 1930s, Korean anarchist poets were increasingly pulled in the direction of proletarian literature. See Cho Doo-Sub, "1920nyeondae hangug sangjingjuuisiui anakijeumgwa yeonsogseong yeongu [A Study on the Relationship Between 1920s Korean Symbolist Poems and Anarchism]," *Ulimalgeul tong-gwon* 26 (2002): 331–385; and Cho Young-Bok, *1920-yeondae ch'ogi si eui inyeom kwa mihak* (*The Ideology and Aesthetics of Korean Poems in the Early 1920s*) (Seoul: Somyeong Ch'ulp'an, 2004).

into the street, pistol in hand, and firing blindly"—the only alternative being to accept a "well-defined place in the crowd,... belly at barrel-level."[10] As a means of dismissing "the crowd" from the poet's room (since, in truth, few Surrealists ever took up arms), the signature Surrealist technique of trance-writing, *écriture automatique*, was both less violent and more effective, letting the writer disavow public responsibility for the published word.

However serious these literary bohemian allies were in their political commitments, a search of the international anarchist press during the period of the greatest avant-garde ferment—the flourishing of Dada, Imagism, Futurism, Surrealism—reveals few traces of their work. These periodicals are not bereft of poems; on the contrary, as Pessin notes, it was quite common for them to print poetry alongside reportage, opinion pieces, correspondence, and statistics (fig. 2).[11] Nonetheless, the anarchist movement did not depend on the productions of the avant-gardes for its poetry. Rather, the movement developed its own poetics—a poetics that, in many respects, appeared intent on affirming and even reinforcing the very kinds of symbolic relations that the avant-gardes had set themselves against. At the same time, these poets, at least at the movement's peak, seem to have been largely unconcerned with the problem of influence in Bloom's sense.

It is this other poetic tradition, the poetry of the anarchist movement, in its broadest historical dimensions, that this chapter is intended to investigate. I would like to ask: What is the relationship of this anarchist movement poetics 1.) to the speech of the past (i.e., to poetic legacies or traditions), 2.) to the adult speaking subject that emerges from this past speech, and 3.) to the public sphere that the speaking subject is supposed to found?

Within anarchist counter-communities, as Clara Rey has observed, poems are usually identified as "anarchist" not by virtue of revolutionary experimentation with form, but by their revolutionary content.[12] Anarchist movement poetics, which has been termed "tra-

---

10 André Breton, *Manifestoes of Surrealism*, trans. Richard Seaver and Helen R. Lane (Ann Arbor: University of Michigan Press, 1972), 125.

11 Alain Pessin, "Anarchisme et littérature au XXe siècle," *Proudhon, anarchisme, art et société: Actes du Colloque de la Société P.-J. Proudhon, Paris, 2 décembre 2000* (Paris: Société P.-J. Proudhon, 2001), 81.

12 Clara Rey, "Poesía popular libertaria y estética anarquista en el rio de la plata," *Revista de Crítica Literaria Latinoamericana* 15.29 (1989): 186.

ditional" or "classical in form," "filled with stereotypes," "rather banal," "unoriginal," "staid," is quite at odds with Pound's "make it new."[13] Even in 1896, while anarchists were rubbing elbows with Symbolists and Decadents in Paris, an anarchist poet like André Veidaux (a.k.a. Adrien Devaux, 1868–1927) could face criticism from peers for *too much* stylistic "novelty" and "originality."[14]

In East Asia, as Kim Gyoung-Bog notes, "modernity seemed to wear a double face": colonial, mechanical, and oppressive in many respects, but potentially also rational, emancipatory, and utopian.[15] Asian anarchists often felt the attractions of literary modernity outweighed its tainted association with the humiliation of colonialism; in particular, for a China repeatedly humiliated and colonized not only by the West but by neighboring Japan, the stigma of backwardness was of pressing concern. Native literary traditions were sometimes too closely identified with the patriarchal, Confucian culture that anarchists, as modernizers and advocates of "New Woman" discourse, were trying to overthrow. Tradition was felt, particularly by students such as Li Shizeng (1881–1973) in the "Paris group," as a constraint, something to be shed, e.g., by importation (the translation of Western political and literary texts into Chinese), simplification (the adoption of *baihua* over old-fashioned "literary" writing), universalization (the replacement of Chinese by Esperanto), or rationalization (shifting from centuries-old forms of poetry to nineteenth-century Western-style narrative prose). "All the classical texts," cried Wu Zhihui (1865–1953), "should be thrown down the toilet."[16] Whereas traditional Japanese poetics had often emphasized simplicity and immediacy, Chinese poetry was associated with a "classical" (*yulu*) literary diction so far removed from everyday speech as to be almost unintelligible to

---

13 Serge Salaün, *La poesía de la guerra de España* (Madrid: Castalia, 1985), 34; Granier, *Les briseurs de formules*, 82; Eric Arthur Gordon, *Anarchism in Brazil: Theory and Practice, 1890–1920* (Ann Arbor, MI: University Microfilms International, 1979), 219; Rosemary Chapman, *Henry Poulaille and Proletarian Literature: 1920–1939* (Amsterdam: Rodopi, 1992), 47.

14 Granier, *Les Briseurs de formules*, 84–85.

15 Kim Gyoung-Bog, *Hangug anakijeum simunhag yeongu* [*A Study of Korean Anarchist Poetry*] (Diss., Pusan National University, 1998).

16 Qtd. in Peter G. Zarrow, *China in War and Revolution* (New York: Routledge, 2005), 137.

ordinary workers—a "hierarchy of genres" reinforcing the class hierarchy that the anarchist educators aimed to overcome.[17] Thus, in Japan, anarchist poets formed avant-gardes modeled after Western Dada and Futurism, such as the "Mavo" group and the short-lived journal *Aka to Kuro* (*Black and Red*, 1923), while Chinese anarchists like Ba Jin (a.k.a. Li Feigan, 1904–2005) tended to retreat from poetry altogether, striving instead to produce a modern prose, modeled after the Western social novel of Zola and Tolstoy, that would be maximally accessible.

Tradition, too, wore a double face: it could represent the ideology binding women and children to patriarchal families, but it could also stand for collective spirit and anti-colonial resistance.[18] Anarchist poets in Korea and Japan seem to have readily drawn on national traditions. If Western anarchists often attempted to root movement poetry in historically deeper cultural traditions, using these to gain leverage against a degraded and "decadent" industrial modernity, so too did Korean anarchist poets turn to their oral traditions, using the centuries-old musical and performance-based lyrical (*sijo*), folk-song (*minyo*), and ballad (*minyosi*) forms, which had the additional benefit of linking them to peasant communities who had been on the move well before the arrival of Western anarchist ideologies.[19] Meanwhile, traditional poetic forms like *kanshi* (Japanese poems written in Chinese characters) and *tanka* were intimately habitual modes of expression for Japanese anarchists, such as Kōtoku Shūsui (1871–1911), Kanno Suga (1881–1911), and Kaneko Fumiko (1903–1926).[20] Japanese anarchist-feminist Takamure Itsue

---

17 Merle Goldman, *Modern Chinese Literature in the May Fourth Era* (Cambridge, MA: Harvard University Press, 1985), 25; Dietrich Tschanz, "Where East and West Meet: Chinese Revolutionaries, French Orientalists, and Intercultural Theater in 1910s Paris," *Taiwan Journal of East Asian Studies* 4.1 (June 2007): 100.

18 Kim Gyoung-Bog, *Hangug anakijeum simunhag yeongu.*

19 Ibid. Gang Hyejin, *Kwon Ku-hyeon si yeongu: anakijeumgwaui gwanlyeonseong-eul jungsim-eulo* (MA Thesis, Yeungnam University, 2010), (Gang Hyejin notes that the Korean anarchist poet Kwon Ku-hyeon used "the traditional form of poetry and folk songs.")

20 Libertaire Group, *A Short History of the Anarchist Movement in Japan* (Tokyo: Idea Pub. House, 1979),107; Helene Bowen Raddeker, *Treacherous Women of Imperial Japan: Patriarchal Fictions, Patricidal Fantasies* (London: Routledge, 1997), 42, 86.

wrote in the *waka* tradition, and her compatriot Ishikawa Sanshirō took inspiration from epics like the *Sangokushi* (*Romance of the Three Kingdoms*).[21] At times, we even find Chinese anarchists, such as the Esperantist and anti-Confucian Liu Shifu (1884–1915), advocating a certain traditionalism *against* modernism, paradoxically aligning themselves with their political enemies, the conservative Confucian scholars. "One is left," remarks Pik-chong Agnes Wong Chan, "with the picture of an individual who, after having smashed the pedestal on which he had been standing, tightly holds on to one of the pieces of debris that have fallen around him, as if not to be totally bewildered by the consequences of his act of destruction."[22]

Instead of dividing into rival avant-gardes competing to be the most modern, anarchist poets often differentiated themselves by the various ways in which they borrowed from the past. In some contexts, anarchist movement poetics presented a revival of romanticism—idealist, sentimental, without modernist reserve. Percy Bysshe Shelley, for example, who stood for all that was embarrassing about romanticism in the eyes of T.S. Eliot, was for German anarchist Ret Marut (a.k.a. B. Traven, ca. 1882–1969) "the greatest lyric poet of world literature."[23] Such a judgment is echoed by Scottish comrade Thomas Hastie Bell (1867–1942), who wrote, in praise of the American philosophical anarchist Charles Erskine Scott Wood (1852–1944), "I put you among our Anarchist poets, such as Burns, Shelley, Whitman, Wilde, Carpenter"[24]—virtually an anarchist canon, judging how often they were

---

21 E. Patricia Tsurumi, "Feminism and Anarchism in Japan: The Case of Takamure Itsue, 1894–1964," *Bulletin of Concerned Asian Scholars* 17.2 (April–June 1985): 5; Maeda Ai, "From Communal Performance to Solitary Reading: The Rise of the Modern Japanese Reader," in *Text and the City*, trans. James A Fujii (Durham: Duke University Press, 2004), 224.

22 Pik-chong Agnes Wong Chan, *Liu Shifu (1884–1915): A Chinese Anarchist and the Radicalization of Chinese Thought* (Diss., University of California, Berkeley, 1979), 66.

23 T.S. Eliot, *Selected Prose of T.S. Eliot*, ed. Frank Kermode (New York: Harcourt Brace Jovanovich, 1975), 81–86; Ret Marut, trans. Michael L. Baumann, qtd. in Michael L. Baumann, *B. Traven: An Introduction* (Albuquerque: University of New Mexico Press, 1976), 100.

24 Thomas Hastie Bell, "On Freedom and Bolshevism: A Letter by T.H. Bell to Charles Erskine Scott Wood," *Freedom* 1.1 (Jan. 1, 1933): 8. The term "philosophical anarchist" generally denotes an embrace of anarchist ideas without a corresponding anarchist practice beyond the conduct of one's personal life.

subjects of anarchist lectures and essays, their poems reprinted in anarchist journals such as *Mother Earth* and *L'Endehors*.[25] "Walt Whitman, the Liberator of Sex," as Emma Goldman called him in the title of one of her lectures, became a touchstone of movement poetry more for his declamatory, prophetic style than for his free-verse experimentalism. "Every Bavarian child," declared Landauer, German translator of his *Leaves of Grass*, ought to "know Walt Whitman by heart"; in the pages of *The Libertarian*, Leonard D. Abbott wrote that "the Anarchist in Whitman is revealed on almost every page he wrote."[26] Similarly, Victor Hugo was embraced by Francophone anarchists such as Louise Michel (1830–1905), while Jewish anarchist poet Joseph Bovshover (1873–1915) committed to memory the verse of Heinrich Heine, a poet equally lionized by German-speaking anarchists.[27]

In the Anglo-American context, this quite frequently meant that, even in the period of high modernist revolt against the "genteel tradition," anarchists such as Voltairine de Cleyre (1866–1912) were continuing to produce poetry on something like a Victorian model, pairing didactic, sentimental content with an ornamental, "oratorical" or prophetic style.[28] "Sometimes the idiom is definitely that of Whitman, sometimes that of the Bible," wrote Louis Untermeyer, describing Wood's poetry—an observation that could be borne out by a reading of passages such as this one, excerpted for the 1929 *Anthology*

---

25 Interestingly, apart from a few early appreciations—e.g., among participants in New York's Ferrer Center (1911–1914), such as the American anarchist James Huneker (1857–1921), who had included him in his *Egoists: A Book of Supermen* (New York: Scribner, 1909)—William Blake seems to have joined this "canon" very belatedly, in the late-twentieth century, well after his rediscovery by early-twentieth century modernists like Yeats.

26 Gustav Landauer qtd. in Ben Hecht, *A Child of the Century* (New York: Simon and Schuster, 1954), 306; Leonard D. Abbott, "The Anarchist Side of Walt Whitman," *The Libertarian* 2.5 (March 1926): 232.

27 Charles J. Stivale, "Louise Michel's Poetry of Existence and Revolt," *Tulsa Studies in Women's Literature* 5.1 (Spring 1986): 41; Julian Levinson, *Exiles on Main Street: Jewish American Writers and American Literary Culture* (Bloomington: Indiana University Press, 2008), 128; Anonymous, note to Heinrich Heine, "The Weavers," *Liberty* 5.10 (Dec. 17, 1887): 1; Michael Schwab, "Autobiography of Michael Schwab", in *The Autobiographies of the Haymarket Martyrs*, ed. Philip S. Foner (New York: Monad Press, 1977), 111.

28 Joseph Harrington, *Poetry and the Public: The Social Form of Modern U.S. Poetics* (Middletown, CT: Wesleyan University Press, 2002), 106.

of Revolutionary Poetry by anarchist editor Marcus Graham (a.k.a.
Shmuel Marcus, 1893–1985) from Wood's *The Poet in the Desert*:[29]

> Oh, Revolution, dread angel of the Awful Presence,
> Warder of the gate of tears,
> Open and set the captive free.
> Dark, silent, loving, cruel and merciful one,
> Hold yourself not aloof.
>
> ....
> Pitch head-long from the cloudy battlements
> And, with heavenly-fire, utterly destroy
> This distorted and mis-shapen world.[30]

Here, it is Biblical language (e.g., the use of archaic senses of the
words "dread" and "Awful," the images of an "angel," "heavenly-fire,"
etc.) that accomplishes the task Theodor Adorno assigned to modernism—the evocation of "perspectives" to "displace and estrange
the world, reveal[ing] it to be, with its rifts and crevices, as indigent
and distorted as it will appear one day in the messianic light."[31] From
such "messianic" perspectives, it is not the anarchist who is aberrant,
eccentric, deviant; it is the botched, the corrupt and broken world.

The search for premodern poetic models brought anarchists such
as Gustav Landauer in Germany and Edouard Rothen in France to
look to the Middle Ages as a high point in the integration of the
arts with society.[32] In other national contexts, such as that of Brazil,
where the sonnet flourished in the pages of anarchist journals such
as *O Sindicalista* and *A Plebe*, anarchist poets such as José Oiticica
took the ancient Greek poets as their model, embracing a classical
ideal in defiance of "decadent" modernity.[33] Similarly taking the side

---

29 Louis Untermeyer, *The New Era in American Poetry* (New York: H. Holt,
    1919), 235.

30 Charles Erskine Scott Wood, "This—Our World," in *An Anthology of Revo-
    lutionary Poetry*, ed. Marcus Graham (New York: Active Press, 1929), 288.

31 Theodor W. Adorno, *Minima Moralia: Reflections From Damaged Life*,
    trans. E.F.N. Jephcott (London: Verso, 1978), 247.

32 Landauer, *Revolution*, 127–137; Rothen, "Littérature."

33 Edgar Rodrigues, *O Anarquismo na escola, no teatro, na poesia* (Rio de Ja-
    neiro: Achiamé, 1992); Tereza Ventura, *Nem Barbárie Nem Civilização!*
    (São Paulo: Annablume, 2006), 18.

of the classical against the romantic school, the Proudhonian worker-educators of *L'Atelier: organe spécial de la classe laborieuse*, who in 1843 declared that romanticism had "done nothing" for the people—a judgment that made sense, perhaps, in a country where a late-arriving romanticism had quickly aligned itself with counterrevolutionary forces, and where the left-wing "social romanticism" of the mature Victor Hugo had yet to emerge.[34] In still other instances, anarchist poetics entailed a turn away from both the "ancient" and "modern" poles of the Western tradition in favor of "primitive," folkloric forms: for instance, Louise Michel drew on the pagan tradition of the Gauls of her native Haute-Marne and her fascination with the Kanak songs and stories she heard in the penal colony of New Caledonia, while the Spanish anarchist poets drew on folkloric traditions of the *verso de romance*, a kind of popular ballad, which linked contemporary realities with the mythic past. Even such a champion of avant-garde modernism as Herbert Read (1893–1968) insisted that Surrealism itself had a precursor in "ballads and anonymous literature."[35]

In nearly all of its varieties, whether romantic, classical, or primitivist, anarchist poetics favored what the German-Jewish anarchist poet Erich Mühsam (1878–1934) called the "tendency-poem" (*Tendenzlyrik*) or "poem of struggle" (*Kampflyrik*), what others would call "committed" poetry—that is, poetry with a clear rhetorical function.[36] Moreover, much anarchist poetry was written not by traditionally educated poets of the middle and upper classes but by working-class men and women, often autodidacts, who self-categorized their work as "proletarian poetry," "workers' poetry," "social poetry," or "popular poetry."[37] This, in turn, implied that whatever elements of exalted style

---

34 Georges Duveau, *La Pensée ouvrière sur l'éducation pendant la Seconde République et le Second Empire* (Paris: Domat-Montchrestien, 1948), 63–64.

35 Louise Michel, *The Red Virgin: Memoirs of Louise Michel*, eds. and trans. Bullitt Lowry and Elizabeth Ellington Gunter (Tuscaloosa, AL: University of Alabama Press, 1981), 16–17, 111–117; Salaün, *Romancero libertario*, 19–20; Read, *The Philosophy of Modern Art* (New York: World, 1953), 119.

36 Walter Fähnders, *Anarchismus und Literatur* (Stuttgart: Metzler, 1987), 98, 64.

37 Ferran Aisa, *La cultura anarquista a Catalunya* (Barcelona: Edicions de 1984, 2006), 264; Gonzalo Espino, *La lira rebelde proletaria* (Lima: TAREA, 1984), 34; Joseph Déjacque, *Les Lazaréennes. Fables et chansons, poésies sociales* (Nouvelle-Orléans: J. Lamarre, 1857); Rey, "Poesía popular libertaria," 179.

might be borrowed from past schools of poetics, the diction of anarchist poetry had to remain accessible and plebeian.

Whereas modernist poetics declared, in the words of Mallarmé, that a poem should express itself "in words that are allusive, never direct, reducing themselves to the same silence"—or, as Archibald MacLeish put it, that it ought to be "mute"—the urgencies of speech, of establishing communication and community against an enforced silence, made directness and accessibility central poetic values for anarchists.[38] Accordingly, anarchist poets would forgo modernist obscurity in favor of "transparency" and "simple symbolism,"[39] emphasizing "narration, affirmation, and basic truths."[40] In short, anarchist poetry was "thetic" with a vengeance—a poetics of the intact, adult speaking subject, staking a place in the public square.

Who, then, is speaking to whom in anarchist poems? It was a Romantic poet who insisted that the poet is "a man [sic] speaking to men [sic]"—a speech situation not unlike the ones we encounter every day.[41] However, if ordinary speech almost always entails a specific somebody addressing a specific somebody else, what Jonathan Culler has called "the extravagance of lyric" consists in the lyric poet pretending to address almost anyone and anything but the actual reader—speaking as if to Death, the wind, an urn, or a flower—while the actual reader pretends to have "overheard" the poet's voice.[42] All of this is supposed to distance the lyric from the language of politics, i.e., from rhetoric: in Yeats's famous formulation, if "we make out of the quarrel with others, rhetoric," then poems spring from "the quarrel with ourselves."[43] We hear an echo of the old lyrical address in Charles Erskine Scott Wood's

---

38 Stéphane Mallarmé, *Œuvres complètes*, ed. Bernard Maréchal (Paris: Gallimard, 1998), 309; Archibald MacLeish, "Ars Poetica," *Poems, 1924–1933* (Boston: Houghton Mifflin, 1933), 1.

39 Ventura, *Nem Barbárie*, 16; Daniel Armogathe, "Mythes et transcendance révolutionnaire dans la poésie de Louise Michel," in *À travers la vie et la mort: œuvre poétique*, eds. Daniel Armogathe and Marion V. Piper (Paris: F. Maspero, 1982), 10.

40 Salaün, *Romancero libertario*, 35.

41 William Wordsworth and Samuel T. Coleridge. *Lyrical Ballads*, ed. R.L. Brett (London: Routledge, 2007), 300.

42 Jonathon Culler, *Literary Theory: A Very Short Introduction* (Oxford: Oxford University Press, 2000), 76; and *The Pursuit of Signs: Semiotics, Literature, Deconstruction* (Ithaca, NY: Cornell University Press, 2002), 137.

43 William Butler Yeats, *Mythologies* (London: Macmillan, 1959), 331.

poem hailing a personified "Revolution," asking it, in quasi-religious tones, to "destroy / This distorted and mis-shapen world," and so on. Is this a pretense on the order of imagining that Blake is actually addressing a tiger? Or might Wood be asking the actual reader to identify himself or herself with the fictive audience, to—in some impossible way—incarnate the idea and *become* "Revolution"?

The case of Lola Ridge (1873–1941), "our gifted rebel poet," as Emma Goldman called her, and founder of the anarchist *Modern School* magazine, might at first appear simpler.[44] It is easy to read Ridge's "Reveille," appearing in Graham's *Anthology of Revolutionary Poetry*, as relatively straightforward propaganda—"a call to the workers of the world to rise up in the name of justice against their oppressors," as Daniel Tobin characteristically puts it:[45]

> Come forth, you workers!
> Let the fires go cold—
> Let the iron spill out, out of the troughs—
> Let the iron run wild
> Like a red bramble on the floors[46]

Ridge's poem asks us to become something that we are not yet; it speaks to something that is not congealed in the self, to formative forces.[47] Likewise, in "The Song of Iron," Ridge addresses a never entirely tamed force, asking it to make her into something she is not, almost as John Donne once asked God to "break, blow, burn, and make me new": "Oh fashioned in fire ... Behold me, a cupola / Poured to Thy use!"[48] In Ridge's anarchist lyric, then, what appears to be speech

44 Goldman, *Living My Life, Vol. 2* (New York: A.A. Knopf, 1931), 706; Paul Avrich, *The Modern School Movement: Anarchism and Education in the United States* (Oakland, CA: AK Press, 2006), 170–171.

45 Daniel Tobin, "Modernism, Leftism, and the Spirit: The Poetry of Lola Ridge," in *Light in Hand: Selected Early Poems of Lola Ridge*, ed. Daniel Tobin (Florence, MA: Quale Press, 2007), xxx.

46 Lola Ridge, "Reveille," *The Dial* 66.791 (May 31, 1919).

47 See Colson, *Petit lexique*, 121–123 and 257–272 on what he calls "*force plastique*" and, after Deleuze, "the power of the outside."

48 Lola Ridge, "The Song of Iron," *The Ghetto, and Other Poems* (New York: B.W. Huebsch, 1918), 15, 17–18; John Donne, "Holy Sonnet XIV," in *Metaphysical Poetry: An Anthology*, ed. Paul Negri (New York: Dover, 2002), 4.

addressed to an impossible other is perhaps to be understood instead as evoking the impossible other that is within oneself. Conversely, we might question whether the "simplicity and immediacy" of an address to "you workers" is quite so simple. Consider, for instance, that the version Tobin quotes, with its breathless dashes reminiscent of Emily Dickinson's, is not actually the original form in which "Reveille" was published. In fact, its first appearance, in 1919, was in *The Dial*—a journal that would shortly become famous for its showcasing of modernists such as Yeats, Eliot, and Pound. Here, Ridge's poem is printed shorn of dashes and outfitted with more thoughtful ellipses, the onward rush of certain phrases ("Let the iron spill out, out of the troughs") blunted by more sedentary lines ("Let the iron cleave to the furnace"):

> Come forth, you workers!
> Let the fires grow cold...
> Let the iron cleave to the furnace...
> Let the iron spill out of the troughs...[49]

This is a version of "Reveille" that might do more to elicit a Yeatsian reading, even if there is still something smoldering inside it that threatens to spill out of containment. Moreover, *The Dial* makes an unlikely medium in which to encounter working-class readers. It even seems a strange place—an estranging place—to find working-class writers: witness Conrad Aiken's patronizing review of Ridge's "The Ghetto" in an earlier issue ("one must pay one's respects," Aiken admits grudgingly, while complaining that the verse "seems masculine," that it "scream[s]" and is "sometimes merely strident," lacking in "subtleties of form").[50]

However, in this period, its political and aesthetic boundaries are very much in play, as the editorial direction is split between the *anarchisant* pacifist Randolph Bourne and his onetime mentor, the pro-war John Dewey.[51] For a time, the magazine hosts poets in the

---

49 Ridge, "Reveille."
50 Conrad Aiken, "The Literary Abbozzo," *The Dial* 66.782 (January 25, 1919): 83–84.
51 Nicholas Joost, *Scofield Thayer and The Dial: An Illustrated History* (Carbondale, IL: Southern Illinois University Press, 1964), 10–11.

Imagist line, some of whom will later turn to fascism, alongside poets and other writers from across the spectrum of the Lyrical Left, such as Carl Sandburg, Kenneth Burke, and Mina Loy; anarchist fellow traveler Margaret Anderson is another collaborator. Nevertheless, "Reveille" seems curiously out of place in *The Dial*; reprinted in Graham's *Anthology of Revolutionary Poetry*, it is as if, exiled from the aesthetic domain, it has been repatriated to its own political nation.

But anarchy is a politics without a territory, without an "own"; witness Ridge herself. It is difficult to "situate" her geographically: should she be read as an Irish poet, since she was born Rose Emily Ridge in Dublin? Is she a New Zealander, since she emigrated there as a child, or an Australian, since her first poems signed "Lola" appeared in the *Sydney Bulletin* in 1901? Or is she really an American poet, since she spent most of her life in the United States, where she published her first book of poems, *The Ghetto*, documenting life among the Jews of Manhattan's Lower East Side? Poems, of course, cross borders even more readily than the poets themselves. Perhaps every time a poem or a poet shifts its ground, encountering different readerships, the question of whom it addresses is raised again. What might this mean for the poetry of anarchists as creatures of movement, pushed around the world by currents of migration?

> I am only passing through, but I like to speak your language. Forgive me if I seem distracted. It's because three quarters of myself spills over every word and collapses into the depths. I only recognize what comes to the surface.
>
> I have not traveled much; on the contrary, a whole host of peoples and centuries have chosen to make their journeys in my person. They stroll about in me, make themselves at home.
>
> ....
>
> I am nowhere entirely, but I also want a bit of myself in that place; nowhere; for that is where we find grace, and it is there that I met you, that I began to speak your language.[52]

The author of these lines, Giovanni Baldelli (1914–1986), born of an Italian father and a French mother, expelled for antifascist activities,

---

52 Giovanni Baldelli, "Épanchement," *Le Pied à l'étrier: poèms* (Rodez: Éditions Subervie, 1969), 13–15.

then interned by the British in Australia as an enemy alien, now writing in French from his exile in Southampton, where he teaches Russian, knows whereof he speaks.[53] For many an anarchist, "grace" is to be found, if at all, in placelessness. As Jens Bjørneboe wrote, in "Emigranten": "I am a child of strange and alien planets."[54]

Not that efforts haven't been made to put these poets in their place. "Brothers, I salute you," writes José Oiticica (1882–1957) from a military jail outside of Rio de Janeiro, after the failed anarchist insurrection of 1918, concluding that "We must welcome our pain, / the pain that does not oppress just men / and that renders the most humble superior."[55] The sonnet he composes "To the Companheiros in Prison," however, will only be published nearly three years later, in *O Sindicalista* of Porto Alegre. To whom is this admonition or wish addressed? The lapse in time and place between composition and publication complicates things. Oiticica writes to imprisoned comrades, but he is in prison when he writes; he would have had no guarantee that anyone else would ever read it. Does he then address himself, counseling stoic patience, compensating for present suffering with the promise of a "superior" self-in-construction?

Poetic self-address as a mode of resistance forms the premise of much anarchist verse. We might compare this with Miyamoto Masakichi's (birth and death dates unknown) "To the Poets" (1932), in which the isolated poet cries out, "Oh, my Self! / Become a hot fire and burn / or freeze and summon your friends / ten million of me facing the tempest / Hear me, you lonely Me among them!"[56] So might Oiticica have been speaking from the perspective of an imagined future self, a self that has lived through and surpassed his present suffering. On this level, the sonnet would represent a promise addressed from the future to the present: if you live through this, you will be stronger. On the other hand, when Oiticica publishes his sonnet in 1921, in shifting from a private to a public speech-situation,

53 Henry de Madaillan, "Introduction," in Giovanni Baldelli, *Quand l'aube se survit: poèmes* (Rodez: Éditions Subervie, 1965), 7.

54 Jens Bjørneboe, "The Emigrant," trans. Esther Greenleaf Mürer, 8 (web).

55 José Oiticica, "Aos companheiros de prisão [To the Comrades in Prison]," in *O Anarquismo na escola*, 307–308 (originally published in *O Sindicalista*, 1921; written in prison, 1918).

56 Miyamoto qtd. in Filler, *Chaos From Order*, 213, trans. Filler.

might it not change its address as well, so to speak, becoming another kind of promise, a gesture of empathy for the suffering of others and a testimony: I have been where you are? And in the dimension of "overhearing" that is brought into being by readers who are not and have never been in prison, could it be that Oiticica invites them to imagine themselves as stoic prisoners, so that the message becomes the grim promise: You may be where we have been? In constructing a plural first person, a "we" composed of many prisoners—present, past, and potential—suffering together, the poem enables all of these readings, dissolving the walls between self and others, between the horror of "today" and the future of the "pure dream," between captivity and freedom.[57]

Perhaps, though, the material context of anarchist poetry is always a kind of captivity. "Poetry," for the anarchist Octavio Brandão (1896–1980), "makes its muse from pain and anger, vehemence and indignation."[58] We often find anarchist poets hurling invective at adversaries real or imaginary—false gods, exploiters, rulers, perpetrators of deception and murder. In "The Gods and the People," originally issued as a pamphlet in Scotland, Voltairine de Cleyre asks, "What have you done, O skies, / That the millions should kneel to you?"[59] Brazil's Ricardo Gonçalves (1883–1916) pours wrath upon the owners of the earth: "Tremble, disgusting vampires! / Tremble in your opulent / golden palaces!" he thunders in the pages of São Paulo's *A Plebe*.[60] Here, poetry acts as a kind of "rehearsal for the revolution," a dramatization of the possibility of one's own power, from the perspective of present powerlessness, as Augusto Boal recommends in his *Theatre of the Oppressed*—or, in the language of syndicalism, as a "revolutionary gymnastics."[61] In the poem's rhetoric, the enemy can be cut down to size—the inverse

---

57 Oiticica, "Aos companheiros de prisão," 8.
58 Yara Aun Khoury, "A Poesia Anarquista," *Revista Brasileira de História* 8.15 (February 1988): 216.
59 de Cleyre, *Selected Works*, 50.
60 Ricardo Gonçalves, "Rebelião [Rebellion]," in *O Anarquismo na escola*, 57–59 (originally in *A Plebe*, 1917).
61 Augusto Boal, *Theatre of the Oppressed*, trans. Charles A. McBride and Maria-Odilia Leal McBride (New York: Theatre Communications Group, 1985), 122; Émile Pouget, *La Confédération Générale du Travail* (Paris: M. Riviére, 1908), 59.

of the mental operation by which the enemy has been imagined as superhuman and omnipotent.

On the other hand, the adversary is not always simply them (the bosses, the generals, the priests and proprietors); it is quite often also us. Under the pseudonym of "Basil Dahl," in Boston's *Liberty*, Joseph Bovshover chastises the vampires' all too willing victims—"I hate your superstition, workingmen, / I loathe your blindness and stupidity"—while fellow Yiddish anarchist poet David Edelstadt berates them: "Wake up, working brother, wake up!"[62] And just as often, as Ridge and Oiticica demonstrate, anarchist poets address real or potential allies against the common foe. From Rosario, Argentina, in the pages of the anarcho-communist *La Voz de la Mujer*, Josefa M. R. Martínez (dates of birth and death unknown) greeted her potential comrades in arms: "Salud, Compañeras! Anarchy / Raises the liberator's banner; / Hurrah, dear brothers, to the fight! / Strong be your arms, serene be your heart!"[63] Barbaric exhortations indeed.

And who is doing the exhorting? Quite often, this is an anonymous voice, or someone who conspicuously and self-consciously identifies as a *non-poet*. "I don't write literature!" declared Antonio Agraz (1905–1956), author of countless poems published in the newspaper of the anarcho-syndicalist CNT union.[64] Nor was he alone in such a declaration. "I am not a poet—I am a worker," declared Edelstadt; "I am writing ... so that every worker will understand me."[65] In statements like these, it is easy for us to hear the echo of anarchist *obrerismo* ("workerism")[66] and to miss what else they tell

---

62 Basil Dahl (Joseph Bovshover), "To the Toilers," *Liberty* 11.22 (March 7, 1896): 5; Edelstadt, "Shnel loyfn di reder [The Factory Wheels Run Fast]," trans. Helena Frank and Rose Pastor Stokes, in *The Yiddish Song Book*, ed. Jerry Silverman (New York: Stein and Day, 1983), 168.

63 Josefa M. R. Martínez, "Brindis [A Toast]," *La Voz de la mujer: periódico comunista-anárquico, 1896–1897*, ed. Universidad Nacional de Quilmes (Buenos Aires: Universidad Nacional de Quilmes, 1997), 44. Originally published in *La Voz de la mujer*, 1896.

64 Agraz qtd. in Steinbeiß, "'Meine Verse sollen Bomben sein.'"

65 Edelstadt qtd. in Melech Epstein, *Jewish Labor in the U.S.A.: An Industrial, Political, and Cultural History of the Jewish Labor Movement, 1882–1914* (New York: Trade Union Sponsoring Committee, 1950), 288.

66 This is a dangerously inexact translation of a Spanish term that has more accurate cognates in Catalan (*obrerisme*), Italian (*operaismo*), and French (*ouvrierisme*), even though they came into circulation at different times.

us about how an anarchist might conceive of poetry and poets.

First, Edelstadt claims to write *as* a worker—a garment-industry sweatshop worker, at that—rather than on behalf of workers.[67] In other words, despite the prophetic tone, the anarchist poet disavows any unilateral right to speak for others: in rejecting vanguardism, anarchists forswear poets' traditional privilege of "prophesying" in an authoritarian mode. Where Shelley ends his *Defence of Poetry* by declaring that "Poets are the unacknowledged legislators of the world," Goodman's *Speaking and Language: Defence of Poetry* asks, "What does he intend? That they should be acknowledged? Then what would they do?"[68]

Secondly, the anarchist poet, frequently a working-class autodidact rather than a traditional intellectual or even a *declassé* bohemian, is writing for an audience of peers. Consequently, the anarchist poet shares with the audience an expectation of understanding—a serious departure, as Nelly Wolf reminds us, from traditions that made the poet a keeper of mysteries: whereas novelists were expected to write in the language of the "new," poets were expected to write in a language of symbols, establishing "a tangible border between the language used inside the poem and the language used outside."[69] An anarchist poet writes without this prophylactic, contaminating

---

The Spanish word, as David D. Gilmore explains, can mean "worker culture," "class cohesiveness," "working-class ideology," or simply "the common denominators of working-class life," "laborers' routine, style of life, and self-images" (*The People of the Plain: Class and Community in Lower Andalusia* [New York: Columbia University Press, 1980], 87); it names, in short, allegiance to a non-branded, non-sectarian politics articulated from the perspective of workers. However, the English term "workerism" is mainly used, in contemporary anarchist discourse, to denote a fetishism of the working classes and ultimately of toil as a good in itself—an ideal that many anarchists of earlier periods, laborers by necessity rather than choice, would have seen as perverse. Even in reaction to the Stalinist cult of work, Camillo Berneri criticized not "*operaismo*" per se but "*operaiolatria*," i.e, "workerolatry," the uncritical celebration of workers per se: see his *L'Operaiolatria*.

67 Morris U. Schappes, *The Jews in the United States: A Pictorial History, 1654 to the Present* (New York: Citadel Press, 1958), 136.

68 Percy Bysshe Shelley, *Shelley's Prose: Or, The Trumpet of a Prophecy*, ed. David Lee Clark (London: Fourth Estate, 1988), 240; Goodman, *Speaking and Language*, 230.

69 Nelly Wolf, *Le Roman de la démocratie* (Saint-Denis: Presses Universitaires de Vincennes, 2003), 23.

an elevated, "poetic" vocabulary and imagery drawn from the past (romantic, medieval, classical, folkloric) with contemporaneous, everyday language. In his study of the anarchist *romance* poems of the Spanish Civil War, for instance, Serge Salaün notes the combination of quasi-medieval archaisms and "epic" features with "popular turns of phrase, puns, old saws, proverbs and sayings, the use of dialect or familiarisms, swearing and trivial words," and so on.[70] In this way, anarchist movement poetics resisted fetishizing the "purity" of genres and national languages and embraced hybridity.[71]

Quite frequently, the mutual understanding of anarchist poets and their audiences could be verified, as anarchists tended to favor the oral circulation of poetry in face-to-face settings—a tradition echoed later in the "Revolutionary Letters" recited by Diane di Prima (b. 1934) from the back of a truck in New York City.[72] It is only in the age of print culture, as Victor Méric (1876–1933) noted in his entry on "Poésie" for the *Encyclopédie anarchiste* (1934), that "poetry is separated from the song," shedding its communal character along with its orality: "Among the contemporaries, verse is tortured, dislocated, gives forth only vague assonances and an approximative music. Poetry willingly flees into the abstruse, escapes all rules, and rejoins prose in its absence of clarity as well as in its offenses against the most elementary syntax."[73] The lack of immediacy in the print medium presented a problem in other ways, too: even if the "enthusiasm and applause" elicited by the spoken word can be superficial, argued an anonymous contributor to the anarchist workers' journal *Le Ça Ira* in 1888, "written thought also has its limitations; whoever reads too much of it loses their ability to act.... What's needed is a balance between the two, so that the spontaneity evoked by the spoken word is joined with the kind of reflection that induces thought itself."[74] Finally, oral modes of circulation accorded well with anar-

---

70 Salaün, *Romancero libertario*, 34–35.

71 Cf. Robert F. Barsky, "Bakhtin as Anarchist?: Language, Law and Creative Impulses in the Work of Mikhail Bakhtin and Rudolph Rocker," *South Atlantic Quarterly* 97.3 (Summer 1968): 629.

72 Diane di Prima, *Revolutionary Letters* (San Francisco: Last Gasp, 2007), 164.

73 Victor Méric, "Poésie," in *Encyclopédie anarchiste*, 2070–2071, trans. mine.

74 Qtd. in Howard G. Lay, "Réflecs d'un Gniaff: On Emile Pouget and *Le*

chist critiques of property: whereas the technologies of print culture were concentrated in relatively few hands, everyone had the potential to participate in the production of oral culture—to add or subtract verses as the occasion and the spirit dictated, exercising a collective creativity.[75] The written word, subject to copyright law, was private property; the spoken word, particularly before the advent of recording technologies, refused to present itself as an ownable, commodifiable object.[76] Accordingly, a re-oralization of poetry was in order.

Even when circulated purely in written form, anarchist poems often took on some of the characteristics of oral culture. Joseph Labadie (1850–1933), for instance, often wrote occasional poems to present as gifts to friends, sometimes in individually hand-copied chapbooks. A typical sample, *To Mr. & Mrs. Mehan, On Their Return from the East*, dated "Detroit, June, 1901," begins: "We welcome you with arms awide, / Greet you as morning's golden gleams, / Your happy smiles like eventide / Bring rhythmic cheer & tranquil dreams."[77] The language and imagery are trite, the rhythm and rhyme mechanically tidy. It cannot be denied, however, that the resources of a certain poetic tradition have been mobilized in the interest of specific, intimate relationships; this is "occasional poetry," lauded by Goodman, following Goethe, as "the highest [form of] integrated art."[78] It is "applied" poetry, poetry that has not fled into a separate realm, as Méric complains, but that renders service to life.

The example of Labadie's occasional poetry—reminiscent of the practices of "poets such as Emily Dickinson" lauded by Simon DeDeo, "whose poetical work merges seamlessly into private communication

---

Père Peinard," in *Making the News: Modernity and the Mass Press in Nineteenth-Century France*, eds. Dean de la Motte and Jeannene Pryzblyski (Amherst, MA: University of Massachusetts Press, 1999), 85–86.

75 Neil Birrell, "Notes on Culture and Ideology," *The Raven* 10.39 (Summer 1999): 193–201.

76 Granier, *Les Briseurs de formules*, 77. Cf. also Proudhon's critique of the very notion of "intellectual property" in *Majorats littéraires* (Paris: Librairie Internationale, 1868).

77 Joseph Labadie, "To Mr. & Mrs. Mehan, On Their Return from the East," unpublished, dated "Detroit, June, 1901" (Labadie Collection, University of Michigan).

78 Paul Goodman, "Advance-Guard Writing: 1900–1950," *Kenyon Review* 13 (Summer 1951): 376.

through letters and notes"—is indicative of another dimension of anarchist movement poetics: the mixture of "private" and "public" forms to evoke a realm that is neither conventionally "public" nor "private."[79] In the correspondence, articles, and speeches of anarchists such as Berkman and Goldman, too, as Kathy Ferguson notes, we find "blurred distinctions between letters addressed to a specific individual and public speech addressed to the generalized other."[80] In so doing, anarchist poets helped to construct a sphere of relations sufficiently opaque to the larger publics inhabited by anarchists to resemble the private realm, and at the same time translucent, "indefinite" in its extent, "mediated by print, theater, diffuse networks of talk," to borrow the language of Michael Warner's *Publics and Counterpublics*.[81] We might extend Ferguson's observations to conclude that anarchist poets are vital architects of an "emergent anarchist counterpublic"—a social world "defined by [its] tension with a larger public," its constituency "marked off from persons or citizens in general."[82]

Such a counterpublic, while maintaining a vigilant and at times painful consciousness of its subordinate or subaltern relationship to the larger (and hostile) public within which it is embedded, would appear to have a number of advantages over the grand public. Its smaller scope—perhaps especially important for anarchists caught up in movements of displacement and migration, whether fleeing from Russian *shtetls* to the Argentine *pampas* or from rural Catalonia to seek factory work in Barcelona—could retain something of the intimacy of village life (even the intimacy of personal bickering), as against the anonymity and impersonality of the great urban centers. Like other counterpublics, as Warner notes, it permits "discussion ... understood to contravene the rules obtaining in the world at large, being structured by alternative dispositions or protocols, making different assumptions about what can be said or what goes without saying."[83] Anarchist counterpublic discourse, thus, can unfold partially

---

79 Simon DeDeo, "Towards an Anarchist Poetics," *Absent Magazine* 1 (December 2006).

80 Kathy E. Ferguson, "Anarchist Counterpublics," *New Political Science* 32.2 (2010): 213.

81 Michael Warner qtd. in Ferguson, "Anarchist Counterpublics" 195.

82 Ibid., 197; Michael Warner, *Publics and Counterpublics* (New York: Zone Books, 2002), 56.

83 Ibid.

outside the range of locally tolerated opinion and expression, the little space between official orthodoxy and the outer limits of heterodoxy—the invisible boundaries of "free" public discourse.

It is when outsiders peer into the counterpublic conversations taking place in an anarchist newspaper like *Golos Truda* (*The Voice of Labor*, 1911–1918) or *Khleb i Volia* (*Bread and Freedom*, 1917–1918) that these conversations, constituted by a universe of references not shared by outsiders, appear to be, as Karen Rosenberg says, "arcane," "a body of esoteric knowledge," reserved for the "initiated," etc.[84] The apparent mysteriousness of anarchist counterpublic discourse is accentuated when it unfolds under intense surveillance, censorship, and repression (e.g., under the Czarist and Communist regimes in Russia). In such conditions, when the only "safe" public discourse is that which mirrors "the flattering self-image of elites," anarchist discourse might be expected to take on the kinds of cryptic, inaccessible forms—carefully coded exchanges of subversive signs—so evocatively described by James C. Scott in his studies of peasants' resistance culture. Sometimes, anarchists did resort to encrypted speech: Bakunin, for instance, was an avid user of ciphers, foreshadowing today's cryptoanarchists.[85] However, the police were all too often capable of countering such evasive maneuvers, as in 1892, when a group of French anarchists using a fairly sophisticated code were arrested, their messages intercepted and deciphered.[86] At other times, anarchists experimented with class-specific dialects that facilitated easy communication among equals while eluding the comprehension of "hostile informatives": such was the case with the use of French argot in Émile Pouget's (1860–1931) *fin-de-siècle* newspaper, the *Père Peinard* (1889–1902).[87]

---

84 Rosenberg, "The Cult of Self-Sacrifice," 178.

85 Scott, *Domination and the Arts of Resistance: Hidden Transcripts* (New Haven: Yale University Press, 1990), 18; Edward Hallett Carr, *Michael Bakunin* (New York: Vintage Books, 1961), 272, 432, 438, 464; Colson, *Petit lexique*, 163.

86 David Kahn, *The Codebreakers: The Comprehensive History of Secret Communication from Ancient Times to the Internet* (New York: Scribner's Sons, 1997), 245.

87 Roger Farr, "The Strategy of Concealment: Argot & Slang of the 'Dangerous Classes,'" *Fifth Estate* 373 (Fall 2006): 19, 54. Even here, however, Maurice Tournier warns us that we ought not to exaggerate the "neologis[tic]" character of Pouget's argot, which he finds "quite readable" ("Le bestiaire anarchiste à la fin du XIXe siècle," *Revue des lettres et de traduction* 8 [2002]: 254).

But even in Russia, where anarchism was an illegal, underground movement, as Michaël Confino observes, the anarchists' vocabulary is no argot; it is "not a clandestine language, the utility of which consists in not being understood by those not privy to the 'secret.'"[88] More often, especially under regimes with even limited freedom of speech and assembly, anarchists chose to openly defy bans and constraints, to make these into the occasion for struggle—the "free speech fights" of Emma Goldman and the IWW, for instance, holding meetings in public and challenging the laws. Anarchist movement poetry, by and large, pursues just this strategy, pushing the boundaries of acceptable public discourse rather than surrendering the field.

---

88 Michaël Confino, "Idéologie et sémantique: Le vocabulaire politique des anarchistes russes," *Cahiers du monde russe et soviétique* 30.3 (1989): 262.

2: THE DEVIL'S BEST TUNES

THERE is a Japanese anarchist song, sometimes dated from 1924, called "Anakisuto no uta [Anarchist Song]." Bizarrely, it is sung to a tune that an American would instantly recognize as "O Christmas Tree." It appears to have been written as a swipe at the Communists, who used the same tune for their anthem, the "Akahata no uta [Song of the Red Flag]." This was a 1921 translation of James Connell's song, "The Red Flag" (1889)—

> The workers' flag is deepest red,
> It shrouded oft our martyred dead;
> And ere their limbs grew stiff and cold
> Their life-blood dyed its every fold.

—which had been written with a Scottish air in mind, but which had been popularized in the IWW's song canon with the tune to a German schoolmaster's revision of an old Silesian song, "O Tannenbaum" (1824).[1] Red flags had belonged to all factions of the international workers' movement—in the so-called Akahata Jiken [Red Flags Incident] of 1908, Japanese anarchists, arrested en masse for singing "socialist songs," had indeed inscribed their slogans on red banners[2]—until the advent of the Russian Revolution and the consolidation of Communist Party power. Confronting former allies turned rivals, then, the anarchists remade the "Akahata no uta" as the

---

1   James Connell, "The Red Flag," *I.W.W. Songs to Fan the Flames of Discontent* (Chicago: I.W.W. Publishing Bureau, n.d., 2nd print); Connell, "How I Wrote the 'Red Flag,'" *The Call* (May 6, 1920): 5.

2   Vera C. Mackie, *Creating Socialist Women in Japan: Gender, Labour and Activism, 1900–1937* (Cambridge: Cambridge University Press, 2002), 66.

"Kurohata no uta [Song of the Black Flag]," now invested with lyrics accusing the Bolsheviks of having "defiled [*yogosu*]" the "sacred [*shinsei*]" symbol.[3] And so anarchists engaged in a public "war of songs" with their authoritarian and reformist rivals.[4]

Is "anarchist song," then, the product of a struggle over sacred symbols—a holy war? Perhaps it is telling that Pierre-Joseph Proudhon's prototypical example of "social art"—and of the value of art for *resistance*—is a "hymn":

> During my captivity at Sainte-Pélagie, in 1849, there were around eighty political prisoners, at a minimal estimate, if one thinks of the thousands of prisoners of that sad period. Every evening, half an hour before the closing of the cells, the detainees gathered in the courtyard and sang the *prière*; it was a hymn to Liberty attributed to Armand Marrast. One sole voice spoke the strophe, and the eighty prisoners gave back the refrain, which then was taken up by the five hundred *unfortunates* detained in the other section of the prison.... That was a *real* music, realist, applied, a *situated* art [l'art *en situation*], like church songs or fanfares in a parade, and no music pleases me more.[5]

Popular song—parallel in form and function, as Proudhon notes, to church hymns—is doubly valued: performed, enacted, it can be "situated" in the concrete, pragmatic needs of a specific community, for whom it enables collective resistance. At the same time, Marrast's song is not primarily propaganda for a belief that would be aimed at converting those outside its circle of the saved; those who sing it are those who already identify with its premises, and their singing serves to intensify that identity. "When one sings," Gaetano Manfredonia observes,

> it is not only for others but also for oneself. At the same time it seeks to mobilize, the song effects a labor of differentiation vis-à-vis

3   "Anakisuto no uta [Anarchist Song]," in *Nihon no kakumeika*, eds. Jirohei Nishio and Tamotsu Yazawa (Tokyo: Isseisha, 1974), 188.

4   See Stephen S. Large for a description of such song-battles in the struggle over direction of the labor movement (*Organized Workers and Socialist Politics in Interwar Japan* [Cambridge: Cambridge University Press, 2010], 41).

5   Pierre-Joseph Proudhon, *Du Principe de l'art et de sa destination social* (Paris: Lacroix, 1875), 332.

Fig. 1: A songbook issued by the *goguette* "La Muse Rouge," illustrated by Félix Lochard (1905).

others and identification between members of the group. It is not directed exclusively to external parties to be conquered but also to militants for whom it reaffirms the validity of the common struggle to be carried out. It helps keep alive the sense of group membership and encourage participation in its system of values. Just like the color of the flag or other distinguishing signs, it constitutes a powerful means to create and strengthen the militants' feeling of belonging to a single school of thought.... Often, the songs are only written and sung for the militants themselves.[6]

Songs could be carried and spread by individuals, but singing was also a communal activity—not only, as Alvan Sanborn observed, in "the little wine-shop concerts of the faubourgs, at which each and every person present is expected to 'do his turn' and all are counted on to help out with the choruses," but in organized workers' singing groups, *goguettes*; one such group, "La Muse Rouge [The Red Muse]" (1901–1939), not only convened monthly but published illustrated sheet music (fig. 1) and a series of seditious journals.[7] It may be logi-

6   Gaetano Manfredonia, "De l'usage de la chanson politique: la production anarchiste d'avant 1914," *Cités* 3.19 (2004): 45.

7   See Gaetano Manfredonia, *La Chanson anarchiste en France des origines*

cal, then, if strange, that according to the French penal code of 1894, the singing of anarchist songs *in public* was a matter for the Assize Court, punishable by a few days in jail, but those caught singing the same songs *behind closed doors* could be hauled before the Criminal Court and subjected to banishment.[8] As one anarchist remarked in São Paulo's union newspaper, *La Lotta Proletaria*: "the notes of our anthems give us spirit!"[9]

This privileging of song as the collective foundation of anarchist poetry is visible not only in the breadth and depth of anarchist song culture, as evidenced by the Argentine *Cancionero revolucionario* (1905) or the IWW's *Songs to Fan the Flames of Discontent* (ca. 1909), but also in the titles of anarchist poems and poetry collections such as Erich Mühsam's "Gesang der jungen Anarchisten [Young Anarchists' Song]" (1914); Alberto Ghiraldo's (1875–1946) "Canción del deportado [Deportee's Song]" (1921); J. William Lloyd's (1857–1940) *Songs of the Unblind Cupid* (1899); Akira Tanzawa's "Kō onna no uta [Factory Woman's Song]" (1929); or Herbert Read's "Song For the Spanish Anarchists" (1940). A great number of anarchist poems are specifically titled in imitation or parody of religious songs, such as Paul-Napoléon Roinard's "Cantique des cantiques [Song of Songs]" (1891), Paul Robin's "Hymne à la nuit [Hymn to the Night]" (1906), Jens Bjørneboe's "Fedrelandssalme [Hymn to the Fatherland]" (1968), Attilio Panizza's "Inno dei malfattori [Criminals' Hymn]" (1891), and innumerable anonymous poems with titles such as "Himno Acrático" or "Himno Anarquista [Anarchist Hymn]". In addition, many poems were given musical settings: thus David Edelstadt's "In Kamf [In Struggle]," composed in 1889, became a popular protest song among anarchist workers by 1903, for instance, and Carlo Monticelli's "L'Inno dei pezzenti [Tramps' Hymn]" (also titled "La Marsigliese del lavoro [The Labor Marseillaise]"), written in 1881,

à 1914: "dansons La Ravachole!" (Paris: L'Harmattan, 1997) and Robert Brécy, *Autour de la Muse Rouge: Groupe de poètes et chansonniers révolutionnaires, 1901–1939* (Saint-Cyr-sur-Loire, France: Editions Ch. Pirot, 1991).

8   René Garraud, *L'Anarchie et la répression* (Paris: Libr. du Recueil général des lois et des arrêts L. Larose, 1895), 67–68.

9   Angelo Scala qtd. in Gordon, *Anarchism in Brazil*, 222; Angelo Trento *Do outro lado do Atlântico: um século de imigração italiana no Brasil* (São Paulo, SP: Nobel, 1989), 243, 223.

was set to music by Guglielmo Vecchi in 1895.[10] Even poems not set to music were often recited publicly: one of the most widespread anarchist cultural forms, the *velada*, a kind of amateur evening variety show, combined recitations with songs, dances, and theatrical skits as well as lectures, debates, and speeches performed by workers and their families for one another.[11] In her study of French anarchist culture, Caroline Granier argues that "'pure' poetry ... holds a minor place in the corpus of the anarchist writers," and that pride of place belongs to the anarchist song.[12]

What kind of place is this world of songs? For an answer, we might look to the *Chansonnier international du révolté* (1906) compiled by Arnold Roller (a.k.a. Siegfried Nacht, 1878–1956) and Max Nomad (a.k.a. Max Nacht, 1881–1973), which presents a cross-section of the global anarchist song canon, at least in the diasporic languages of continental Europe (other tongues are absent). Out of sixty-five songs included, eleven are in French, twelve in German, nine in Yiddish (with some duplication), seven in Russian, six in Polish, five each in Spanish, Italian, and Czech, and just one in Ukrainian. Only thirteen songs are attributed to songwriters, most of these representing radical classics by fellow-travelers among the mighty dead—e.g., Heinrich Heine, Adam Mickiewicz, Eugène Pottier, William Morris, Josef Boleslav Pecka, and Max Kegel; the rest, of more recent date, are by anarchists. Evidently, the place of anarchist song is as international as the book's title—in other words, placeless. "Go forth into the world, little songbook," the editors write: "accompany, in their struggle and on their journey, the homeless, the wandering, expelled, banished comrades, and with the sound of your songs, the home of the homeless, the fatherland of the antipatriots—becomes the whole earth, becomes all mankind."[13]

---

10 Karen Ahlquist, *Chorus and Community* (Urbana, IL: University of Chicago Press, 2006), 207–208.

11 Maria Antonia Fernández, "Evolución de la propaganda anarquista española en la etapa fundacional del movimiento (1868–1897)," *Cuadernos Republicanos* 56 (Otoño 2004): 72–73; Shaffer, *Anarchism and Countercultural Politics*, 196–197; Gordon, *Anarchism in Brazil*, 221–222. The "format" of the *velada* seems to derive from the liberal tradition in Spain: see Navarro Navarro, *A la revolución por la cultura*, 265; and Angel Smith, *Anarchism, Revolution and Reaction: Catalan Labour and the Crisis of the Spanish State, 1898–1923* (New York: Berghahn Books, 2007), 157.

12 Granier, *Les Briseurs de formules*, 81.

13 Arnold Roller and Max Nomad, "Les Chants de Revolte/Rebellen-Lieder,"

If a certain kind of vagrancy is part of the condition of much anarchist poetry, it is doubly so for anarchist song. As the book's editors acknowledge, the prototypical creator and transmitter of the anarchist song is not the proletarian, but a more marginal type, a lumpenproletarian: the tramp, the itinerant, possessing only the most tenuous ties to the world of work. In France, this "quasi-mythical" figure, elevated to the status of an ideal, was called the *trimardeur* (from *trimancher*, in French argot, "to walk along the road"): the voluntary vagrant, who, having refused employment and citizenship alike, is free to be a full-time militant. As a "total anarchist," the *trimardeur* was imagined as escaping the dilemma of vocation that haunted proletarians; as Pessin observes, "with the practice of the '*trimard*,' anarchy is no longer a belief, a conception, or an activity separate from the rest of the individual's existence."[14] Known in Italian as *cavalieri erranti* (knights-errant), in English as the hobo, this nomad is the privileged carrier of song to whom the Nacht brothers intend to provide a paper "travelling companion":

> As soon as one comes into a new country, among comrades of other languages, one wants to share their enthusiasm before one can speak with them, one wants to sing their songs with them; one quite often learns the language from revolutionary songs, and later carries this song back to the homeland, a warm memory in happy hours, which one has brought back from the circles of comrades in other lands.[15]

The anarchist song, then, is first and foremost a means of international communication. Or is it? If no one language is shared among the singers, then whatever specific statement or demand the songs

---

Le Chansonnier international du révolté (London: Broschüren-Gruppe des Comm. A.-B.-V., 1906), 6.

14 John G. Hutton, "Les Prolos Vagabondent: Neo-Impressionism and the Anarchist Image of the Trimardeur," *The Art Bulletin* 72.2 (June 1990): 296–309; Pessin, *La rêverie anarchiste*, 79. Hutton emphasizes the imaginary nature of the trimardeur, whose reality was more often "dismal" than emancipatory, citing an 1891 study finding that the homeless unemployed were "so enervated that they have not the strength of will and purpose to accomplish such a revolt" ("Les Prolos Vagabondent," 302).

15 Roller and Nomad, "Les Chants de Revolte," 5–6.

might make—e.g., "Tsar Alexander, go home!" ("Warszawianka"), "What did the British Empire ever do for us?" ("The Starving Poor of Old England"), or "I'm ready to die for the cause" ("Das Testament" / "Mayn Tsavoe")—is not transmitted, no more than the content of punk lyrics screamed over guitar feedback in a noisy basement club. What is transmitted, at such moments, is not necessarily content, but comradeship: communion, not communication. The song's meaning, then, would consist less in what it says (its "constative" message, as philosophers of language put it) than in what it does (its "performative" function).

If anarchist songs are primarily intended to produce or "perform" harmony—the social kind by way of the musical kind—then why does the constative content matter? Wouldn't the comrades do just as well to sing school fight songs, dance-floor hits, or gospel tunes? In fact, a preeminent strategy of anarchist songwriting is to place dissident contents into just such familiar musical settings. Perhaps the easiest way to imagine this is as a radical equivalent of Weird Al Yankovic or the Capitol Steps—i.e., what Tuli Kupferberg (1923–2010) dubbed the "parasong":

> Parasong: a song using new and original lyrics set to an older (generally a popular) melody. Martin Luther set many of his religious hymns to the popular songs of that period. His reasoning: "Why should the devil have the best of tunes?" And in our time, the Wobblies repaid the compliment by resetting many old hymns to new radical Labor anthems!

And so, thanks to Kupferberg, the Christian classic "Jesus Loves Me" (1860) becomes "Nixon Fucks Me" (1971); the gentle liberal hymn, "Will The Circle Be Unbroken" (1907), becomes, courtesy of contemporary Wobbly Darryl Cherney (b. 1956), "Will the Fetus Be Aborted" (1988);[16] and in the hands of the Swedish-American Wobbly *trimardeur* Joe Hill (a.k.a. Joel Emmanuel Hägglund, Joseph Hillström, 1879–1915), the old hymn "In the Sweet By and By" (1868) becomes "The Preacher and the Slave" (ca. 1911):

---

16 Tuli Kupferberg, *Listen to the Mocking Bird* (Washington, NJ: Times Change Press, 1971), 21; Paul Lewis, *Cracking Up: American Humor in a Time of Conflict* (Chicago: University of Chicago Press, 2006), 130–131.

IN THE SWEET BY AND BY	THE PREACHER AND THE SLAVE
There's a land that is fairer than day,	Long-haired preachers come out every night,
And by faith we can see it afar;	Try to tell you what's wrong and what's right;
For the Father waits over the way	But when asked how 'bout something to eat
To prepare us a dwelling place there.	They will answer in voices so sweet:
Refrain	*Chorus*
In the sweet by and by,	You will eat, bye and bye,
We shall meet on that beautiful shore;	In that glorious land above the sky;
In the sweet by and by,	Work and pray, live on hay,
We shall meet on that beautiful shore.	You'll get pie in the sky when you die.

The relation of song to parasong is something like the relation of host to virus: the subversive lyrics insinuate their radical DNA into the ready-made reproductive apparatus of the cell, forcing it to crank out copies of the enemy as its integrity degrades. The key is successful mimicry: the matching of rhythms, first of all (anapestic trimeter, roughly, for the verses), but also of rhyming words—not vertically, from one line to the subsequent, or even internally (although pie-sky-die is already a savage punchline), but laterally, from parody to original ("In the sweet"/"You will eat")—and the echo of imagery ("beautiful shore"/"glorious land"). The audience is expected to hear the match, to recognize the original in the mimic—the better to appreciate the inversion of meanings, from spiritual otherworldliness to the materiality of the body, and of affects, from ascetic piety to the insistent demands of the body. The overturning of the world of values projected by the hymn is swift and complete, a musical instance of what Mikhail Bakhtin called "carnivalization," evoking that satirical condition in which feasting trumps fasting, laughter replaces prayer, and "life is subject only to its laws, that is, the laws of its own freedom."[17]

Hill's parodic re-appropriation of the Lord's tunes for the Devil's works, a tactic that would later be called *détournement*, was by no means the only mode possible. If Wobbly bards such as John

---

17 Mikhail Bakhtin, *Rabelais and His World*, trans. Hélène Iswolsky (Bloomington, IN: Indiana University Press, 1984), 7.

Brill, T-Bone Slim (a.k.a. Matti Valentine Huhta, c.1890–1942), and countless anonymous Fellow Workers delighted in plundering hymns and show tunes for songs like "Dump the Bosses Off Your Back" (to the tune of "What A Friend We Have In Jesus"), "The Popular Wobbly" (to the tune of "They Go Wild, Simply Wild, Over Me"), or "It's a Long Way Down to the Soupline" (to the tune of "It's a Long Way to Tipperary"), there are perhaps even more cases where the relation between sound and sense was rather less overtly hostile.

Observe: a Methodist camp-meeting tune ("Say, Brothers, Will You Meet Us"), wedded to the joke-song-become-abolitionist-tribute "John Brown's Body," then dressed up by Julia Ward Howe as the patriotic "Battle Hymn of the Republic,"[18] gives Ralph Chaplin (1887–1961) a setting for the IWW anthem, "Solidarity Forever." The end result has something of the pious fervor of the religious revivalist, abolitionist, and patriotic instantiations, albeit given a new direction and rationale ("what force on earth is weaker than the feeble strength of one? / But the Union makes us strong"). Another example: a Polish national-liberation song, the "Marsz Żuawów" (the "Zouaves' March," popularized during the Rebellion of 1863), supplies the music for a labor song, the "Warszawianka" (1883), written in prison by the socialist Wacław Święcicki (1848–1900); in translation, Święcicki's song gets taken up by some German anarcho-syndicalists, who bring it with them to Spain, where it catches on among the young comrades. It is then to this thrice-translated tune Valeriano Orobón Fernández (1901–1936) sets "A Las Barricadas (Marcha Triunfal)" (1933), battle anthem of the C.N.T.[19] In this form, it retains the labor and national-liberation inspirations of its earlier incarnations, but with a difference. The valences and connotations of music and words alike are repeatedly transformed in ways that suggest something more like co-evolution—mutualism, not predation. Instead of reversing the music's ideological signs, an-archist lyrics might add to or amplify them.

18 Sarah Vowell, "John Brown's Body," in *The Rose & the Briar: Death, Love and Liberty in the American Ballad*, ed. Sean Wilentz (New York: W.W. Norton, 2005), 85–86.

19 Apparently, the "Warszawianka" also caught the ear of Chinese anarchist educator Lu Jianbo (1904–1991), who set his own "revolutionary song" to its tune ("Lu Jianbo Ba Jin yanzhong de 'Zhongguo Gandi,'" *Chengdu Ribao* [Feb. 13, 2012], web).

One of the uses to which anarchists put their stolen tunes, indeed, was not mockery but dignification. If Marx—contemptuous of the ways in which the radicals of 1848 presented their ideas in words and images borrowed from the Revolution of 1789—could complain of the slavish imitation of "the tradition of all the dead generations," insisting "the social revolution of the nineteenth century cannot draw its poetry from the past, but only from the future,"[20] this was not so evident a necessity for his anarchist counterparts. On the contrary, as C. Alexander McKinley has shown, French anarchists of the late-nineteenth century, struggling to popularize their movement, saw that a way to reach working-class audiences—many of whom were illiterate, but who knew the songs of the French Revolution—was to use the old songs as a fulcrum for their own ideological work. Thus, if workers who were wary of identifying themselves with Ravachol's bombings of the judiciary nonetheless identified with the bloodthirsty heritage of the sans-culottes associated with songs like the "Carmagnole" and "Ça Ira," it made perfect sense to set the song "La Ravachole" to the tune of "Ça Ira" and to give it the subtitle "The New Carmagnole."[21] The newer, more radical content is couched in terms of an already-assimilated, seemingly safe context that is still pregnant with a radical content of its own. Indeed, to sing "La Ravachole" is to demonstrate that the past and its poetry are not spent forces, mere weights upon the living. Thus, Yvetot argues that this unique relation to the past is precisely the greatest virtue of song as an art form: where the visual arts preserve a distance between the spectator and the image of history, anyone who sings a *chanson* becomes a participant in it, "intimately involved in the life of what it recounts or recalls, criticizes or glorifies." In that sense, it "gives us the truest picture [*la plus réelle image*] of the past"—a past which, as the latter-day Wobbly singer Utah Phillips (1935–2008) reminds us, "didn't go anywhere."[22]

---

20 Marx, in *Marx-Engels Collected Works*, 11.103, 106.
21 C. Alexander McKinley, "Anarchists and the Music of the French Revolution," *Journal for the Study of Radicalism* 1.2 (2008), 3–4.
22 Georges Yvetot, "Chanson," *Encyclopédie anarchiste*, 320; Phillips and Di-Franco. See Daniel Colson's meditations on the ontology of "the past" in anarchism, sketched briefly in "L'Ange de l'Histoire," (*Le Monde Libertaire* 1377 [November 18–25, 2004]) and at greater length in his essay on Nietzsche's notion of "eternal return" in the *Petit lexique*, 99–108.

Part of what is at stake in anarchist song, indeed, is the future of the past. If, as Bakunin declared, all the products of "collective thought" and experience are the "intellectual and moral patrimony" of the people as a whole, then the progressive appropriation of that patrimony to the profit of a few is as monstrous a form of exploitation and expropriation as any.[23] In this sense, the official adoption of the "Marseillaise" as the French national anthem in 1879, ostensibly a victory for the forces of Republicanism and progress, is actually a dispossession, monopolizing a song that belongs to everyone. Rather than simply abandoning the "Marseillaise" in disgust, however, French anarchists spent the next two decades fighting its officialization, rewriting it and overcoding it with their own ideology.[24] Well after the turn of the century, we can find innumerable songs in Italian, Portuguese, German, and even English with the title "Anarchist Marseillaise," and among Latin American anarchists, as Iris M. Zavala notes, "the Marsellaise ... [remained] popular and entirely compatible with new re-accentuations."[25]

Observing the shifting relations of the anarchist song to its historical contexts and sources, we see a process of cultural contestation, a continuous "stealing back and forth of symbols," as Burke would call it, that speaks to the nature of resistance culture in relation to the culture of the past. These matters much occupied the mind of Dr. Félix Martí-Ibáñez (1911–1972), living in a Barcelona that had

23 Bakunin, *Bakunin on Anarchism*, 241.
24 McKinley, "Anarchists and the Music of the French Revolution," 6–10.
25 Iris M. Zavala, *Colonialism and Culture: Hispanic Modernisms and the Social Imaginary* (Bloomington, IN: Indiana University Press, 1991), 172. For instance, there is Carlo Ponticelli's "Marsigliese del lavoro" (1895), Erich Mühsam's "Generalstreik-Marseillaise" (1905), Ricardo Flores Magón's "Marsellesa Anarquista" (1907), the anonymously authored "Workers' Marseillaise" that appears in the ninth edition of the IWW songbook (1917), and Raymundo Reis's "Marselhesa Anarquista" (1933). There are accounts of German, Italian, and Russian anarchists around the world singing the "Marseillaise" with enthusiasm throughout the heyday of the movement, and Moses Rischin recounts that, in 1890, the same Russian-speaking Jewish anarchists who sang antireligious parasongs at their "Grand Yom Zom Kippur Ball" in Brooklyn promoted the event with flyers promising not only a Kol Nidrei to be sung by Johann Most (author of *The Deistic Pestilence*) but the singing of "[the] Marseillaise and other hymns against Satan" (Rischin, *The Promised City: New York's Jews, 1870–1914* [Cambridge, MA: Harvard University Press, 1978], 154–155).

birthed the Spanish Revolution but was being torn apart by the Civil War in 1937. Even in these precarious conditions, however, the doctor (about whom we shall hear more later) insisted that it was a "dangerous error" to disregard the importance of culture in the revolutionary struggle, to see it as subsidiary to economic or military struggle: "to work for a dignified and humanist culture," he wrote that October, "is ... to defend the Revolution, forging a revolutionary conviction, a wall of souls against which fascism will crash." A revolution, he argued, was preeminently a process of cultural transformation—the crumbling of a "decrepit" system of ideas and values, the construction of a new order of the "spirit":[26]

> A Revolution is ... a period of social abnormality in which, all the integral factors of society that give it its personality are thrown into a confused chaos ... At moments of danger or commotion—like a Revolution—in order to admit the lived moment into consciousness, to orient ourselves to it, temporally and spatially, and adapt to it, proto-images or *archetypes*, coming from and arising within our mental life, become the guides of our actions.[27]

Accordingly, in an extended pamphlet published by the anarchist journal *Tierra y Libertad*, Martí-Ibáñez pursued his *Psicoanálisis de la Revolución Social Española* (1937).

An enthusiast of Freud and Jung, Martí-Ibáñez's point of departure for understanding this "crisis of the soul of the people" was the "pubertal crisis," the developmental narrative according to which children are transformed into adults, and its social analogue, the speculative prehistory sketched by Freud in *Totem and Taboo* (1913). A society in the process of overcoming authority, Martí-Ibáñez reasoned, paralleled the historical process whereby (according to Freud) humanity had overcome its abject submission to a primitive "patriarchal tyranny." Just as the sons of the primal horde had to kill and castrate the obscene, greedy Father to gain access to his women, the Spanish people had to overcome the violent, plutocratic State and strip it of its force in order to gain access not only to the Land

---

26 Martí-Ibáñez, "La Cultura," 11–12.
27 Félix Martí-Ibáñez, *Psicoanálisis de la Revolución Social Española* (Barcelona: Ediciones "Tierra y Libertad," 1937), 17.

("Mother Earth") but to all the other symbols of value (likewise traditionally represented by archetypal female figures): "Freedom," "Justice," "Peace," etc.[28]

In light of Martí-Ibáñez's theory of cultural revolution as positive symbolic "parricide" and "incest," then, anarchist song might not
be an attempt to differentiate the individual artist from the matrix
of poetic tradition at all costs, but precisely as an attempt to wrest
valuable, potent symbols away from the Father, the nexus of social
authority, who possesses and controls them. To put it another way:
why should the Good Lord have all the best tunes?

---

28 Ibid., 14–15, 23.

3: TWO CRISES OF LANGUAGE

IF song is the foundation of anarchist poetry, then we can only wonder at the difference between the kind of songwriting characteristic of the *Chansonnier international du révolté* or *Songs to Fan the Flames of Discontent*, on the one hand, and the sound of the music that is now most widely recognized as "anarchist": punk. The change has been neither continuous nor instantaneous; even well before the advent of the Sex Pistols, someone grounded in the tradition of the anarchist movement could observe, with Utah Phillips, that "There's a big difference between 'How many miles must a white dove sail before it can rest in the sand' and 'Dump the bosses off your back'!" Curiously, as Phillips observes, it is precisely as protest songs became more "poetic"—their lyrics more "introverted," "harder to understand"—that anarchist poetry became less song-like.[1] What was happening?

There is a collection of essays, published by the Free Society Group of Chicago in 1951, titled *The World Scene from the Libertarian Point of View*. It is a gloomy book. The contributors—Spanish, Russian, German, Japanese, many of them writing from political exile—struggle against despair; a few dare to hope that capitalism and its false alternatives may yet some day collapse, but the assessment of the present, from every corner, is almost uniformly dismal. It is not only that capitalism has survived its crisis, Stalin has remained in power, the labor movement has been bureaucratized and co-opted: all the

---

1   Utah Phillips, in Utah Phillips and Jeffrey Lewis, "The True Tall Tale of
    Utah Phillips, Folk Legend and 21st Century Wobbly," in *Wobblies!: A
    Graphic History of the Industrial Workers of the World*, eds. Paul Buhle and
    Nicole Schulman (New York: Verso, 2005), 251.

old modes of cultural resistance, too, have been outflanked. More and more, the ways that anarchists knew of constructing a counterpublic sphere—pamphlets, speeches, agitation, theater—no longer work; there is no longer an opening to a wider world. "By the fifties," Jerry Zaslove reflects, social hopes for an "authentic public sphere" had fallen into eclipse: it seemed instead that "any public culture would have to be clumsily made up of fragments of lost polises, mythical remnants of stories of vanished places ... sacred reminders and traces lost in collective memory."[2] Nor would this shrinkage of public space leave the counterpublic of anarchist movement poetics unscathed.

Writing in 1964, Herbert Read credits Mallarmé with having first identified the basic "predicament of modern poetry," "a problem affecting not only the poet, but social communication in general": "the evident fact that the language of our western civilization had become too corrupt for poetic use."[3] If this attribution seems to be a bit of an overstatement—Percy Bysshe Shelley, for instance, had warned almost a century before Mallarmé that unless it is perpetually renewed by poets, "language will be dead to all the nobler purposes of human intercourse"—it is still telling that Mallarmé serves as Read's prophet, and that the prophecy is seen as *already* having come true: by the mid-twentieth century, it can be taken as given that language *is*, for all the nobler purposes of human intercourse, dead.[4]

What has killed language? More specifically, what has put it beyond poetic repair? Frederic Jameson reads the 1960s as the moment when capitalism attained its maximum reach, assimilating "the last vestiges of Nature"—i.e., not only "the Third World," via the so-called Green Revolution of agribusiness, but also, via the new techniques of commercial media culture, "the unconscious" itself.[5] This may be a fair assessment, and more than one commentator has noted how

---

2 Jery Zaslove, "The Public Sphereoid—Following the Paths in the Millennial Wilderness, or 'Lost Without a Utopic Map' in the Spheres of Hannah Arendt and Robin Blaser," in *The Recovery of the Public World: Essays on Poetics in Honour of Robin Blaser*, eds. Charles Watts and Edward Byrne (Burnaby, BC: Talonbooks, 1998), 435.

3 Herbert Read, "The Resurrection of the Word," in Arlene Zekowski, *Abraxas* (New York: Wittenborn, 1964), 5.

4 Shelley, *Shelley's Prose*, 278.

5 Frederic Jameson, *The Ideologies of Theory 2: The Syntax of History* (Minneapolis: University of Minnesota Press, 1989), 207.

this last development spelled doom for a whole host of oppositional avant-garde ways of making art, as seemingly everything from Surrealism to Abstract Expressionism to graffiti were converted into marketing materials by "hip consumerism."[6] By 1968, the euphemistic language of "pacification" in Vietnam could bring Denise Levertov to despair: "O language, mother of thought, / are you rejecting us as we reject you?"[7] However, the damage is not confined to Vietnam or to the United States. In a recent interview, the Swiss anarchist writing under the *nom de plume* of "p.m." (Hans Widmer, b. 1946) reflected on his rationale for inventing a "weird secret language" for the elements of his utopia, *bolo'bolo* (1983): "European left-wing terminology was no longer viable," he reflects, because it only conjures up images of the "gulag" or of a tepid reformism; "all of the other standard left-wing expressions such as 'solidarity,' 'community,' they're all contaminated and no longer useful."[8] Indeed, the global eclipse of radical working-class poetics had begun much earlier, during the crisis that had marked anarchism's finest hour (and, in most conventional historical accounts, its last stand): the transition from the Great Depression to the Second World War.

We can see this shift taking place perhaps most clearly in the U.S. and Britain. Repression following the First World War and the Red Scare—lynchings, raids, trials, deportations—had taken a tremendous toll on the ability of American anarchists to operate and organize, and increasing restrictions on immigration cut off the further influx of workers such as the Jews, Russians, and Italians who had formed the backbone of the movement.[9] By the end of the 1920s, American activists like the Russian-born Joseph Spivak (1882–1971) were asking: "Why is it that the anarchist movement is so weak? Why

6   Andrei Codrescu, *The Disappearance of the Outside: A Manifesto for Escape* (Reading, MA: Addison-Wesley, 1990); Thomas Frank, *The Conquest of Cool: Business, Culture, Counterculture, and the Rise of Hip Consumerism* (Chicago: University of Chicago Press, 1997).

7   Denise Levertov, "Prologue: An Interim," *Poems 1968–1972* (New York: New Directions, 1987), 29–30.

8   p.m., "bolo'bolo: Transcription of a video by O. Ressler, recorded in Zurich, Switzerland, 24 min., 2004," *european institute for progressive cultural policies* (web), 1. See Part III, Chapter 6 for more on this language.

9   Bill Ong Hing, *Defining America Through Immigration Policy* (Philadelphia: Temple University Press, 2004), 67, 215–216.

is it that our influence upon the population of this country is so negligible?"[10] By the time the Depression hit, anarchists were too poorly positioned to respond to the crisis; instead, other labor organizations—confrontational, but with far more circumscribed goals—and the Communist Party became the privileged organs of working-class contestation. Indeed, particularly during the period of the Popular Front (1934–1939), when Communist Parties sought broad alliances with liberal and progressive forces against the fascist right, we see writers on the Communist left increasingly appropriating and adopting the poetics that had once typified the anarchist movement.

Marcus Graham's 1929 *Anthology of Revolutionary Poetry*, capturing and codifying what anarchist movement poetics had been, became a touchstone for the Rebel Poets, whose work, in turn, became seminal for an entire "genealogy" of left-wing American writers.[11] A broad meeting ground for "communists, socialists, anarchists, and other nonaffiliated proletarian poets," the Rebel Poet group had been convened in the previous year by Jack Conroy (1899–1990), who later in life admitted being "more of a philosophical anarchist than anything."[12] Among the co-authors of the Rebel Poets' 1931 manifesto were the authors of the Preface to Graham's anthology, Ralph Cheyney (1896–1941), who also defined himself as a "philosophical anarchist," and Lucia Trent (1897–1977); the *Unrest* anthologies of 1929, 1930, and 1931 were co-edited by Conroy and Cheyney, with Harry Crosby (1898–1929), who also called himself an anarchist,

10 Joseph Spivak, "What is Wrong with Our Movement?," *The Road to Freedom* 4.9 (April 1928): 2. See also A. Blecher, "Problems of Freedom and Practice," *The Road to Freedom* 2.11 (August 1, 1926): 7–8; Samuel Polinow, "Propaganda and Education," *The Road to Freedom* 2.10 (July 15, 1926): 5–6; and W.S. Van Valkenburgh, "What is Wrong with Our Movement?," *The Road to Freedom* 4.10 (May 1928): 3.

11 Douglas Wixson, *Worker-Writer in America: Jack Conroy and the Tradition of Midwestern Literary Radicalism* (Urbana, IL: University of Illinois Press, 1999), 164; James Edward Smethurst, *The New Red Negro: The Literary Left and African American Poetry, 1930–1946* (New York: Oxford University Press, 1999), 19–20.

12 Walter B. Kalaidjian, *American Culture Between the Wars: Revisionary Modernism & Postmodern Critique* (New York: Columbia University Press, 1993), 107; Jack Conroy qtd. in David Ray and Jack Salzman, "Introduction," in *The Jack Conroy Reader*, eds. Jack Salzman and David Ray (New York: B. Franklin, 1979), xv.

joining them on the 1930 anthology.[13] The first two issues of their house organ, *The Rebel Poet* (1931–1932), reported on Graham's sedition trial and featured poems by anarchists Jo Labadie ("The Unemployed") and Charles Erskine Scott Wood ("Authority").[14]

While the group's manifesto insisted that "nothing but general sympathy with our aims is required of members" and that it was "affiliated with no political party," it already insisted on "defense of the Soviet Union against the enemies that are massing for attack."[15] Conroy and the rest of the group drifted towards an increasing acceptance of Communist Party orthodoxy, leading Cheyney to withdraw in 1933, when the *Rebel Poet* journal was retitled *The Anvil: Stories For Workers*, and the group itself renamed the Proletarian Writers' League.[16] Indeed, Conroy, finding himself increasingly marginalized within his own groupings, was already warning fellow worker-writers against collaboration with Roosevelt's New Deal in October of that same year: "The ancient lies have only been refurbished."[17]

In Europe, anarchists were dealing with similar challenges. Henry Poulaille (1896–1980), literary editor of the Confédération Générale du Travail's daily paper, *Le Peuple* (1924–1939), and author of *Nouvel âge littéraire* (1930), championed a conception of "proletarian literature" with roots in the nineteenth-century anarchist tradition of Pierre-Joseph Proudhon and Bernard Lazare, but which, in foregrounding the anti-vanguardist aspects of anarchism, was to remain non-sectarian, identified simply with the working class.[18] By 1935, Poulaille was fending off friendly overtures from both the Populistes and the Communist Party-affiliated Association des Écrivains et des Artistes Révolutionnaires (AEAR) proposing a "Front littéraire commun" against the common enemy: fascism. "At this moment,"

---

13 Wixson, *Worker-Writer in America*, 274; Harry Crosby, *Shadows of the Sun: The Diaries of Harry Crosby*, ed. Edward Germain (Santa Barbara: Black Sparrow Press, 1977), 205.

14 First and second issues of *The Rebel Poet*, January and February 1931.

15 Conroy et al., "Manifesto," qtd. in *The Little Magazine in America: A Modern Documentary History*, eds. Elliott Anderson and Mary Kinzie (Yonkers, NY: Pushcart Press, 1978), 118.

16 Wixson, *Worker-Writer in America*, 301–302.

17 Jack Conroy, "American Proletarian Writers and The New Deal," *The Jack Conroy Reader*, 214.

18 Henry Poulaille, *Nouvel âge littéraire* (Paris: Valois, 1930), 16–17.

warned the ex-Surrealist poet Louis Aragon on behalf of the AEAR, "there is but one single organization of antifascist writers, and that is ours. To divide efforts, today, is to play into the hands of the enemy." Poulaille's response: "We are within the Proletariat and remain there, and that is where we want to remain."[19] The creation of the Fédération du Théâtre Ouvrier de France (FTOF) in 1931, likewise under the tutelage of the Communist Party, posed a dilemma for the surviving members of La Muse Rouge; after a painful split, the "revolutionary poets and songwriters" opted to remain faithful to their anarchist theory and non-sectarian practice, but found themselves increasingly isolated, ostracized by workers' groups, and dissolved in 1939.[20]

With few significant differences, this was how the story ran in Latin America as well. In the early 1920s, anarchist poets such as Brandão were quickly drawn into the newly formed Partido Comunista Brasileiro.[21] In Chile, Pablo Neruda (1904–1973) makes a similar transition away from the anarchist politics he espoused in the 1920s, when he was active with the anti-authoritarian Federación de Estudiantes de Chile (FECh), to Communist Party membership in the 1940s, following in the path of his friend, Louis Aragon.[22] Another friend of Neruda's, the Peruvian César Vallejo (1892–1938), took a similar trajectory from the influence of the anarchist Manuel González Prada (1844–1918) to that of the Comintern.[23] Perhaps fewer deserted anarchism in Argentina, but some of the most vigorous radical writers of the mid-twentieth century—e.g., Elías Castelnuovo (1893–1982), Álvaro Yunque (1889–1982)—would, without quite renouncing their libertarian sympathies, remain in the communist cultural orbit.[24]

---

19 Aragon qtd. in Chapman, *Henry Poulaille and Proletarian Literature*, 84; and Poulaille qtd. Ibid., 86.

20 Manfredonia, *La Chanson anarchiste en France*, 300.

21 John W. F. Dulles, *Anarchists and Communists in Brazil, 1900–1935* (Austin: University of Texas Press, 1974), 181–183.

22 Neruda qtd. in Rita Guibert, *Seven Voices: Seven Latin American Writers Talk to Rita Guibert* (New York: Knopf, 1973), 13; Hernán Loyola, *Neruda: la biografía literaria* (Santiago: Seix Barral, 2006), 77, 97, 197; Greg Dawes, *Verses Against the Darkness: Pablo Neruda's Poetry and Politics* (Lewisburg, PA: Bucknell University Press, 2006), 54–55, 74–75.

23 Franco, *César Vallejo: The Dialectics of Poetry and Silence* (Cambridge: Cambridge University Press, 1976), 7–8, 20, 150.

24 Carlos M. Rama and Angel J. Cappelletti, *El Anarquismo En América Latina* (Caracas, Venezuela: Biblioteca Ayacucho, 1990), XIII, LIII–LIV.

Central to the dynamic that the Japanese refer to as the *ana-boru ronso* (anarchist-Bolshevik controversy) in the 1920s was the dispute between anarchists and Marxists over how a new feminist and proletarian culture should be constructed. In the 1920s, Japanese anarchists such as Ōsugi Sakae (1885–1923) and Nii Itaru (1888–1951) struggled against the notion that only an intellectual vanguard could constitute the authorship or even the audience for radical verse, advocating a kind of "proletarian poetry" that would be both for and by the working classes themselves.[25] Anarchist writers like Takamure Itsue and Uemura Tai (1903–1959) from Japan, Kim Hwa-san (a.k.a. Bang Jun-gyeong, 1905–1970) and Yu Seo (1905–1980) from Korea, and Ou Shengbai (a.k.a. Qu Shengbai, 1893–1973) from China tended to resist the narrowly instrumentalist, class- and Party-centered conceptions of the Marxists.[26] Organizations such as the NAPF (Nippona Artista Proleta Federacio) and KAPF (Korea Artista Proletaria Federacio) as well as journals like *Funü sheng* (*Women's Voice*, 1921–1922) in China and *Bungei sensen* (*Literary Battleground*, 1924–1930) and *Nyonin geijutsu* (*Women's Arts*, 1928–1931) became sites for this contestation; ultimately, they were captured by Marxists, and anarchists were expelled.[27] Resisting Communist Party demands for "committed" literature, anarchist poet Tsuboi Shigeji (1897–1975) insisted, in 1927, that "the literary theory of anarchism is ... the negation of 'the Communist political party in literature' or, in extreme terms, the negation of 'political party literature' in general."[28] Regardless, increasing

---

25 Thomas A. Stanley, *Ōsugi Sakae, Anarchist in Taishō Japan: The Creativity of the Ego* (Cambridge, MA: Council on East Asian Studies, Harvard University, 1982), 116; George Tyson Shea, *Leftwing Literature in Japan: A Brief History of the Proletarian Literary Movement* (Tokyo: Hosei University Press, 1964), 87; Filler, *Chaos From Order*, 209.

26 Ha Ki Rak, *History of the Korean Anarchist Movement* (Taegu, Korea: Anarchist Publishing Committee, 1986), 39–51; Dongyoun Hwang, "Korean Anarchism Before 1945," in *Anarchism and Syndicalism in the Colonial and Postcolonial World, 1870–1940*, eds. Steven Hirsch and Lucien Van der Walt (Leiden: Brill, 2010), 113.

27 Kim Yun-sik, "KAPF Literature in Modern Korean Literary History," *positions: east asia cultures critique* 14.2 (Fall 2006): 412–413; Filler, *Chaos From Order*, 22; Angela Coutts, "Imagining Radical Women in Interwar Japan: Leftist and Feminist Perspectives," *Signs* 37.2 (Winter 2012): 351–52.

28 Tsuboi qtd. in Seiji M. Lippit, *Topographies of Japanese Modernism* (New York: Columbia University Press, 2002), 254n55.

government persecution largely stifled proletarian poetry and the anarchist movement as a whole well before the start of World War II.[29] When the lights came back on, the anarchists had largely been swept from the stage.

Among the many writers on the American left who disregarded warnings against Popular Front-style collaboration was the head of the Federal Writers' Project, Henry G. Alsberg (1881–1970). In younger days, Alsberg had flirted with radicalism, traveling to Russia as a journalist to bear witness to the Bolshevik experience and meeting Emma Goldman, Alexander Berkman, and Peter Kropotkin. Disgusted by the new regime and impressed by the intransigent morality of his anarchist friends, he called himself a "philosophical anarchist"—a label he still used to describe himself in the 1930s, when he was appointed to the government post, although the passage of time had obviously softened his politics. Alsberg drew many talented radical writers into the Federal Writers' Project, including Conroy himself, the anarchist Leonard D. Abbott (1878–1953), and, in San Francisco, an American Wobbly and poet, Kenneth Rexroth.[30]

Rexroth, who had previously styled himself a Marxist and attended Communist Party meetings, quit his WPA Federal Writers' Project job in 1939 in anger over appeasement of the fascists by the Western powers and the Soviets alike.[31] Their eventual realignment against fascism in the Popular Front and World War II would only confirm their hypocrisy. In 1947, writing for the British anarchist literary journal *Now*, Rexroth would recall that

> years of the expedientialism of Lenin, Stalin, and/or Trotsky
> and/or John Dewey had accomplished a miracle of surgery.
> Thousands of people woke up one day to discover that their
> backbones had been painlessly removed.... The W.P.A. Writers'

---

29 Ibid.

30 Jerre Mangione, *The Dream and the Deal: The Federal Writers' Project, 1935–1943* (Syracuse, NY: Syracuse University Press, 1996), 55–56; Reed Harris, in United States et al., *Executive Sessions of the Senate Permanent Subcommittee on Investigations of the Committee on Government Operations* (Washington, DC: U.S. G.P.O., 2003), 666 ; Paul Avrich, *Anarchist Voices: An Oral History of Anarchism in America* (Princeton, NJ: Princeton University Press, 1995), 479 n34.

31 Mangione, *The Dream and the Deal*, 132.

Project changed its name to the Office of War Information; salaries were upped handsomely.... These people are not innocent with invincible ignorance. They all knew they were selling their souls for a mess of government vouchers.[32]

Gathering around himself a nexus of like-minded dissidents from what had become the mainstream of the left—pacifists, homosexuals, anti-statists—Rexroth formed the San Francisco Anarchist Circle (ca. 1945–1948), one of the primary vehicles for the regeneration of a shattered and enervated American anarchist movement and, not incidentally, a flashpoint for postwar American poetry. Among the libertarian poets who gathered, first in Rexroth's apartment, then in an old Arbeiter Ring hall, were Kenneth Patchen, Jack Spicer (1925–1965), and Robert Duncan (1919–1988), as well as William Everson (a.k.a. Brother Antoninus, 1912–1994), Philip Whalen (1923–2002), Robin Blaser (1925–2009), and Philip Lamantia (1927–2005).

Rexroth also formed links between these poets and their anarchist counterparts on the east coast of the U.S., where the journals *Why? An Anarchist Bulletin* (1942–1947), its successor, *Resistance* (1947–1954), Dwight Macdonald's *politics* (1944–1949), and *Retort: An Anarchist Quarterly of Social Philosophy and the Arts* (1942–1951) were the anchors, as well as in England, where George Woodcock's journal *Now* (1943–1947), featuring the work of anarchist poets Herbert Read, Louis Adeane (b. 1922), Derek Savage (1917–2007), and Alex Comfort (1920–2000), served a similar purpose for the antiwar remnant of British anarchism.

It is in the very first issue of *Retort* that we find an attack, penned by one of the journal's editors, Holley Cantine, on one of the grand patriarchs of anarchist poetry—Walt Whitman himself. The Whitman who appears in Cantine's essay is almost unrecognizable as the poet hailed by Bell, Goldman, Landauer, and Abbott. In 1907, a writer for Goldman's *Mother Earth* could simply declare, without fear of objection, that "Walt Whitman is the poet of democracy"; in 1942, *Retort* retorts that his effusions over "the common man" were "not enough to make a real democrat"—indeed, that his exaggerated

---

32 Kenneth Rexroth, "Letter From America," *Now* 7 (February–March 1947): 61–62.

respect for "the 'popular will'" amounted to the belief that "whatever a majority of the people happened to believe at any particular moment was by definition both true and good," a fascist notion.[33] In 1919, the German anarchist newspaper *Freie Jugend* (1919–1925) could print translations of Whitman's "To a Foil'd European Revolutionaire" alongside an appeal to Communist Party members to "hear his ardent calls" and "renounce blood and power";[34] in 1942, American anarchists instead read Whitman through the lens of the Popular Front and the war-propaganda machine that has seized on his works. During the lead-up to the war, Cantine recounts, "liberal interventionists" argued that

• Walt Whitman was the Great Affirmer of Democracy;
• Walt Whitman sanctioned the fighting of a war for democracy;
• Therefore: how can anyone who professes to believe in democracy fail to support American participation in the present war?[35]

What is at stake here is much, much more than just a tussle over the political ownership of the Good Gray Poet. What is revealed by this dispute, instead, is the opening of an even greater fissure between public and counterpublic. As Cantine observes, he, the intelligentsia of the liberal States, and their Left allies can all agree that "Whitman sanctioned the fighting of a war for democracy," but cannot agree on a.) whether or not what Whitman affirmed was "democracy"; b.) whether or not the war against the Axis powers is a "war for democracy"; c.) what *counts* as "democracy"; or d.) whether or not a "war for democracy" is a contradiction in terms. In short, while the *facts* are not a matter of dispute, the *values* assumed by these two universes of discourse are so different that it is *almost as if* they refer to two different universes.

Whitman and the discredited language of the entire prophetic-populist tradition, on the one hand, and the ancestral figures associated with the rhetoric of mass organizing on the other. It is at this point, ironically, that the anarchist poets published in journals such as *Now*

---

33 Elisabeth Burns Ferm, "The Democracy of Whitman," *Mother Earth* 1.12 (February 1907): 18; Holley R. Cantine, "A Footnote on Walt Whitman," *Retort* 1.1 (Winter 1942): 54, 52–53.

34 Qtd. in Walter Grünzweig, *Constructing the German Walt Whitman*, (Iowa City, IA: University of Iowa Press, 1995), 162–163, trans. Grünzweig.

35 Cantine, "A Footnote on Walt Whitman," 51.

and *Retort* actually are placed in something like the position described by Kristeva's *Revolution in Poetic Language*. By 1951, Goodman will retrospectively describe this as a "crisis of alienation."[36]

After Kronstadt, after the Moscow show trials, after the Bloody Week in Madrid, after the Molotov-Ribbentropp pact, it is in vain that Read will counsel his fellow anarchist poets "not [to] be afraid to use the word 'brotherhood' ... simply because it has sentimental associations."[37] Falsified, betrayed, the word has now become a sign of falsehood and betrayal. Indeed, "brotherhood" increasingly appears not as a "concrete existential bond" but as an empty abstraction, and Pound's Imagist counsel—"Go in fear of abstractions"—is becoming an imperative.[38] Times are inauspicious for anarchist speech in public; anarchist poetry, accordingly, will turn away from the apparently blocked channels of democratic and plebeian discourse, back toward the bohemian-aristocratic poetics that had been so assiduously developed by that long series of avant-gardes stretching from the Symbolists to the Surrealists.

In *Retort*, we see an alternation between the old and new modes. The first issue, appearing immediately in the wake of Pearl Harbor, features Rexroth's "Again at Waldheim," an elegy in homage to de Cleyre's "Light Upon Waldheim," itself an elegy for the Haymarket anarchist martyrs buried in Waldheim Cemetery in Chicago (subsequently the resting place of Emma Goldman and de Cleyre herself as well). Dated "London, October, 1897"—nearly ten years after the execution of George Engel, Adolph Fischer, Albert Parsons, and August Spies:

> Light upon Waldheim! And the earth is gray;
>   A bitter wind is driving from the north;
> The stone is cold, and strange cold whispers say:
>   "What do ye here with Death? Go forth! Go forth!"[39]

---

36 Goodman, "Advance-Guard Writing," 375.

37 Herbert Read, "Chains of Freedom (II)," *Now* 9 (July–August 1947): 21.

38 Ibid., 21; Ezra Pound, *Literary Essays of Ezra Pound*, ed. T.S. Eliot (New York: New Directions, 1968), 5.

39 Voltairine de Cleyre, "Light Upon Waldheim," *Selected Works of Voltairine de Cleyre*, 66.

Rexroth's half-century late reply addresses the fallen precursors: "when every voice / Was cowed, you spoke against the coalitions / For the duration of the emergency— / In the permanent emergency / You spoke for the irrefutable / Coalition of the blood of men."[40] This relatively simple piece, written in a restrained free verse, is linked to the traditions of anarchist poetry by more than allusions and ideas. At the same time that it repudiates false identities ("coalitions / For the duration of the emergency"), it communicates, eliciting and embodying a true community (the "irrefutable / Coalition"); it is a poem of and for a movement, written for an occasion (the onset of war, the dissolution of hopes). It is an artifact of anarchist resistance culture, summoning the forces of memory and example—the "tradition of the oppressed," as Walter Benjamin put it, that "teaches us that the 'state of emergency' in which we live is not the exception but the rule"[41]—against the hopelessness bred by "permanent emergency." At the same time, Rexroth's rhetoric of mourning cuts quite against de Cleyre's imperative: "Stand not to weep for these." If the former imagines the statue urging us to "Go forth!" the latter seems to answer, "Where?" Even the closing invocation of a "Coalition of the blood of men" seems more a consolation than a charge. Rexroth's poem confirms, in a way that de Cleyre's did not, Auden's quintessentially late-modernist conclusion: "poetry makes nothing happen."[42]

More indicative of the new direction, in *Retort*, are the poems of Dachine Rainer (a.k.a. Sylvia Newman, 1921–2000) and Jackson Mac Low (1922–2004). Here, although some traces of nostalgia for them remain,[43] the old oral-musical forms and genres—revolutionary

---

40 Kenneth Rexroth, "Again at Waldheim," *Retort* 1.1 (Winter 1942): 27–32. The substitution of "rain" for "light" was corrected in subsequent editions of "Again at Waldheim."

41 Benjamin, *Illuminations*, 257.

42 Or, one might add, to Holley Cantine's contention that art is, in its pre-capitalist essence, "activity that has no direct practical value" ("Art: Play and its Perversions," *Retort* 4.1 [Fall 1947]: 6).

43 See, for instance, the reprinting of the original French version of Eugène Pottier's "L'Internationale," followed by Jackson Mac Low's original translation of it, in *Retort* 3.2 (Spring 1946), 3.3 (Winter 1947), respectively. In an accompanying note, Mac Low explains that he has chosen, in the interests of "literalness," to partially "dispense with rhyme" and "strict meter," maintaining only "some sort of singability with the usual tune" (Mac Low, "The International," *Retort* 3.3 [Winter 1947]: 39n).

hymn, proletarian ballad, lyrical call to arms—fall away entirely as the scope of potential readership radically diminishes, abandoned in favor of quieter, more private and meditative modes, elegies not only for the passing of a moment but that of community and meaning. The stylized abstractions of Rainer's "The Psychoneurotic" only hint obliquely at concrete social realities:

> the incident is principle
> a rationalized focal shift
> each new center a rosary and an axe.
> fixed upon the cross, disciplined
>
> nails still hold the moldy order
> of charred bone....[44]

Out of a cloud of empty terms and phrases vaguely reminiscent of the jargon of psychiatry ("psychoneurotic," "incident," "principle," "rationalized focal shift") precipitate a series of concrete images ("rosary," "axe," "cross," "nails," "charred bone") that imply both prayer and torture. It is up to the reader to infer the relationships between these ideas: perhaps psychiatry (as a new form of "order," in contrast to the "moldy order" of the Church) is being likened to a form of religious "discipline," such as confession. This was, indeed, a common theme in the experiences of pacifist prisoners documented in *Prison Etiquette: The Convict's Compendium of Useful Information* (1950), a book Rainer edited with Cantine, where many testify to the practice of "bugg[ing]," or labeling recalcitrant prisoners insane in order to have them transferred to the "psychoneurotic ward[s]" of prisons with harsher regimes.[45] At the same time, the poem suggests relationships between the concepts of a "focal shift," a "new center," and a "cross" (in the sense of an intersection), together with a dichotomy between "rosary" and "axe": if someone,

---

44 Dachine Rainer, "The Psychoneurotic," *Retort* 3.3 (Winter 1947).

45 Holley R. Cantine and Dachine Rainer, eds, *Prison Etiquette: The Convict's Compendium of Useful Information* (Bearsville, NY: Retort Press, 1950), xxxix, 31, 89. Contributions to this anthology were solicited in the pages of *Retort*, and an excerpt—Clif Bennet's "Resistance In Prison"—was published in *Retort* 4.3 (Winter 1949).

perhaps a "psychoneurotic" under analysis, is shifting focus, each new "center" of attention can serve as a vehicle for guilty submission (the function served by a "rosary") or as a means of aggression directed outward (like an "axe"). A fragmentary, obscure drama of violence and resistance is being played out here for only the most attentive among a tiny circle of readers.

Jackson Mac Low's poetic contributions to *Retort* were often much more in keeping with the older traditions of movement poetry than the kinds of experimental verse he had been working on since his teens. Compare, for instance, "H U N G E R ST r i kE wh A t d o e S lifemean" with an untitled poem he published in *Retort* in 1947:

> Men are sheep today, savage as tigers,
> destroying at command, loosing unwilled vengeance,
> repudiating themselves, repudiating nature,
> not repudiating their masters![46]

The precocious experimentalism of the earlier poem is strongly reminiscent of modernists like Guillaume Apollinaire and Gertrude Stein, while the second, in its emotive, rhetorical directness, would not have been out of place in the pages of a journal like *Mother Earth* or *Blast*, or even, as Louis Cabri suggests, the Communist *New Masses*.[47] The invective against "men ... today" and "their masters" perhaps reflects the influence of the older generation of immigrant anarchists—stalwarts like Sam Dolgoff (1902–1990) from the Stelton Colony, the IWW, and the Vanguard Group— who had mentored Mac Low, Goodman, and the other young men and women of the *Why?/Resistance* circle.[48] The intergenerational tensions that divided these paternal anarchists from their intellectual offspring might provide one reason for Mac Low to reject what had been, after all, the parents' poetry. Yet his poem for *Retort*, in its apprehension of a depraved world, also does much to explain why

---

46 Jackson Mac Low, Untitled poem ["Men are sheep today, savage as tigers"], *Retort* 4.1 (Fall 1947): 20.

47 Louis Cabri, "'Rebus Effort Remove Government': Jackson Mac Low, *Why?/Resistance*, Anarcho-Pacifism," *Crayon* 1 (1997): 53.

48 Stoehr, "Introduction," *Drawing the Line*, XVI; Sam Dolgoff, in Avrich, *Anarchist Voices*, 425.

Mac Low would turn back to a modernist poetics—for why should
a poet bother to address such a depraved audience? This is the question posed by another such poem Mac Low had published in *Now*
earlier that same year:

> We who by addiction and by choice
> address the public in our private voice
> can, if we reach, but little hope to please
> ears that have only heard the public wheeze ...
> ....
> When taste is formed on corporation prose
> the candid protest seems a mannered pose:
> by private anger, cloth'd in "outworn" styles
> provokes in private readers public smiles.[49]

Here, in language closer to Heine or Hugo, if not to Alexander
Pope—"mannered"? "cloth'd"? "outworn"?—than to Apollinaire
or Stein, Mac Low demonstrates why it won't do to write like this.
Such language *is* "too corrupt for poetic use." It belongs to a "public," corrupted by "corporation prose," which is unreachable, willfully ignorant, determined to misread. As Paul Goodman lamented,
in an article published in *politics* that same month, poets are able to
"strengthen the sense of community" only if "the sense of community
is [already] strong."[50]

Faced with this impasse, the features of Anglo-American anarchist poetry that had once rendered it maximally accessible, forming
a porous and open-ended counterpublic sphere—rhyme, rhythmic
regularity, concrete imagery, narrative, grammatical coherence—faded away. There was less concern with position-taking; all the available
positions had been occupied by the agencies of institutionalized coercive power and a corrupt, anonymous social authority. "I am not
concerned with the practicability of a programme," Read declared
in *Poetry and Anarchism* (1938); "I am only concerned to establish
truth, and to resist all forms of discipline and coercion.... It is the
only protest an individual can make against the mass stupidity of the

---

49 Jackson Mac Low, "Post Victoriam—Neque Dulcem Neque Decoram,"
    Now 7 (February–March 1947).
50 Paul Goodman, "Occasional Poetry," *politics* (March–April, 1947): 59.

modern world."[51] Just as Mallarmé had declared, in the spirit of Rimbaud's "I'm on strike," that the poet was "on strike against society," postwar anarchist poets went on H U N G E R ST r i kE.[52]

---

51 Herbert Read, *Poetry and Anarchism* (London: Faber and Faber, 1938), 17.

52 Arthur Rimbaud, *I Promise to Be Good: The Letters of Arthur Rimbaud*, trans. Wyatt Alexander Mason (New York: Modern Library, 2004), 28; Stéphane Mallarmé, *Selected Prose Poems, Essays, & Letters*, trans Bradford Cook (Baltimore: Johns Hopkins Press, 1956), 22.

4: "A NEED WITHOUT A HOPE"

IT is during this postwar period, fortuitously, that the Surrealists around André Breton and Benjamin Péret make their final turn away from the Communist Party and toward anarchism. Between 1947 and 1953, a group of Surrealists published a series of overtures to the French anarchist movement in *Le Libertaire*. Breton wistfully recalls a moment when the Symbolist avant-garde—spiritual ancestors of Surrealism—had been close to the anarchist movement, averring, "It is in the black mirror of anarchism that surrealism, long before it achieved self-definition, first recognized its own reflection"; Péret, who had gone into the Spanish Civil War as a Trotskyite but ended up fighting with Buenaventura Durruti's anarchist militia, assured anarchist readers that "the enemies of poetry" were their own enemies as well—as was grimly emphasized by the Falangist assassination of Federico García Lorca.[1]

Surrealism exercised a profound appeal for young English-speaking anarchist poets—such as Philip Levine, Carlos Cortéz (1923–2005), Bob Kaufman (1925–1986), Franklin P. Rosemont (1943–2009), and Adam Cornford (b. 1950)—seeking an alternative to the seemingly foreclosed language of a past anarchist movement, who greeted Surrealist elders (Lorca, for Kaufman and Levine; the quasi-surrealist Patchen, for Cortéz; Breton, for Rosemont and Lamantia; Nanos Valaoritis, for Cornford) not as seducers but

---

1   André Breton, "Tower of Light," *Free Rein*, trans. Michel Parmentier and Jacqueline d'Ambroise (Lincoln, NB: University of Nebraska Press, 1998), 265; Benjamin Péret, "Poète, c'est-à-dire révolutionnaire," in *Surréalisme et anarchie*, ed. José Pierre (Paris: Plasma, 1983), 77.

liberators. Nonetheless, this rapprochement was at first viewed with skepticism by anarchists. In *Le Libertaire*, a "group of militants" expressed reservations about Surrealist complicity with the "hermeticism" and search for "originality for originality's sake" endemic to modern art; writing for *Now*, Jean Trieux doubted whether Péret and Breton could dislodge surrealism from "the zone of inertia in which it rests at the moment."[2] Other anarchists were more pointed in their criticism: as editor of *Twentieth Century Verse*, Julian Symons scrapped what was to have been a special Surrealist issue, publishing instead an editorial, "Against Surrealism," while in *Ark*, Robert Duncan castigated what he saw as the cynical "diabolism" of the U.S. surrealist journal *View*—"the aesthetic of the insane and the sadistic"—for its complicity with the mundane cruelty of the State and its wars. For his part, Kenneth Rexroth discouraged Philip Lamantia from associating himself further with Breton, who had attempted to take the young poet under his wing in 1943.[3]

Surrealism, in its belated anarchist acceptance, both invited and repelled these anarchist critiques. On the one hand, in the spirit of Lautréamont's aphorism—"Poetry shall be made by all, not by one alone"—Surrealists rejected the ethos of the poet as craftsman.[4] If Symons complained that "it has no standards of craftsmanship ... so that ... every crackpot can write a poem that may be called surrealist,"[5] this was not in the least troubling to Lamantia, once he had rejoined the Surrealist fold: rejecting the etymological connection between "poetry" and the Greek *poiesis* ("making"), the surrealist

---

2   Un groupe de militants [Roland Breton, Serge Ninn, and Paul Zorkine], "Le vrai sens d'une rencontre," *Surréalisme et anarchisme: écrits pour débattre* (Lyon: Atelier de Création Libertaire, 1992), 18; Jean Trieux, "French Writing Today," trans. Marie-Louise Berneri and George Woodcock, *Now* 8 (1948): 20.

3   Robert Duncan, "Reviewing *View*: An Attack," *The Ark* (1947): 62–67; Franklin Rosemont, "Surrealist, Anarchist, Afrocentrist: Philip Lamantia Before and After the 'Beat Generation,'" in *Are Italians White?: How Race is Made in America*, eds. Jennifer Guglielmo and Salvatore Salerno (New York: Routledge, 2003), 131, 126.

4   Qtd. in Roger Cardinal, "André Breton and the Automatic Message," in *André Breton: The Power of Language*, ed. Ramona Fotiade (Exeter, UK: Elm Bank, 2000), 34 n5.

5   Julian Symons, "Against Surrealism," *Twentieth Century Verse* 3 (April–May 1937): 42.

also "reject[s] 'craftsmanship'" in favor of a subjectivist "sovereignty of mind, the primacy of human desires and oneiric exaltation."[6]
Driving a wedge between poetry-as-expression and poetry-as-craft,
however, had paradoxical results. On the one hand, it argued for a
rejection of formalism in favor of expressive content—placing the
speaking subject back at the center. At the same time, insofar as
self-expression was privileged over communication with others, it cut
the poet loose from the judgment of the audience, the "other men" to
whom the speaker was obligated. Rather than emphasizing the poem
as an autonomous object, a well-wrought urn, anarchist surrealism
emphasized the autonomy of the poet.

Accordingly, the wedding (or remarriage) of surrealism to anarchist poetry was accompanied by a resurgence of interest in the
hermetic—both in the sense of secrecy and in the sense of magic.
Certainly, some kind of "Orphic mysteries and magics in poetry,"
as Duncan put it in retrospect, seemed necessary to undo the spell
of resignation and complacency that held sway over the industrialized countries in the period of postwar affluence.[7] Mallarmé and
the Symbolists had long before flirted with the notion of poetry
as a form of mysticism, but this had put them at odds with the anarchists' materialism and populism. Was not esoteric poetry, by
definition, antithetical to the popular? "Poetry," argued Argentine
Surrealist Aldo Pellegrini (1903–1973), son of anarchist militants,
merely "keeps its door hermetically sealed against idiots," i.e., those
for whom "value is only given by the exercise of power."[8] Serge Ninn
(a.k.a. Jean Senninger, Serge Senninger, etc., b. 1921), a founding
member of the French Fédération Anarchiste after the war, and
who would later become an adept of Alfred Jarry's Pataphysics, was

6 Philip Lamantia, "The Crime of Poverty," in *The Forecast is Hot!: Tracts
   & Other Collective Declarations of the Surrealist Movement in the United
   States, 1966–1976*, ed. Franklin Rosemont et al. (Chicago: Black Swan
   Press, 1977), 206–207.

7 Robert Duncan, "Preface," Jack Spicer, *One Night Stand & Other Poems*,
   ed. Donald Allen (San Francisco: Grey Fox Press, 2006), XIII.

8 Pellegrini's 1961 manifesto is reprinted by a subsequent generation of
   Argentine anarchists (Aldo Pellegrini "Se llama poesía todo aquello que
   cierra la puerta a los imbéciles," *Caos* 5 [1980]: 34). See also Ruben Dan-
   iel Méndez Catiglioni, "Aldo Pellegrini y el surrealismo en Argentina," in
   César Moro y el surrealismo en América Latina, ed. Yolanda Westphalen
   Rodríguez (Lima: Fondo Editorial de la UNMSM, 2005), 47.

quick to adopt the rhetoric of his surrealist comrades in London, rhapsodizing over "the magic of the word": "We seek the philosopher's stone of language," he wrote in the anarchist journal *Plus Loin*.[9] In the 1950s and 60s, Jack Spicer, Robert Duncan, and Diane di Prima, too, would turn toward the hermetic tradition as a "wisdom of other times" for which, as di Prima put it, "spirit and matter, man and cosmos, were one."[10] Thus the spiritual was translated into the material and esoteric into the popular—but not, by the same token, into the public.

A strangely similar poetic strategy is urged by Paul Goodman. In the very same 1951 essay for *Kenyon Review* in which he reexamined the premises of the last half century of avant-garde poetics, Goodman argued that the most vital task for "present-day advance-guard efforts" would be not to shock and confuse the audience (the old modernist strategy of *épater la bourgeoisie*) nor to pander so as to compete for audience approval on mass culture's commercial terrain (*flatter la bourgeoisie*) but to attempt "the physical reestablishment of community." Taking up Goethe's maxim that "occasional poetry is the highest kind," Goodman proposed

> to solve the crisis of alienation in the simple way: the persons are estranged from themselves, from one another, and from their artist; he takes the initiative precisely by putting his arms around them and drawing them together. In literary terms this means: to write for them about them personally. It makes no difference what the genre is, whether praise or satire or description, or whether the style is subtle or obscure, for any one will pay concentrated attention to a work in which he in his own name is a principal character. But such personal writing about the audience itself can occur only in a small community of acquaintances, where everybody knows everybody and understands what is at stake.[11]

---

9 Serge Ninn, "Liberté de mouvement," *Plus loin* 1 (March 1946): 21.

10 Diane di Prima, "Paracelsus: An Appreciation," in *The Hermetic and Alchemical Writings of Aureolus Philippus Theophrastus Bombast, of Hohenheim, Called Paracelsus the Great*, ed. Arthur Edward Waite (New Hyde Park, NY: University Books, 1967), xii.

11 Goodman, "Advance-Guard Writing," 372, 375.

This strategy—neither to attack the reigning culture nor to surrender to it, but to retreat to a more favorable terrain—met with an enthusiastic reception among many poets inhabiting the countercultural margins of the world of official culture—notably among those based in San Francisco/Berkeley, New York, and the experimental Black Mountain College of North Carolina. Charles Olson immediately felt that Goodman had clarified what he and his friends were actually already doing: "all this damn funny recent verse," he wrote to Robert Creeley, was "directed to actual persons, composed, actually, by and for OCCASION." Frank O'Hara responded with excitement to Goodman's "delicious message," and later, in a letter to Creeley, cited as justification for his own poetic practice "that remark of Goodman-Goethe: 'Occasional poetry is the best kind.'"[12] Jack Spicer would later declare that "certainly we belong to a community rather than a society, we poets"—having specified: "if you mean what [Paul] Goodman means by the word 'community.'"[13]

What Goodman seemed to mean, for postwar anarchist and *anarchisant* poets, was less the public sphere than the intimate circle, the coterie, perhaps even the cabal or conspiracy. They might say, with the Australian Harry Hooton (1908–1961), that "ordinary people / Don't want / My poems," that "My poems are ... / For extraordinary people."[14] Their poetry was increasingly directly addressed to individuals, populated with insider references, allusions to proper names and shared memories. Spicer and a friend jokingly founded a secret society, "the Interplanetary Services of the Martian Anarchy," with its own language (in "North Martian" and "South Martian" dialects).[15] In 1957, Spicer and Duncan held

---

12 Creeley qtd. in Lytle Shaw, *Frank O'Hara: The Poetics of Coterie* (Iowa City, IA: University of Iowa Press, 2006), 83; O'Hara qtd. in Andrew Epstein, *Beautiful Enemies: Friendship and Postwar American Poetry* (Oxford: Oxford University Press, 2006), 110.

13 Jack Spicer, *The House That Jack Built: The Collected Lectures of Jack Spicer*, ed. Peter Gizzi (Hanover, NH: University Press of New Hampshire, 1998), 167.

14 Harry Hooton, "MYPOEMS," "Harry Hooton (1908–1961): Poet and philosopher of the 21st Century," *Radical Tradition: An Australasian History Page*, April 2001 (web).

15 Lewis Ellingham and Kevin Killian, *Poet Be Like God: Jack Spicer and the San Francisco Renaissance* (Hanover, NH: University Press of New England, 1998), 57.

a "Poetry as Magic" workshop for a select group of fifteen poets, featuring "assignments" such as "Write a poem concerning some magic sacrifice" and "Evoke magic spirits."[16] At the same time, Duncan, too, in the poems he would publish under the ironic title *The Opening of the Field* (1960), was swerving from the occasional overt statement, couched in an almost public rhetoric—

> Hear! Beautiful damnd man that lays down his law lays down himself creates hell
> a sentence unfolding healthy heaven.

—to esoteric allusions:

> The Earth shakes. Kore! Kore! (for
> I was thinking of her—She
> who shakes the stores of ancestral grain)

—to a kind of private rumination, sprinkled with proper names and references to personal experiences only half-disclosed:

> Writing it down now, it is the aftermath, the silence, I remember, part of the dance too, an articulation of the time of dancing ... like the almost dead sleeping is a step. I've got it in a poem, about Friedl, moaning in the depths of. But that was another room that summer ...

—to the cryptic and sometimes downright opaque:

> After a shower, the mirror
> shows the body spreading, orange in time,
> reveals accumulations
> of my uses, beyond all earliness ...[17]

---

16 Ibid., 81, 83.

17 Robert Duncan, *The Opening of the Field* (New York: New Directions, 1973). "Friedl" was the name of a friend and lover of Duncan's, "a middle-aged German refugee," in the summer of 1945, when he worked at an inn in the Catskills (Ekbert Faas, *Young Robert Duncan: Portrait of the Poet as Homosexual in Society* [Santa Barbara: Black Sparrow Press, 1983], 171).

A reader trained to the standards of an Ezra Pound or a T.S. Eliot might conceivably understand the word "Kore" as an allusion to the myth of Persephone (daughter of Ceres, goddess of grain); only a close friend or a posthumous biographer could hope to recognize the name "Friedl"; recognition and reference meet a dead end in the "body spreading, orange in time." Thus, anarchist poets re-construed mystery, obscurity, and encryption as tactics of resistance culture.

But what of the communitarian and public dimensions of anarchism? In the essay that had excited such enthusiasm among postwar anarchist poets, Goodman had suggested:

> In our estranged society, it is objected, just such intimate community is lacking. Of course it is lacking! The point is that the advance-guard action helps create such community, starting with the artist's primary friends. The community comes to exist by having its culture; the artist makes this culture.[18]

The "community" so described is not a "public" but, once again, a counterpublic. Nonetheless, a hermetic counterpublic would seem to be much less porous or expansive than that engineered by Emma Goldman and her comrades. This acceptance of opacity, the withdrawal of poetry into the "personal and parochial," seems to have troubled Goodman in time, as did the popularity of mysticism and irrationalism. "Young people say that science is anti-life," he mourned.[19] As his friend Hayden Carruth (1921–2008) remarked, "Goodman was too thoroughly Aristotelian and psychoanalytic in his bias to accept ultimately the idea of a secret, mystical, supraverbal logos."[20] Finding an alternative to the cryptic or esoteric in poetry seemed imperative.

It is in these circumstances that a certain nostalgia for a lost or eclipsed populist tradition is stirred up. Even Spicer, with his love of the magical and the secret, mourned the absence of a broad audience for poetry, the lack of public relevance, and remembered, by contrast, the appeal of his father's Wobbly songs. "If I could write

---

18 Goodman, "Advance-Guard Writing," 375–376.
19 Paul Goodman, *New Reformation: Notes of a Neolithic Conservative* (New York: Random House, 1970), 6.
20 Hayden Carruth, *Suicides and Jazzers* (Ann Arbor, MI: University of Michigan Press, 1992), 86.

popular songs, I'd do it," he admitted; "Certainly the IWW songs—Joe Hill—did have some effect."[21] For Utah Phillips, likewise, the authentic protest tradition is firmly on the side of communication: "Talk to each other, by God!"[22]

Lawrence Ferlinghetti tried to revive interest in populism, not only the populism of Whitman but that of Vachel Lindsay (1879–1931), Edgar Lee Masters (1868–1950), and Carl Sandburg (1878–1967): "I liked the way these writers communicated directly. None of them was obscure." Fifteen years after having gone on record as an advocate of "getting the poet out of the inner esthetic sanctum where he has too long been contemplating his complicated navel ... [and] getting poetry back into the street where it once was," Ferlinghetti issued the first in a series of "Populist Manifestoes," calling on fellow poets to "come out of your closets, / Open your windows, open your doors": "Secret words & chants won't do any longer. / The hour of oming is over ... / Stop mumbling and speak out / with a new wide-open poetry / with a new commonsensual 'public surface' / with other subjective levels / or other subversive levels." Recalling Whitman's blending of individualism and collectivism, Ferlinghetti invited them to "Of your own sweet Self still sing / yet utter 'the word en-masse'— / Poetry the common carrier / for the transportation of the public / to higher places / than other wheels can carry it."[23]

It would not be hard to see a number of postwar anarchist poets as already pursuing this kind of project, particularly Americans like Levertov, Levine, Carruth, and Goodman. Goodman's poetic bias toward transparency and self-revelation leads Alicia Ostriker to call him a "poet of indecorum," a self-exhibitionist who "means everything literally"[24]—an affront to readers schooled in the canons of New Criticism, watchful against the "pathetic fallacy" and

---

21 Spicer, *The House That Jack Built*, 162–163.

22 Phillips, in John Malkin, *Sounds of Freedom: Musicians on Spirituality & Social Change* (Berkeley: Parallax Press, 2005), 82.

23 Neeli Cherkovski, *Ferlinghetti: A Biography* (Garden City, NY: Doubleday, 1979), 24; Ferlinghetti qtd. in Thomas Parkinson, *A Casebook on the Beat* (New York: Crowell, 1961), 124; Lawrence Ferlinghetti, "Populist Manifesto No. 1," *Who Are We Now?* (New York: New Directions, 1976), 61–64.

24 Alicia Ostriker, "The Poet of Indecorum," in *Artist of the Actual: Essays on Paul Goodman*, ed. Peter Parisi (Metuchen, NJ: Scarecrow Press, 1986), 89.

"the heresy of paraphrase": "Paul Goodman annoys his reader," one complained, "by the bald statement of his ideas. Every important situation and feeling is not only presented, it is explained. Its composition or significance is formulated ... in the language of ideas, by the author as lecturer to the reader."[25] His other sin against modernism, of course, was precisely his resort to "decorous" traditional forms—not only the borrowed Eastern finery of the *hokku* taken up by anarcho-Beats Rexroth, Whalen, and Gary Snyder (b. 1930), as well as by Pound long before them, but also Western genres such as the ballad, the *ballade*, and, not insignificantly, the sonnet—"These hand-me-downs of Milton that I wear."[26] By turns self-conscious, playful, reverent and irreverent, Goodman's sonnets employ a personal address and expressive use of space characteristic of postwar anarchist poetry, but in a classical guise.

And so it was that Hayden Carruth, discharged from a mental institution in 1955, latched onto Goodman's flexible adaptation of the sonnet form, inventing what he called the "paragraph," his own fifteen-line stanza, just hinting at the traditional sonnet's music, but more discursive, more "abundant," than the "severe" form would allow. Darkly lyrical in his autobiographical "The Asylum" (1959), Carruth's "Paragraphs" allowed for a kind of essayistic mode when linked together in *Brothers, I Loved You All* (1978). The voice here is by turns ambitious and despairing. It is ambitious in its will to invoke and convoke a "public"—even in violation of the regional customs of respect for privacy and property—and at the same time, attempting to speak in a popular idiom, even a regional vernacular. Lamenting the sale of farms to real-estate developers "all / for a hot pocketful of dollars," Carruth points fingers: "Yes, townsmen, friends, I name *you*, / Andy and Jake, against every rule of Yankee decorum, / I name you in your public guilt." The use of personal names here is no longer an exercise in the construction of a counter-community as bohemian "coterie," à la Frank O'Hara, but a direct address to members of an existing (non-literary) community; it is an attempt to summon up the very forces of social disapproval that it runs up against, calling

---

25 Jacob Lititz, "Notes on Some Works of Paul Goodman," *The Black Mountain Review* 2.5 (Summer 1955): 40.
26 Paul Goodman, "On the Sonnet," *Collected Poems*, ed. Taylor Stoehr (New York: Random House, 1974), 217.

to account those who have sold out, who have betrayed the loyalties of custom and place.

But Carruth's awareness that the buck of "public guilt" does not stop there dislodges him from what might otherwise be the position of the bard or griot as keeper of community morals. Looking outward, the poem registers a "floating despair" in its apprehension of larger, more mobile and global forces at work, the economic powers that are rendering this intimate landscape into something "ugly, evil, dying"—forces that cannot be shamed, for they have no personal names or community attachments, no face to lose, no social capital to risk. The force of mourning in this poem forecloses any hope of consolation. Even equipped with an ingenious social ecopoetics, a way of writing capable of evoking community memory and the spirit of place, Carruth is unable to achieve much more than an elegy for the death of a landscape and the culture it sustained. In the absence of solidarity, even a vision of revolutionary redemption ("Black / is the color of my only flag / and of man's hope") flickers out quickly:

> Will revolution bring the farms back?
> Gone, gone....
>
> ....
> ... Someday we will be free,
> someday when it's too late.
> It's true, the real revolutionary is one who can see
> all dark ahead and behind, his fate
> a need without a hope: *the will to resist.*
> The State is universal, the Universe is a state.
> Now ask me if I am really an anarchist.[27]

If "Paragraphs" is determined, in the face of this dying lifeworld, to manifest an anarchist "will to resist," this resistance appears to have shrunk to something like the size of an individual; there is no culture of resistance to be had. The vision of an ecological Waste Land, worthy of a T. S. Eliot or a Theodor Adorno—"The State is universal, the Universe is a state"—renders perilously tentative what would otherwise be a dare, a rhetorical turn toward closure made all the more

---

27 Hayden Carruth, "Paragraphs," *Brothers, I Loved You All: Poems, 1969–1977* (New York: Sheep Meadow Press, 1978), 93–94.

dramatic by its placement, hedged by suddenly heavy end-rhymes, at the last line of the fifteen-line stanza: "Now ask me if I am really an anarchist." What, in this state (this condition, this dominated territory), could that really be?

5: FIGHT OR FLIGHT?

BUT who am I to talk? If, as Whitman and Rimbaud would have it, the self is always a multitude, other to itself, who is represented by the word "I"? Kristeva argues that poetry is not responsible for conveying any definite "message" because its real task is to disrupt the illusion of the unified self: "the univocal enunciation of such a message would itself represent a suppression of the ethical function as we understand it."[1] The problem lies in the very "voice" of lyric poetry, the subject who says "I." "The poet," masking the creative multitude behind a singular persona, is perhaps already a falsification, warns Robin Blaser—"a reduction."[2]

To see why the uniqueness of the poet's voice might pose a problem for anarchists, we turn to "Confessions of a Mild-Mannered Enemy of the State," the anarchist *Bildungsroman* of Ken Knabb (b. 1945). Living in Berkeley in October 1970, he recounts, "One of my few remaining heroes was Gary Snyder ... [who] himself was more or less an anarchist":

> Then one day I learned that he was coming to Berkeley to give
> a reading of his poetry.... Did I still think such an event was a
> good thing? Or was it "spectacular"—did it contribute toward
> people's passivity, complacency, star worship?[3]

---

1 Kristeva, *Revolution in Poetic Language*, 223, emphasis mine.
2 Robin Blaser, "The Practice of Outside," in *The Collected Books of Jack Spicer*, ed. Robin Blaser (Los Angeles: Black Sparrow Press, 1975), 271.
3 Ken Knabb, *Public Secrets: Collected Skirmishes of Ken Knabb, 1970–1997* (Berkeley: Bureau of Public Secrets, 1997), 113.

Stated in this way, the question answered itself: of course the event would be just another spectacle—a spectacle of "enlightenment," "significan[ce]," the "beautiful." In a later essay, "Ode on the Absence of Real Poetry Here This Afternoon: A Poem in Dialectical Prose," Knabb reflects: "As with the spectacle in general, the communication of a poem is unilateral. The passive spectator or reader is presented with an image of what was lived by the poet."[4] At the same time, Knabb, member of the audience, *identifies* with that image of the great poet, an identification that allows him to vicariously participate in all the things the poet stands for—including "anarchism." Feeling conflicted ("I scarcely thought I could compare myself with Snyder"; "I became hesitant"; "How did I dare attack Gary Snyder this way?" etc.), Knabb came to the uneasy realization that it was not only a matter of respect for Snyder's work that was producing the hesitation to criticize the spectacle of the poet; it was that he was already anticipating a criticism of Snyder's *image* as an injury to his own ego-ideal.[5]

This is a perilous moment. In the chain of symbolic exchanges by which poetry comes to be reified into poems, which then are identified with the poet, with whom the reader/listener identifies in turn, we can recognize the same authoritarian magic by which, as Read warned, the imagination of the Leader as "Father of his People" encourages us to "transfer to this figure-head all sorts of imaginary virtues which we ourselves would like to possess":

> Through generations we have spent our blood and expended our utmost efforts on getting rid of the leadership of priests and kings ... only to find ourselves with the same infantile longing to be led.... We are children seeking a father, children full of mutual jealousy and suspicion, repeating on a national scale the neurotic conflicts of the family.[6]

Knabb wrote, pasted together, and copied a broadside. On the day of the poetry reading, he waited for the right moment to present itself:

---

4   Ibid., 163–164.
5   Ibid., 114.
6   Herbert Read, *The Philosophy of Anarchism* (London: Freedom Press, 1940), 13; and "The Cult of Leadership," *Now* 1 (1943): 13.

There was an audience of several hundred people. Snyder started off by saying that before he got under way with the poetry he'd like to "say a few words about the revolution." He made a few remarks on that topic which were a bit vague, but not bad. When he finished, the audience *applauded.*

That did it. Nothing could have made the spectacular nature of the whole occasion more clear. The applause was the glaring sign that his words would not be taken up practically, but would merely serve as one more tidbit for passive titillation. (People would probably go home after the reading and tell their friends, "He not only read a lot of great poems, but he even said some far out stuff about revolution!") I was outraged at the situation. The most insulting aspects of my leaflet were only too appropriate. I took them out, threw them into the crowd and ran away.[7]

Even with its dramatic concluding demand (a line repurposed from Lautréamont: "POETRY MADE BY ALL—OR NOT AT ALL"), the leaflet, "Do We Need Snyder For Poet-Priest?" makes for less absorbing reading than Snyder's poems.[8] As an act of public speech, Knabb admits, it was ineffectual: "after a few seconds' pause the reading continued." However, as a private ritual of self-expression, it was, for its author, exhilarating, "liberating," a "real breakthrough." And so it is that later, when Knabb proudly displayed his work to certain radical mentors (who "were aware of my admiration for Snyder"), they paid him the highest compliment: "Hmm. I see you've been subverting yourself as well as others!"[9] As in the old Zen saying, the anarchist, meeting the Buddha-poet on the road, has killed him.

Knabb, Duncan, and Kristeva are by no means the first to conceive of anarchist poetics as entailing a certain extinction of the "I," a disruption of the illusory coherence and self-containment that is the mark of adulthood. The Dadas had envisioned this decades earlier: thus, Tristan Tzara devised his infamous cut-up technique for, in the words of Hugo Ball, "discard[ing] the ego like a coat full of holes":

---

7 Knabb, *Public Secrets*, 114.
8 Ibid., 161.
9 Ibid., 114–115.

a poem randomly assembled from fragments of newspaper "will resemble you ... an infinitely original author of charming sensibility, even though unappreciated by the vulgar herd."[10] Tzara's deliberate embrace of randomness renders laughable, in advance, any question of "origin[ality]" or "author[ship]"; if the cut-up poem resembles the poet, this is not because an poet's personality is the source of poetic meaning, but because poem and personality alike are the product of chance, contingency, and chaos; the resemblance is not a sign of paternity but of fraternity.

Unaccompanied by any expression of collectivity, however, this avant-garde disruption of the lyric "I" remained a nihilistic gesture rather than forming part of an anarchist resistance culture. As Hans Richter put it, Dada was the product of, rather than the antidote to, social dissolution: "Belief in belonging to anything is missing, and we thank your form of 'society' (oh state) for this, your 'community.'"[11] Even balanced by an equal contempt for the "infinitely original author," Dadaist contempt for "the vulgar herd" was all too genuine. By contrast, for contemporary anarchist poet Michael Halfbrodt (b. 1958), one of the "key moments" of anarchist poetics is "that of collectivity: anarchist literature is not an individual construct composed at a desk, but the result of debate and discussion, which is a collective practice."[12] Such a collective poetics could more readily take inspiration from Whitman's democratic embrace of the "seething multitudes around us, of which we are inseparable parts":

> Democracy consists in not that half only, individualism, which isolates. There is another half, which is adhesiveness or love, that fuses, ties and aggregates, making the races comrades, and fraternizing all.

---

10 Ball, *Flight Out of Time*, 29; Tristan Tzara, *Seven DaDa Manifestos and Lampisteries*, trans. Barbara Wright (London: Calder, 1977), 39.

11 Hans Richter, *Hans Richter*, trans. Cleve Gray (New York: Holt, Rinehart and Winston, 1971), 96.

12 Michael Halfbrodt in Bernd Drücke, Ralf Burnicki, and Michael Halfbrodt, "Poetry for Anarchy: Ein Interview zum zehnten Geburtstag des libertären Literaturprojekts Blackbox," *graswurzelrevolution* 294 (December 2004).

This image of revolutionary *fraternité* not as a state but as a continuous process of dynamic mixture, "fraternizing," is marked by a pluralism no doubt attractive to anarchists, suspicious of uniformity in fraternal guise. Whitman's pluralistic conception of the "multitudes around us" is mirrored by his conception of the "multitudes" within—"I am large ... I contain multitudes"—so reminiscent of Rimbaud's "I is another."[13] Similarly, Baldelli's exile perceives himself as an ocean, a vast and diffuse space traversed by "peoples and centuries," while Landauer imagines the subjectivity of the poet as an inner space traversed by "living people that have collected in them, that are buried in them and will be resurrected out of them": when this truth is recognized in revolutionary solidarity, "the people shall be the poet, the poet shall be the people."[14]

If, indeed, "what one usually calls the individual," as Landauer observes, is not "an isolated unit" but a "community," then social revolution might have to entail a liberation of one's "inner being," a recovery of the "many personalities" masked by identity. "The I kills itself so that the World-I can live," Landauer had written; "Do not kill others, only your Self." In poetic terms, this might translate into an anarchist program for the disruption of authorial identity—an assassination of the Author as Author-ity, the sovereign guarantor of all coherence and meaning. "You have to interfere with yourself," Jack Spicer says, to act as a "medium" for poems that are not your property: "You have to, as much as possible, empty yourself for this." Thus, in a letter to Robin Blaser, Spicer urges the poet to "Go mad. Commit suicide. There will be nothing left / After you die or go mad, / But the calmness of poetry."[15]

In the open space left by this withdrawal of the Creator from the Creation—a kind of poetic *zimzum* (the "act of divine contraction," "concealment and limitation," in Kabbalah, by which God makes room for the universe) or *kenosis* (an "emptying," "humbling,"

---

13 Walt Whitman, *Complete Poetry and Collected Prose* (New York: Library of America, 1982), 87, 661, 949.

14 Landauer, *Der werdende Mensch*, 359; and *For Socialism*, 33.

15 Landauer, *Revolution*, 96–97, 88–89; Spicer, *The House That Jack Built*, 13–14; Spicer, "A Poem Without A Single Bird In It," *My Vocabulary Did This to Me: The Collected Poetry of Jack Spicer*, eds. Peter Gizzi and Kevin Killian (Middletown, CN: Wesleyan University Press, 2008), 73.

or "self-abnegation" of the divine, in the Christian tradition)[16]—the anarchist poem might take meaning from the activity of the reader. Juliana Spahr (b. 1966) argues that this is precisely the way in which poetry can promote autonomy, equality, and community: by creating gaps and ambiguities, "the work allows readers self-governance and autonomy," evoking "dynamic participation" rather than passive consumption, so that "the reading act is given as much authority as the authoring act." Rather than reading the strange signs of avant-garde poetry as simply "nonsense, or private, or encoded, or presymbolic," Spahr rereads them as invitations to create meaning collectively rather than unilaterally—a "poetry created by all," in a sense.[17] "Adhesiveness," then, would be evoked by permitting the "multitudes" to fraternize within the space of the poem.

This, indeed, is what Mac Low aimed at in his experimental poetic text/performances, which systematically incorporated randomness, unpredictable processes of permutation, and multiple participants to produce poems without any single author. The point was not to make a text representing an author's "ideas"—not even anarchist ideas—but to "embody such ideas in microcosm" by

> creat[ing] works wherein both other human beings, their environments, & the world "in general" (as represented by such objectively hazardous means as random digits) are all able to act.... The poet creates a situation wherein she or he invites other persons & the world in general to be co-creators. The poet does not wish to be a dictator but a loyal co-initiator of action within the free society of equals which it is hoped the work will help to bring about.

Mac Low's inclusion of "the world in general" in the creative process is significant; the anarchy that he envisions is one in which

> the elementary actions of the world itself & of "all sentient beings" are regarded as being on the level with those of humans. One

---

16 Gershom Scholem, *Kabbalah* (New York: Meridian, 1978), 129; Bloom, *The Anxiety of Influence*, 87, 91.

17 Juliana Spahr, *Everybody's Autonomy: Connective Reading and Collective Identity* (Tuscaloosa, AL: University of Alabama Press, 2001), 14, 6, 13.

comes to a situation where "even plants have rights": one doesn't chop down a tree unless there's a *damn good reason to* do so.[18]

As Colson explains, anarchists have denounced the humanist assumption that "man as pure subject, guided by reason, free and responsible for his actions" faces "the world as pure object, open to man's manipulation," insisting, instead, that human beings are "not distinct from the reality through which they move and in which they are embedded."[19] In this sense, Mac Low's goal might be to make Landauer's "World-I"—a contradiction in terms, from the perspective of humanist individualism, as if he had spoken of an "Object-Subject"—actively, effectively real.

One might question, however, whether a poetics that assassinates the image of the Author is necessarily non-authoritarian per se. It is troubling, for instance, that Knabb's smashing of his own poetic idol elicits emotions that combine the aggressive with the regressive: "As I ran from the auditorium I felt *like a child again*, as excited as *a grade school kid playing a prank*."[20] The conclusion of the episode, too, evokes childhood, albeit this time on the register of the Good Boy rather than his Naughty counterpart: beaming under the gaze of his "subversive" friends, Knabb behaves something like a kid proudly showing his parents the test he has just aced. Has the authority, the Patriarch/Poet, been destroyed or simply displaced? The sheer repetitiveness of Knabb's own writing, its ceaseless reiteration of the catchphrases and formulas of his radical models (e.g., Guy Debord), sometimes threatens to collapse the difference between Knabb's rejection of the Author's claim to originality, his embrace of "plagiarism" as "necessary"—in theory, a poetics of subversive appropriation, contesting literary property and propriety—and what, in practice, looks disturbingly like a mere reproduction of the Same.[21]

---

18 Jackson Mac Low, *The Pronouns: A Collection of Forty Dances for the Dancers, 3 February–22 March, 1964* (Barrytown, NY: Station Hill Press, 1979), 75.

19 Colson, *Petit lexique*, 120–121; Daniel Colson, "Subjectivités anarchistes et subjectivité moderne," *La Culture Libertaire: Actes du Colloque International, Grenoble, mars 1996*, ed. Alain Pessin (Lyon: Atelier de Création Libertaire, 1997), 149.

20 Knabb, *Public Secrets*, 115, italics mine.

21 Lautréamont, qtd. by Guy Debord, in Mustapha Khayati "Captive Words:

And if Mac Low's goal, as anarchist poet, is to collapse the distance between the two poles of subject and object, to construct situations in which the self no longer stands apart from the non-self, might we also see this poetics as a reproduction of the *chora*, the indivision of baby-subject from mother-object? Or is this another way of saying that Mac Low's self-generating poems babble? That, like the baby suspended in its matrix, it owes an unreturnable debt to that structuring agency—"the general framework & set of 'rules'"—as Mac Low acknowledges, that are "given by the poet"?[22] That in abandoning communication, they also lose the sense of community? That, far from achieving Whitman's vision of "adhesion," they evoke nothing so much as the anomie of life under capitalism? That in undoing the illusion of a coherent subject, they fail to imagine another kind of social selfhood to put in its place?

These doubts seem to haunt Mac Low, who never definitively abandons his earlier, more accessible style (well after what Louis Cabri identifies as Mac Low's turning point in 1954, he is still contributing work in something like the prewar mode of *Tendenzlyrik* to radical journals such as *Liberation* [1956–1977] and *Win: Peace and Freedom Thru Non-Violent Action* [1965–1983]). In a 1988 conversation with Language poet Bruce Andrews, Mac Low confesses that

I feel sometimes I ought to speak in a way that a larger number of people here and there might be interested in; you might not

---

Preface to a Situationist Dictionary," trans. Ken Knabb in *Situationist International Anthology*, ed. Ken Knabb (Berkeley: Bureau of Public Secrets, 2006), 171.

22 Mac Low, *The Pronouns*, 75. The debt, if unreturnable, is not unacknowledged: as Bruce Andrews recounts, Mac Low made a conscientious practice of "append[ing] elaborate notes to his work, detailing the process by which the works were generated, so that the reader would be brought into the process but not the realm of the significance or the value of what they were actually reading ... as if the part of the reader's experience that Mac Low wanted highlighted was the reader's experience of being intrigued or impressed by the process by which the work was generated, regardless of what it meant" (Dan Thomas-Glass and Bruce Andrews, "Bruce Andrews Interview," *The Argotist Online*, web). Nonetheless, the solitary writer's control over the process and its range of possible outcomes disturbs the pretense of self-organization: behind what might look like autopoiesis, there is still a poet, a giver of laws from the outside.

just have the converted, but those on the line, etc.—by bringing in a lot of things that are efficacious, in the sense of a rhetorical poetry ... a more basic poetry.[23]

Rather than regarding this as a refutation of the premises of his more experimental work, he urges Andrews to consider the two modes as alternatives appropriate to different occasions and purposes—a kind of poetic "diversity of tactics": why not, he suggests, pursue "a tandem project of social writing," devoting some time to "radical disruptive writing" and some to writing "that might be, if not efficacious, at least understandable to a wider audience without the background, etc."? Why should poets have to choose only one mode?[24] Jens Bjørneboe makes just this assessment in a 1970 essay, "Diktning og kritikk—middel til kamp eller flukt? [Writing and Criticism—Fight or Flight?]," in which he lashes "modernist" critics who demand that "literature shall be written in free verse, without punctuation and with lower-case letters," and, on the other hand, those critics who would impose "the same dictatorship, but with the opposite sign," demanding that poets "write for the masses," producing only "positive and edifying" works. Refusing both demands, he declared: "I declare myself an adherent of 'engaged' writing.... But, to bring the matter into balance: that doesn't mean that I'm opposed to 'pure' writing."[25]

This suspension, this hesitation between alternatives—or is it a refusal of the alternatives on offer?—is reminiscent of what DeDeo describes in his recent manifesto, "Towards An Anarchist Poetics." In terms strikingly similar to Bjørneboe's, DeDeo writes that, in the face of "the current crisis of language" that is simultaneously "the current political crisis," poems can engage in "flight" away from any public language or in a "fight" to wrest that language away from its powerful abusers. Flight takes poetry away from its potential readers; fighting is all but impossible. In this light, it might seem that Mac Low's "tandem project" is a choice of fight *and* flight—for

---

23 Mac Low in Bruce Andrews, *Paradise & Method: Poetics & Praxis* (Evanston, IL: Northwestern University Press, 1996), 68.

24 Ibid., 66–67.

25 Jens Bjørneboe, "Writing and Criticism—Fight or Flight?," trans. Esther Greenleaf Mürer, web.

DeDeo, a choice of two opposed and equal impossibilities. Laudable as the motives might be, opting for a poetic "diversity of tactics" might only amount to a helpless hesitation between mutually exclusive, equally unacceptable alternatives, a decision not to decide between them.[26] The problem, as DeDeo succinctly frames it, remains: "Given the brute obviousness of power, its massive colonization of the actual daily use of words, how can the poet create a work that challenges or renounces this power without becoming incomprehensible to the ear?"[27]

One answer to this impossible question might look something like Spahr's *This Connection of Everyone With Lungs* (2005), a title that doubles down on the wager of her book of criticism, *Everybody's Autonomy: Connective Reading and Collective Identity* (2001). It is gutsy: who can still pretend to speak to "everyone"? What can "connect" us, atomized as we are? *This Connection of Everyone With Lungs* collects a series of poems, named "Poem Written after September 11, 2001" and "Poem Written from November 30, 2002 to March 27, 2003," in response to the pervasive sense of helplessness that comes from watching video images of airplanes full of people smashing into enormous office buildings, over and over again, a helplessness assuaged, for many, by militaristic vengeance. Spahr's response is not more subtle than this pageant of power. The difficulty in reading it is of another order altogether.

In her search for that which connects, after something like the manner of Snyder's or Carruth's ecopoetics, Spahr begins from the biological:

> There are these things:
> cells, the movement of cells and the division of cells
> and then the general beating of circulation
> and hands, and body, and feet

---

26 I am thinking, here, of Herman Rapaport's distinction between a philosophical "undecidability" and mere "indecision" (*The Theory Mess: Deconstruction in Eclipse* [New York: Columbia University Press, 2001], 121–122). The phrase "diversity of tactics" has long been used, in the anti-capitalist/altermondialiste movement, to signal the coexistence of conventional, nonviolent demonstrations with more disruptive forms of protest such as property destruction.

27 DeDeo, "Towards an Anarchist Poetics."

and skin that surrounds hands, body, feet.
This is a shape,
a shape of blood beating and cells dividing.[28]

The body, then, as the foundation: "cells," "hands," "feet," "skin,"
"blood," and "lungs" are precisely what connect "everyone." But this
is only a point of departure for an investigation of the "space in the
room that surrounds the shapes of everyone's hands and body and
feet and cells and the beating contained within": "Everyone with
lungs breathes the space in and out as everyone with lungs breathes
the space between the hands in and out."[29] "In" and "out" are not distinct, bounded spaces but repeating moments in a process ("in and
out"), the cyclical process of breathing that connects "everyone with
lungs," which could be abbreviated, much as we fail to recognize it every day, as simply "everyone." The individual body, a world in itself, is
also internally defined by its relation to its "outside," a relation so intimate that the very word "outside" is inadequate, misleading—a totally commonplace observation, albeit one that cannot be recognized
by governments and corporations, fatally required to apprehend the
world as something that is "outside," controllable and possessable.
There is nothing esoteric about this, and nothing yet that is an argument, except perhaps for the pathos of remembering the fact of being
this microcosm, a body: its frailty and its incompleteness, its radical
dependence on what it cannot contain, and, once more, its universal-
ity. Spahr's meditation on the fact of lungs, on breathing and embodiment, expands and expands until it encompasses the globe.

There is no nonsense here, no Cubist pyrotechnics, nothing the
least bit surreal: this is as realistic, as literal, as deadly earnest as we
can get. The language is relatively simple and straightforward, though
lyrical in its own way, and although it manifests a certain humil-
ity—a cautiousness (sticking close to the observable, the intuitive)
and a reticence (waiving, or at least exercising very carefully, its right
to make demands on us, to endorse or denounce, to bring any more
strenuous rhetoric to bear on us)—that might amount to a kind of

---

28 Juliana Spahr, "Poem Written After September 11, 2001," *This Connection
of Everyone With Lungs: Poems* (Berkeley: University of California Press,
2005).

29 Ibid.

communicative nonviolence, reminiscent of the kind of textual openness Spahr has praised in more "difficult" poets. We can see Gertrude Stein's influence, maybe, in the plain diction and the use of slow repetition, but where a work like *Tender Buttons* enforces the modernist law against the heresy of paraphrase, Spahr is not concerned to do so.

One of the very few places that Spahr alludes to anything less contemporary than Fox News or Mariah Carey is in the section marked "January 20, 2003." The allusion is to Sappho's Fragment 16, sometimes called "The Anactoria Poem" or "To an Army Wife, in Sardis":

> Some say thronging cavalry, some say foot soldiers,
> others call a fleet the most beautiful of
> sights the dark earth offers, but I say it's what-
> ever you love best.[30]

This fragment of poetic antiquity returns—is it Marx's "tradition of all the dead generations," that "weighs like a nightmare on the brain of the living"?—in contemporary costume:

> Some say 120 Challenger Two tanks, or infantry, or a fleet of ships.

> There are those who say a host of cavalry, M1A2 Abrams tanks, and others Bradley fighting vehicles.

> Some say others of infantry, and others of ships, and others of 155 mm howitzers.

> Some say thronging Warrior combat vehicles, some say foot soldiers, others call a fleet the most beautiful of sights the dark earth offers.

> Some say that the fairest thing upon the dark earth is a host of anti-armor AH-64 Apache attack helicopters and others again a fleet of ships.

---

30 Sappho, "LP 16," *The Poetry of Sappho*, trans. and ed. Jim Powell (New York: Oxford University Press, 2007), 7.

Some say that the most beautiful thing upon the black earth is an army of AS90 self-propelled guns, others, infantry, still others, ships.

On this dark earth, some say the thing most lovely is the thirty thousand assault troops from Britain today joining the sixty two thousand from the US mobilized in the past ten days and a further sixty thousand from the US on their way.

On this black earth, over the coal-black earth, some say all of this and more.

But I say it's whatever you love best.[31]

The juxtaposition of Sappho's classical diction ("a host," "thronging," "the dark earth," "the coal-black earth") and the discourse of a *Jane's Military Vehicles and Logistics* catalog ("120 Challenger Two tanks," "155 mm howitzers") is jarring. It is the *Jane's* discourse, the numbing discourse of the displays at international arms fairs, with its rhetoric of technical mastery, the promise of control at a distance, that is recycled by the news media, so that thousands upon thousands of living bodies, the kind Spahr has led us to think about for many pages now, become effectively abstract, part of this endless parts list. The gap between the two languages, between that ancient music and this terrible new sense, creates an opening for possibilities of meaning. It could be that, just as in the modern poetry of an Ezra Pound or a T.S. Eliot, the classical serves as an anchor for a shaky modern consciousness, "fragments I have shored against my ruins."[32] Perhaps the beauty and glamor of Sappho's elevated diction is being ironically contrasted with the ugly, resolutely anti-heroic mundanity of contemporary war-making. On the other hand, maybe Sappho and Spahr are more alike than different in that both draw a contrast between the perspective of the lyrical "I"—"but I say"—and the perspective of the "others," now as then, who are perverse enough to find killing "the most beautiful."

31 Spahr, "January 20, 2003," *This Connection.*
32 T.S. Eliot, "The Waste Land," *The Waste Land and Other Poems*, ed. Frank Kermode (New York: Penguin Books, 2003), line 430.

The reader can fill the gap with a number of possible meanings, but this last possibility seems the most persuasive, and this leads me to see parallels between the way "January 20, 2003" talks to us and the way Armand Marrast's song spoke to Proudhon in the prison of Sainte-Pélagie. In both cases, poetry enacts a we, a "collective identity," as Spahr has it; it commits us to the values that tell us who we are, setting us even more firmly against the forces that endanger them. We are not killers-at-a-distance, admirers of war. We are lovers, the people who love:

> It's what one loves, the most beautiful is whomever one loves.
>
> I say it is whatsoever a person loves.
>
> I say for me it is my beloveds.
>
> For me naught else, it is my beloveds, it is the loveliest sight.
>
> I say the sight of the ones you love.
>
> I say it again, the sight of the ones you love, those you've met and those you haven't.
>
> I say it again and again.
>
> Again and again.
>
> I try to keep saying it to keep making it happen.
>
> I say it again, the sight of the ones you love, those you've met and those you haven't.[33]

With this incantation, the speaker of the poem struggles not to justify but to enact a value ("to keep making it happen"), to perpetuate it in the mind against the entire force of a world that is indifferent to it; to persuade, not others, in the mode of propaganda, but herself ("I say for me"), that her perspective is real at all. But if we are the

33 Spahr, "January 20, 2003."

likely readers of this poem, and if we are not made of stone, then it is hard not to feel that the "I" who desperately "say[s] it again and again" is also one's own.

If there is a rhetoric at work here, it is something less like Aristotle's instrumentalist "means of persuasion" and more like Burke's "identification": "You *persuade a man* [*sic*] only insofar as you can talk his language by speech, gesture, tonality, order, image, attitude, idea, *identifying* your ways with his."[34] Or is it, in another way, Goodman's "physical reestablishment of community"? It is, in any case, a poetry that, in a quietly determined manner, renounces the kind of rhetorical power that sends planes into buildings and rains cluster bomblets upon children while remaining entirely comprehensible to the ear. It is both a kind of public speech, an exercise in solidarity—global, universal—and terribly intimate. Here is a woman speaking to other women and men in public space. She hails them as "my beloveds": as her own.

---

34 Aristotle, *Rhetoric*, trans. W. Rhys Roberts, in *The Rhetoric and the Poetics* (New York: Random House, 1977), 1355b; Kenneth Burke, *A Grammar of Motives and A Rhetoric of Motives* (Cleveland: World Pub. Co., 1962), 579, emphasis mine.

PART III

A man [*sic*] who cannot imagine away from the actual soon cannot move, because he is like Zeno's arrow, which cannot move where it is and cannot move where it is not.

— Paul Goodman, "On a Writer's Block."

We cannot ask reason to take us across the gulfs of the absurd. Only the imagination can get us out of the bind of the eternal present, inventing or hypothesizing or pretending or discovering a way that reason can then follow into the infinity of options, a clue through the labyrinths of choice, a golden string, the story, leading us to the freedom that is properly human, the freedom open to those whose minds can accept unreality.

— Ursula K. Le Guin, *Dancing at the Edge of the World*.

1: WHITE ROOMS

THE tramp who is the protagonist of Bernard Lazare's *Les Porteurs de Torches* (1898) is indeed named Juste; Justice, in the world of private property, is homeless. And so it is not surprising that he should meet, on his travels, another traveler who claims to be from a "country ... where all belongs to all"—a homeland Juste recognizes immediately: "That is a utopian idea, sir." Of course, within the reality of Lazare's novel, this recognition (which amounts to saying "nonsense!") is really a misrecognition: the other country is every bit as "real" as this one, and indeed, as the dialogue progresses, it is *our* world that comes to seem implausible, fictive, notional, a tissue of flimsy "ideas."[1] It is within this system of ideas that the adjective "utopian" means "unreal," a judgment embedded in its very coinage: as Lazare was surely aware, Thomas More invented the term "utopia" as a pun on *eu-topos*, "good place," and *ou-topos*, "no place."

There is almost literally no place for anarchist fiction in literary history. That is to say: as soon as "literature" is defined as imaginative works of poetry and narrative prose, the only place allotted for anarchism is that of the "no-place," utopia—that "pigeonhole allotted for daydreams and paradoxes," as Lazare puts it.[2] Utopias are taken to form a comfortably self-contained genre of their own, marginal to literature, more akin to political philosophy; if they are undeniably imaginative works of prose, they are more akin to the essay than to any narrative genre. "The Utopian text," Frederic Jameson writes, "furnishes a blueprint" for "a kind of machine"; it

---

1   Bernard Lazare, *Les Porteurs de Torches* (Paris: Armand Colin, 1898), 4.
2   Ibid., 259.

"does not *tell a story* at all."[3] Blueprints can be pretty, of course, but even when utopias happen not to be merely "uninspired mixtures of technological reform in fictional guise," in the words of Judith Sklar, they are essentially static images rather than tales in the process of being told.[4] In other words, beyond the purely explanatory and persuasive functions, which belong to the vulgar, utilitarian world of politics ("technological reform") rather than the aesthetic realm of literature, utopian writing is supposed to be a kind of picture-painting; it is visual, spatial ("a blueprint") rather than narrative. To the extent that utopian writing breaks out of this static, spatial model, e.g., by the injection of conflict and contradiction, it is no longer properly utopia but "heterotopia" or "critical utopia"— underscoring the extent to which we are encouraged to think of utopias as monolithic and uncritical (even if their very existence as writing stands as a criticism of the existing, non-fictional reality). If, as we are told, "conflict" is the essence of fictional narrative, utopias, by their very nature, are free from conflict and contradiction, hence from plurality and diversity; as dreams of uniformity, they are constituted by repression, that is to say, by exclusion, just as Plato formed his Republic by the exclusion of poets. By such paradoxical arguments, literary history, that Republic of Letters, excludes anarchists.

There are at least two dominant versions of the history of the novel, for instance, which perform this kind of exclusion, having decided in advance that utopias are not to be counted, but that there is at least such a thing as a radical stance in fiction—a critical stance. One version assumes that authentic political radicalism, in the field of the novel, is essentially Social Realism; the other version, standing the first on its head, assumes that the authentically radical tradition in fiction is to be found in anti-realist, formalist experimentation, i.e., what Anglo-American literary historians were content, until recently, to simply call Modernism. Seen from this perspective, the question is whether the true model of the radical novel ought to be

---

3 Frederic Jameson, *The Seeds of Time* (New York: Columbia University Press, 1994), 56, emphasis mine.

4 William V. Spanos, *Heidegger and Criticism: Retrieving the Cultural Politics of Destruction* (Minneapolis: University of Minnesota Press, 1993), 77–78; see also Russell Jacoby, *Picture Imperfect: Utopian Thought for an Anti-Utopian Age* (New York: Columbia University Press, 2005), 136.

considered to be Upton Sinclair's *The Jungle* or James Joyce's *Finnegan's Wake*. The emergence of cultural studies has punctured this conversation about literary history by opening up the category of "culture," forcing us to read high-culture works (e.g., Jane Austen or Charles Dickens) alongside their disavowed mass-cultural kin (e.g., the paperback romance or the soap opera). Yet even this opening has merely produced another pair of authoritative narratives-about-narrative. On the one hand, we find accounts of mass-cultural narrative that, loyal to a high-culture vision of "the writerly text" as against the text as mass-market commodity, calculated to pander to a slovenly, plebeian readership, write the latter off as yet another safety valve for the discontents of life under patriarchy and capitalism, offering just so many varieties of escapism, consolation, and accommodation. On the other hand, there is an account according to which these mass genres positively brim with subversive energies, reflections of radical desires, and opportunities for readerly "agency," so much so that the snobbish label "mass culture" must give way to the democratic embrace of "popular culture." Finally, we are offered a grand synthesis under the auspices of Frederic Jameson's theories: the high-culture fiction of the postmodern era (and postmodernism, we are informed, is merely "the cultural logic of late capitalism") is so thoroughly imbued with references to mass culture, and the distinctions between social reality and media-generated simulacra have become so thoroughly blurred, that the distinction between the "avant-garde" and the "popular" falls away entirely, and we can speak without embarrassment of an "avant-pop" in which all contradictions are happily resolved.[5]

What would "anarchist fiction" look like, then—John Dos Passos's *1919*? Henry Miller's *Nexus*? Thomas Pynchon's *The Crying of Lot 49*? All of these writings manifest an anti-authoritarian imagination, striving against what Louis Marin calls "the traps of narrative"; all are notable for experimentation with narrative form (multiple points of view, stream of consciousness, dream imagery, lyricism, denial of resolution, etc.), verging on "antinarrative," a refusal to narrate. Moreover, all of them bear tantalizing traces of historical encounters with anarchism— knowing references to Wobbly culture and "anarchist picnic[s]," rosy

---

5   Mark Amerika and Lance Olsen, eds., *In Memoriam to Postmodernism: Essays on the Avant-Pop* (San Diego: San Diego State University Press, 1995).

memories of Red Emma, moldering copies of *Regeneración*.[6] Yet none of these authors self-identifies as anarchist or writes with explicit political commitments; none of these works emerges from an anarchist movement or is circulated within anarchist counter-communities. Readers of Dos Passos, Miller, or Pynchon encounter anarchism only as a vague atmosphere—or in scholarly footnotes.

For some critics, on the contrary, it is difficult to tell the difference between anarchist "social art" and Marxist "socialist realism." María-Luisa Siguán finds works of fiction by Spanish anarchists to be "perfectly similar to those of [Marxist] 'party literature'"—unremittingly "positive," "didactic," "exemplary" tales of proletarian heroism.[7] Conversely, avant-garde movements in the arts had relatively little impact on anarchists' writing before the Second World War; the work of writers like Joyce, Woolf, Kafka, and Proust goes all but unnoticed by anarchist critics, and when they refer to trends such as Symbolism or Futurism, it is typically with derision: "It is enough for us to open a symbolist book," writes a critic in the pages of the Argentine anarchist literary journal *Los Nuevos Caminos*, "to be convinced that this book is the product of a disordered brain," while for Federica Montseny, "Futurism is caught like the measles."[8] This frequently reiterated analogy of modernism with disease[9] is carried to its satirical extreme in Ret Marut's (a.k.a. B. Traven) "Mein Besuch bei Dichter Pguwlkschrj Rnfajbzxlquy [My Visit to the Writer Pguwlkschrj Rnfajbzxlquy, 1919]," in which the adulatory critic finds his

---

6 John Dos Passos, *1919* (Boston: Houghton Mifflin, 2000), 335, 338; Henry Miller, *Nexus* (New York: Grove Press, 1987), 83, 315; Thomas Pynchon, *The Crying of Lot 49* (New York: HarperPerennial, 1999), 98.

7 Siguán, "La Novela Ideal," 419–420.

8 Manuel Laranjeira, "Algunos apuntes sobre arte contemporaneo," *Los Nuevos Caminos* 1.1 (Mayo de 1906): 68; Federica Montseny, "El Futurismo," *La Revista Blanca* 2.1.1 (June 1, 1923): 8.

9 See, for instance, de Cleyre's "Literature the Mirror of Man," in which she bemusedly wonders at the prevalence in modern literature of "madmen explaining their own madness, diseased men picking apart their own diseases, perverted men analyzing their own perversions, anything, everything but sane and normal men" (*Selected Works*, 378), or José Peirats's admonition to fellow anarchists not to "catch the disease" of avant-garde "blabla-blaism" ("Por un lenguaje libertario que se entienda [For a Libertarian Language That Can Be Understood]," *Bicicleta: Revista de comunicaciones libertarias* 20 [October 1979]: 45).

subject, the avant-garde writer with the unpronounceable name and the unreadable *oeuvre* (the fact that his works are "impossible to understand" is taken as "confirmation" of his superior genius), in his natural setting: "the Clinic for the Incurably Insane."[10]

The imperative, for writers emerging from and working within the anarchist movement, is not innovation or originality in style—"the decadent lunacy that is called originality," as Montseny puts it[11]—but effectiveness in conveying a content, and establishing contact between this textual content and a non-textual reality that moves, evolves, and changes. Thus, echoing Bakunin's admonition that good art, while dealing with "general types and general situations," nonetheless "recalls to our minds the living, real individualities which appear and disappear under our eyes," Francisco Caro Crespo declares that the novel must "bear the stamp of life."[12] Indeed, this is precisely the ambition of anarchist writers such as Alfonso Martínez Carrasco: to present the reader with an "exact transcription of a page from the sublime book of Life."[13]

At times, this aspiration seems to call for a hard-edged realism—for instance, in Japan, where anarchist writers like Miyajima Sukeo (1886–1951) helped create what became known as "Proletarian Literature" (*puroretaria bungaku*), featuring "journalistic-style realistic reporting on the lives of the poor," or in Brazil, where the anarchist newspaper *Novo Rumo* published gritty slice-of-life stories (e.g., a series of anonymous "*Placas Fotográficas*" or snapshots) about the realities of the modern urban centers.[14] The Italian individualist anarchist Leda Rafanelli called these short, quasi-journalistic narrative pieces *Bozzetti Sociali* ("social sketches"):

> The *social sketch* reflects, in a few pages of impressions, the feelings and sensations experienced, the varied aspects of modern

---

10 B. Traven, *To the Honourable Miss S... and Other Stories*, ed. and trans. Peter Silcock (Westport, CT: L. Hill, 1981), 67, 69.

11 Federica Montseny, "La estética y la originalidad en la literatura," *La Revista Blanca* 2.1.7 (September 15, 1923): 11.

12 Bakunin, *God and the State*, 56–57; F. [Ferdinando] Caro Crespo, "Juicios sobre la novela," *La Revista Blanca* 4.65 (February 1, 1926): 26.

13 Alfonso Martínez Carrasco, "¡Pero mató a un burgues!," *La Novela Proletaria* (1932–1933), ed. Gonzalo Santonja (Madrid: Ayuso, 1979), 125.

14 Filler, *Chaos From Order*, II; Photographo, "Placas Fotográficas, 1," *Contos anarquistas* (100–1) and "Placas Fotográficas, 2" (52–3).

life. In the gray mist of evening chill and frost, in the gloomy shadows of the slum, in the modern abysses of the workshops, and also in the glare of the waterfront, more beings that the novelist cannot see.... They live in houses, shacks, in the depths of mines, in the cold solitude of prisons, in the quiet of convents, all the victims of torture and pain, all those subject to the conventionality of the present laws ... the castaways of life ... without any to pass them the lifeline of salvation.

These "short and true [*brevi e vere*]" descriptions of the lives of modern society's "victims" have their genealogy not in Dada (nor even in Futurism, which had attracted Rafanelli for a time) but in Italian *Verismo*, as well as in the Naturalism of Émile Zola and Leo Tolstoy's passionate Christian-humanist realism.[15] Indeed, Zola's novels *Germinal*, *Paris*, and *Travail* were avidly read by anarchists from Chicago to Chengdu—at least eight journals (in Yiddish, Spanish, French, Italian, and Portuguese) and an untold number of anarchist children were named "Germinal" in honor of the first alone—and Tolstoy's work, published in translation by anarchist journals such as *La Revista Blanca* in Spain, *La Battaglia* in Brazil, *Wohlstand für Alle* in Austria, *Tianyi Bao* in Japan, and *Mother Earth* in the U.S., was also highly influential in the anarchist milieu.[16]

At the same time, however, we find anarchists repeatedly *distancing* themselves from what they refer to, often disparagingly, as "realism." This begins with Proudhon himself, who kicks off his book-length defense of his friend, Courbet, by denying the distinction between "idealism" and "realism" ("art is, by its very nature, at once realist and idealist"), and concludes that "the real is not the same as the truth": "The early schools of art departed from truth by

15 Leda Rafanelli, *Bozzetti sociali* (Milan: Casa editrice sociale, 1921), 5–6; Franco Andreucci, "Rafanelli, Leda (1880–1971)," *Italian Women Writers Database* (University of Chicago Library, 2004), web. For Rafanelli's links to Futurism, see Günter Berghaus, *Futurism and Politics: Between Anarchist Rebellion and Fascist Reaction: 1909–1944* (Providence, RI: Berghahn Books, 1996), 53 and 85n20; and Alberto Ciampi, *Leda Rafanelli—Carlo Carrà: un romanzo* (Venezia: Centro Internazionale della Grafica, 2005).

16 Vittorio Frigerio, *Émile Zola au pays de l'Anarchie* (Grenoble: ELLUG, Université Stendhal, 2006), 37; Litvak, *La Mirada Roja*, 34, 134n93, 9, 129–130 n1; Chan and Dirlik, *Schools Into Fields and Factories*, 22.

way of the ideal; do not yourself depart from it by way of the real." In remarkably similar terms, Kropotkin suggested that "realistic description," if deprived of any "idealistic aim," would in fact be falsified; literature must tell the truth, not only of the concretely present, but of "desire."[17] Just as Zola's pretension to "photograph" reality objectively is rejected by Bernard Lazare as pitiably "incomplete," so for José Prat (1867–1932), art "has to be something more than a photography that paints the vices and the virtues that we have; it also must point out new courses to humanity."[18] Mécislas Golberg (1869–1907), likewise, calls this photographic style of realism "sterile"—a kind of self-neutering capitulation to what Freud would call the reality principle. Cleaving to the pole of objectivity, this would-be literature of protest turns out to be precisely the kind of writing that allows us to write off alternatives to the status quo as "utopian."[19]

And yet—surprisingly—we will just as consistently hear the same anarchists denounce "utopias" and "utopian" thinking. The entry for "Utopia" in the *Encyclopédie anarchiste* immediately notes that the common usage of the word is entirely negative, something to be disavowed rather than claimed: "all that is impossible to achieve."[20] "Taken in its usual current sense," Kropotkin argued, "the word 'Utopia' ought to be limited to those conceptions only which are based on merely theoretical reasonings as to what is *desirable* from the writer's point of view"; anarchism, on the contrary, is "based ... on an analysis of *tendencies of an evolution that is already going on in society*," something "*already developing*."[21] Society is plural and mobile; a utopia is the product of a single intellect, a fixed idea. To wish to impose one such idea on everyone, for Proudhon, is already to dream of

---

17 Proudhon qtd. in James Henry Rubin, *Realism and Social Vision in Courbet and Proudhon* (Princeton, NJ: Princeton University Press, 1980), 94, trans. Rubin; Kropotkin, *Ideals and Realities*, 85–86. Lest this notion of "truth" sound too Platonic, it might help to read it against Zo d'Axa's statement: "We aren't going to bother ourselves with eternal Truth—with a capital T [*la sempiternelle Vérité—avec un grand V*]" ("Nous," *L'En-dehors, Anthologie, 1891–1893* [s.l: Chamuel, 1896], 125).

18 Lazare, *L'Écrivain et l'art social*, 29, 27; José Prat, "Teatro nuevo," *Ciencia social* 2.3 (September 1898): 48.

19 Golberg, letter to Zola, May 29, 1896, qtd. in Frigerio, *Émile Zola*, 24.

20 A. Blicq, "Utopie, Utopiste," *Encyclopédie anarchiste*, 2829.

21 Kropotkin, "Modern Science and Anarchism," *Evolution and Environment* (Montréal: Black Rose Books, 1995), 60.

dictatorship: "no one on earth is capable, as Saint-Simon and Fourier were said to be, of providing a complete system, made from scratch, that one simply has to put into practice."[22] As Jean Grave puts it, "Given the diversity of temperaments and characters, establishing a single mode of organization to which everyone has to conform and that we would impose immediately after the Revolution would be a utopia"—very much in the sense of "impossible to achieve."[23] Accordingly, for Paul Goodman, writing on the other side of the age of revolutions, "the best solutions are usually not global but a little of this and a little of that."[24] To imagine "global" solutions, societies "made from scratch," is to dream of eliminating the messiness of actual history, of actual human beings, in the purity of a Year Zero—"the terrifying void," as Colson writes, "in which the 'imagination' of the revolutionary leaders ... can finally deploy itself without obstruction."[25] In short, the concept of "utopia," from these perspectives, stands for all that anarchism *opposes*.[26]

Consider Voltairine de Cleyre's Gothic tale, "The White Room," first published in the freethinking journal *The Open Court* (1896). An artist creates the perfect home, "the White Room," for his perfect wife, "herself the whitest thing, his pure-faced Scandinavian girl ... with that beautiful, meek, white patience of hers": white walls, ceiling, floors, furnishings, décor, etc. He is intent on the imitation of nature: "the dazzling beauty of the ceiling was like a broken arc from a cave's roof, so white and gleaming was it with the strange substance

---

22 Proudhon, letter to Antoine Gautier (May 2, 1841), in *Correspondance de P.-J. Proudhon*, ed. Amédée Jérôme Langlois (Paris: A. Lacroix et Cie., 1875), 1.326.

23 Jean Grave, *La société au lendemain de la revolution* (Paris: Bureau de La Révolte, 1893), 4.

24 Goodman, *New Reformation*, 204.

25 Daniel Colson, "Anarchist Readings of Spinoza," trans. Jesse Cohn and Nathan Jun, *Journal of French Philosophy* 17.2 (2011): 104. Colson's phrase, here, could almost serve as a plot summary of Le Guin's *The Lathe of Heaven* (New York: Scribner, 1971), in which one well-intentioned man actually *does* gain the ability to shape the perfect world from his own "imagination"; the ensuing technocratic nightmare is an authentically anarchist anti-utopia.

26 For a more in-depth exploration of anarchist anti-utopianism, see Michel Antony, "Les libertaires face à l'utopie: entre critiques, analyses, expérimentations et projets," *Ressources sur l'utopie, sur les utopies libertaires et les utopies anarchistes* (Académie de Besançon, Nov. 8, 2008): 1–35.

he had made; and the walls had all the wild fantastic tracery of the frost-forests on our winter windows, which God paints—but no man." So meticulous is he that he does not notice his beloved pining away with boredom and neglect in their grubby garret, until the day he finishes the work—and returns to find her gone, of course. When she turns up years later, "in the gutter, quite drunk and dying," he takes her in, allowing her to die in her White Room, "soil[ing]" it, leaving behind this final curse: "Ugh! The horrid fancies in the liquor. It looks all white, WHITE, like a Dead-house!"[27] The White Room is, of course, a work of art, and as such bears no small resemblance to the centerpiece of Edgar Allan Poe's "The Oval Portrait"—a painting that takes on increasingly lifelike qualities at the expense of the very life-force of its subject, the artist's wife, who dies on its completion. Each story could be described, in the words of de Cleyre's fellow anarchist, E. Armand, as an "'extraordinary' case of the transfer of the vital element from a living body to a representation of this body," a lesson on the dangers of representation.[28] Eugenia C. DeLamotte reads it as a critique of the nineteenth-century notion of the virtuous woman as "the Angel in the House" and, incidentally, as an allegory of the way in which we are all led to define ourselves by what we are not (e.g., not perfect, not pure). Just as the real woman is forever excluded, while living, from the ideal room, we create our identities by "abjection"—by deciding that some stuff is "beneath" us, "beyond the pale," "not for me"—so that, paradoxically, this "outside" is what shapes and defines our "inside," so that it is in a sense part of us, an inner-outside.[29] But the White Room is also a *place*, intended to be perfect: it is, in the classical sense, a kind of utopia. And it is uninhabitable, at least by the one for whom it is constructed; it cannot support life.

And aren't books also a kind of White Room—a space of representation that attempts to fix and capture life? Anarchists seek to tunnel out of the White Room of idealist or utopian representation,

---

27 Voltairine de Cleyre, "The White Room," *The Open Court* 10.459 (June 11, 1896): 4945–4946.

28 Émile Armand, "Edgar Poe, le conteur de l'extraordinaire," *Profils de Précurseurs et Figures de Rêve* (Paris: Editions de l'En Dehors, 1931), 75.

29 Eugenia C. DeLamotte "Revolution of the Mind," *Gates of Freedom: Voltairine de Cleyre and the Revolution of the Mind: With Selections From Her Writing* (Ann Arbor, MI: University of Michigan Press, 2004), 119.

a closed space that cannot accommodate the messiness of real women, real bodies, or real life. But isn't the very mark of the book the fact that it can be *closed*, that it has a beginning and an end, unlike life? What "realistic" representation could ever present anything but an infinitely tidier version of the real? A "closed system," Andrew M. Koch points out, "always omits an element contained in the object it seeks to describe."[30] In that case, it would seem, anarchist resistance to representation entails a resistance to realism as well.

Are the anarchists, then, to be seen as realists or anti-realists, chroniclers of the dystopian everyday or intransigent utopians? Perhaps they are both at once, or neither? José Martín (1892–1930), writing in the *Revista Blanca*, proposed that "the novel ... should be neither realistic nor utopian": "We live in reality, there is no need for us to read it; the utopia, as such, is chimerical and chimeras cannot and should not substantiate anything. Between reality and utopia is an area of darkness that the novel should illuminate."[31] The staging ground for anarchist narrative is precisely this heterotopian space caught "between reality and utopia," between—in the title of Teresa Claramunt's banned play of 1896—*El mundo que muere y el mundo que nace* (*The World That Is Dying and the World That Is Being Born*). And here we are: in the area of darkness. We have wandered off the maps of literary history. *Here be dragons.*

As usual, tracing the history of anarchist resistance culture will require a more careful kind of reconstruction, looking beyond old and new canons. At the same time that anarchist writers, pushing against the constraints of literary convention, evoke a sense of strangeness, courting the limits of antinarrative, they are also impelled toward classical and popular forms of narrative—both to avoid estranging readers and in order to overcome those other orders of alienation that persuade us that we are not the authors of our own lives, that forbid the imagination to venture beyond certain bounds, that obscure the possibilities inherent in the real.

---

30 Andrew M. Koch, "Poststructuralism and the Epistemological Basis of Anarchism," *Philosophy of the Social Sciences* 23.3 (1993): 337.

31 José Martín, "Estudios: La novela," *La Revista Blanca* 3.48 (May 15, 1925): 29.

2: VARIETIES OF ESTRANGEMENT

IN Havana, Cuba, 1903, a new book of short stories bearing the insouciant title *Cuentos Inverosímiles* ("Implausible Stories") appeared in a series published by the Biblioteca Pro-Vida. The author, a Catalan anarchist named Adrián del Valle (1872–1945), who was also the director of the *Revista Pro-Vida*, house organ of the Institución Naturista Cubana Pro-Vida (dedicated to the cause of "social nudism"), had been publishing stories under such noms de plume as "Palmiro de Lidia," "Fructidor," and "Hindus Fakir." The collection begins, appropriately enough, with a story about a talking cello ("El Músico Polaco [The Polish Musician]").

"Nothing can surprise me," remarks the impoverished cellist, William Koseck, when his instrument strikes up a conversation with him. "You have suffered a lot of disappointment.... It was your own fault," admonishes the cello. "Don't be cruel," the musician pleads.[1] The violation of verisimilitude—we know from experience that cellos are things, not people, and do not talk—is not unprecedented, of course. In fairy tales, harps, swords, and gingerbread cookies are routinely heard from. The premise could have come from Hans Christian Andersen or the Brothers Grimm: a poor but virtuous man is on the verge of starvation, when he is addressed by a magical voice... But we are not in a fairy tale; the non-realist element is abruptly annulled a third of the way through (Koseck wakes up—it had been only a "strange dream"). More fundamentally, the magical laws that should fill the Polish musician's empty belly are not in force, and after futile

---

1   Adrián del Valle, *Cuentos Inverosímiles* (Havana: Imp. "Cervantes," 1921), 3–4.

attempts to sing and beg for his supper, Koseck will end up dangling by the neck from the unhappy end of his own cello string. What is happening here?

A psychoanalyst might quickly diagnose the voice of the cello as a projection of Koseck's own; ventriloquizing, the failed artist places in the mouth of his instrument accusations that make sense of his failure ("It was your own fault"). More precisely, the cello speaks with the chastising voice of a super-ego, berating a diminished ego for having fallen short of its ego-ideal. But the accusation it levels at Koseck is quite otherwise. The "strange dream" section of the story runs like a kind of Socratic dialogue in reverse, in which the philosophical cello mercilessly demolishes every one of the ideals to which Koseck has attached his ego: "'Ah,' exclaimed Koseck. 'Poor me, who have spent my life dreaming of art, longing for glory, to learn at the end of my journey, old, poor and forgotten, that life, art and glory are nothing more than wishful fictions!'"[2] It seems to be the musician's inability to fully learn this lesson that dooms him: losing all hope of assuaging his hunger by getting others to pay him for his music, he pawns "his beloved cello"—"repaying its service with the blackest ingratitude," as he thinks of it, "simply to satisfy the material demands of the stomach, to extend his miserable existence a few days." It is for this, finally, that he commits suicide.[3]

A good materialist, of course, would know just what to do with the insolent cello, this means of production that seems to take on life at the expense of the producer. It is all too similar to the famous passage in Marx's *Capital* in which he explores the "metaphysical subtleties and theological niceties" that appear when wood, hewn and assembled into a table, enters the marketplace: "so soon as it steps forth as a commodity, it is changed into something transcendent. It not only stands with its feet on the ground, but ... stands on its head, and evolves out of its wooden brain grotesque ideas, far more wonderful than 'table-turning' ever was"—referring to the Spiritualist practice of communing with the dead through table-rapping.[4] In other words, if your stuff appears to talk back to you, this is a symptom of "the fetishism of commodities," a general phenomenon of life

---

2   Ibid., 6.
3   Ibid., 8.
4   Marx, in Marx and Engels, *Collected Works*, 35.81–82.

under capitalism. Alienated from his product, it is the wage-worker who is "a mere instrument, an object without a soul," as Koseck objects. No wonder he has consoled himself with fantasies of being elevated above material considerations by art, "transported to ethereal regions, far from the earth, far from men."[5]

Much as he is estranged from "men," Koseck is *not* alienated, at least as far as his labor goes. If the cello is his means of production, it is small, and he owns it; technically, even though he is destitute, that would place him in the class of the petit bourgeois. Moreover, he is an artist: the sensuous act of making music, for him, carries its purpose in itself. An artist might be in a good position to achieve what Emma Goldman, following Nietzsche, liked to call "the transvaluation of all values": in other words, to refuse to allow others to judge for me what is beautiful or ugly, good or bad, worthwhile or worthless, to decide that what is valuable *to me* is valuable *in itself.* Koseck takes up a passive stance with respect to values, receiving rather than creating them for himself. This is why it is so devastating for him to realize, belatedly, that he has no idea what he means by "art" or even by "life," and that a posthumous "glory" seems pointless; this is why, having been found worthless by the standards of a utilitarian society, he helplessly agrees to act as his own executioner. Pawning his one true love for a little bread, he has allowed the capitalist economy in which he is marooned, an economy that fails to assign value to his actions, to invalidate his values. Thus, when he tries to trade music for food, his offer is received as begging: "If you want to eat, pay in more solid cash; music is money that blows away in the wind." To be an artist, in such a world, is to face a continual threat of death by starvation in a world where art, as Koseck observes, "matters little before the materiality of life."[6] What is truly implausible, grotesque, is not so much that an object should take on life to which "an object without a soul" should have no claim—indeed, for del Valle, a philosophical vitalist, this claim is not at all spurious.[7] What is unthinkable is that a thinking, feel-

---

5 There are, interestingly, no women visible in this story, though he embraces his cello as if it were his "lover [*amante*]" and "with a mother's caresses [*caricias de madre*]" (del Valle, *Cuentos Inverosímiles*, 9).

6 Ibid., 9–10.

7 An element of vitalism runs through anarchist philosophy; Bakunin denies that there is any such thing as *mere* "matter," i.e., matter devoid of move-

ing, creative subject should be reduced to the status of a mute and meaningless object.

This transposition of subject and object, of self and non-self, is an important motif of anarchist fiction.[8] In Francisco Pi y Arsuaga's parable, "Lo Que Dicen los Máquinas [What the Machines Say]," for instance, we hear a machine literally admonish the worker who tends it: "Don't be proud! In no way are you different from me. An instrument of labor like me, your stomach, like my indispensable coal furnace, receives just sufficient food to keep you engaged in your mechanical function."[9] To be the tool of another, to be exploited, is to be

ment, spontaneity, activity, even "intelligence" (*God and the State* 12–14, 49). Del Valle frequently returns to this idea, both in his philosophical writings for intellectual journals such as *Revista de Filosofía* and in his stories. Thus, he has the talking cello opine that "everything that exists has sensation, to varying degrees" (*Cuentos Inverosímiles*, 5). In another of the *Cuentos Inverosímiles*, "Un Rayo de Sol [A Beam of Sunlight]," it is a talking sunbeam who informs the narrator that what he has heretofore incorrectly understood as "soul" is really only "matter reflected in itself," while "matter" is really only "soul reflected in itself" (181–182). Similarly, in "El Medio Social Como Factor Psicológico" (published in translation as "Social Environment as a Psychological Factor" in *Inter-América* 7.8 [August 1924]), del Valle proposes "the existence of psychism in all the manifestations of life" and even "psychic manifestation in every form of energy" (471).

8   Thus, Curtis Marez astutely notes that Ricardo Flores Magón's stories, too, "often represent a modern world filled with commodities and machines that come to life and speak, as in fantastic dialogues involving inanimate objects such as man and machine ['El Obrero y la Máquina'], an expensive pen and a cheap pen ['Las Dos Plumas'], and a fancy coat and a workman's smock ['La Levita y la Blusa']. Like early cartoons, these animated engines, pens, and coats represent what Walter Benjamin would call a new sensorium of urban life where commodities seem to have a thrilling life of their own. Yet in contrast to Marx's famous analysis of fetishism, in which commodities appear to be alive because they displace living human labor, Magón's commodities make speeches about the labor theory of value, reminding readers that, from cars to clothes, commercial goods are the product of work" (Marez, "Pancho Villa Meets Sun Yat-sen: Third World Revolution and the History of Hollywood Cinema," *American Literary History* 17.3 [Fall 2005]: 490).

9   Francisco Pi y Arsuaga, "Lo que dicen los máquinas," *Regeneración: Semanal revolucionario* 4.92 (June 1, 1912): 1. This particular motif of the human changing places with the machine is echoed in numerous other stories, including Anselmo Lorenzo's "Os Homens Máquinas [The Machine-Men]" (1908) and Han Ryner's "La Révolte des Machines [Revolt of the Machines]" (1896). A related motif: the transformation of human beings into animals or insects, as in Ba Jin's "Gou [Dog]" (1931), Octave Mirbeau's *Dingo* (1913); Charles Malato's "Entre los Gorilas: Cuento simbólico [Among the Gorillas: A Symbolic Tale]" (1904) and (under the

made a victim, and many anarchist stories are indeed fictions of social victimization under oppressive forces—of militarism, colonialism, and religious bigotries, of grinding poverty and the cruel juridical machineries of punishment, of the petty tyrannies of the patriarchal family, the marriage bond, and the educational system, and especially of the predatory sexism practiced in prostitution and rape. What Granier says about French anarchist novels could be applied, with some justice, to the work of anarchists around the globe: "They are novels of denunciation, first and foremost."[10]

This focus on the victims might seem an obvious choice for writers of fiction affiliated with the anarchist movement, a politics often defined in terms of the negative. The denunciations on which these stories center make them, in the heading of one series that ran in *Le Libertaire*, "Bitter Tales [*Contes amers*]," or, in the subtitle of Ernesto Herrera's story collection, *Su Majestad el Hambre* (*His Majesty, Hunger*, 1910), "Brutal Stories [*Cuentos brutales*]." But they are quite as often presented as frankly "Implausible Stories," "Mysterious Stories [*Cuentos misteriosos*]," "Phantasmagorical Stories [*Cuentos fantasmagóricos*]," "Marvelous and Prodigious Stories [*Cuentos de maravilla y prodigio*]" "Prophetic Stories [*Contes prophétiques*]," "Incredible Tales [*Histoires Incroyables*]," or even "Impossible Tales [*Fábula impossível*]."[11] What is apparently one of the earliest pieces of anarchist fiction in China—an unsigned short story, "Yu chu jin yu: Renrou lou [A Modern Yu Chu Story: House of Human

---

pseudonym of "Talamo") *Les Mémoires d'un Gorille* (*Memoirs of a Gorilla*, 1901); or Han Ryner's *L'Homme-Singe* (*The Ape-Man*, 1894) and *L'Homme-Fourmi* (*The Ant-Man*, 1901). In Félix Fénéon's "Les Ventres [The Bellies]" (1883), as Granier points out, this "inversion of lexical fields" operates in both directions: "Thus, the animals 'dine [*mangent*]' while the villagers 'swill [*bâfrent*],'" and vagrants are treated as human "game," to be "hunted" (*Les Briseurs de formules*, 362–363). Similarly, Maurice Tournier shows how Émile Pouget's denunciatory rhetoric makes use of the portmanteau—e.g., "cléricochons" or "cléricafards" (from *cléricaux*, of or pertaining to the clergy, plus *cochons*, pigs, or *cafards*, cockroaches)—to create an imagery of "chimeras," monstrous hybrids ("Le bestiaire anarchiste," 257–258).

10 Granier, *Les briseurs de formules*, 111.

11 See "Yu chu jin yu: Renrou lou" *Xinmin Congbao* 1.5 (Apr. 8, 1902): 97–100; and Geng Chuan Ming, "Wu zhengfu zhuyi yu zhongguo xiandai wenxue xiandai xing de qiyuan," *Hua Dong Shi Fan Da Xue Xue Bao* 6 (1998): 25–26.

Flesh]," published in the *Xinmin Congbao* [*New Citizens' Journal*] in 1902—is just such a tale: a satirical attack on the faltering Qing regime, presented as "A Modern Yu Chu story" or "Yu Chu in Contemporary Language." "Yu Chu" was a name synonymous with the weird or tall tale, dating back to the Han Dynasty. The imagery is accordingly outrageous, symbolically representing exploitation as a form of cannibalism (predating Lu Xun's use of the same motif in his famous "Kuangren Riji [Madman's Diary]" by a decade and a half). Thirty years later, Ba Jin's "Gou [Dog]" (1931) strikes a similarly Kafkaesque note with its most unreliable narrator: a Chinese man who, brutalized by poverty and colonialism, comes to think of the people with "fair skin, blond hair, green eyes, big noses, and tall, strong bodies" as the true "human beings," viewing himself as "a stone," "a lost object," ultimately, "a dog, or something like it."[12] Of course, even in its extremity, this distorted self-perception mirrors China's colonial reality: "Decades ago," as Ba Jin laconically notes in a reflection of 1958, "on the entrance door of a park in the Shanghai Concession, there hung a plaque with the words, 'No Chinese or dogs admitted.'"[13] These are conditions not to be believed, but to be rejected.

Western anarchist stories often take something like the form of the "scientific romance" *à la* Hawthorne or Poe before modern science fiction—along the stricter lines laid down by Verne and Wells—appeared. In del Valle's collection, for instance, we encounter a scientist driven mad by his belief that he can bring back the dead ("Vitalis"), a jealous lover who kills his rival with a thought ("Cerebralis"), a despondent dreamer lectured on the nature of the soul by a sentient beam of sunlight ("Un Rayo de Sol"), and so on. Jules Lermina (1839–1913), author of *L'A.B.C. du Libertaire* (1906) and contributor to the Argentine anarchist newspaper *La Protesta Humana*, also penned scores of *Histoires Incroyables*

---

12 Ba Jin, "Dog," trans. Lance Halvorsen, in *The Columbia Anthology of Modern Chinese Literature*, eds. Joseph S. M. Lau and Howard Goldblatt (New York: Columbia University Press, 2007), 113, 110–111.

13 Ba Jin, *Selected Works*, trans. Sidney Shapiro and Wang Mingjie (Beijing: Foreign Languages Press, 1988), 4.134. He also notes that such distortion—what Iris M. Zavala calls an "anatropic" or "inverted" representation of the world (*Colonialism and Culture* 1)—was one way to smuggle anti-colonial critique past the censors (4.133).

(1885, 1888) and science-fiction novels inspired by Bulwer-Lytton. The fictional work of Han Ryner (a.k.a. Henri Ner, 1861–1938) is just as adventurous in exploring the possibilities of the *roman d'anticipation*, from his futuristic tale of robot insurrection, "La Révolte des Machines [The Revolt of the Machines]" (1896) to his post-human epic, *Les Surhommes, Roman Prophétique (The Superhumans: A Propetic Novel*, 1929), in which hyper-intelligent mastodons have inherited the Earth from a defunct human race. Novels advertised in Gilded-Age anarchist journals such as *Lucifer, the Light-Bearer* often featured what Brigitte Koenig refers to, not unfairly, as "an extraterrestrial prophet": a "Marsite" in Henry Olerich's (1851–1927) *A Cityless and Countryless World* (1893), a Venusian in William Windsor's (b.1827; date of death unknown) *Loma, a Citizen of Venus* (1897).[14] Even the protagonists of John Lloyd's *Dwellers in Vale Sunrise* (1904) "were as messengers from another world" in their sheer otherness: "A sort of god-like dignity and health seemed to hang about them."[15] Indeed, in *The Dispossessed: An Ambiguous Utopia* (1974), when Ursula K. Le Guin deploys her anarchist protagonist, Shevek ("The First Man From the Moon," as his hosts call him), to the authoritarian world of Urras, she rediscovers a century-old tradition.[16]

Nor did anarchist writers, for all their enthusiasm over science and technology, confine their violations of realism to the rationally possible, "*domesticat[ing]* the impossible" along the lines laid down by the Fabian socialist Wells.[17] On the contrary, they were often fascinated by the mythic and folkloric, regarding them as the as-yet undomesticated remnants of oral cultures hostile to regimentation

---

14 Brigitte Koenig, "Visions of the Future: Reproduction, Revolution, and Regeneration in American Anarchist Utopian Fiction," in *Anarchism and Utopianism*, eds. Laurence Davis and Ruth Kinna (Manchester: Manchester University Press, 2009), 175.

15 J. William Lloyd, *The Dwellers in Vale Sunrise: How They Got Together and Lived Happily Ever After* (Westwood, MA: Ariel Press, 1904), 15.

16 Ursula K. Le Guin, *The Dispossessed: An Ambiguous Utopia* (New York: Harper & Row, 1974), 20. One is also reminded of the "mysterious stranger" in Pietro Gori's often-performed play, *Primo Maggio* (Barre, VT: Pallavicini, 1896), who represents "the fate that guides us/to a peaceful and harmonious future" (1).

17 H.G. Wells, *The Scientific Romances of H.G. Wells* (London: Gollancz, 1933), VIII.

and the State.[18] Thus, from their prison-colony exile in New Cale-donia, Louise Michel (with the help of her friend and fellow anar-chist exile, Charles Malato) avidly collected the tales of the native Kanaks, which she compared to "the Eddas, the Sagas, the Romance-ro, the Niebelungen" (1885).[19] She had already published a volume of French regional folklore, *Le Gars Yvon, Légende Bretonne* (1882), as had her comrade in arms, André Léo (a.k.a. Victoire Léodile Béra, 1824–1900), who collected tales from her husband's native region, Corrèze, in *Légendes Corréziennes* (1870). Other French anarchist writers around the turn of the century experimented with the fairy-tale form as well, from Bernard Lazare's *Porte d'Ivoire* (*The Gate of Ivory*, 1897) to Ryner's *L'Homme-Fourmi* (*The Ant-Man*, 1901).

Nor was this fascination with the folkloric by any means confined to France. In Germany, both Gustav Landauer ("Der gelbe Stein: Ein Märchen [The Yellow Stone: A Fairy Tale]," 1910), and Ret Marut ("Khundar: Ein deutsches Märchen [Khundar: A German Fairy Tale]," 1920) try their hands at the fairy-tale form, the first of these adapting a story from the Welsh Mabinogion, the latter a more idio-syncratic allegory with vague echoes of Percy Bysshe Shelley's *Alas-tor*.[20] Shortly thereafter, in the mid-1920s and 1930s, we find Marut, writing under the name of B. Traven, collecting and adapting the oral literature of his adopted country, much as Manuel Rojas Sepúlveda (1896–1973) was doing for his native Chile around the same time.[21]

18 For Louise Michel, for instance, the folklore of her native Haute-Marne symbolizes the resistance of the Gauls to the Roman Empire (Edith Thom-as, *Louise Michel* [Montréal: Black Rose Books, 1980], 53), while Voltair-ine de Cleyre sees the fairy tale as representing both a victory of the human spirit over the mythic fear animating religion and a domain of the "imag-ination" resistant to industrial rationality (*Selected Works*, 363, 374); in a similar vein, Félix Martí-Ibáñez proposes that fairy tales allow children to negotiate, in the form of "play," their struggle to carve out a realm of auton-omy against "forces in the adult world that threaten to devour the child's ego" (*Ariel: Essays on the Arts and the History and Philosophy of Medicine* [New York: MD Publications, 1962], 34–35).

19 Louise Michel, *Légendes et Chants de Gestes Canaques* (Paris: impr. de A. Reiff, 1882), 3, trans. Mitch Abidor.

20 Susanne Schmid, *Shelley's German Afterlives, 1814–2000* (Basingstoke: Palgrave Macmillan, 2007), 146.

21 E.g., B. Traven, *Land des Frühlings* (Berlin: Büchergilde Gutenberg,1928) and *Sonnen-Schöpfung: indianische Legende* (Zurich: Büchergilde Guten-berg, 1936); Manuel Rojas, *Hombres del Sur, Cuentos* (Santiago, Chile: Na-scimento, 1926), "El Colocolo," in *El Delinquente* (Santiago, Chile: Imp.

Meanwhile, the Korean anti-colonial historian Shin Chae-ho (a.k.a. Tanjae, 1880–1936) rewrote national folklore into a revolutionary allegory, *Yonggwayong ui daegyeokjjeon* (*Battle of Dragon Against Dragon*, 1928).[22] Even the usually rather bluntly pragmatic Ōsugi Sakae (1885–1923) resorts to the fantastic and allegorical in his story, "Kusari kōjō [The Chain Factory]" (1913):

> One night, when I opened my eyes, I suddenly found myself in a strange place.
>
> As far as the eye could see, there were only countless masses of human beings, everyone individually working on something. I was making a chain.
>
> A fellow right next to me took a long, extended chain, wrapped it once around his body, and passed the end to the person next to him. The person next to him extended the chain further, wrapped it around his body, and passed the end to yet the next person. While this was happening, the first fellow received a chain from the person next to him, and as before stretched it out, wrapped it once around his body, and passed the end to the fellow on the other side of him. All repeated the same action over and over—and this took place at a dizzying speed.

The bizarrerie of the scene, the fantastic element, underlines the absurdity of human self-enslavement: "Chains," a fellow worker solemnly informs the narrator, "are sacred things which protect us and make us free." When the narrator protests the irrationality of manufacturing one's own chains, he recalls Hegel's admonition: "Everything real accords with reason, and everything that accords with reason is real."[23] Clearly, this "reality" is not all it is cracked up to be.

This fascination with the irrational and unreal coincided rather than conflicted with the writing of more conventionally realist "victim of society" narratives. Thus, in her collected works, Luisa Capetillo directly follows her short story "La Igualdad Humana [Human

Universitaria, 1929), "El Hombre de la Rosa" and "El León y el Hombre" in *Travesía: Novelas Breves* (Santiago, Chile: Editorial Nascimiento, 1934), and *La Ciudad de los Césares* (Santiago, Chile: Ediciones Ercilla, 1936).

22 Song Chae-so, "The Changes of Tanjae's Thought," 24–28.

23 Ōsugi Sakae, "Kusari kōjō," *Kindai shisō* 1.12 (September 1913): 2, trans. Stephen Filler, qtd in Filler, *Chaos From Order*, 9–10; Ibid., 10.

Equality]," in which the narrator speaks with an allegorical eagle and a "radiant, splendid, magnificent figure wrapped in a white transparent tunic with a diadem on it that in sparkling letters read: '*Anarchy*'" with "El Cajero [The Cashier]," a melodrama of working-class frustration, revenge, and escape.[24] Rather than opting for "Sacco" over "Sappho," as Muriel Rukeyser put it, anarchist writers of fiction like Capetillo were capable of shifting between materialist and mythical modes—a "*mélange d'antique et de moderne*," as Bernard Lazare's narrator puts it in *La Porte d'Ivoire*.[25]

Indeed, the materialistic and the mythic, the ancient and the modern often overlapped in the form of anarchist fables or parables, such as Multatuli's "Geschichte der Autorität [Tales of Authority]" (in *Minnebrieveri*, 1861, reprinted in *Der freie Arbeiter* 1907), Francisco Pi y Arsuaga's "El Cuervo" (in *Preludios de la Lucha*, 1886, reprinted in the Flores Magón brothers' *Regeneración* in 1911), Lillian Browne's "Parable of the Benefactor" (*Mother Earth*, 1910), or Gertrude Nafe's "The Woman Who Stood in the Market Place" (*Mother Earth*, 1914). All of these closely match Vittorio Frigerio's description of a prominent subgenre of the French anarchist *nouvelle*, the "allegory," featuring "highly symbolic characters"—"the lion" (Multatuli), "the woman" (Nafe), "the crow" (Pi y Arsuaga)—"installed in what is often a geographically and temporally indecipherable setting"—"the plain," "the market place," "the land tilled by a man who works it."[26] Like their Greek or Christian counterparts, these anarchist fables are openly didactic; indeed, they are often written for expressly pedagogical purposes by educators such as Nafe and Browne. In this way—as in many others—anarchist fiction forms part of the materials of anarchist pedagogy, and demands to be read as such.

---

24 Capetillo, *Absolute Equality*, 78–82, 82–88.

25 Bernard Lazare, *La Porte d'Ivoire* (Paris: A. Colin, 1897), 4.

26 Vittorio Frigerio, "Éléments pour une rhétorique de la nouvelle anarchiste," *Rhétorique des discours politiques*, eds. Pierre Marillaud and Robert Gauthier (Toulouse: C.A.L.S./C.S.T., 2005), 174; Multatuli "Geschichte der Autorität," *Der freie Arbeiter* 4.4 (January 26, 1907): 2, 7; Lillian Browne, "The Parable of the Benefactor," *Mother Earth* 5.6 (August 1910): 199; Zoais [Luis García Muñoz], "¡Golondrinas!," *Tierra y Libertad* 4.289 (January 19, 1916): 2; Gertrude Nafe, "The Woman Who Stood in the Market Place," *Mother Earth* 8.12 (February 1914): 380–384; Pi y Arsuaga, "El Cuervo," 1.

This is not to say, however, that the didacticism of these works is exactly the same as that of Aesop or the Gospels. "A book is not a gospel," Kropotkin warns us; "It is a suggestion, a proposal—nothing more. It is for us to reflect to see what it contains that is good, and to reject whatever we find erroneous in it."[27] Thus, not only might the moral content of an anarchist parable differ from its classical antecedents, but the presentation of the content takes on a rather different form: it invites not a passive but an active reading. This, too, was consistent with the goals of anarchist pedagogy as it had been articulated by educators such as Paul Robin (1837–1912), Francisco Ferrer y Guardia (1859–1909), and Madeleine Vernet (a.k.a. Madeleine Eugénie Cavelier, 1878–1949) against the rote-learning style of the schools erected by Church and State, a system that naturally produced copyists rather than creators; "Let the child make his own discoveries," urged Robin, "so that his mind continues its own efforts, and above all, refrain from imposing on him ready-made, banal ideas, transmitted by unthinking and stupefying routine."[28] Anarchist fables, likewise, could not merely present moral maxims for the pupil-reader to memorize and repeat; as Granier points out, anarchists often engaged not so much in retellings of fables and legends as in reworkings of them—indeed, "*détournements*" (violent appropriations) or "*déformations*" (parodic undoings) of the originals.[29] Rather than merely soliciting our reading, such stories seem to elicit (and perform) a kind of *re*reading, as if they were designed to teach "the

27 Peter Kropotkin, "Preface," in Émile Pataud and Émile Pouget, *How We Shall Bring About the Revolution: Syndicalism and the Co-Operative Commonwealth*, trans. Charlotte Charles and Frederic Charles (London: Pluto Press, 1990), XXXI.

28 Ali Nematollahy, "Jules Vallés and the Anarchist Novel," *Nineteenth-Century French Studies* 35.3–4 (Spring–Summer 2007): 578; Paul Robin qtd. in Christiane Demeulenaere-Douyère, *Paul Robin (1837–1912): un militant de la liberté et du bonheur* (Paris: Publisud, 1994), 217.

29 Granier, *Les Briseurs de formules*, 353. While Granier is speaking of French anarchist writing, the observation can be applied to works far afield. For example, as John Fitzgerald notes, in "Xinnian Meng [New Year's Dream]" (1904), Cai Yuanpei flips the genre of the "dream" narrative, so that rather than projecting himself into an ideal future and awakening with wistful yearning, his dreamer "reliv[es] the hopes of his youth in his dream," then "awakens ... to discover [to his horror] that *nothing has changed*" (*Awakening China: Politics, Culture, and Class in the Nationalist Revolution* [Stanford: Stanford University Press, 1996], 61).

habit of *reading* twice, or at least with a *double* intent" recommended by Voltairine de Cleyre: i.e., in an empathetic or recollective reading that allows the reader "to feel what the writer felt" (a Romantic "hermeneutics of recollection") and in a skeptical reading that places the text at a distance from the reader (an Enlightenment "hermeneutics of suspicion").[30]

Bernard Lazare's *Les Porteurs de Torches* (*The Torch-Bearers*, 1897) and *La Porte d'Ivoire* (*The Gate of Ivory*, 1897) are particularly noteworthy for the way in which they consistently invert or bracket the "ready-made" meanings that these "transmitted" stories seem to suggest. One way that Lazare achieves this destabilization of conventional meaning is by playing with the generic code of the frame-story; just as, in *The Arabian Nights*, individual tales are embedded within the story of the storyteller (Scheherazade's game of survival, forestalling her death one night's tale at a time), Lazare presents his fables within a single, overarching narrative about their narrators. It might even be more accurate to say that he lets us *overhear* them, for the manner of the narration emphasizes orality: within these stories, tellers are often interrupted or challenged by listeners, and there is often a discussion of the tale's meaning subsequent to the telling which complicates or reverses its apparent meaning. Thus, in "Le Triomphe de l'Amour [The Triumph of Love]," we are presented with a pseudo-Oriental fable of a familiar form. The young nobleman, Çandilya (based loosely on a Hindu sage) ventures into the world to seek wisdom, achieving an impressive but superficial degree of learning, then is "humbled" into a sudden recognition of "the vanity of knowledge"; he subsequently retires into asceticism, becoming famous instead for being able to "spen[d] six months without taking food, standing on the toe of his right foot with his left leg resting on his loins." The encounter that humbles him is with a boy who repeats to him a tale *he* heard from an old woman on the banks of the Ganges concerning the lovers Sambadar and Saranya: while Sambadar is away on a voyage, his betrothed, Saranya, is bitten by a snake and dies, but after Sambadar prays to the love-god Kama, Saranya is miraculously resurrected. The moral of the story, claims the boy, is that "love was the highest of the gods," with the further significance that "to learn this truth, I did not even need to leave the banks of the Ganges."

30 de Cleyre, *Selected Works*, 379.

Thus, as "an old philosophy professor" comments, "Çandilya owed his saintliness to the words of an old woman, repeated by a child."[31]

At this point, it seems that we have a standard bit of Eastern mysticism: worldly knowledge, born of travel and education, is worthless beside the untutored virtues of love and piety, inverting social hierarchies (so that the poor knows better than the rich, the woman better than the man, the child better than the adult). There seems to be an additional symmetry between Çandilya's voyaging and the voyage of Sambadar, as if to suggest a repetition of the theme: in both cases, the greater value (truth, love) is to be found at home, not abroad.

However, the narrator of Çandilya's story is Western; it is Lazare's protagonist, Anselme, who himself has the story second hand from the "old philosophy professor"—whom Anselme introduces to us as a thoroughly disreputable source, a hypocrite who "seemed to delight in contradicting his thoughts by his actions." Moreover, Anselme does not allow the professor's gloss to stand as the last word. If "Çandilya owed his saintliness to the comments of an old woman, repeated by a child," he argues, this in turn implies that "he also owed it to one who was basically feeble-minded, for stupidity is a prerequisite for saintliness." We are abruptly jerked out of the Romantic frame of the folkloric narrative and returned to a suspicious, critical perspective from which the ready-made conclusion can be questioned and perhaps undone:

> Had Çandilya been more intelligent, he could have replied to the young man that he had not had in mind the selfish and particular love celebrated by the old woman from the outskirts of the city, but the vast, profound, subtle, intelligent love that allows one to know, understand, and serve men. But travel could teach Çandilya nothing, for Çandilya was a fool, and he was born to believe that wisdom resides in the wailings of the simple-minded as interpreted by sophists and soft-headed skeptics, philosophers of uncertainty—that is to say, the most conceited and foolish of men. That is why the only effort of which the prince found himself capable, after years of reflection, was to place his left foot on his loins.[32]

31 Lazare, *La Porte d'Ivoire*, 15–17.
32 Ibid., 17.

The swiftness of this second inversion might leave the reader reeling, uncertain of the direction of narrative gravity: Which narrator is to be trusted: Anselme? The professor? The boy? The old woman? Was Çandilya foolish to have thought to have found wisdom through worldly travel and learning, or was he foolish to have dismissed this wisdom too quickly as folly? Perhaps we are meant to adopt the latter position in the end, since the last words of this story—"That is why the only effort of which the prince found himself capable, after years of reflection, was to place his left foot on his loins"—echo those of the introduction to Çandilya's tale, in which we are made to marvel at "the ascetic Çandilya" who is capable of "spen[ding] six months without taking food, standing on the toe of his right foot *with his left leg resting on his loins.*" Since narrative conclusions are marked by symmetries like these, then it might seem that the weight of judgment is being thrown behind the value of active "effort" rather than ascetic passivity. All of this is given an additional twist of complication if we recall Anselme's comment that when he encountered this story in the professor's book, "I took the extreme pleasure of a child from that reading."[33] If reading like a child means being "simple-minded," i.e., overly trusting (the boy takes the old woman's words as true without question) and overly concrete (the boy confuses sensual, erotic love with intellectual, philosophical love), and if Anselme's relationship to the professor parallels the relationship between the old woman and the boy, is Anselme to be trusted?

This proliferation of ambiguities is deliberate. For Lazare, as Granier explains, the anarchist fable is calculated to produce, not to reduce, "uncertainty as to the meaning to be assigned to the work."[34] If this is a gospel, a means of transmitting the anarchist Idea and will to the reader, then it also attempts to ensure that this transmission requires the receiver to be active rather than passive, to exercise skepticism. It attempts to prevent the perpetuation of "followership," in Howard J. Ehrlich's term—the condition of Vallès's "Victimes du Livre."[35]

In this respect, too, the anarchist fable bears a certain resemblance to Christ's parables, which are also constructed so as to

---

33 Ibid., 10.

34 Granier, *Les Briseurs de formules*, 365.

35 Howard Ehrlich, "Anarchism and Formal Organizations," *Reinventing Anarchy, Again*, 65.

prevent a superficial, too-quick understanding, the solidification of the life-giving Word into the dead and deadening Letter. For all the (fully reciprocated) hostility of anarchism to the Church that makes a cult of "the rotting corpse from Nazareth,"[36] indeed, anarchists have frequently expressed their admiration for Jesus as martyred man of conviction (an honorary member of a long list of secular figures in the anarchist "martyrology"—of which more later) and itinerant idealist—at once a figure in the most powerful victim narrative ever told and a kind of extraterrestrial visitor. According to Temma Kaplan, the Spanish anarchists "often referred to Christ as the first anarchist, to themselves as Christians, and to their leaders as apostles"—sincerely, if also with self-conscious irony.[37] And so it is that, in anarchist stories, from the anonymously penned satire "The Christmas Adventures of Jesus" (1907)[38] to Han Ryner's novel-length *Cinquième évangile* (1911), a recurring character is none other than "the vagabond carpenter from Galilee," as the Mexican anarchist Antonio Díaz Soto y Gama called him, or in Gaston Couté's more pungent phrase, "the great anarchist tramp."[39]

---

36 Jason McQuinn, "The Life and Times of *Anarchy: A Journal of Desire Armed*: 25 Years of Critical Anarchist Publishing," *The Anarchist Library*, May 21, 2012 (web), 13.

37 Temma Kaplan, *Anarchists of Andalusia, 1868–1903* (Princeton, NJ: Princeton University Press, 1977), 85. Reimaginings of Jesus as anarchist are scattered throughout French, Portuguese, and Spanish anarchist literatures: see Granier, *Les Briseurs de Formules*, 118, 141–144, 352; João Freire, *Freedom Fighters: Anarchist Intellectuals, Workers, and Soldiers in Portugal's History*, trans. Maria Fernanda Noronha da Costa e Sousa (Montréal: Black Rose Books, 2001), 145; Gordon, *Anarchism in Brazil*, 220–221; Reinhold Görling, "El anarquismo como cultura proletaria en Andalucía: acercamiento al proceso de conservación y reforma de una cultura popular," in *El Anarquismo Español y sus Tradiciones Culturales*, ed. Bert Hofmann et al. (Frankfurt am Main: Iberoamericana, 1995), 150; and Jerome R. Mintz, *The Anarchists of Casas Viejas* (Bloomington, IN: Indiana University Press, 2004), 66–67.

38 *Mother Earth* 2.10 (Dec. 1907): 427–430.

39 Soto y Gama qtd. in John M. Hart, *Anarchism & the Mexican Working Class, 1860–1931* (Austin: University of Texas Press, 1978), 124; Couté qtd. in Granier, *Les Briseurs de formules*, 118.

3: OUTCAST NARRATIVES

"**I** created for myself a delusional role of a shadowy stranger, a roughish nomad," writes "Mack," the pseudonymous author-hero of *Evasion* (2001). Originally a zine, later released as a kind of autobiography (albeit one in which "all events ... are purely fictional—so, no, you can't use this as evidence") by the CrimethInc. Ex-Workers' Collective, *Evasion* promotes the romance of a train-hopping, nomadic lifestyle, supported by dumpster-diving, petty larceny, and a catalog of clever "scams" for the avoidance of work. While omitting much overt reference to the historical specifics (apart from a few coy references to "old hobo books"), *Evasion* can be placed in a tradition of anarchist road stories, ranging from fictional and allegorical novels, such as George Bonnamour's *Le Trimardeur* (1894), Adolphe Retté's *Similitudes* (1895), or Han Ryner's *Voyages de Psychodore, philosophe cynique* (1903), to life-writing in the manner of Robert Reitzel's *Abenteuer eines Grünen* (*Adventures of a Greenhorn,* 1900/1902), Harry Kemp's *Tramping On Life: An Autobiographical Narrative* (1922), or *Sister of the Road: The Autobiography of Boxcar Bertha* (1937), this last from the pen of the notorious Ben Reitman.

Reitman, the radical doctor and orator known in his day as "King of the Hoboes," also penned a long sequence of poems (never published) about sundry others of the men and women he met while riding the rails, which he called *Outcast Narratives*. A rather small selection of these short, sometimes stark, sometimes affectionate portraits, excerpted in a recent biography of Reitman, reveals that while each of these narratives—"Buffalo Slim," "Blinkey Morgan," "Ohio Skip"—can stand alone, they also demand to be read together:

Buffalo Slim

Buffalo Slim was a Tramp,
Twenty-two, and raised in the Buffalo Reform school.
He had a great passion for travel;
Had beat it from Coast to Coast in eight days.
He would deck it from Buffalo to Chicago in a night.
He was a member of the Lake Shore Gang....
That night in the Jungle when he saw
Blinkey look at Skip's Punk,
He knew there was going to be trouble.
As Skip was reaching for his gat he knifed him.
When Slim lay dying with a bullet in his lung, he said:
"Kid please go see my mother, and tell her—."

Blinkey Morgan

Blinkey Morgan was a Bum,
Fifty-three years old hailed from Boston.
He knew all the saloon keepers
In every division town between Boston and Chicago.
He was a bird at finding "blind pigs" in dry towns.
He was a member of the Lake Shore Gang....
One night when the Gang was having a gump stew
With three half barrels and a gallon of white line,
Blinkey whispered to Slim: "Get Skip stewed.
We Will cop his Punk and make the Fair at Fostoria."
Skip shot Slim and Blinkey.
As Blinkey died he said:
"Kid, if you want to see life, stick to the road."

Ohio Skip

Ohio Skip was a Hobo.
He was 37 and born in Columbus.
He used to work around Cleveland and Toledo.
His moniker was on all the water tanks,

On the B. &. O., Lake Shore and Pensie.
He was a member of the old Lake Shore Gang....
One night Skip blew into the Jungles.
With a 15-year-old Punk that he picked up in Toledo.
Blinkey and Slim tried to snare the Kid.
They were all stewed and an awful fight started.
When Skip lay dying with a knife in his kidney.
He said: "Kid go home. This is how we all end."

In Slim's story, Blinkey (his lover) and Skip (his killer) are third-person characters; in Skip's story, Blinkey (who is after Skip's lover) and Slim (who kills him in revenge for killing Blinkey) are third-person characters; and so on. Each intersection modifies how we understand each event (jealousy, anger, murder) and each participant (as victim, villain, both, neither). We are denied a stable position from which to adjudicate right and wrong. We are kept *on the move*.

The peculiar affinity, here, between form and content—the poems are narratives *about* "outcasts," and the manner in which they narrate these lives is *also* a casting-out, a perpetual wandering, a refusal of the safe shelter of destinations or conclusions—signals something of broader importance about how anarchists tell stories. It is not only due to the historical association of anarchism with immigrant populations or with radicalized hoboes that anarchist fiction displays a distinct obsession with characters who are in transit, with mobility and flight, with the nomadic condition. "My relatives were nomads," remarks the eponymous narrator of Manuel Rojas's novel, *Hijo de Ladrón*, "migrants from city to city, from country to country ... resisting, with varying success, the advances of the eight-hour work day, modern production methods and the regulation and regimentation of international travel." This resistance, he notes, makes them pariahs, "generally held in contempt, and not infrequently cursed, to whom the world, envious of their freedom, gradually bars all roads."[1] The potency of this image of "nomadism" as simultaneously a kind of curse (the archetype of the Wandering Jew is never far away) and a nobility (the Italian anarchist exiles liked to call themselves *cavalieri erranti*, "knights-errant") is not at all limited to the specific historical

---

1   Manuel Rojas, *Born Guilty: A Novel*, trans. Frank Gaynor (New York: Library Publishers, 1955), 10–11.

and material conditions that produced anarchist experiences of no-madism.[2] It is also a reimagination of the worker as, in the phrase of Deleuze and Guattari, "the heir to the nomad in the Western world."[3] As Pessin observes, even when anarchist organizing shifts toward more sedentary working-class populations, the figure of the tramp remains "a generative axis of the libertarian dream."[4] In libertarian fiction, the narrative of movement becomes one of the most potent figures for the movement of narrative itself.

Anarchist narratives attempt to deterritorialize the reader, to make us lose our spatial and temporal bearings, and thereby to dislodge us from our false consciousness, to pull us out of the "hierarchy where we know our place," as the narrator of Han Ryner's *Les Pacifiques* (1914) puts it. This "reactionary I-narrator ... steeped up to his ears in bourgeois ideas," as one anarchist reviewer puts it, will impart a perversely subversive thrust to Ryner's work.[5] A French traveler known by the single name "Jacques" (the same as Ryner's own given name: Jacques Élie Henri Ambroise Ner), he is a conservative soul, profoundly shaken by his encounter with the peaceful people named by the title, the inhabitants of an island utopia. Revolted by the Atlanteans' lack of respect for the pieties of French life (patriarchal order, military valor, marital rectitude, commercial success, the work ethic, and above all, "Progress"), Jacques retreats:

> Although reinstalled in my beloved fatherland and my old habits, there remains in my heart I know not what disturbance.... Whoever wants happiness and peace of mind must, I believe, descend far enough to see nothing other than the life to which he is condemned, to become incapable of even entertaining other possibilities or of failing to find them crazy and ridiculous.... Woe unto he who no longer asserts the immobile solidity of his horizon....
>
> From now on, I shall be the wise man who looks at everything from his own home, who refuses to leave behind his solid point

2 Dimas Antonio de Souza, *O Mito politico no teatro anarquista Brasileiro* (Rio de Janeiro: Achiamé, 2003), 72–74.

3 Gilles Deleuze and Félix Guattari, *A Thousand Plateaus: Capitalism and Schizophrenia* (London: Continuum, 2008), 623n61.

4 Pessin, *La Rêverie anarchiste*, 78–80.

5 Fritz Oerter, "Han Ryner: *Nelti*," *Der Syndikalist* 24 (1930): 1.

of view as a Frenchman and a man of the twentieth century. I will not consider anything under the aspect of eternity, I will not consent to the heartbreaking and humiliating effort of looking at my life from the perspective of Sirius or even of Atlantis. I know my duty: to lock myself in my enclosure and in my moment.[6]

Here, putting words in the mouth of his double, Ryner redoubles the rhetoric of "place" ("fatherland," "home," "point of view," "perspective," "horizon," "enclosure," etc.) as if to lay it on so thick that we can no longer see through it. Jacques's desire for security is so fierce that we are almost compelled to pull away from him, to experience his repulsion as repulsive. If this wish to be "at home" means being "immobile," "solid," "locked up," then I want nothing of it. I want to be able to "imagine away from the actual," as Paul Goodman puts it, to leave home, to wander, to be a traveler, a nomad.

"For anarchists," according to the Brazilian scholars Francisco Foot Hardman and Antonio Arnoni Prado, "the most significant works are those that have no known author, or rather those whose author is called the popular spirit or collective soul."[7] Is it any mystery then, that perhaps the most famous anarchist author in the world is at the same time—and *for the same reason*—the most obscure? In 1925, in a note attached to the German manuscript for his novel *Das Totenschiff* (*The Death Ship*)—which Albert Einstein supposedly once named as one of the books he would take with him to a desert island—the author, who signed himself B. Traven, wrote, "I would like to state very clearly: The biography of a creative person is absolutely unimportant. If that person is not recognizable in his works, then either he is worth nothing or his works are worth nothing. The creative person should therefore have no other biography than his works."[8] But Traven had, by that time, already gone to extreme lengths to disguise his own identity, and would continue to do so up to *and beyond* his death in 1969.

---

6   Han Ryner, *Les Pacifiques* (Paris: Eugène Figuière & Cie, 1914), 289–292.

7   Antonio Arnoni Prado and Francisco Foot Hardman, "Introduçã," in *Contos Anarquistas*, 17.

8   John Anthony West, "Foreword," in B. Traven, *The Death Ship: The Story of An American Sailor* (Brooklyn: L. Hill Books, 1991), iii; Traven qtd. in Will Wyatt, "Introduction," in B. Traven, *To the Honourable Miss S... And Other Stories*, ed. and trans. Peter Silcock (Westport, CT: L. Hill Books, 1981), vii.

If literary historians are not completely mistaken—and it is difficult to know how far they are mistaken—then the Death of the Author
was the very condition under which the writer who also called himself, at various times, Hal Croves, T. Torsvan, Traven Torsvan, Traven
Torsvan Croves, Berick Traven Torsvan, and Richard Maurhut, could
live. His birth date and original name are doubtful, but it seems apparent that the man known as Traven had previously written for the
anarcho-syndicalist newspaper *Der Ziegelbrenner* under the name
Ret Marut, another pseudonym.[9] The last issue of *Der Ziegelbrenner*
appeared in 1921, in defiance of the German authorities; Marut was a
wanted man, having barely escaped summary execution at the hands
of the paramilitary Freikorps for his enthusiastic participation in Bavarian revolt of 1919.[10] Fleeing Germany, briefly jailed in London,

---

9   Nobody agrees on where, when, and under what name the man who
    signed his writings "B. Traven" was born. He may, at various times, have
    been a restaurant owner, a dancer, an archaeologist, a sailor, an actor, a
    deadbeat dad, a student of philosophy. He died a Mexican citizen, living
    under another false name. Some biographers claimed that he had been
    an American, born in Chicago, possibly a Wobbly, who had emigrated
    to Mexico after spending time at sea. Others claimed that he had proba-
    bly been Swedish or Norwegian. More exotic identities were attributed
    to him: he was said to be a pen name for Jack London, for Ambrose
    Bierce, for the boxer and Surrealist poet Arthur Cravan, for an illegit-
    imate child of Kaiser Wilhelm II (Larry Rohter, "His Widow Reveals
    Much Of Who B. Traven Really Was," *New York Times*, June 25, 1990,
    C13, C16). John Huston, the American director of the film adaptation
    of Traven's *Treasure of the Sierra Madre*, suspected (but was "never com-
    pletely convinced") that a man who arrived on the set presenting himself
    as Traven's "agent," Hal Croves was actually Traven (Roy Pateman, *The
    Man Nobody Knows: The Life and Legacy of B. Traven* [Lanham, MD:
    University Press of America, 2005], 6). Complicating things, Traven's
    works were published in English, German, and Spanish, and it is not
    always clear which versions were the originals (Sheilah R. Wilson, "The
    Fantasy of Bruno Traven: Macario," *Latin American Literary Review* 3.6
    [Spring, 1975]: 17n1; Michael L. Baumann, "The Question of Idioms in
    B. Traven's Writings," *The German Quarterly* 60.2 [Spring 1987]: 171–
    192). One biographer claimed, in 1981, to have finally identified him
    as Otto Feige, born on February 23, 1882 in Schwiebus, Germany, now
    part of Poland (Wyatt, "Introduction," XII–XIII). This theory has since
    been disputed, and the International B. Traven Society biography merely
    declares: "Place and date of birth are unknown" ("About B. Traven: Brief
    Biography," 2010 [web]).
10 Wyatt, "Introduction," IX–X.

then somehow slipping the traces and making his way to Tampico, Marut reinvented himself as B. Traven—a name that, as his widow observed, sounds a little like the English word "betrayed."[11] But by withholding his "real" name from the world, B. Traven fulfilled, rather than betrayed, the ambition of Ret Marut, who resisted too-curious questions from readers as so many "attempt[s] ... to pin me down," declaring: "I want to be nothing but—the word."[12] In exile, he became "freer than anybody else," capable of endless self-reinvention: "I am free to choose the parents I want, the country I want, the age I want."[13] Contrast this with the poor monarch in Marut's fable, "Der Schauspieler und der König [The Actor and the King]" (1919), who cannot so choose. The king is amused by the fact that his friend the actor can "play" a king, but insists that "there remains an unbridge-able abyss between a real king and a theatrical king": "However re-markable your performance as a king, you cease to be a king as soon as the curtain descends.... Whereas I, my dear fellow, I remain a king even when I lie in my bed!" The actor harshly reminds the king that he, too, derives his power from an audience: "If these people should ever cease to play their parts as unpaid extras, then you also—and not only in your bed, but also in the clear light of day—you also, my friend, will cease to be a real king!"[14] Identity is revealed to be a fic-tion—an alibi, a passport, an indictment on trumped-up charges. Its power and its poverty are two sides of the same phenomenon.

What would it mean, Marut and Traven ask us, to leave both the power and the poverty of identity behind? To be "freer than anybody else"? The author bio accompanying Félix Martí-Ibáñez's short story collection, *All the Wonders We Seek: Thirteen Tales of Surprise and Prodigy* (1963), presents, on the contrary, a man who is thoroughly decorated with identifications:

> Born in Cartagena, Spain, Felix Marti-Ibanez received his Doc-torate in Medicine from the Medical School of the University of Madrid. He then practiced psychiatry in Barcelona and lectured

---

11 Donald O. Chankin, *Anonymity and Death: The Fiction of B. Traven* (Uni-versity Park: Pennsylvania State University Press, 1975), 123n42.

12 Marut qtd. in Wyatt, "Introduction," ix.

13 B. Traven, according to Rosa Elena Luján qtd. in Rohter, "His Widow," C16.

14 Traven, *To the Honourable Miss S...*, 28–29.

throughout Spain on psychology, medical history, art and literature. During this period, he also edited several medical and literary journals and wrote novels and many books on the history of medicine and psychology. In 1937 he was appointed General Director of Public Health and Social Services of Catalonia, and later, Secretary of Public Health and Social Service for Spain. Dr. Marti-Ibanez came to reside in the United States in 1939 and subsequently became an American citizen. He has participated in the International Congresses of History of Medicine, History of Science, Psychology, and Psychiatry, held in Amsterdam, Paris, Stockholm, Nice and Zurich.[15]

And so on for three more paragraphs of awards and publications. What is left unmentioned, in this apparently exhaustive list of distinctions, is that at the time of his service to Catalonia and Spain, it was unclear whether these nations numbered one, two, or three: the Spanish Civil War was in full swing, and the anarchist CNT-FAI faction had agreed, in order to fight off the fascist forces of Generalissimo Franco, to enter into the Catalonian and Spanish Republican governments. The young doctor Martí-Ibáñez was working as a representative of the anarchist faction, and in order to emigrate to the U.S., he had to flee for his life across the Pyrenees with the remnants of the antifascist forces. He in fact was, and had long been known as, an anarchist.

Born in 1911,[16] his polymath abilities were evident early on: as a

---

15 Félix Martí-Ibáñez, *All the Wonders We Seek: Thirteen Tales of Surprise and Prodigy* (New York: C.N. Potter, 1963), 449–450.

16 Strangely, even such a basic fact of his biography is widely disputed by the literature. J.J. López-Ibor has the year of his birth as 1903 ("Félix Martí-Ibáñez, 1903–1972," *Actas luso-españolas de neurología, psiquiatría y ciencias afines* 2.2 [March 1974]: 147), and according to Rafael Llavona and Javier Bandrés, Martí-Ibáñez was born on Christmas Day in 1911 ("Psicología y Anarquismo en la Guerra Civil Española: La Obra de Félix Martí-Ibáñez." *Psicothema* 10.3 [1998]: 669), and while Richard Cleminson, an expert on the subject, refers to him as having been "born in Cartagena, in southeast Spain, in 1913" ("Sexuality and the Revolution of Mentalities," *Anarchist Studies* 5.1 [1997]: 46), the finding aids to Martí-Ibáñez's personal papers at Yale, established some thirty years ago, have his birth date as 1915 (Yale University Library, *Preliminary Guide to the Félix Martí-Ibáñez Papers*, 2012, 3 [web]). I am relying on the account of José Pardo Tomás in "Félix

medical student at the University of Madrid specializing in psychiatry, he wrote his dissertation on the psychology and physiology of Indian mysticism (1935) while making a reputation for himself through his contribution to anarchist publications like *Estudios, Tiempos Nuevos*, and *Ruta* of articles on sexual issues.[17] His take on sexuality and gender norms is refreshingly libertarian and egalitarian for the times, and, while he exercised authority, he made it a priority to provide working-class women with unrestricted access to abortion and family-planning services—putting Catholic Catalonia well in advance of the rest of Europe. In the middle of all this, the young doctor penned two novels: *Yo, Rebelde: Novela Juvenil y de Inquietudes*, published by the Biblioteca Estudios (1936), and *Aventura: Poema de Juventudes* (1938), published by the FIJL (Federación Ibérica de Juventudes Libertarias, or Libertarian Youth Federation, the youth wing of the FAI).

All the Wonders We Seek is dedicated to William Somerset Maugham, whose short stories, according to Maugham's biographer, were much prized by Martí-Ibáñez after he discovered them while recovering from wounds sustained in battle. "The writer of fiction," Maugham counseled the young emigré, "must take care that his special interests do not cause harm to his fiction"; in particular, he disapproved of a story Martí-Ibáñez had sent him which amounted, in his opinion, to "propaganda in condemnation of the atom bomb."[18] Was the counsel heeded? The fiction Martí-Ibáñez wrote in exile—like his essays—meticulously avoids reference to anarchism.[19] However, we can also detect a certain refusal to surrender the libertarian dream. "In our hurried life," the doctor writes, "[we] do not dream enough, and daydreams are important." He admits to being a "romantic": "To be romantic means that a man lets his heart go to

Martí-Ibáñez (1911–1972): perfil(s) d'un metge del segle XX a les portes del segle XXI," in *Salut i societat a les portes del segle XXI: Memorial Félix Martí-Ibáñez*, eds. José Pardo Tomás and Álvaro Martínez Vidal (Barcelona: Residència d'Investigadors CSIC-Generalitat de Catalunya, 2006).

17 Richard Cleminson, "Anarchist, Poet and Sex Radical: the *Estudios* writings (1934–7) of Dr. Félix Martí-Ibáñez," *International Journal of Iberian Studies* 12.1 (1999): 17, 21.

18 Martí-Ibáñez, *All the Wonders We Seek*, IX; Ted Morgan, *Maugham* (New York: Simon and Schuster, 1979): 493.

19 A forthcoming study (with Montserrat Feu-López) will look more closely at the degree to which Martí-Ibáñez may indeed have sold his ideals and his soul in the New World.

his head ... [adopting] a quixotic attitude, a sort of magic lens that transfigures the world and its inhabitants so that they can be viewed in a different perspective."[20]

Martí-Ibáñez sent stories to American science fiction and fantasy magazines.[21] They are florid, dreamy, filled with a kind of exuberance that is at the same time strangely melancholy. A "recurring theme," Evelyn C. Leeper notes, is "the desire to escape from 'the common-place and hopeless.'"[22] In "The Star Hunt," for example, a grouchy, punctilious pharmacist, Don Zoilo, "goes out one morning on an er-rand and finds himself drawn into a series of extraordinary adventures far beyond his normal banal existence." Yet Don Zoilo experiences all of this as an assault on his person, on his sense of what is right, "re-spectable," rational, and real. "I think I am going mad," he protests to one of his magical abductors, a violet-eyed girl who frequents his shop but whom he has never noticed before; "You must be joking." "There's nothing funny about this," the girl retorts:

> Your world is confined to your drugstore and your bottles. Your imagination stops at your prescriptions. You never even noticed the young girl who day in day out sat at her sewing machine looking out her window at a tiny fragment of street. One can stand that sort of existence only so long and no more. One day something bursts in one's heart like a spring, and one can bear it no longer. Either one escapes from the cage or one suffocates.[23]

"The cage" seems to be something like what Freud called the "real-ity principle" (the tendency to avoid pain, as opposed to the "pleasure principle" that drives us to seek greater pleasure); indispensable as a means of self-preservation and adjustment to the contours of the nat-ural and social worlds, pain-avoidance can overtake pleasure-seeking

---

20 Martí-Ibáñez, *Ariel*, 35; *The Mirror of Souls, and Other Essays* (New York: C.N. Potter, 1972), 296.

21 *Magazine of Fantasy & Science Fiction* publishes "Senhor Zumbeira's Leg" (December 1962) and "Niña Sol" (May 1963); *Weird Tales* carries "Be-tween Two Dreams" (May 1953), "A Tomb in Malacor" (September 1954), and after his death—appropriately—"The Buried Paradise" (Fall 1973).

22 Evelyn C. Leeper, "This Week's Reading," *The MT Void* 27.46 (May 15, 2009).

23 Martí-Ibáñez, *All the Wonders We Seek*, 36.

to such an extent that we hobble ourselves, limiting our explorations to what social conventions have decreed safe. No wonder the process that takes Don Zoilo out of his tidy routine, which others experience as self-fulfillment and liberation, feels to him like a threat to his very being, a cracking-apart of the world. What would our world look like if the pleasure principle were given a wider field for expression, if we were not the prisoners of our identity-fictions but their authors?

In "The Threshold of the Door," Martí-Ibáñez imagines such a world in the form of a parallel dimension. A visitor from the parallel-dimensional Caracas teaches an inhabitant of the mundane Caracas to step sideways into his "poetic world" where the desires of each intersect with the desires of every other—a heady, magic-realist take on the utopian socialist Charles Fourier's "new loving world," one might say. In Fourier's utopia, nobody would ever "work"—i.e., do anything he or he didn't want to—but productive activity would be constant, driven by "passional attraction." Likewise, in Martí-Ibáñez's "poetic world," as the mysterious visitor explains, "everyone's desires complement everyone else's":

> "In *your* world you are a wheel that spins around things. Here, everything spins around you. Why do you think all these people have listened to you all day? Why have they willingly given you caviar and champagne instead of coffee and toast? Why did the conductor steer the streetcar into a street where there are no tracks? Why did the girl accept your love? Because in this world everything centers around *you*."
>
> "But what about the others?"
>
> "Everyone here is lord and master of himself. If they followed you in your desires and whims, it was because these fitted in perfectly with their own desires and whims. In carrying out your fantastic dreams you were actually helping the others to carry out theirs. You are the center diamond in the crown, but so are the others. That is what is so marvelous about this world.... The waiter who served your exotic breakfast had always dreamed of doing just that; the aviary attendant had dreamed many times of freeing his birds, and so on down the line. In this world, unrealized desires, the lost I's, the unlived lives, all are fulfilled."

If this fantasy seems purely fantastic, it is only by way of literary flourish. The organizing principles of the "poetic world" are essentially the same as those of the CNT-FAI: when individuals join in mutual aid, their egoistic pleasure-seeking becomes a social principle. Pierre-Joseph Proudhon borrows a similar metaphor from Pascal to describe the non-authoritarian structure of anarchy, comparing it to a sphere: "*its centre is everywhere, its circumference nowhere.*"[24] If there is a gap between Proudhon's rational description of anarchy (mutuality, free contract, federation...) and Martí-Ibáñez's romantic description of it (absurd coincidences, parallel worlds, mysterious convergences of strangers...), it is the gap between 1936 and 1963. The possible, having lost its chance to become real, returns disguised as the impossible.

This is how dreams live in exile. "The wideness of the world used to provide a constant escape," the Czech novelist Milan Kundera reflects in an interview. "A soldier could desert from the army and start another life in a neighboring country. Suddenly, in our century, the world is closing around us."[25] This closure of the world, its "transformation into a trap," would seem to make impossible the kind of novel that allowed for radical imagination in the age of Enlightenment—Diderot's *Supplement to the Voyage of Bougainville* (1772), for instance, or Swift's *Travels into Several Remote Nations of the World* ... or, *Gulliver's Travels* (1726/1735); once the world is thoroughly mapped, carved up into territories by empires, traversed by steamships, railways, and telegraph lines, photographed and cataloged by anthropologists, there are no longer any empty oceans for a Laputa to float above; no spaces left for Diderot's "noble savage," Orou, to speak from, denouncing the hypocrisies and miseries of European civilization. This conquest of space eliminates the interstices between the nodes of "civilization" within which alternatives could unfold in relative peace, left alone for a while, such as the utopian colonies of Nauvoo, New Harmony, or Modern Times in the United States of America, or refuges from capitalism like the escaped slaves' *quilombos*, the anarchist Colônia Cecília, or the settlement of Canudos

---

24 Pierre-Joseph Proudhon, *General Idea of the Revolution in the Nineteenth Century*, trans. John Beverley Robinson (Mineola, NY: Dover Publications, 2004), 282.

25 Milan Kundera, *The Art of the Novel* (New York: Grove Press, 1988), 27.

in Brazil. Narratives that rely on movement through space to achieve a change of perspective become more desperate, more fleeting. They become fugitive narratives.

The trope of the anarchist as nomad (fugitive, exile, immigrant) permits anarchist fiction to turn the condition of placelessness into a technique for displacing the reader, jarring us out of *our* fixed identities. In "El Trampolín [The Springboard]" (1929), Manuel Rojas invites us to make just such a leap. A transnational figure like Traven or Martí-Ibáñez (born in Argentina to Chilean parents, growing up in the proletarian milieus of both countries), Rojas is attuned to border-crossings, to margins and those who dwell on them, to boundaries and those who transgress them. "There are many who do not believe in luck," the narrator of his story tells us:

> They say that everything is determined and that nothing happens that does not obey fixed, unchanging laws, leading to such-and-such facts, and that man cannot escape what fate has in store. But there is undoubtedly a wide margin of unforeseen events, a sort of escape hatch from the determined and prescribed, a refuge from the fatal, a trampoline for blind leaps into the unknown [*saltos de la suerte*].[26] It can be coincidence, happenstance, whatever you like, but it exists, and I want to prove it by telling you about a particular case.[27]

The case is as follows: a pair of friends taking the train from Valparaíso to Santiago find themselves seated behind a police officer ("*el agente*") escorting a prisoner to jail. Talking to the officer and his charge, the officer informs them that the prisoner murdered his friend, a fellow worker in the nitrate mines. The prisoner explains that it was all a drunken accident, playing with a knife, but in the eyes of the law, he has been found guilty. At a stop, the officer leaves his seat to buy a snack from one of the vendors on the platform, but takes the wrong door, and stepping out in front of an oncoming locomotive, is instantly killed. The narrator instantly realizes:

---

26 *Saltos de la suerte* could more accurately be translated as "lucky breaks," but not without losing the metaphor of the *salto*, the leap.
27 Rojas, *El Delincuente*, 55.

Death had opened an escape hatch for the man to escape the pre-
scribed and determined, and I was the only one who could step
through it or close it again, because nobody but me, the casual ob-
server of the accident, could recognize a police officer in that heap
of flesh and tell what happened. Did the man deserve to be given
an opportunity to get rid of his sentence? I think so and thought
so as well considering that he was innocent, at least in principle.
His remorse and sorrow were already enough of a weight on his
soul. Moreover, the only interested party, under compulsion of his
job, which served the sentence of the man, was the officer, and the
officer had died. Justice, the abstract person, had lost its representative; until another appeared, the man was free. I thought...

But I did not think; I entered the car and decided to help the
man jumping on the trampoline of luck.

To land where he may.[28]

The passing train has made the neatest possible slice between the moral
and the legal, interrupting the sad, pitiless automatism of the law to
present a moment of stunning clarity. Instead of assuming their roles
as "agents" of the law (*agent*: one who acts *in place of*, a deputy or delegate, a representative), the narrator and his friend act instead as free
agents (*agent*: one who *acts*). They take the leap, refusing to identify
with the "abstract person" of legal justice: they help hide the prisoner's
handcuffs until they can free him from them, urging him to run away.

Evasion, as we have seen, is one name of the game in a post-sixties
U.S., in a time and place where revolution has vanished behind the
historical horizon. In such a situation, it is perhaps no surprise that
anarchist resistance culture should seize upon the old theme of the
hobo, "prefiguring" the abolition of the class system by deserting the
working class unilaterally. That the resistance this presents to capitalism and the State is minimal, that the freedom it produces is private and transitory, are the subject of Murray Bookchin's widely read
broadside (1995) against what he gave the enduring label of "lifestyle
anarchism"—"a playground for juvenile antics," "'personal insurrection' rather than social revolution."[29] Indeed, Mack's picaresque

---

28 Ibid., 60.
29 Murray Bookchin, *Social Anarchism or Lifestyle Anarchism: An Unbridge-
able Chasm* (Oakland, CA: AK Press, 1995).

(anti-)narrative, with its deliberate defiance of any teleological direction (the chapters are numbered in reverse order, from "5" to "1"), seems to invite Bookchin's critique of an aesthetic centering on "episodic adventures," which he traces to

> the steady withdrawal of self-styled anarchists these days from the social domain that formed the principal arena of earlier anarchists, such as anarcho-syndicalists and revolutionary libertarian communists ... into a crude egotism that feeds on the larger cultural decadence of present-day bourgeois society.[30]

The publishers of *Evasion* are, of course, aware of such objections. In a postface, "Holden Caulfield, Commando for CrimethInc. People's Liberation Front" answers these charges in advance:

> *Mere temporary, partial, individual solution!* will cry the radical old guard, always suspicious of anyone whose resistance to capitalism begins with her own life and for her own sake—and they're right, of course. But that is exactly what is called for right now ... since without them we are simply paralyzed, hopeless, unable to find even a starting place.
>
> These solutions are *temporary*, because it is absurd to seek a sustainable life in an *unsustainable* world—better do whatever it takes to create new options, and go from there. They are *partial* solutions, for each of us is a fragment of the world that makes us, and can only act back on it as such. And they are *individual*, so other individuals can take them, revise them, apply them in their own ways in their own lives, without needing to wait for a mass movement to come along to save the day. That mass movement will proceed from the solutions hit upon by individuals, or else it will never come at all.[31]

That these "solutions" are more easily practiced by certain "individuals" does not escape Bookchin's attention, however. Without explicitly naming gender, age, ability, and racial privilege as such (though with a sharp eye to class privilege), he observes that

30 Ibid., 2.
31 In Mack, *Evasion* (Atlanta, GA: CrimethInc, 2003), 119.

the *intentional* poverty, homelessness, unemployment, and vagrancy of the neo-hobo is, perversely, a "luxury" that not everyone can afford.[32] Such narratives run the risk of rewriting Huck Finn's infamous "evasion"—the retreat into a white fantasy of escape, at the slave's expense.[33]

Where is there to run, in a world where all the magic doors have been closed? Is the no-place called "utopia" still accepting immigrants at all?

---

32 Bookchin, *Social Anarchism*, 24; Laura Portwood-Stacer, *Lifestyle Politics and Radical Activism* (New York: Verso, 1999), 139–140.

33 See *The Adventures of Huckleberry Finn*, ch. 39. Interestingly, "Mack" has since resurfaced to endorse a friend's business-success manual (Sophia Amoruso's *#Girlboss*)—a transition he finds totally unastonishing: "If I had to sum up the fundamental shift undergone by anyone who takes the (very few) good parts of anarchy-ism and brings them onward to greener pastures, I think it is best captured in this quote from serial entrepreneur Eben Pagan: '[the transition requires] moving from a value extraction paradigm to a value creation paradigm.'" Nonetheless, he smugly quotes Amoruso: "You know, those tricks we used to do... I use them in business every day" ("From the Food Bank to Making Bank," *Huffington Post*, May 6, 2014). For most anarchists of any time and place, it would be hard to write a more damning indictment of *Evasion*, and perhaps of CrimethInc, than this.

4: FROM CRETINOLÂNDIA TO COMMON-SENSE COUNTRY

STEP aboard the train to utopia—do you have a second-class ticket, or are you perhaps clambering aboard a boxcar, hoping to hell the railroad bulls don't find you?—and let Zoais (a.k.a. Luis García Muñoz, instructor at the Institución Libre de Enseñanza de Valladolid and regular contributor to the anarchist journals *Tierra y Libertad* and to *El Látigo*, where this story appears) be your conductor:

SWALLOWS!

(Ideal Voyage)

All along the way, like a magical pentagram, run the telegraph cables upon which the black swallows perch, looking like diabolical notes in fantastic dances, warbling and trilling the arpeggios to the beautiful hymn of their morning song, like a chant of honor offered up to a new day being born in the East.

The diamond beads of dew forming a charmingly decorated diadem, the colorful little flowers with their unfurling corollas offered a kiss of love to the breaking dawn.

The train is running its vertiginous race like a monstrous serpent of iron, its black exhalations forming a wake like a sad streamer of expired night, gnashing its iron muscles with a hammering sound.

As if through a movie-theater screen, scenes of light and beauty appear in the windows, and the trees seem to pass as swiftly as warriors in a vegetable army.

The shrill whistle of the locomotive announces the entry of the vehicle into a tunnel. The darkness is all-consuming, and the iron echoes are louder. It looks as if we are on a path leading into the infernal abyss. Time passes. The light comes forth to kiss us. The tunnel is behind us, and the monster ventures proudly from his burrow. The smoke that bursts forth is white, like incense spilled in praise of the Sun that extends its life-giving rays over the horizon.

The scenery looks more beautiful, and even the swallows are happy.

We have arrived.

"Anarchy. An eternity!" repeats the powerful voice that vibrates like a judgment.

"Freedom, Happiness, Love!" resonates in space. We have reached the end of our voyage. We are in the Free Land.[1]

The breathless lyricism of this "ideal voyage" could make us miss the poetics of horror that initiate it: *diabolical, vertiginous, monstrous, infernal.* Why should this Dantesque language be the vehicle for a journey to the Free Land? Perhaps before we are ready to leap into utopia, we need to experience the present as something other than concretely, mundanely, incontestably real. Otherwise, fear bars the way.

If utopia is, by definition, the vision of our desires fulfilled, then it would seem to be the least frightening thing in the world: can we want *not* to get what we want? The reception-history of utopias after the French Revolutions of 1789 and 1848 (and even more so after the Russian Revolution of 1917) can be read as a series of attempts to answer that question "yes." In a humor magazine from 1893, thus, we find an image of anarchy *as* a state of misery—indeed, something very like Hobbes's notion of the State of Nature as a war of all against all, if the crows picking at the bones of the dead lying in the street are any indication. Crippled, ragged, and above all friendless, the "limited member of the Future Society" is precisely a member of nothing; the caricaturist takes it as self-evident that anarchy is the opposite of "society," that an anarchist "civilization" is a contradiction in terms (fig. 1). This figure of the miserable tramp is the scarecrow posted at the gates of our civilization, now as then. We are scared away

---

1   Zoais, "¡Golondrinas!"

IDÉAL ANARCHISTE, par Assus.

Un membro réduit de la Société de Demain.

Fig. 1: "THE ANARCHIST IDEAL, by Assus / A limited member of the Future Society," from *Le Charivari oranais et algérien*, Dec. 17, 1893.

from thinking of a better world by the production of images of our fears: fear of poverty, of violence, and above all (for this is what they amount to), *fear of one another*.

Utopia has been successfully transformed into an object not only of ridicule, but of terror, by the evocation of a series of such scarecrows:

• *The demon within*: Utopias ignore the greed and violence inherent in human nature.

• *The demon without*: Utopias, as perfect societies, cannot stand contamination from "the outside"; they crumble at the least contact.

• *The ignorant masses*: Utopian ideals—including sexual freedom, internationalism, and atheism as well as the abolition of money and government—are hatched by eggheads, bohemians, rootless intellectuals; they will never be popular among ordinary, uneducated people, who are by nature conservative, nationalistic, and backwards-looking, fearful of change.

• *The impossibility of rupture*: Utopias require violent beginnings; there is no possible transition from the status quo to another system except through unthinkable disruption and cruelty.[2]

What is needed, to resist these appeals to fear of the unknown, is encouragement. "If you walk straight toward the [door] frame without fear," the mysterious stranger in Félix Martí-Ibáñez's "The Threshold of the Door" tells the narrator, "I promise you that you shall enter the poetic world whole and safe."[3] So Vicente Carreras ends his utopian sketch, "Acraciápolis," published in *La Revista Blanca* (1902):

> Those who read this description and like it, if they want to go there, just tell them that the road is well known: always follow the road of social revolution.
>
> They will encounter many obstacles and dangers during the journey, but they must not lose heart; if they have courage and perseverance, it will come; have no fear, it will come.[4]

And so it is that the way to Acraciápolis happens to run through Cretinolândia, where the worst has *already happened*.

If the name Cretinolândia—the title of a story by an anarchist writing under the name "Lanceta" in Gigi Damiani's (1876–1953) São Paulo journal, *Guerra Sociale*, in 1917—does not appear on any of our maps, it nonetheless seems to have a capital, Cretinópolis (the title of a 1901 story by Charles Malato, appearing in *La Revista Blanca*), and forms part of the larger continent of Anathemasia, as described by social geographer Louisa S. Bevington (1845–1895); Ben Reitman's 1910 lecture on "The Geography of the Underworld and the Mental Topography of the Educator" would seem to place Cretinolândia somewhere in the "Ocean of Despair," possibly adjacent to the "Land of Respectability."[5] In "this special region of the globe,"

---

2 Cf. Paul Goodman: "In a modern massive complex society, it is said, any rapid global 'revolutionary' or 'Utopian' change can be incalculably destructive" ("Anarchism and Revolution," *Drawing the Line*, 266).

3 Martí-Ibáñez, *All the Wonders We Seek*, 288.

4 Vicente Carreras, "Acraciápolis: Cuento," *La Revista Blanca* 1.6.103 (October 1, 1902): 234.

5 Malato's Cretinópolis is run by monkeys (significantly bearing the names

the land of stupidity, Lanceta says, "what was going on was fantastic, absurd, inconceivable":

> In this country there existed *tantalic* hunger, a kind of hunger that did not exist in other regions because the natives were starving to death in front of crowded grocery stores.
>
> On the crowded pier were sacks and sacks of sugar, beans, and other foodstuffs, which were exported abroad for a dirt-cheap price. Within the country these same things cost three times more than the price at which they were sold abroad.[6]

Of course, the paradox of exporting food while starving at home could serve as a description of the conditions that are guaranteed to arise from time to time anywhere the commodification of the means of living has made the very lives of their producers a secondary consideration. This is, however, the most literal description of what was happening in Brazil at the time of writing: Brazil's bean exports, for instance, negligible as recently as 1914, jumped more than ten-thousandfold over the next three years, three-quarters of this bounty flowing into the United States, while its domestic food prices spiked, soaring twenty to 150 times their previous levels in the first half of 1917.[7] The intolerability, the irrationality and injustice of the situation is brought into glaring focus precisely by defamiliarizing it, by displacing it, setting it in another kind of nowhere: a dystopia.

---

of established authors) who cage human beings, in an "world turned upside down" reminiscent of *Planet of the Apes*; Louisa S. Bevington's Anathemasia has a mock-credo featuring such motley articles of faith as "the Mammon of the Money-Bag, of the Statute, and of the Holy Church is all one.... This is the Capitalistic Faith, which except a man believe faithfully he may possibly be saved. / Glory be taken from the Money-Bag, and from the Statute, and from the Holy Church. / As it was in the beginning so it isn't now, nor ever will be again. Progress without end. Amen" (*Chiefly a Dialogue: Concerning Some Difficulties of a Dunce* [London: "Freedom" Office, 1895], 14). For Reitman's "geography," see Tim Cresswell, *The Tramp in America* (London: Reaktion, 2001), 72–8.

6 Lanceta, "Na cretinolândia," *Contos Anarquistas*, 58–59, italics mine.
7 *Encyclopedia Americana: A Library of Universal Knowledge* (New York, Chicago: Encyclopedia Americana Corporation, 1918), 4.434–435; Dulles, *Anarchists and Communists in Brazil*, 43.

A kind of dystopian or "delirious" realism—the careful representation of the present and real as a nightmarish impossibility—is a hallmark of many works of anarchist fiction;[8] indeed, it is only one extension of the principle of *inverosimilitud* employed by Adrián del Valle and others. As Auguste Linert wrote in the journal *L'Art Social:* "It seems to me that drama must be terrible to be true, or at least sincere."[9] Surprisingly, it is a feature of many anarchist utopian fictions as well. Joseph Déjacque's utopia, *L'Humanisphère* (1859), employs just such devices.

L'Humanisphère, serialized in Déjacque's journal *Le Libertaire*, opens with a grandiose history of humanity's errancy, culminating in the all-too-recent bloodbath that was the suppression of the 1848 revolutions. Thus he conjures up the spectacle of an army "conquer[ing], with a very military bravery, the boulevards of Paris, these boulevards where one faced an army of marchers, arm in arm, of all ages and all sexes," as well as an entire litany of

> Judges, informers, legislators and torturers,... Priests,... Bankers, tradesmen, usurers, leeches upon the production for which the producer is such an easy prey,... Rich men,... Lawyers,... Baliffs, solicitors and notaries,... Doctors of public instruction, who have the faculty to develop the children of the society in the name of scholarly or clerical cretinism,... All of you, finally, who are opulent in opprobrium, abusers of authority upon whom fortune smiles in the way that prostitutes smile from the threshold of houses of disrepute; debauched by Christian decadence, corrupting and corrupted ...

—a veritable "phantasmagoria of titled, mitered, braided, silver- and copper-plated, verdegrised ghosts" that will flee before the new humanity.[10] Technological progress is rendered monstrous by its one-sidedness: steam power is personified as "the monster with the iron body, the raucous voice, the lungs of flame, leaves far behind it

---

8   Granier, *Les Briseurs de formules*, 317.

9   Linert qtd. in Xavier Durand, "L'art social au théâtre," *Le Mouvement Social* 91 (April–June 1975): 16–17.

10 Joseph Déjacque, *L'Humanisphère* (Bruxelles: Administration, 1899), 65–69.

the horse-drawn carriage and the stagecoach," "the slave at a million wheels."[11] We watch in horror as a "Civilization ... infected with an incurable disease"—"the disease [that] bears the name of authority," "*usurian* disease"—grows from error to error, takes a "poison that it mistakes for an elixir": "This poison, a mixture of nicotine and arsenic, has but one word on its label: *God*."[12] We are invited to recoil in disgust before the prospect of sexual relations in "civilization," a word that comes to sound increasingly dirty, as all desires are made "filthy" by coercion and bribery: "In the civilized world ... the spirit is a sewer of contemptible thoughts, the flesh a drain for filthy pleasures. In this epoch, men and women don't make love, they do their duties." Women, not free to love as they choose, are "sold" like "cashmere," "petticoats," or "beef stew." "If the men of the future could have an image of ... this profanation of the flesh and of human thought, this crapularisation of love," Déjacque writes, "they would shiver in horror as we ourselves would shiver, in a dream, at the thought of a dreadful reptile squeezing us in his cold, fatal coils and gushing its tepid, poisonous spittle in our faces."[13] Only by converting the world we take for real and normal into a nauseating "phantasmagoria" can Déjacque make us believe in his alternative vision: "Civilized, civilized, I say to you: the mirage is not a mirage, the Utopia is not a Utopia; what you take for a phantom is the reality!"[14] And vice versa, what you take for reality is a phantom.

This, too, is the technique favored by Louise Michel in *L'Ère Nouvelle* and *Le Monde Nouveau* (*The New World*, 1888). Both of these futuristic, utopian narratives begin in something very close to the style of her denunciatory novels of the present, such as *Les Microbes Humains* (*The Human Microbes*, 1886), which indeed forms a kind of first volume to *Le Monde Nouveau*, or *Le Claque-Dents* (*The Grifter*, 1890). All feature mutually entangled parallel plotlines involving such events as "kidnappings, abductions of children by an unscrupulous pimp, serial murders carried out by a respectable scholar, arrests of innocent victims"—they are, as her biographer complains "impossible to summarize"—drawing mainly on the traditions of

---

11 Ibid., 58.
12 Ibid., 80–81, 142, 158, 30.
13 Ibid., 106.
14 Ibid., 86.

Gothic melodrama and the serial novel associated with Eugène Sue's *The Mysteries of Paris*, but blended incongruously with the adventure novel, detective fiction, and burlesque, and characterized by a dark, grotesque style. If they are absurd, what could be more absurd than the fact that "those who created everything lack everything"?[15] What nightmare, if you think about it, could be more ghastly than life under the reign of capital, which is dead labor—in the title of the opening section of *Le Monde Nouveau*, "the nightmare of life"?[16]

All are to some extent narratives of victimization, with the victims typically young, working class, and female (a classic anarchist motif); all thematize this victimization as the hunting of prey by predators, with the predators often cast in the role of decadent bourgeois gentlemen. With the antagonists being continually compared to spiders, vipers, wolves, the prose is thick with metaphors of animals and insects, as the very atmosphere is thick: thus, the opening scene of *Les Microbes Humains* unfolds in a shady bar where "the smoke is so thick that Jupiter could hide behind the cloud."[17] Indeed, the writing itself has been thickened in something like the manner of the paint on an Impressionist canvas: there is no pretense of transparency, of detached observation.

"The constant use of comparisons and metaphors," Granier observes, "has the effect of evoking a parallel world behind the visible world ... a world in which the possible has taken refuge."[18] Utopian spaces appear, in Michel's work, as refuges: they are founded far from civilization, in the extremes of the Earth—the polar deserts, the jungles of equatorial Africa—by tribes of those who have "wearied of the evils done them, or sickened by the evils they did to others."[19] They draw on the energies of disgust, on what Julia Kristeva called "the powers of horror." If a Naturalist novel like Upton Sinclair's *The*

---

15 Louise Michel, *L'Ère Nouvelle: Pensée dernière: Souvenirs de Caledonie* (Paris: Librairie Socialiste Internationale, 1887), 3.

16 Louise Michel, *The New World*, trans. Brian Stableford (Encino, CA: Black Coat Press, 2012), 10.

17 Caroline Granier, *Quitter son point de vue: quelques utopies anarcho-littéraires d'il y a un siècle* (Paris: Monde libertaire, 2007), 56; Louise Michel, *The Human Microbes*, trans. Brian Stableford (Encino, CA: Black Coat Press, 2012), 20.

18 Granier, *Quitter son point de vue*, 56.

19 Thomas, *Louise Michel*, 265; Michel qtd. in Ibid.

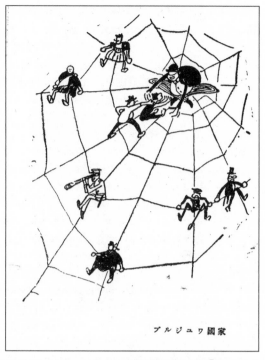

ブルジュワ國家

Fig. 2: Capitalist as spider, worker as fly: Mochizuki Kei (with Ōsugi Sakae),
Manbun Manga, 1922.

Jungle taps into the same sources, it is all in service of the restoration of a norm, the correction of an error; it is fundamentally reformist. In the extremity of her descriptions, in her insistence on the grotesque, Michel resists reformist as well as conservative forces. A "spider," unlike a factory boss or a President of the Republic, is innately predatory, not reformable (cf. fig. 2); thus, Granier argues, "Louise Michel seems to indicate to the readers that society is not reformable: a new society will be able to be built only in a radical elsewhere, on the ruins of the old world."[20] Here, Michel seems to offer a surprising answer to what George Goodin terms the "problem of hope" posed by narratives of victimization. If utopian dreaming seems to be primarily a matter of hoping for something better, even victim-of-society stories, which would appear to be anything but utopian—indeed, they are often classics of literary reformism, as in Dickens's *Hard Times* or

20 Granier, *Nous sommes les briseurs*, 2.2.2.8.

Harriet Beecher Stowe's *Uncle Tom's Cabin*—also require a certain quantity of hope for improvement: if there is no hope, then the narrative collapses into "excessive pessimism," squandering its accumulated energies of sympathy and indignation.[21] For Michel, on the contrary, if *too much* hope is offered, the utopia is unnecessary; if there is no dystopia to escape, then there is no impetus to utopia.

And yet the process of exposition, once the thunder of denunciation subsides, and the properly utopian moment of the text arrives, is a rational, "programmatic activist discourse."[22] Thus, the lyrical-denunciatory opening of Michel's *L'Ère Nouvelle* (*The New Era*, 1887)—"She is dying, the old ogress who has drunk human blood from the very beginning in order to prolong her accursed life"—gives way to a kind of Socratic exposition of the bases for a new society. Anticipating the usual questions ("How will the lazy live? How would envy, jealousy be arranged for under a system of equality?"), Michel reasons: if laziness is a kind of aberration caused by life under the system of exploitation, it can be expected to vanish with that system; however, like those living with other "infirmities," "The lazy ... are entitled to life, and they will live, or rather vegetate, without harming anyone." The motives of jealousy and envy, likewise, are premised on a scarcity that stands to be eradicated forever once "the machine will be at the service of man, and working for the benefit of all."[23] Here, rather than narrate the journey of an outsider into utopia (in the classical manner) or simply explicating the utopia's principles in an abstract manner, Michel articulates the good society *against* and *through* the objections that we cannot help raising to it. A rhetoric of ridicule deftly inverts the expected relations of topia to utopia: rather than allowing the here and now to be automatically justified—"the real is the rational," as Hegel so smugly put it—whereas the imagined world must be defended, Michel presents the imaginary as self-evident and the here and now as questionable, dubious, ephemeral. Conversely, as prisoners of the dystopian present, we are given reasons to doubt

21 George Goodin, *The Poetics of Protest: Literary Form and Political Implication in the Victim-of-Society Novel* (Carbondale, IL: Southern Illinois University Press, 1985), 132.

22 Roger Bozzetto, "Louise Michel, une utopiste libertaire?," in *Transformations of Utopia: Changing Views of the Perfect Society*, ed. George E. Slusser et al. (New York: AMS Press, 1999), 253.

23 Michel, *L'Ère Nouvelle*, 18.

our own grasp on what is possible and impossible, what is likely and what is unlikely: "Do you know how we will see that the old world no longer exists?" she asks. "Those who have returned from a dungeon to light, to safety, they alone could tell."[24]

This is the procedure favored by Ricardo Mella, the rationalist pedagogue, in *La Nueva Utopía* (1890). "Why kill," he asks, "where the death of one's neighbor [*semejante*] has no purpose, nor does theft, nor jealousy, nor ambition, nor envy? Why place oneself in open battle with the constituted society when it guarantees the satisfaction of all our desires in the natural order of life?"[25] Even the dismal perception of human beings as a conformist herd can be made to work in favor of utopian hope: how many would be willing to bite the hand that feeds them?

A similar logic runs through Émile Pataud (1869–1935) and Émile Pouget's utopian work, *Comment Nous Ferons la Révolution* (*How We Shall Bring About the Revolution*, 1909)—a title that results from a printer's error, the prefatory note explains; since, "as you all know it, the Revolution is over!—Capitalism is dead," the title was intended to have been "COMMENT / NOUS AVONS FAIT / LA RÉVOLUTION [HOW / WE BROUGHT ABOUT / THE REVOLUTION]."[26] The book narrates how the revolution *was* brought about in the past tense, lending the air of a *fait accompli* to what otherwise might seem daring speculations:

> The Revolution had brought about a marvel [*un prodige*] which, up to the time of its triumph, had appeared as fantastic as the search for the squaring of the circle,—the friendly blending of opinions.
>
> The reconciliation was effected on the economic ground, and the foundering of the whole superstructure of the State had cemented this accord and made it lasting. Men came to laugh at their past folly. They were astonished that they could have hated each other so much, persecuted each other so bitterly, under the foolish pretext of discordant political ideas.

---

24 Ibid., 15.
25 Ricardo Mella, "La Nueva Utopía," in *El cuento anarquista*, 228.
26 Pataud and Pouget, *How We Shall Bring*, xxxviii; *Comment nous ferons la Révolution* (Paris: J. Taillandier, 1909), v.

The same phenomena were observed in religious matters. Peace was made. The disagreement in individual beliefs no longer set men quarrelling. They ceased to hurl invectives at each other because of philosophical or metaphysical differences; they no longer cursed each other because their ideas about the universe and the problems of life and death were opposed.

Thus, still more distant than political quarrels, more profoundly buried in the limbo of history, seemed the epochs of barbarism in the course of which men killed each other in the name of religion.

Following a defensive anticipation of the reader's objection of unlikelihood ("a marvel," "fantastic"), the rhetoric of retrospection ("up to the time of its triumph," "distant," "buried in the limbo of history," "epochs of barbarism") reverses this objection into a protest against the unlikelihood of the *actual* ("Men came to laugh"; "They were astonished"; etc.). But the more substantive argument, underneath this narrative sleight of hand, makes a wager, with Mella, that "the economic ground," will prove more fundamental: "the satisfaction of all our desires" will trump ideology and theology, material common sense will trump metaphysics.[27]

In short, the utopia of Pataud and Pouget, no less than that of Mella (in spite of its geographical location in France), is adjacent to what Bevington names "Common-Sense Country," "a country where Common-sense ... was as common as lunacy is in a madhouse":

In Common-sense Country all the commodities and goods, all the instruments, utensils, and appliances—in short, all the "things"—had very simple and unadventurous biographies, and,

27 This is an ideological maneuver *par excellence*, at least if we can subscribe to Michael Freeden's notion that the typical function of an ideology is to "decontest meanings": it attempts to remove something from discussion, to place it outside of the disputable, the conflictual (*Ideologies and Political Theory: A Conceptual Approach* [Oxford: Clarendon Press, 1998], 76). Of course, every attempt to declare peace in this way is itself contestable, and this particular notion has been contested on *other* anarchist grounds; thus, Gustav Landauer regards the "materialism" of the Marxists as short-sighted, emphasizing instead the need to evoke a common "spirit [*Geist*]" of community. See Landauer, *For Socialism*, 47–104.

if they could have spoken, they would not have had much harrowing information to impart about the ravages of their tissues and textures caused by moth and rust, not yet of vicissitudes incurred at the hands of thieves breaking through to steal. "I was needed: I was made: I was conveyed: I was applied: I was consumed." That would have summed up the history of a thing in the country where things went right: only five short chapters. In most countries, of course, all sorts of distressing and distracting other chapters intervene. Thus: "I was coveted: I was done without: I was lied for: I was hated for: I was speculated in: I was adulterated: I was advertised: I was legislated about: I was sold (and my buyer with me): I was squandered: I was hoarded: I was quarrelled over: I was fought for: I was burgled: I was bombed."[28]

The simplifying force of rationality pushes against the complicating force of narrative. For Mella, too, "The social system of the 'New Utopia' is an admirable simplicity." "Our whole problem boils down to this: meeting social needs as well as possible with the least amount of force required, developing as far as we can the sphere of our knowledge and our pleasures."[29] Indeed, why would anyone ever want to do otherwise, if they did not live in Cretinolândia? The appeal to self-interest, a motive usually taken to render the anarchist utopia impossible by its very existence, is in fact a major component of anarchist utopias. In a short utopian fiction, "A Year of Jubilee," published in *The Firebrand* in 1895, we are asked to imagine not only the outbreak of the revolution in town—the critical moment, during a strike, when popular anger tips against the police and military—but the jubilation of a farmer on reading the news of capitalism's fall (naturally, in the new issue of *The Firebrand*):

> Farmer Jones who is just getting back from town, having seen the sight and heard all the news, and when in sight of home, waves the late[st] issue of THE FIREBRAND aloft and yells like a comanche indian, so that the team came very nearly running away, and his wife rushes out to see what is the matter. "Holy

---

28 Louisa S. Bevington, *Common-Sense Country* (London: James Tochatti, "Liberty" Press, 1890), 3–4.
29 Mella, "La Nueva Utopía," 235.

pumpkins, old girl, come here and hold me or I'll bust. Gee wit-taker,—whoop!" "What is up Abe, you have not been drinking, have you?" "No, nothing of the kind, but I am full just the same, full of good news. The mortgage is paid, mother; no more interest, no more slaving from morning till night to keep the old homestead from the money sharks; no more scraping around for taxes." "But what has happened Abe, I don't understand." "Why the revolution, about which the papers have been talking about, for ever so long, has come and gone, and we did not know anything about it. You know I drove to town to sell some potatoes, to get money to pay the interest on the mortgage. But there was no chance to sell anything, every thing was in an uproar, such as I never saw before.

"They were just blowing up the armory with dynamite when I got there, and all them tin soldiers in it went to glory; golly that was a sight. The city is turned upsidedown, the workingmen are on top. The Courthouse and City hall with all their records wiped out, burned down. The rich have fled or hunted their holes, and for the time being the people rule. They have declared the co-operative commonwealth, and from now on they are going to run things to suit themselves. You remember I was always opposed to these Socialists and Anarchists, but I don't know about it now, it strikes me rather favorably, we can keep our farm, have no more taxes or interest to pay and I think I'll stay with the boys." "Why of course, Abe, what better could you do, we can go and work now, with a heart and live again as we did, when we got married and the farm was free of encumbrances. But what have you got in the wagon?" "Well, let me talk for once and I'll tell you everything. After driving around a while, I was directed to the food committee, which has charge of all the provisions on hand, and coming in. They told me to leave my potatoes with them and I could take anything I needed. They gave me some groceries, we had to have in the house anyway. I picked out a pair of shoes for myself and some calico for a dress for you and then I thought I had about as much as the taters were worth, and started to drive home, but they stopped me and asked if I did not want a new cultivator plough, harness or some thing of that kind, you bet I do, sez I. Well then take it along, old man, they said, and put it in the wagon; we have no use for it here in town and you have. And here is something for you, Sally, here wrapped up in paper." "What is it Abe?" "Look and see for yourself." "Why the idea a new fashionable bonnet, just the thing I wanted, you better put up the horses Abe, while I run in the house and try on the bonnet."

The amateurish writing style—I have corrected the spelling here, out of mercy, but left the grammar and punctuation verbatim—again makes a rhetorical appeal to authenticity, to certain beliefs about how farmers and their wives think and talk; it also identifies the narrative voice fairly closely with those voices. The dialogue, conducted in a countrified dialect, attempts to imagine why protagonists like these might sign on to a revolution that is inspired by an ideology whose terms and representatives—"these Socialists and Anarchists"—are foreign to them. For them, the revolution appears as a "jubilee" in the Biblical sense (another idiom commonly shared by American farmers): a lifting of the yoke of debt slavery, a setting-free of the bondsman from the mortgage that makes property a kind of legal theft. And this it is that softens the blow:

"I knew that would strike her," said the old man "but where is the hired man?" "Hey Ben, where are you, come along and help me to unhitch the team, what have you been doing?" "None of your business." "What's up." "Nothing only I read The Firebrand and know what is going on. I am going to leave you and move on to the old Kearny place; I talked with the neighbors about it and they said I was entitled to it, being so long around here, and what is more your daughter Lizzy is going to keep house for me." "Well I'll be blowed," gasped the old man, "and not even ask my permission or nothing?" "We are all equals now, and you might as well act according to it. I like her and she likes me and that is all there is to it."

"Well, well, Ben, I did not think of that, this comes kinder sudden; will you please help me then with the team and you'll stay for supper anyway, won't you?" "Why of course, now you are talking, go in and rest yourself and I'll tend to the stock." Old man Jones strokes his whiskers meditatively and goes up to the house where he finds his wife trying on the new bonnet.

Of course Farmer Jones has something to lose. Almost everyone does: one of the few ingenuities of hierarchy is that it provides so many subjects with someone who is subject to them, lower in the pecking order. But here the spirit of equity balances out the loss of relative privilege (and the spirit of jubilee sweetens it all). If it is difficult to imagine, outside of certain chapters of the Christian Identity movement, an ordinary American farmer so radical as to rejoice at watching soldiers blown sky-high, let alone to subscribe to an anarchist newspaper like *The Firebrand*, is it beyond belief that the Joneses might be ready to live as equals with their old hired hand?

5: STRONGER LOVING WORLDS

THE fate of former masters and lackeys after the revolution is, in fact, a frequent preoccupation of anarchist utopian writing. If "everyone connives with the prince," as Proudhon put it[1]—the police and army are supported by and composed of the people, who elect the governments that pay them; white workers conspire with their employers to exploit and humiliate their black coworkers; bosses boss foremen, who boss their subordinates, who go home and boss their wives, who boss their children, who boss smaller children, etc.—then a key component of anarchist dreaming is the process of reconciliation and reintegration that would constitute a society of equals without producing another Terror. In the absence of the accustomed laws and hierarchies, what will we do? To start with the oldest customary arrangements: how will men and women get along—or will they? Who will take care of the kids?

The patriarchal family is a primary target of anarchist critique; much anarchist fiction could say, with André Gide, "Families, I hate you!" "Poets, novelists, playwrights, priests, judges, educators," fulminated Francisco Ferrer, "you said that however lethal the family may be, the 'self' would still find there the care and affection that would dress and heal its wounds! You have lied!"[2] In anarchist fiction, escape from this brutal, authoritarian micro-society—from the toxically conformist household in Jules Vallès's Jacques Vingtras trilogy (*L'Enfant* [*The Child*, 1879], *Le Bachelier* [*The Graduate*, 1881], and

---

1   Proudhon, *Selected Writings*, 116.
2   Ferrer qtd. in Caroline Granier, "Le désordre du 'je' ou l'ordre en jeu," *Cahiers Octave Mirbeau* 10 (2003): 53.

L'Insurgé [*The Insurgent*, 1886]) to the stifling gerontocratic atmosphere of the Kao household in Ba Jin's *Jia* (*Family*, 1933)—tends to involve a deviation from the traditional pattern of the *Bildungsroman*, the nineteenth-century "novel of education"; indeed, Granier argues, these can be called novels of *failed* education. She describes the narrative pattern as follows:

> — failure of an early "institutional" education,
> — revolt,
> — opposition to the family,
> — the completion of education with the help of a friend who serves as "tutor."[3]

This, indeed, describes not only the plot of other nineteenth-century anarchist narratives, such as Georges Darien's (1862–1921) *Biribi* (1890) or Octave Mirbeau's (1848–1917) *Sébastien Roch* (1890),[4] but also late-twentieth and early-twenty-first century examples, e.g., the first volume of Grant Morrison's comic book series *The Invisibles* (1994–1996) or the various editions of Mike Gilliland's *The Free* (1986, 1990, 2011). Taking the place of little Jacques Vingtras are Morrison's teen hooligan, Dane McGowan, a.k.a. Jack Frost, and Gilliland's Linda Moon, a.k.a. Maxie. Both undergo a change of names signaling their transition from psychological and physical bondage—to a creepy faith-based boarding school reminiscent of *Sébastien Roch*, in Dane's case, and to abusive Catholic-school teachers and an incestuous father, in Linda's. Both revolt against their official educator-captors and families, and in the wake of these failed educations, find friends and guides (Tom O'Bedlam and Maggie, respectively) who serve as their tutors in freedom. In particular, both learn to overcome the bitterness and shame that help keep them pinned in their gender roles.

What seems to shift, comparing these late-twentieth-century novels to their late-nineteenth-century precursors, is the emphasis: where the earlier versions give greater narrative weight to the forces holding children captive, fixed in their identity as victims—*Biribi* is set in a notorious French prison colony, and *Sébastien Roch* ends in the protagonist's senseless death—the later versions emphasize the

---

3   Ibid., 55.
4   Ibid.

children's mobility, their positive capacity for self-reinvention. Indeed, the second edition of *The Free* takes a turn toward the utopian, as Gilliland extends this pedagogical imagination into the wider world, letting us watch as new forms of social and ecological life appear to replace the failed institutions of a dying civilization. However, from the nineteenth century right through the present, anarchist narratives of childhood have often entailed the construction of *alternative* forms of kinship and family life.[5]

In Gilliland's *The Free*—first written in the era of the Poll Tax Riots and the miners' struggles (1986), then rewritten for the age of the "two crises" of economic slump and climate change (2011)— runaway Linda, cagey but battered and frightened, finds the unconditional love and support she has been missing in Maggie Bellows:

> I can see Maggie still, that first time, coming sudden in the door.
> And I wish I could see her still.
> A big tall red haired woman, wide mouth and a few big freckles, wearing a worn orange coat and bright yellow trousers.
> Speechless I stared at her. Seeing spots from looking at the sun....
> —"So what brings you to this part of the world?"—says she.
> But I held my silence. Looking in my grey tea and figuring out a good story. Then I looked up, and suddenly right into her warm orangey eyes.
> —"You can trust me, you're my sister."—she said strangely.
> And stranger still I began immediately to tell her the true story. It seemed like Maggie was the first really honest person I'd ever met, and I took to her at once. As if I'd always been waiting to meet her.
> I started to tell her the truth, as I saw it, and it wasn't that easy. I told her about my problems at school and at home. Though *not* about my Dad molesting me. I was still too panicky for that.
> I ended up crying on her shoulder. Getting my black eye bathed with a hot flannel, and laughing together, and making more tea.[6]

---

5   David Der-Wei Wang finds a striking example of this in Ba Jin's "Dier de muqin [The Second Mother]" (1932).

6   Mike Gilliland, *The Free*, 3rd ed. (n.l.: n.p., 2011), 47–48.

Is Maggie a "sister" merely in the sense of the cliché, or does she become a kind of surrogate kin? Is her relation to Linda sisterly, in fact, or mothering? In any case, the significance of the imagery of light and warmth (red, orange, yellow, "warm orangey eyes," "spots from looking at the sun") is unmistakable. As Maggie puts it: "*There's all kinds of families you know*."[7]

Novels like Rosa Graul's *Hilda's Home: A Story of Women's Emancipation* (1899) seem calculated to dispel "fears," in the words of Moses Harman, "that under Freedom the Home and the Family would cease to exist, or that woman will be less loving and lovable, or that man will be less manly and honorable."[8] Following a familiar strategy, Graul begins by sketching a portrait of the present in terms of exactly those fears: the protagonist, Imelda, has been thrown into a condition of total precarity by the very laws and customs ("honor," "virtue," "decency," "legitimacy," and so on) commonly imagined as protecting women and children. Only some drastically different arrangement could offer women something other than this terribly raw deal:

> We hear the cant of freedom, of liberty, of a "free country," all around us, when in reality it is all a miserable sham! Every word must be guarded, every action fettered. We must eat, drink, sleep, walk and talk all according to a prescribed fashion; must bow to fashion, to custom. We may not even welcome a child to our arms when we desire it, unless we have first allowed shackles to be placed upon our freedom; unless we have first bartered our womanhood for motherhood—often turning what should be a priceless boon to a most bitter curse.[9]

The "future cooperative home," then, is the place where this Faustian social compact has been nullified by a combination of material and moral egalitarianism. Hilda's vision of the communal life blends "sacred privacy," enlarged domestic spaces such as the "common parlor," the collective "nursery," and the shared "dining hall," and a richly public realm of "the lecture hall and the theater," "grand

---

7   Ibid., 80.
8   Moses Harman, in Rosa Graul, *Hilda's Home: A Story of Woman's Emancipation* (Chicago: M. Harman & Co, 1899), I–II.
9   Ibid., 289.

conservatories," "spacious halls where the ardent searchers after knowledge of any kind might find their teacher"—more gracefully bridging the gendered private and public realms. It combines a sensual vision of a "life of unconventionality" and "abandon" with images of a new sexual contract in which men "wait and abide [women's] invitation," becoming partners in "sweet co-operation and planning."[10] This is anarchist communism as constructed from the perspective of "the prospective mother," no longer dependent on the resources of a single man—faithful, in the case of Imelda's and Cora's father, broken by the burden, or fickle, in the case of Cora's lover, leaving her in her distress. All resources are pooled; all are shared. The word "sweet" is repeated four times in the space of a paragraph, lending its taste and fragrance by turns to "dream[s]," "blossoms," "welcome[s]," and finally, "co-operation and planning"—as if Logos itself, to calm our fears of abandonment and exposure, were in need of Eros's sweetening touch.

Rather than locating utopias in inaccessible, other-worldly locales, one anarchist tactic is to place happiness literally within arm's reach. "The Idea is a lover," writes Joseph Déjacque, "who, in her impetuous embraces, bites you to make you shout, and does not let you go for a single moment, breathless and exhausted, except to prepare you with renewed and more burning caresses." "Literally my ideal text would *draw* to me someone to *embrace*," echoes Peter Lamborn Wilson, writing more than a century later.[11] Idealized representations of romantic and familial love present us with micro-utopias, little worlds governed by mutuality and caring, a fact that has perhaps always been behind the popularity of the romance genre: "Truly, love is always free. It escapes all morality and all convention," remarks the male protagonist of Mariano Gallardo López's *Mujeres Libres: Novela sexual* (ca. 1937) (fig. 1).[12] In this sense, romance has frequently been taken to be one of the depoliticizing devices of mass entertainment: discontentment and desire is channeled into the search for a perfect mate, culminating in a vision of domestic bliss that leaves the larger, loveless, ugly society unchanged. However, anarchist romances—a

10 Ibid., 377–378.
11 Déjacque, *L'Humanisphère*, 76–77; Wilson, "Amoral Responsibility," 57.
12 Mariano Gallardo López, *Mujeres libres (Novela sexual)* (Barcelona: Revista Blanca, s.d.), 7.

Fig. 1: Cover of Mariano Gallardo's *Mujeres libres: novela sexual* (from the Novela Libre series).

surprisingly rich and extensive genre—attempt to harness these utopian yearnings, to link them to broader social visions.

Lloyd's free-love utopia is prefaced with the admonition: "*It is not meant, O Reader, that you should live life as this man lived it, but only that you should fearlessly and gladly live your own life.*"[13] As individualistic as this might sound, Lloyd's emphasis on the intimate, personal dimension of joy is calculated to distance Vale Sunrise from the more programmatic or prescriptive visions of the classical utopias, rather than to prevent us from imagining shared, social joy. On the contrary: from the moment we are first invited to enjoy, from the perspective of the outsider (the free-spirited artist Theodora Earle), the sight of "a naked man, or nearly so" galloping bareback through the fields (the even more free-spirited Forrest Westwood, the "natural

13 Lloyd, *The Natural Man*, 7.

man" of the title, keeper of what becomes the Vale Sunrise colony),
we are also invited to imagine a world of Theodoras and Forrests, of
sensual pleasures and easy living:

"It was so beautiful there [said Forrest], and so delightful to lie
on one's back and look up into the sky, and hear the bees mur-
mur in the tree tops."

"It was indeed [replied Theodora], I quite envied you, for I
used to do just that when a child."

Instantly his shyness vanished in the enthusiasm of one who
utters a favorite thought.

"And why do you not do it now? You would enjoy it just as
much now as you did then. Nay more, for the adult mind can
interweave more charms, can be more consciously happy, can receive more wide delights than the child mind. Why do you, why
does every one, pine for the joys of childhood and yet refuse the
means that childhood instinctively takes to attain its pleasures?"[14]

The slide from "I" to "you" to "every one" turns a moment of private,
inward, bodily enjoyment into a universalized, socialized longing for
pleasure, for "joy." What emerges at the end of this romance, as in
Hilda's Home, is a domestic bliss so enlarged as to become public, a
society in miniature and incipiently in grand scale (as developed further by *Dwellers in Vale Sunrise*).[15]

We find a similar movement between the personal and the political at work in Gallardo López's *novela sexual*, which begins as the
attempt of the male protagonist, Paúl, to convince Dolores, Flora,

---

14 Ibid., 17–18.

15 Authors such as Jules Lermina (*Le Fils de Monte-Cristo* [*The Son of Monte-Cristo*, 1881]) and Michel Zévaco (*Le Chevalier de la Barre* [*The Knight
of La Barre*, 1899] and *Les Pardaillan* [*The Pardaillan*, 1905–1918]) enact
a similar enlargement of the scope of the adventure novel. For instance,
Lermina's reworking of Dumas's *Count of Monte Cristo* has the eponymous
Count seek revenge not only on his individual tormentors but on he social system they represent: as Vittorio Frigerio puts it, "individual action
becomes social action, individual responsibility disappears and society is
clearly indicated as the sole entity responsible for the wickedness of those
it perverts" ("Romans d'aventures et idéologie: Réflexions autour du cas de
Jules Lermina," in *Poétiques du roman d'aventures*, eds. Alain-Michel Boyer
and Daniel Couégnas [Nantes: Editions Cécile Defaut, 2004], 127).

Sabina, and Rosario to sleep with him, but which turns into a series of philosophical dialogues about sexual ethics, ending in consummation and a new vision of a world transformed by "love-friendship [*amor-amistad*] and sexual friendship [*amistad amorosa*]." "Today, my friend Rosario," Paúl laments, just as individuals are taught to think of life as a war of all against all, "almost all men look at women, not as friends or companions, but as things"; ergo, "revolutionaries in love need to struggle with atavistic prejudices," especially "the idea of personal property which man has over the woman he loves."[16] The importance of *consent* in the new, non-proprietary relationships—both sexual and social—is evidence in favor of Paúl's assertion that free love might set a pattern for free life.

While rape and sexual violence are not explicitly addressed in *Mujeres Libres*, anarchist serial novels and short stories, as Litvak notes, frequently present working-class female protagonists—for example, any number of hapless victims in Louise Michel's *Les Microbes Humains* (1886), Lucy in José Prat's "A Caza de Carne [On the Flesh Hunt]" (1893), Laura in J. D. González's (birth and death dates unknown) *El Suplicio de Laura [Laura's Torments]* and *La Expósita [The Abandoned]* (1901), Rosa Maria in Antonio Penichet's (birth date unknown, d. 1964) *La Vida de un Pernicioso* (1919), Oh-Kwa in Kwon Ku-hyeon's "In-yugsijang jeomgyeong [Scenes of the Human Flesh Market]" (1933)—as prey to wealthy pursuers who stand in for the bourgeoisie; in these cases, the violation or coercion of women's sexual consent is directly identified with capitalist exploitation, their humiliation with "the humiliation of an entire class."[17] Conversely, consensual sexuality represented the highest possibilities for mutuality, equality, and freedom within the confines of the present, as Graul suggests:

> Turning to Hilda and kneeling at her feet Cora laid her face upon her knee.
>
> "Is the curse never to be lifted?"
>
> "Yes! When woman is ready to be blessed; when she has learned to keep herself pure; when the sacred temple of her body no longer is invaded by the curse of lust; when man no longer

---

16 Gallardo López, *Mujeres Libres*, 62–63.
17 Litvak, *El cuento anarquista*, 35–37.

dares to intrude, to force his unwelcome attentions upon her, but patiently bides his time at a respectful distance."

"You speak of the 'millenium,' of the perfection of the race. Must our lives be one long sacrifice to secure that end?" Hilda shook her head as with both hands she lifted the tear-wet face.

"I hope not! Whilst we all have a work to perform in the meantime, I believe we may yet be able, in our own lives, to so far lift ourselves out of and above all the pains that make life such a weary round of toil, as to be able to enjoy just a little in advance, of what the coming future will bring the now enslaved race. When we are brave enough, when we are strong enough to live as our inmost convictions tell us is right and true and pure, we may then hope for a little happiness, or perhaps a great happiness, just as we make ourselves ready to receive and appreciate it. And I feel so sure, so sure that here, just right here around us, a band is forming, true and staunch, that by its unity will enable us yet to realize what now seem but dreams!"[18]

This foretaste of emancipation, one of the "present-tense dimensions" of anarchism of which Uri Gordon speaks so eloquently, gives substance to Gustav Landauer's characteristic statement that anarchy "is not a matter of making demands ... [but] of how one lives," that it is "a matter of the present."[19] Reading the anarchist romance, one is taken into the arms of the Idea.

From an anarchist standpoint, just as sexual relations between men and women, presently damaged by inequality and soured by hypocrisy, are nonetheless potentially liberatory, the family, inadequate as it may be, contains a utopian embryo. Antonio Penichet declared that in spite of its authoritarian aberrations, the family was the "best field for experimentation," since the moral and material "bond" between its members "indicates the march toward communism."[20] This sense of a domestic life as the potential kernel of a

---

18 Graul, *Hilda's Home*, 289–290.

19 Uri Gordon, "Liberation Now: Present Tense Dimensions of Contemporary Anarchism" (paper presented at *Thinking the Present: The Beginnings and Ends of Political Theory* conference, Berkeley, CA, May 27–28, 2005); Landauer, *Revolution*, 87.

20 Penichet qtd. in Kirwin Shaffer, "The Radical Muse: Women and Anarchism in Early-Twentieth Century Cuba," *Cuban Studies* 34.1 (2003):

communist world—grounding, in its core ethic of fidelity, the solidarity of an entire society—is perhaps most powerfully captured by Le Guin's *The Dispossessed*. Here, "free love" takes the primary form of what the Spanish anarchists called the *union libre*—the consensual commitment of a couple to monogamy without State or religious sanction, dissolvable, like any other such pact, by the withdrawal of consent:

> Partnership was a voluntarily constituted federation like any other. So long as it worked, it worked, and if it didn't work it stopped being. It was not an institution but a function. It had no sanction but that of private conscience.[21]

This is pretty precisely the "free union" championed by publications like *La Revista Blanca* (ca. 1898–1904) and in pamphlet series such as *Propaganda Anarquista entre las Mujeres* (1895), contrasted with "bourgeois and religious marriage" as a form of "prostitution," "guaranteed only by will and pleasure," with "freedom to break the bond at all times," and forming a "family based on true love and affection," as Laura Fernández Cordero summarizes.[22] According to the anarchist ethos of Annares, "freedom to change," rather than "invalidat[ing] the idea of promise or vow, in fact the freedom made the promise meaningful":

> A promise is a direction taken, a self-limitation of choice. As [the anarchist philosopher] Odo pointed out, if no direction is taken, if one goes nowhere, no change will occur.... So Odo came to see the promise, the pledge, the idea of fidelity, as essential in the complexity of freedom.[23]

The keeping of faith, of trust, between Shevek and Takver—strained to the extremes by separation and hardship—underlines the strength of their love, and it underwrites the force of their idea: a world

143, trans. Shaffer.

21   Le Guin, *The Dispossessed*, 244.

22   Laura Fernández Cordero, "Queremos emanciparos: anarquismo y mujer en Buenos Aires de fines del XIX," *Izquierdas* 3.6 (2010): 13.

23   Le Guin, *The Dispossessed*, 244–245.

brought into being by "loyalty, which asserts the continuity of past and future, binding time into a whole."

> Fulfillment, Shevek thought, is a function of time. The search for pleasure is circular, repetitive, atemporal. The variety-seeking of the spectator, the thrill-hunter, the sexually promiscuous, always ends in the same place. It has an end. It comes to the end and has to start over. It is not a journey and return, but a closed cycle, a locked room, a cell. Outside the locked room is the landscape of time, in which the spirit may, with luck and courage, construct the fragile, makeshift, improbable roads and cities of fidelity: a landscape inhabitable by human beings.[24]

Here, then, is another kind of anarchist vision: another "stronger loving world to die in."[25]

---

24 Le Guin, *The Dispossessed*, 334.
25 J. J. Cale qtd. in Alan Moore and Dave Gibbons, *Watchmen* (New York: DC Comics, 1986), 12.32.9.

6: FROM *TERRE LIBRE* TO *TEMPS DE CRISES*

"**IT** is easiest to think of it [utopia] as growing in virgin territory with new people," write Paul and Percival Goodman—as in Charlotte Perkins Gilman's decidedly non-anarchist utopia *Herland* (1915), severed from civilization by an epic rockslide. Some anarchist utopias take advantage of the logic of place, suppressing our doubts about the fragility of utopias by locating them in a remote or protected elsewhere. Vicente Carreras's "Acraciápolis" (1902), isolated from "a corrupt and criminal society" by "countless impenetrable forests inhabited by enormous snakes, tigers, lions and countless other beasts that threaten the lives of people who dare to cross them," sets the tone.[1] Islands are popular: Jean Grave's *Terre Libre* (1908) reimagines the Communards' exile in Nouméa as the founding of a new society, and in *Les Pacifiques* (1914) Han Ryner locates his colony of "Nelti" on Atlantis. Closer at hand, we find the far less dramatically secluded "Vale Sunrise" of J. William Lloyd's *The Natural Man* (1902) and *Dwellers in Vale Sunrise* (1904), located vaguely "in the mountains" (just down the road from rural "Rippleford") and the extraterrestrial utopias of Denis Parazols's *Rêve à Vénus* (1935) and Le Guin's *The Dispossessed* (1974).[2]

---

1   Goodman and Goodman, *Communitas*, 220; Charlotte Perkins Gilman, *Herland and Selected Stories* (New York: Signet Classic, 1992), 64; Carreras, "Acraciápolis," 223.

2   Jean Grave, *Terre libre (Les pionniers)* (Paris: Librairie des Temps nouveaux, 1908); Ryner, *Les Pacifiques* (1914); Lloyd, *The Natural Man* (1902) and *The Dwellers in Vale Sunrise* (1904); Denis Parazols, *Rêve à Vénus: Anticipation*

More often, however, anarchist fictions locate utopia in the future, presenting us with a *uchronia*. Instead of planting their flag on Grave's *Terre Libre* (free land), we might say, they let us glimpse a better world through Jules Jouy's "*temps de crises*" (crisis times). The *sommaire* at the head of the sixty-page "Prologue" to Sébastien Faure's uchronian novel *Mon communisme: le bonheur universel* (1921), the body of which is set "fifteen years after the liberation movement," gives us the sense of how such plots move:

> Jobless—The Durands join, in Brazil, their friends the Picards—
> Events in France—The Social Revolution—Looking Back—The
> Great War—After the War—In extremis—Atop a volcano—
> Revolution breaks out—The insurgency spreads; daring raids—
> All of Paris in the power of the Insurgents—The movement
> triumphs in the provinces—The advent of Communism—The
> expatriates come to visit France.[3]

Thus, Pataud and Pouget open their account of *How We Shall Bring About the Revolution* with scenes of a Paris construction workers' strike "during a Sunday afternoon in the spring of the year 19__," stirred into a general strike by police provocation.[4] Likewise, Capetillo's utopian sketch, "La humanidad en el futuro: Huelga general y sociedad futura" ("The Humanity of the Future: General Strike and Future Society," 1910) begins on "May 14th, a splendid and beautiful day" in an unnamed island nation not unlike Puerto Rico, when a wage dispute erupts into a general strike.[5] In both cases, we see the structures of the future world germinating in the cracks of a conflictual present: the very efforts of the ruling classes to starve out the strikers, in Capetillo's narrative, force them to spontaneously invent the kinds of self-reliant, autonomous institutions needed to resist: cooperatives, common funds, rotation of tasks, barter networks.[6]

---

sociale (Marseilles: Chez l'auteur, 1935); Le Guin, *The Dispossessed* (1974).

3 Sébastien Faure, *Mon communisme: le bonheur universel* (Paris: Édition du Groupe des amis de Sébastien Faure, 1921), 5–6, 9.

4 Pataud and Pouget, *How We Shall Bring*, 1–3, 12.

5 Luisa Capetillo, "La humanidad en el futuro: Huelga general y sociedad futura (relato utópico)," *Los Escritos de Luisa Capetillo*, ed. Arcadio Díaz Quiñones (Rio Piedras: Ediciones Huracán, 1992), 127.

6 Ibid., 127–131.

In a more recent example, Gilliland's *The Free* takes as one of its fundamental premises that the government of the island nation in which it is set, a place suspiciously like Ireland, has devolved into a fiscal wreck, flattened by declining revenues from offshoring industries: "times had changed, irrevocably, as the private sector collapsed, and the State itself tottered towards bankruptcy."[7] In this climate, elements of the "deals" that forestalled revolution in the early-twentieth century are nullified: the welfare net is shredded, upward mobility vanishes, "and the power of the Unions was broken." Without these institutions as buffers, all the State has left, increasingly, is force, further alienating the already desperate population. Into the gap step a number of non-State actors, including some right-wing (the Brother-Hood) or politically ambiguous (the CLANs), and one libertarian movement, The Free. It is this last that proves most successful, building alternative institutions such as collectively-owned Co-Ops, radical workers' Free Unions, and the Pools (collectivized resource bases and credit unions), fielding "De-Schools" and "Free Uni[s]" to replace the derelict school systems, and taking advantage of the increased disrespect for legality in order to push their tactics of squatting real estate and reclaiming abandoned plants ever further. At the very beginning of the novel, a condition of dual power already exists, growing more tense by the day, until ultimately, it breaks out into open warfare.

In plotting scenarios like these, authors like Gilliland, Pataud, Pouget, Capetillo and others attempt to overcome one of the traditional weaknesses of the uchronian genre, the absence of a credible "causal history," as Santiago Juan-Navarro puts it, spanning the gap between a non-revolutionary present and a post-revolutionary future: "The changes were given, the new order was in place, and [it] functioned properly and without question."[8] Instead, anarchist uchronias attempt to *narrate* anarchy, to present utopia as a *process* rather than only as a result.

In keeping with the Proudhonian notion of revolution—that there is but one continual Revolution in history, advancing or receding—Alfonso Martínez Rizo (1877–1951) gives his *1945: El*

7   Mike Gilliland, *The Free*, 2ⁿᵈ ed. (London: Attack International, 1990), 55; *The Free* 3ʳᵈ ed., 86.

8   Santiago Juan-Navarro, "The Anarchist City of America: Libertarian Urban Utopias in the New World," *Atenea* 29.1 (2009): 103.

Advenimiento del Comunismo Libertario (1933) a relatively deep chronology:

HISTORICAL SUMMARY

The year 1945 closes a cycle of twelve years, one of those fateful cycles in the history of Spain ...
Year 1861—Cholera.
1873—Uprising of the cantons.
1885—Cholera.
1897—War in America.
1909—Military defeat at Barranco del Lobo [Morocco] and the Tragic Week.
1921—Military defeat at Anual [Morocco].
1933—Separatist uprising in Catalonia.
1945—Implementation of libertarian communism.[9]

For his part, the pseudonymous "p.m." authoring *bolo'bolo* (1981), while flippantly minimizing the length of the struggle that would be necessary to establish a global civilization of self-reliant *bolo* settlements (after just five years, *bolo'bolo* covers the planet!), does give that civilization another realistic credential: a date of death. It reigns uncontested, we are told, until 2346, when a strange "cultural epidemic" called "the whites" replaces the *bolo* as a social form, and the civilization falls apart; after that, a period of "Yuvuo" makes its advent, and "Tawhuac" brings what has in retrospect been a mere "pre-history" to a close by "put[ting] a new floppy disc in the drive"—as if everything up to now had been an illusion anyway.[10]

What is "Yuvuo"—some cosmic cycle of creation and destruction, perhaps, as in the Mayan or Hindu calendars? Could "Tawhuac" be some Aztec god? Why the peculiar disregard for science and rationality here, when these have been the hallmark of so much anarchist utopian writing since the late-nineteenth century? It might be a mistake to take these gestures at face value; rather, p.m. seems to be responding to the popular disregard into which science and reason

---

9   Alfonso Martínez Rizo, *1945: El Advenimiento del Comunismo Libertario* (Valencia: Mañana, 1933), 10.

10   p.m., *bolo'bolo* (New York: Autonomedia, 2011), 68–69.

themselves have sunk—the suspicion under which the rationalistic and scientistic style of utopianism has come. By comically foreshortening the period of social transformation and then comically truncating the era of utopia with events that fall entirely outside the scope of rational-utopian speculation, he is signaling an intent *not* to govern the future—strategically "baffling" or "weakening" the prescriptive force of his utopian discourse, as Barthes would have it.

Émile Pataud and Émile Pouget, for their part, are far more detailed about the revolutionary *process*, offering a tangibly detailed version of how the utopia might emerge from the shadow of all the forces that preclude it. Their principal concern, Granier suggests, is the question: "How can utopia be thought as realizable?" which they translate, in good revolutionary syndicalist fashion, into "the question of power: what power do we have to produce a perfect life?"[11] The answer they supply is also typically syndicalist: it is, above all, "a negative action," the *interruption* of work in the general strike, that deflates both Capital and the State.[12] As Daniel Colson writes: "Where can this freedom emerge? In interstices and pauses, when one dreams for a moment or when a cigarette is rolled."[13] In the interval produced by the strike, a kind of suspension of the daily grind, workers find themselves at once deprived of the thing that gave them their identity—work—and, face to face with one another, possessed of a new identity:

> In the furnace of these meetings, where brains were highly charged; and where, at the flame of reality, ideas surged up and became clear; by the side of those timid ones, who were always hesitating, there were those who were more impatient, who were exasperated by the slowness of events. The latter found the strides too short, and dreamed of doubling the pace....
>
> From this conflict of ideas, this mixture of proposals ... there separated out a compound, which constituted a new phase in the struggle.[14]

---

11 Granier, "Une uchronie anarchiste?: *Comment nous ferons la révolution* d'Émile Pouget et Émile Pataud," in Émile Pouget and Émile Pataud, *Comment nous ferons la révolution* (s.l: Les Éditions Invisibles, 2009), 288–289.

12 Pataud and Pouget, *How We Shall Bring About the Revolution* 22.

13 Colson, *Petit lexique*, 40.

14 Pataud and Pouget, *How We Shall Bring About the Revolution*, 41–42.

This "innumerable multitude," "this ocean of heads," "this human sea"—a new "collective being," as Proudhon would have called it— is endowed not only with a "collective force" but also a "collective reason," a qualitatively distinct "compound" cognitive process greater than the sum of its parts, as underscored by the utter absence of proper names, the anonymity of all the protagonists: even the "impatient" and "timid ones" are merely types, instances, tendencies, passing moments in the process.[15] Paradoxically, at the same time that the process of revolution is of a collective nature, it also permits the unfolding in every direction of the individual: it is the collectivization of housekeeping, for instance, that emancipates women from their unpaid labor, and it is "grouped, like men, into Trade Unions" that they find themselves "on a footing of equality with them," equipped with a new "material and moral independence."[16]

Alfonso Martínez Rizo, also writing within the syndicalist movement (he was vice president of the CNT's Sindicato de Obreros Intelectuales in Barcelona), also spends some time imagining possible organs of revolutionary action in his *1945: El advenimiento del comunismo libertario* (1933), including not only the (real enough) Sindicatos of the CNT and affinity groups of the FAI, but also an organization of his own invention, a shadowy federation of *tertulias* called "The Explorers of the Future [*Explotadores del Porvenir*]," reminiscent of Jorge Luis Borges's conspiracy of encyclopedists in "Tlön, Uqbar, Orbis Tertius," engineering a fictional world into existence (1940). However, more so than Pataud and Pouget, he takes the "material" aspect of the revolution for granted, giving even closer attention to the "moral" process of emancipation, a process that does not unfold at the same rate for everyone. The complexities of this transformation emerge especially in brief dialogues between Martínez Rizo (or his 1945 persona) and various persons for whom the moral revolution has not yet taken place. In one, taking place "on the night of that famous Thursday" of the revolutionary uprising, an old friend who has joined the police seeks him out to ask "what you will do with us":

—You know that I joined the guards just to be able to bring home a little bread for my children, and I have always sympathized

15 Ibid., 37, 41–42; Proudhon qtd. in Colson, *Petit lexique*, 120–121.
16 Pataud and Pouget, *How We Shall Bring About the Revolution*, 230.

with the way you think ... But there is such fear that even I'm getting worried. I tried to reassure them that I knew you, you're one of the leaders ...

—Stop!—I interrupted: among us, there is no boss.

—Well, you understand what I mean. I have assured them that I know you well and know that you're a true gentleman [*caballero*].

—Don't be stupid—I interrupted again—A real man, yes. Chivalry [*caballerosidad*] is a hoax.

—Come on, I mean that I have assured them that you were a very good person and that if others were like you, they wouldn't do anything wrong to us. They did not want to believe it and assured me that all of the F.A.I. are bloodthirsty and ferocious, and they were sure they were just waiting to see the first guard to do him in. They even insisted on asking me to go out in civilian clothes and find you to ask what you are going to do to us, the capitalist unions.

I reassured him completely, took him to the Ayuntamiento, got him to talk to the local committee, and initiated negotiations which resulted in the security guards arresting their leaders and surrendering their weapons.[17]

The differences that Martínez Rizo's friend sees as merely semantic—what's the difference between a "leader" and a "boss," a "gentleman" and a "very good person"?—are, in fact, part of a new structure of meanings that have been emerging within the anarchist and syndicalist milieus, and what we are watching is the kind of process by which this structure is rapidly diffused throughout a society. Written well before the uprising of July 19th, 1936, it is remarkably similar to the kind of linguistic transformation Orwell witnessed in the freshly liberated Barcelona: "Servile and even ceremonial forms of speech had temporarily disappeared.... Human beings were trying to behave as human beings and not as cogs in the capitalist machine."[18] In a scene reminiscent of "Year of Jubilee," Martínez Rizo imagines the delicacy of conversation, in a liberated café, with a waiter:

---

17 Martínez Rizo, *1945*, 46–47.
18 George Orwell, *Homage to Catalonia* (New York: Harcourt Brace, 1952), 5–6.

—What do the comrades want from those who serve [*sirva*] them? A waiter asked us when we were seated.

—Why don't you ask us what we want you to bring us?

—Be careful—I interposed. It's degrading to serve [*servir*] a master, but not a compañero.

—Libertarian communism—Olesa said to me—has to change the lexicon and delete the words that recall the former abjection. "To serve [*servir*]" comes from "servitude [*servidumbre*]" and "slave [*siervo*]."

—Everything will come in good time,—I said, but slow down. Don't you think you could provide us with [*nos aporte*] some ice cream?

—Yes, provide us with [*nos proporcione*] two large iced coffees.

—I'll distribute them to you immediately [*distribuírselos a ustedes*].[19]

Olesa's proposal, here, foreshadows the direction taken by anarchist utopias after the Second World War. After, as George Steiner recalls, the degradation of language at the hands of fascist and Stalinist regimes, "something of the lies and sadism ... settle in the marrow of the language"; the lyrical promise of utopian language can no longer be heard in the same way.[20] Under the weight of accumulated cynicism, and pushed aside by the dull but concrete projects of social engineering launched by the Western democracies, anarchist utopias of the 1940s, like Ethel Mannin's *Bread and Roses* (1944) and Ishikawa Sanshirō's *Go-jū-nen ato no Nippon* (*Japan Fifty Years Later*, c. 1946), don't stand a chance; they are *deprived of the word*. And so the anarchist utopias that emerge out of the ashes, from Le Guin's *The Dispossessed* to p.m.'s *bolo'bolo*, propose a certain reinvention of language.

The title of Le Guin's novel, in addition to playing on the title of Dostoyevsky's *The Possessed*, refers to a central feature of the anarchists' artificial language, Pravic: its utter lack of possessives. The creation of a new language is thus posited from the very outset as the central revolutionary fact, the act that sets the utopia in motion.

19 Martínez Rizo, *1945*, 52–53.
20 George Steiner, *Language and Silence: Essays on Language, Literature, and the Inhuman* (New York: Antheneum, 1970), 101.

Where Chris Ferns sees Pravic, within the framework of Le Guin's imaginary society, as "designed to reinforce the break with past habits of thought and perception," it arguably has much more to do with allowing readers to break *their* habits of imagining the worst about human beings and their nature.[21] Taking up the famous Sapir-Whorf hypothesis about the influence of language over thought—a speculation central to the most notorious dystopia of the century, Orwell's *Nineteen Eighty-Four*, in which "Newspeak" is imagined to permanently destroy our ability to even *think* disobediently—Le Guin recasts it into a utopian speculation: if a language is an agreement to "cut nature up, organize it into concepts, and ascribe significances" in a particular way, what if our language cut around, and not between, the concepts "work" and "play"?[22] What if our language "lacked any proprietary idioms for the sexual act" because it largely lacked *any* proprietary idioms whatsoever? What if "order" and "orders" were dissonant rather than consonant terms?[23]

Just as each Annaresti child is given an entirely unique name by a random computer program—a name free from gender categories, from precedents, from ancestral baggage—their vocabulary, in so far as we are allowed to hear it (rather than having it translated into English by the narrator), is undamaged by history.[24] How else could we allow ourselves once again, after the collapse of the last utopian hopes of the 1960s, to imagine greeting strangers as "brother" or "sister," if not by replacing both with a made-up word ("ammar")?[25]

A similar move is at work in p.m.'s *bolo'bolo* in the invention of a new universal "auxiliary language," *asa'pili*, the vocabulary of which provides most of the structure of the book as a kind of nonlinear catalog, a lexicon or glossary after the manner of Milorad Pavic's *The Dictionary of the Khazars* or J. G. Ballard's "The Index" (if not, once

---

21 Chris Ferns, "Future Conditional or Future Perfect?: *The Dispossessed* and Permanent Revolution," in *The New Utopian Politics of Ursula K. Le Guin's The Dispossessed*, eds. Laurence Davis and Peter Stillman (Lanham, MD: Lexington Books, 2005), 251.

22 Benjamin Lee Whorf, *Language, Thought, and Reality: Selected Writings of Benjamin Lee Whorf*, eds. John B. Carroll and Stuart Chase (Cambridge, MA: MIT Press, 1993), 213; Le Guin, *The Dispossessed*, 92.

23 Ibid., 53, 58, 45.

24 Ibid., 250.

25 Ibid., 49.

again, of Borges's *First Encyclopaedia of Tlön*).[26] In *asa'pili*, a smatter-
ing of concepts essential to the new global social contract (the *sila* /
∨) are encoded in two-syllable glyph-words, with a few higher-order
concepts built out of their combination (forming a compound idea,
with the first word specifying the sense of the second) or doubling
(forming an "organic plural"). Thus, the word *asa'pili* / ○⊟ is formed
from *asa* / ○ (world) and *pili* / ⊟ (communication), and *bolo'bolo* /
◩◩ signifies the system of all the *bolos* linked together, civilization.[27]

As with Le Guin's Pravic, the necessity of *asa'pili* is twofold—
first, in terms of the imaginary world within the book, and secondly, in terms of our world, where the book faces a jaded, cynical,
post-leftist audience. "It's impossible," p.m. argues in a footnote, to
"choose an existing international language": they are too freighted
by the history of imperialism to be acceptable to all. Hence, "the
only solution is a completely random, disconnected, artificial 'language' without any cultural links"—although he notes elsewhere
that its phonetic palette is drawn from "Polynesian sound systems"
("I was in Samoa once," he explains, "and I really liked it there. There
are certain parallels there, remnants of relatively intact societies").[28]
This is consonant with the utopia's strange blend of the futuristic
(a planetary language, electronic communication networks, science,
social experimentation) with the neo-primitive: *bolo'bolo* is an agrar-
ian society with a highly rudimentary transportation system (*fasi* /
⊖) and low energy consumption, with relations between semi-no-
madic individuals (*ibu'ibu* / ⊙⊙), communes (*bolo'bolo* / ◩◩),
neighborhoods (*tega'tega* / ⊞⊞) municipalities (*vudo'vudo* / ▣)
and regions (*sumi'sumi* / ⊗⊗) governed by such medieval codes
as personal reputation (*munu* / [an imageless concept]), hospital-
ity (*sila* / ∨), gift-exchange (*mafa* / ⵜ), barter (*feno* / ⌗), and
the possibility of a duel or limited war (*yaka* / ⵝ).[29] A synthetic,
history-less language that nonetheless bears traces of the experience
of non-capitalist societies seems well suited to such a paradoxically
pre-modern, post-capitalist world.

At the same time, of course, it is well suited to *our* need for a

---

26 p.m., *bolo'bolo*, 131.
27 Ibid., 161–162n10.
28 p.m., "bolo'bolo: Transcription," 1.
29 p.m., *bolo'bolo*.

language capable of communicating utopian hope without carrying echoes of the worst exercises in year-zero thinking. As p.m. remarks in an interview:

> I don't want to suffer because of terminology for which I am not to blame; instead, I'd rather create my own. It would probably take longer to explain that the communism that I am talking about is not the one that I saw. It is easier to simply say I am for *bolo'bolo*, and then everyone starts to think of the things all over again, to re-think them.[30]

The renewal of utopian language, then, is an act of "re-think[ing]," an attempt to undo the damage done by time. There is something healthily regressive about it, a childlike playfulness—making language into a game of codes, into something that is *made* rather than simply received. Or, as Paul Goodman has it, it fulfills one of the primary functions of literature as such: "repeat[ing] the meaning and reviv[ing] the spirit of past makings, so they are not a dead weight, by using them again in a *making that is* occurring now."[31]

---

30 p.m., *bolo'bolo: Transcription*, 1.
31 Goodman, *Speaking and Language*, 160.

7: BARBARIZING VISIONS

IF anarchism is often stigmatized as "primitive" rebellion—perhaps appropriate to an age of small, self-reliant villages or independent tribal groups, but unsuited to the realities of urban, technological, modern civilization—then it is no surprise that one anarchist response has been to identify anarchism as much as possible with narratives of science and progress.[1] Another strategy, however, has been to attack the narratives of "modernity" and "civilization" for which anarchy can only figure as something like the mythical state of nature that must give way, naturally, to the rational State (fig. 1).[2] Many anarchists' deviations from literary realism seem aimed at undermining these ideologies by viewing the modern world from the perspective

---

1   See, for instance, Proudhon's *Philosophie du Progrès* (Bruxelles: A Lacroix, Verboeckhoven, 1868) and Kropotkin's *Mutual Aid: A Factor of Evolution* (Montréal: Black Rose Books, 1988).

2   Thus, in anarchism's first period, we find Joseph Déjacque dismissing the entire Christian era equivocally as "these eighteen centuries of barbarism or civilization,—whichever one prefers to call them" and calling civilization a "daughter of barbarism who has savagery for a grandmother" (*L'Humanisphère*, 51, 80), while Ernest Cœurderoy (1825–1862) imagines revolution in the form of an invasion by wild "cossacks" (*Hurrah!!! ou la révolution par les Cosaques* [London: s.t., 1854]; see also Ezequiel Adamovsky, "Russia as a Space of Hope," *European History Quarterly* 33.4 [October 2003]: 411–449). In the second period, a minority tendency of "naturians" emerges, declaring that "*to kill, steal from, or eat one's own kind are acts which are completely* CIVILIZED" (Zisly, *Réflexions* 8), and accordingly producing anti-civilizational utopias such as Henry Zisly's *Voyage au Beau Pays de Naturie* (Paris: chez l'auteur, 1900)—precursors to, if not progenitors of, the "anti-civilizational" anarchism of John Zerzan, John Moore, Fredy Perlman, and others in the third period.

Fig. 1: A barbaric vision of the "civilizers": led by a priest in a bloody cassock, the colonial powers massacre and pillage in Asia. Théophile–Alexandre Steinlen, *L'Assiette au Beurre* 47 (Feb. 28, 1902): 748–749.

of the far future or the distant past—sometimes both at once. When the utopian visitor in Lazare's *Porteurs de Torches* fails to understand terms like "honor" and "stealing," it is the inhabitant of our own world—himself a victim of the private-property system and its ideology of "honor" that forbids him to steal to save his own life—can only exclaim, in bewilderment: "Sir, you are just a barbarian."[3] Joseph Déjacque, writing some forty years earlier, asks us to picture his utopia of a thousand years hence by a similar exercise in reversals:

> Imagine a savage of the first ages, snatched from the heart of his primitive forest and thrown forty centuries ahead, without transition, into the midst of present-day Europe, in France, in Paris. Suppose that a magic power unleashed his intelligence and promenaded him through the wonders of industry, agriculture, architecture, all arts and all sciences, and that, like a *cicerone*, it shows them to him and explains all their beauties to him. And now judge the astonishment of this savage. He will fall in

---

3   Lazare, *Les Porteurs de Torches*, 5. Cf. also Patricia Leighten's analysis of anarchist strategies of anti-colonial caricature in "The White Peril and *L'Art nègre*: Picasso, Primitivism, and Anticolonialism," *The Art Bulletin* 72.4 (1990): 609–630.

admiration before all these things; he will not be able to believe his eyes or ears; he will cry miracle, civilization, utopia!

Now imagine a civilized person suddenly transplanted from the Paris of the 19th century to the dawn of humankind. And judge his amazement before these men who have yet no other instincts but crude ones, men who feed and bleat, who low and ruminate, who roar and bray, who bite, scratch, and howl, men for whom fingers, language, and intelligence are tools that they do not know how to handle, a mechanism the cogs and wheels of which they cannot understand. Imagine this civilized man, thus exposed to the mercy of savage men, the fury of wild animals and the untamed elements. He will not be able to live among all these monstrosities. It will be for him disgust, horror, chaos!

Very well! The anarchist Utopia is to civilization what civilization is to savagery.[4]

Thus, where Ryner's *Les Surhommes* (*The Superhumans*) imagines humanity supplanted by its evolutionary precursors, Gérard de Lacaze-Duthiers (1876–1958) devotes more than a thousand pages, over the course of fourteen years, to a saga reimagining the ideal life of a prehistoric man, *Le Roman de Mauer, homme fossile: Récit de l'âge d'or* (1923–1937), culminating in a satirical dream sequence in which the unfortunate "fossil man" is transported to modern-day Paris, only to be arrested for indecent exposure, interrogated and beaten by police who seem representative of an all-too-"savage" civilization.[5] In a similar vein, Albert Libertad's "Légende de Noël" (1899) ostentatiously addresses itself to an absent audience located in the future.[6] "Dedicated to the little children of the year 3000 (or beyond)," the story presents itself as a kind of nightmarish fairy tale about life in a modern city:

Once upon a time, a long time ago, around the year 1900, there was a great heap of stones and mud that the inhabitants in those

---

4 Déjacque, *L'Humanisphère*, 81–83.
5 Gérard Lacaze-Duthiers, "Mauer Chez le Commissaire," *Pages Choisies: 1900–1930* (Paris: F. Piton, 1931).
6 Likewise, Granier finds that Michel, in her fiction, sometimes "seems to address herself to readers of the future, for whom the reality of the nineteenth century will seem quite strange, quite foreign" (*Les Briseurs des formules*, 322).

times called Paris.... Approaching these piles of stones, fighting off the foul odors rising from them, one could see that it was criss-crossed by paths of all kinds: some wide, lined with beautiful houses, others narrow, crowded on each side by tight rows of houses that looked like mousetraps. On that day, the year was coming to an end; it was a holiday in this city, but nature seemed to sulk, and snow fell in large flakes. Despite that, all along the streets, stores gave forth streams of light and eyes were drawn by bizarrely stocked masses of victuals.

The walkers, the shoppers were numerous: some, covered in warm furs, were blissfully smiling, laughing at the cold, while others, on the contrary, walked timidly, were covered with rags, through which their flesh and bones showed.

From time to time, the latter struck poses of supplication before the former which you do not know, dear children, but which consisted in reaching out one's hands, speaking incoherent words in a mournful tone. They were asking for "alms": that is to say, they were praying the fortunate to give them a share of their abundance in order to acquire necessities for themselves and their children.[7]

Defamiliarizing modernity by viewing it from the perspective of a more genuinely civilized future, Libertad "barbarizes" it, so to speak, so that its very center ("the capital of the nineteenth century," as Benjamin dubbed it), appears nothing more than "a great heap of stones and mud." This rhetorical maneuver is sharpened by framing the readers as children, innocent of historical evil (the forms of everyday degradation and iniquity, utterly familiar to modern readers, that "*you* do not know"). Youth and maturity, progress and decline, the primitive and the civilized, all are made to change places. It is as if Libertad intended to shake us up, to disorient us—or, perhaps, to orient us properly to an upside-down world.[8]

---

7   Albert Libertad, "Légende de Noël," in *Nouvelles anarchistes: la création littéraire dans la presse militante (1890–1946)*, ed. Vittorio Frigerio (Grenoble: ELLUG, 2012), 244.

8   Guy Debord, *Society of the Spectacle*, trans. Fredy Perlman (Detroit: Black & Red, 1983), 9. Cf. Granier's description of the narrative strategies of Octave Mirbeau's *The Torture Garden* (London: Bookkake, 2008): "For critical thought to emerge, the readers must first lose their points of reference" (*Les Briseurs de formules*, 368).

B. Traven's "The Night Visitor" (1928) demonstrates another mode of barbarization, enacting the "displacement in time" for the reader via a displacement in space.[9] Thus we encounter Gerard Gales, American-born expatriate and ex-sailor (in *The Death Ship* [*Das Totenschiff*], 1926), ex-tramp and migrant worker (in *Die Baumwollpflücker/Der Wobbly*, 1926), and ex-alligator hunter (in *Die Brücke im Dschungel*, 1927), now an amateur homesteader somewhere in rural Mexico. Caretaker for the *ranchito* of his "neighbor," fellow expatriate Doc Cranwell, who has gone away on business, Gales falls increasingly under the enchantment—more literally than figuratively—of Mexico's pre-Columbian past, voraciously reading his host's books on the archaeology and anthropology of the region: "I was soon completely under the spell of the histories and mythologies. I forgot the present." It is in this reverie that Gales receives visitations from a spectral guest, a strange and mournful Indian, who beseeches him:

> Oh, sir, it is ever so horrible. How can I make you understand? To know that I am so utterly helpless and without any means for defense against the gruesome attacks of those ugly beasts. Pray, señor, pray to all the powers of providence that never in all eternity may befall you so great a misfortune as the one I am suffering. It will not be long now before those loathsome monsters will gnaw at my heart. They will suck my eyes out of my head. And then there will come the day of all days of horror when they come to eat my brain. Oh, sir, by all that is sacred to you, please do something for me. Help me in my pains so bitter that I have no power in my words to describe them to you.[10]

We are eventually led to believe this uncanny figure to be the ghost of an Aztec noble whose mummy Gales finds in a half-crumbled burial mound violated by roaming hogs. For reasons not quite consciously understood, he fails to return the mummy's ornaments to the earth—an omission that occasions a further turn in the narrative.

It would be easy to see Gales as the antithesis to the image of the traveler as colonizer immortalized in *The Ugly American*; rather than

---

9 Ibid., 325.
10 B. Traven, *The Night Visitor and Other Stories* (Chicago: I.R. Dee, 1993), 26–27.

insisting on the rightness of his own customs and culture in contempt of his foreign surroundings, he is quick to admire them. In this respect, however, he is not entirely different from the protagonist of Traven's "Assembly Line" ("Der Grossindustrielle"), one "Mr. E. L. Winthrop of New York ... on vacation in the Republic of Mexico," quick to appreciate the beauty and potential cash value of the Oaxacan basket-weaver's art.[11] Likewise, reading Cranwell's books, Gales is readily delighted to find "great civilizations had existed in the Americas at a time when the Romans were still semi-savages and the Britons ate the brains of the bravest of their enemies slain in battle."[12] Making a vocation of a wandering life, Gales has come to think of himself as equally at home everywhere: "Home is where I was, and nowhere else."[13] Yet this is precisely the danger. Even as a marginal expatriate, Gales retains his white-skin privilege, and by stealing from the dead, he has become another kind of conquistador, another plunderer.[14] For this, he is punished with a series of harrowing nightmares in which, "strolling about the market places of ancient cities," he finds himself the outsider—moneyless, hungry, pursued by "naked Indian policemen"; in which he finds himself alternately "fighting on the side of the conquistadores" and "fighting on the side of the Tabasco Indians," a captive of the Aztecs sacrificed to the war god and a captive of Spaniards who, "nearly mad with joy, danced around me, yelling that they were glad to get another American for breakfast."[15] Through a series of rapid reversals, Gales is placed in the position of the barbarous outsider and pariah within native civilization, then as a native experiencing firsthand the barbarity of the conquest. Disoriented, terrified, humbled, he surrenders the stolen treasure, and the visitor vanishes.[16] But even these reparations do not relieve Gales's sense of "horror":

Welcome? Am I really welcome?

---

11 Ibid., 73.

12 Ibid., 13.

13 Ibid., 10.

14 As Manuel González Prada puts it, "Every white man is, more or less, a Pizarro" (*Free Pages and Other Essays: Anarchist Musings*, trans. Frederick H. Fornoff, ed. David Sobrevilla [New York: Oxford University Press, 2003], 194).

15 Traven, *The Night Visitor*, 38–41.

16 Ibid., 45–46.

No. I was not welcome. I was not welcome there any longer. Something had been destroyed, inside of me, or outside of me, or somewhere in the far distance. I could not tell what had been destroyed, nor where. I was no longer the same—at least not to me. I felt horror where before I had felt heavenly quiet.[17]

In his last desperate attempt to escape this "horror," he is ultimately engulfed by it, running up against "the wall of the bush":

A wall, dense, dry, dreary, greenish-gray, now looking black, looking in the darkness as though it were stooping slowly though irresistibly upon me where I sat, threatening to suck me into its fangs, intending to swallow me, to swallow all of me, bone, flesh, heart, soul, everything....

The air was filled with chirping, whispering, murmuring, fiddling, whining, whimpering, now and then shrills and shrieks of fear and horror.[18]

Freud reminds us that the German word *unheimlich*, translated by the English "uncanny," is also the opposite of the *heimlich*, "belonging to the house [*heim*], not strange, familiar, tame, intimate, friendly, etc."[19] If anything, this final scene makes clear how thoroughly Gales has lost his sense of being "at home." The chime-like repetition of the word "horror," here, reminds us of Joseph Conrad's *Heart of Darkness*, with its final refrain: "the horror! the horror!"[20] This resemblance is not ac-

---

17 Ibid., 50.

18 Ibid., 55–56.

19 Sigmund Freud, *The Standard Edition of the Complete Psychological Works of Sigmund Freud*, ed. James Strachey et al. (London: Hogarth Press, 1953), 17.222.

20 Joseph Conrad, *Heart of Darkness and The Secret Sharer* (New York: Signet Classic, 1983), 147, 153, 157. Alfred Opitz, too, makes this comparison ("Traven im Kontext der Lateinamerika-Literatur der ersten Jahrhunderthälfte," in *B. Travens Erzählwerk in der Konstellation von Sprachen und Kulturen*, ed. Günter Dammann [Würzburg: Königshausen und Neumann, 2005], 138). Note that although "The Night Visitor" was first published in German under the title "*Der Nachtbesuch* im Busch," it was, according to Traven's account in a letter to his publisher, "written ... originally in English" (qtd. in Karl S. Guthke "In 'A Far-Off Land': B. Traven," in *German Novelists of the Weimar Republic: Intersections of Literature and*

cidental. The excessive negativity of Conrad's narration of the African "bush," with its "heavy, mute spell," identifies the colonial Other as the source of a seductive, omnipresent evil—"the gleam of fires, the throb of drums, the drone of weird incantations"—while at the same time revealing that this horror is to be found within the colonizers themselves.[21] Like Traven's protagonist, Conrad's Marlow recalls that Britain, now in possession of an empire that claims to civilize the world, was once itself a "savage" colony of the Roman empire: "this also ... has been one of the dark places of the earth."[22] But whereas for Conrad, Kurtz's real crime consists in his having gone native, failing to live up to the European colonial ideal, Gales's crime consists in having gone colonial, having repeated the conquistadores' act of theft. Even more clearly than Conrad, then, Traven bears witness to the Freudian truth of the uncanny (*unheimlich*): what is encountered, in the experience of the uncanny, as radically other is "in reality nothing new or alien, but something which is familiar," i.e., precisely the *heimlich*, which has been disavowed, "project[ed] ... outward as something foreign."[23]

We can recognize similar strategies of defamiliarization and unmasking at work in one of Octave Mirbeau's most infamous novels, his *Jardin des Supplices* (*The Torture Garden*, 1899). At first, the novel might appear merely to reproduce, in a fairly repulsive manner, the standard tropes of a classic colonial discourse—the very discourse so thoroughly dissected by Edward Said in *Orientalism*. Here, we are given to behold, through the eyes of a nameless European narrator, a scene to rival the worst excesses of Sax Rohmer:

> Tall porters with grimacing faces, frightfully emaciated, their chests bare and scarred beneath their rags, were holding baskets of meat above their heads, in which the sun was accelerating decomposition and hatching swarm of maggots. They were specters of crime and famine, images of nightmare and massacre, demons materialized from the darkest and most terrifying legends of China. Nearby I saw one whose laugh exposed a slash of saw-toothed

Politics, ed. Karl Leydecker [Rochester, NY: Camden House, 2006], 172).

21 Conrad, *Heart of Darkness*, 143.

22 Ibid., 67–69.

23 Freud, *The Standard Edition*, 17.236. As long as we're etymologizing, the anarchist thing to point out might be the common root of *domestication* and *domination* in the Latin *domus*: "home."

mouth with its betel-lacquered teeth, and extended to the edge of his billy-goat beard, sinister and distorted. Some were cursing and cruelly pulling each others queues; others, with the gliding movements of felines, were slipping through the human thicket, picking pockets, cutting purses, snatching jewels and then disappearing with their loot.... And the smells that arose from the crowd—smells of the latrine and the slaughter-house, the stink of corpses and the perfumes of living flesh—nauseated me and chilled me to the marrow.[24]

The exoticism of the scene—"an imaginary of Chinese cruelty and decadence," as Granier puts it—is all too familiar to the reader of Orientalist discourse; the Eastern other is simultaneously abject (emaciated, bare, ragged, famished) and ferocious (grimacing, saw-toothed, sinister, distorted, cruel), subhuman (goatish or feline, a vegetative "human thicket") or supernatural (spectral, demonic), brutish and repulsive (smelling of the latrine and the slaughterhouse) but also decadent in ornament (perfumed).[25] Here, then, is the East as "irrational," "depraved," and "different," in Said's words—that mirror image of the West against which Europeans can confirm their own image as "rational," "virtuous," and "normal."[26]

But this confirmation is denied us. On the contrary, it is violently subverted at every turn by direct comparisons with the depredations of Europe, both at home and abroad: "Listen!" cries Clara, the sadistic libertine who simultaneously seduces and repels the narrator,

I've seen robbers hung in England; I've seen bullfights, and anarchists garroted in Spain. In Russia I've seen beautiful young girls whipped to death by soldiers. In Italy I've seen living phantoms—spectres of famine—disinter the bodies of cholera victims and eat them eagerly.

The language Clara uses to describe European law and order, the vaunted civilization of the West, deliberately echoes the imaginary of the eponymous Torture Garden—but with the difference that it has

---

24 Mirbeau, *The Torture Garden*, 114–115.
25 Granier, *Les Briseurs des formules*, 367.
26 Edward W. Said, *Orientalism* (New York: Vintage, 1978), 40.

real referents: for instance, the allusion to the notorious spectacle, just three years prior to the publication of the novel, of anarchists subjected to military trial, imprisonment, torture, and execution in the dungeons of Montjuich in Spain.[27]

Yet more complications undermine any sense that the West constitutes a norm against which the East can be safely pitied or condemned. The entire narration of the story titled "The Garden" is embedded within two other narratives, each quite as disturbing: first, a third-person frame-story, the "Frontispiece," which situates all the rest within an evening of discussion among a group of thoroughly cynical, jaded bourgeois at a dinner party in Europe, and then "The Mission," purportedly a manuscript read by one of the dinner guests narrating the scandalous circumstances which led him, the nameless narrator of "The Garden," to quit France for China, aided by his old ally, the corrupt Minister, Eugène Mortain. These extra layers of narrative place even more brackets and question marks around the sadistic scenes staged in the Torture Garden, as they reveal that the man who narrates them to us—increasingly unhinged by what he witnesses—is a thoroughly fraudulent representative of an utterly corrupt "civilization." No element of the self-representation of Europe is left untarnished or spared mockery, including its pretense to objective, scientific knowledge: the narrator himself, who has never so much as studied biology, embezzles money intended to finance a research expedition, presenting himself as an "embryologist" charged with searching for the origins of life.[28] Decadent, murderous, licentious, cruel—and, on top of all that, preposterously pious—the Europe from which the narrator departs is only too exactly mirrored by this phantasmagoric "China." In the end, the East becomes the mask or the uncanny double of the West, rather than its complementary or antagonistic opposite, so that there is nowhere to "escape" to:

> It seems I shall never be able to escape from myself again.... The universe appears to me like an immense, inexorable torture-garden. Blood everywhere ... I should like, yes, I should like to be reassured, cleanse my soul and brain with old memories, with the memory of friendly, familiar faces. I call Europe and its

27 Mirbeau, *The Torture Garden*, 97.
28 Ibid., 49–50.

hypocritical civilization to my aid, and Paris—my joyful, laughing Paris. But it is the face of Eugène Mortain I see grimacing on the shoulders of the fat, loquacious executioner who, at the foot of the gallows, in the flowers, was cleaning his saws and scalpels.[29]

There is no solace in the "familiar" or the exotic; the distinction between them has collapsed.[30]

In the words of Peter Lamborn Wilson, "no Heaven balances this Hell," no remainder is spared from the universal condemnation: "Life, love, pleasure—all is death, all is shit and disease."[31] It appears that the nihilistic "Clara" not only *is* the last word in the novel—"Clara! Clara! Clara!" cries the distraught narrator—but that she *has* the last word:

> "Dear Clara," I objected, "is it really natural for you to seek sensuality in decomposition, and urge your desires to greater heights by horrible spectacles of suffering and death? Isn't that, to the contrary, a perversion of that nature whose cult you invoke, in order perhaps to excuse whatever criminal and monstrous qualities your sensuality involves?"
>
> "No!" said Clara, quickly, "since love and death are the same thing!"[32]

The collapse of opposites into one another (or perhaps the one into the other) threatens to subvert the entire adversarial direction of the

---

29 Granier, *Les Briseurs des formules*, 367; Mirbeau, *The Torture Garden*, 181–182.

30 The Uruguayan anarchist playwright Florencio Sánchez (1875–1910), writing under the pseudonym "Jack the Ripper," enacts a very similar reversal in his short story, "La Justicia en China," originally published in *El Sol* (1900): after a farcical proceeding in which the ostensibly rigorous judge Tio Kin reverses himself four times in deference to the rank of the accused, he turns around and instantly sentences to death a humble tea vendor for failing to bow before the sovereign. Sánchez anticipates his readers responding in horror: "What terrible things happen in China!" to which he responds laconically: "Yes—it seems they happen here, too" ("La Justicia en China," *El Cuento anarquista en Latinoamérica*, ed. Darío A. Cortés [Granada: Emgraf C.B., 2003], 121–123).

31 P. Wilson, "Amoral Responsibility," 56.

32 Mirbeau, *The Torture Garden*, 109.

novel—to subvert the subversion, in a sense. The poison of domination taints everything, so that there appears to be no outside:

> The universe appears to me like an immense, inexorable torture-garden.... What I saw today, and what I heard, exists and cries and howls beyond this garden, which is no more than a symbol to me of the entire earth.[33]

If there is no transcendent escape (what is there besides "the entire earth"?), no alternative to Mortmain and Clara, the narrator cannot fail to conclude in advance: "There is nothing real, then, except evil!"[34] And if this is true, then we are left with nothing else to hope for; we can only give ourselves over to the horror or despair of it. Mirbeau does not seem to wish for either response; rather, he banks everything on the revulsion that he hopes to transform into revolt. But this is not, historically speaking, a safe bet. A generalized *misanthropy*—the inclusion of everything and everyone under the sign of disgust, resentment, hatred—is at least an equally likely outcome for those who do not recoil from *The Torture Garden* as vigorously as it recoils from the world of dominations.

---

33 Ibid., 182.
34 Ibid., 77.

8: A SOCIAL SPECTACLE?

ON March 21, 1969, a forum would test the boundaries of speech and audience, the divisions that Jacques Rancière calls "the partition of the sensible."[1] The Brotherhood Synagogue at 28 Gramercy Park (formerly a Meeting House for the local Society of Friends) was, indeed, a well-partitioned space, as Robert Brustein later reflected: "The white auditorium, in which both participants and audience were arranged in pews, provided what seemed a good atmosphere for rational discussion."[2] That evening, it would host a Theatre of Ideas symposium, provocatively titled: "Theatre or Therapy?" On the list of speakers were Brustein (drama critic for the *New York Review of Books*), Judith Malina and Julian Beck (representing the Living Theater), Paul Goodman (erstwhile playwright for the Living Theater, currently hosting Malina and Beck at his apartment), and *Village Voice* writer Nat Hentoff.

Brustein, the lead speaker, was there to underscore the "or." The new experimental dramaturgy, as represented by Julian Beck and Judith Malina's Living Theater (especially notorious for its debut, that year, of a performance titled *Paradise Now*, performed entirely in the nude, and occasionally featuring live sex acts with spectators) might be a kind of psychotherapy, but it was no longer recognizably a "play." Brustein had previously praised the Living Theater's *The Connection* (1959) as having "somehow managed ... to break down barriers

---

1   Jacques Rancière, *Dissensus: On Politics and Aesthetics*, trans. Steve Corcoran (London: Continuum, 2010), 36.
2   Robert Brustein, "Monkey Business," *New York Review of Books* 12.8 (April 1969): 44.

between what was going on onstage and what was going on in life,"[3] but the intervening decade had cooled his ardor; like Goodman, he now drew analogies between the experimental theater and the left-wing youth movements, which he saw as having devolved from the stuff of high tragedy, "noble acts of non-violent resistance by highly serious individuals," into mere "disruptive and histrionic acts by infantile 'revolutionaries.'"[4] This was the substance of his remarks:

> I believe the theatre to be served best when it is served by supremely gifted individuals possessed of superior vision and the capacity to express this in enduring form. In short, I believe in the theatre as a place for high art....
>
> I do not believe the theatre changes anybody, politically or psychologically, and I don't believe it should try to change anybody.

This is, rather, what Brustein *intended* to say, for he was quickly interrupted by one of the members of the Living Theater in the audience:

> HECKLER: We're all supremely gifted individuals.
> BRUSTEIN: I doubt that very much.
> HECKLER: Up against the wall.[5]

Judith Malina, the third speaker, objected: "Everybody has it in him to be an artist—there's no such thing as special individuals who are supremely gifted." Audience members, untrained, could produce theater "better than Shakespeare or Euripedes." Nonetheless, she too was heckled from the balcony: "Fuck Shakespeare. Fuck Euripedes."

> MALINA: I dig Shakespeare sometimes. But I also want to speak in my own voice, in my own person. I mean there's Hedda Gabler and there's Judith Malina, and I want to be Judith Malina.
> HECKLER IN BALCONY: I'll give you Hedda Gabler: "The candle is on the table." That's Hedda Gabler. Now I'll give you

---

3   John Tytell, *The Living Theatre: Art, Exile, and Outrage* (New York: Grove Press, 1995), 158.
4   Brustein, "Monkey Business," 44.
5   Robert Brustein, *Revolution As Theatre: Notes on the New Radical Style* (New York: Liveright, 1971), 34–35.

me: Fuck Ibsen. Fuck all liberal intellectuals and their fucking discussions ... [6]

The event dissolved in a hurly-burly; Goodman stalked out of the synagogue and hailed a cab, followed by an apologetic Beck, pleading with him to stay: "Clearly," Goodman reflected later, "my role in the psychodrama was to leave. I did. I always dutifully play it straight.... But I told him that it was a lousy play because the actors (we) were treated too anonymously."[7]

What was at stake in this "psychodrama," if that's what it was? Was Goodman right to regard the Living Theater as an example of failed or soured anarchist art, an experimental attack on aesthetic hierarchies degenerating into sheer anti-intellectual rancor? Didn't the disruption merely reproduce the alienation it was intended to interrupt? Had Malina and Beck, along with their old friend, fallen victim to their own Frankenstein's monster (having just mounted, a year earlier, what was said to be a very successful production of *Frankenstein*)? Was the intervention—or the entire modus operandi of the Living Theater—anarchist at all?

Hardly any anarchist of the second period would have said "Fuck Ibsen."[8] Indeed, Ibsen was part of their global dramatic canon, performed countless times, lauded in lectures by the likes of Emma Goldman. However, Ōsugi Sakae (fig. 1) might have been willing to stake a claim for the place of the Living Theater in the anarchist tradition. As the proponent (and practitioner) of a theory of positive "heckling," Ōsugi also struck an anti-intellectual stance at times; "your writings are jokes," he taunted the radical literati, "as long as ... [they] touch not on the reality of subjugation or on opposition to it."[9] However, he insisted that he interrupted other radicals' speeches "not for the purpose of simply destroying ... [but] for the purpose of constructing

---

6 Ibid., 34–35.

7 Paul Goodman, "Playing It Straight," *New York Review of Books* 12.10 (May 22, 1969): 46.

8 Nor even "Fuck Shakespeare." "To tell the truth, it was only Shakespeare who really struck me in the course of my literary education," said the anarchist tramp-poet, Jehan Rictus (1867–1933) (qtd. in Eugène Porret and Étienne Chipier, *Jehan-Rictus et la Misère* [Neuchatel: Éditions de la Roulotte, 1947], 86). See also Landauer's Shakespeare lectures, below.

9 Ōsugi qtd. in Stanley, *Ōsugi Sakae*, 66.

大杉栄君

Fig. 1: Portrait of Ōsugi Sakae—in a typical pose—by Mochizuki Kei (1922).

at all times and all places the new lifestyle and the new order step by step."[10] In this "new order," Ōsugi postulated, the sense of deference would give way to an egalitarian, populist spirit. This had to extend to the arts, which were presently "the privilege of a few people": "The people are alienated from the arts. Those who are most numerous in the nation, the most vibrant part, do not have any representation in any kind of art."[11] Accordingly, an anarchist theater would be a popular theater, accessible to all, and also an egalitarian theater, polyvocal rather than univocal:

> Long speeches are the special characteristic of old plays; in the new plays, short dialogues will succeed....
>
> Listening silently to a person's long speech is only to be swept up in a marching song: it is what is done vis-a-vis upper-class people. Among people of the same class, long speeches will

---

10 Ōsugi qtd. in Ibid., 120.
11 Ōsugi Sakae, "Atarashiki sekai no tame no atarashiki geijutsu [A New Art for A New World]," *Zenshū* (Tokyo: Sekai Bunko, 1963): 5.23–45.

disappear and short dialogues will succeed. From long monologues to short dialogues: this is the evolution of conversation.
This is the evolution of humanity.[12]

This seems a satisfying fit between form and content. Mikhail Bakhtin suggests that the monologue is an inherently authoritarian form,
while dialogue connotes dissent and plurality. Monologue requires a
silent other, and eliciting passivity; dialogue elicits active engagement.
So the theory goes. On the other hand, many an anarchist the-
atergoer has enjoyed a good monologue—"a modality privileged by
the anarchists," Eva Golluscio de Montoya asserts.[13] Consider Jean
Roule's fourth-act monologue in Mirbeau's popular *Les Mauvais
Bergers* (*The Bad Shepherds*, 1897), urging the striking workers not to
turn to the politicians for help:

> JEAN: The boss is at least a man like yourselves! You have him be-
> fore you—you speak to him—you make him angry—you threat-
> en him—you kill him. At least he has a face, a breast into which
> you can thrust a knife! But go now, and move that being without
> a face that is called a politician! Go kill that thing that is known
> as politics! That slippery and fugitive thing, that you think you
> have, and that always escapes you—that you believe is dead, and
> it begins once again—that abominable thing by which all has
> been made vile, all corrupted, all bought, all sold—justice, love,
> beauty! Which has made of the venality of conscience a national
> institution of France—which has done worse yet, since with its
> foul slime it has soiled the august face of the poor—worse yet,
> since it has destroyed in you the last ideal—the faith in the Rev-
> olution! Do you understand what I have desired of you—that
> which I still demand of your energy, your dignity, your intelli-
> gence? I have desired, and I desire, that you shall show for once,
> to the world of political parasites, that new example, fecund and
> terrible, of a strike made, at last, by yourselves, for yourselves!
> And if once more you have to die, in this struggle which you
> have undertaken, know how to die—one time—for yourselves,

---

12 Ōsugi qtd. in Stanley *Ōsugi Sakae*, 120.
13 Eva Golluscio de Montoya, "El monólogo: una convencíon de la escena
libertaria (Río de la Plata, 1900)" (Teatro del Pueblo / SOMI, April 1990)

for your sons, for those who will be born of your sons—and no more for those who trade upon your suffering, as always![14]

The language combines the political harangue *à la* Henry V's Saint Crispin's Day speech, the soapbox denunciation, and the philosophical lecture.[15] It is both diegetic speech ("heard" by an audience of other characters on stage) and an exegetic discourse (intended to be "overheard" by the audience in the theater and applied to their own situation).[16]

In short, this is where the pedagogical function of the anarchist drama is most visible: we are being schooled in revolution. Li Shizeng's (1881–1973) *Ye wei yang*, a Chinese translation of Leopold Kampf's stage melodrama *Le Grand Soir* (1907), one of the earliest works of anarchist culture in Chinese (in fact, one of the very first *huaju* or Chinese spoken-word plays, as opposed to opera), was explicitly conceived in this way: "schools have a tendency to instruct students in scientific understanding and application," Li reflected, "but as to the sentimental education of mankind, schools are often ineffective and one should make drama into the school for this task."[17] Such "class-struggle plays" were subsequently performed at schools with significant anarchist participation, such as Liming Gaozhong [Dawn Senior Middle School] in Quanzhou, where one student theater group actually named itself the *Ye wei yang ju she* (Grand Soir Drama Club).[18] In Argentina, likewise,

14 Octave Mirbeau, "The Bad Shepherds," in *The Cry for Justice: An Anthology of the Literature of Social Protest*, ed. Upton Sinclair (Philadelphia: The John C. Winston Co., 1915), 628, trans. unknown, modifications mine.

15 Golluscio de Montoya, "El monólogo."

16 What is astounding, considering how widely this particular play traveled along the anarchist circuits of publication, dissemination, and performance—it played in Greece, Germany, Japan, Argentina, Catalonia, the U.S.—is how often spectators felt that it was talking about *their* situation. For instance, the same Act IV monologue reproduced above from a collection of social protest literature, edited by Upton Sinclair (1915), is cited by Gustav Landauer, the German translator of the play, in the context of a polemic (1899) against the Social Democrats (Walter Fähnders and Christoph Knüppel, "Gustav Landauer et *Les Mauvais bergers* d'Octave Mirbeau," *Cahiers Octave Mirbeau* 3 [1996]: 79).

17 William Dolby, *A History of Chinese Drama* (New York: Barnes & Noble Books, 1976), 279n13; Tschanz, "Where East and West Meet," 94.

18 Gotelind Müller, *China, Kropotkin und der Anarchismus* (Wiesbaden: Harrassowitz, 2001), 606; Dongyoun Hwang, "Korean Anarchism Before 1945," 117.

many performances of plays such as this were mounted by groups affiliated with *centros de estudios libertarios*.[19] And since, as we have seen, anarchist resistance culture is thoroughly imbricated with the project of education, the monologue, carrying much of the "didactic force" of the play as a whole, occupies a special place in anarchist dramaturgy in a way that it does not in more traditional drama.[20]

Well, then: if the anarchist monologue requires a maximum of reverent silence from the diegetic (on-stage) audience, and if the exegetic (in-theater) audience is given to self-assertive heckling, what results? According to Juan Suriano, journals such as *La Protesta* register complaints about the audience's lack of decorum: talking during the performance, laughing at tragic moments, "juvenile insolence," smoking in the theater, failing to doff hats, and other such affronts drew harsh criticism from anarchist journals as ideologically disparate as the pro-organization *La Protesta* and the anti-organizationalist *El Rebelde*, both of Buenos Aires.[21]

Should anarchist theater then be regarded as a kind of (fortunately?) failed experiment in "acculturating" the uncultured working class? Analyzing a posed photograph of the attendees of a Brazilian syndicalists' conference, Francisco Foot Hardman notes a "tension between *solemnity* and *relaxation*: the need to pose, the search for *respectability*, the use of suits and hats, the solemn character marking the aspiration of the workers' associations to 'civilize' the world."[22] We can see the same codes of solemnity on display in film footage of the 1931 Congreso Extraordinario of the CNT-AIT in Madrid, held during a sweltering week of June in the Teatro Conservatorio: the speakers on the stage (including such luminaries as Ángel Pestaña, Rudolf Rocker, and Augustin Souchy) are almost all wearing suits as well as ties, despite the fact that they are visibly sweating, and most of those in the jam-packed auditorium, if they aren't wearing vests, at least have their shirt-sleeves down and collars buttoned (there are scarcely any women to be seen in the place). A collective water-jug (*el botijo*) is passed around the floor. We see the delegates, who pour out into the street after a session of the

19 Juan Suriano, *Paradoxes of Utopia: Anarchist Culture and Politics in Buenos Aires, 1890–1910* (Oakland, CA: AK Press, 2010), 22.

20 Golluscio de Montoya, "El monólogo."

21 Suriano, *Paradoxes of Utopia*, 111, 279n91.

22 Francisco Foot Hardman, *Nem Pátria, nem Patrão: vida operária e cultura anarquista no Brasil* (São Paulo, Brazil: Brasiliense, 1983), 48–49.

congress, light up cigarettes, but having *put on* their coats and hats.[23] Perhaps a similar tension between the recalcitrant body and the spirit of solemnity is at work in the theaters of Buenos Aires. If the anarchists saw theater as primarily a means of propaganda, of recruitment, then wouldn't the interruption of that process represent workers' resistance to being recruited, their rejection of "the Idea"?

A number of facts complicate this interpretation. First of all, while anarchist theater is often framed by solemn genres (dramas of denunciation, scenarios of confrontation and revolution, social tragedies), and somber occasions (dates from the martyrological calendar), it also spans the comedic genres; it includes satires like Charles Malato's *Barbapoux* (1900) and *César, pièce satirique* (n.d.), Li Shizeng's adaptation of the "short farce" *L'Echelle* as *Ming bu ping* (*Cry of Injustice*, 1908), and Tsuji Jun's comic opera *Tosukina* (1919), send-ups of bourgeois morals and institutions like Georges Darien's *L'Ami de l'ordre* (1898) or Octave Mirbeau's one-act *Farces et Moralités* (1898–1904), and anarchist "vaudevilles en 1 acte" like Malato's "Mariage par la dynamite" (1893) or Émile Chapelier's "Au confessionnal" (1910).[24] The ascetic streak in Spanish anarcho-syndicalism and the rigors of the struggle there entailed a certain contempt for "buffoonery," as a writer for *Acracia* called it (1937), and Carlos Fos claims that only "a minority in Argentine anarchism defended comedy and entertainment as channels for the expression of the ideal," while their Chinese counterparts were concerned to distance themselves from the frivolous and exploitative elements of their own opera traditions; however, Juan Suriano notes that offerings at the anarchist theaters of Buenos Aires also regularly included "*juguetes cómicos*" and farces—and *festas* held in São Paulo were not complete without a comic skit like *O Tio Padre* (*Uncle Father*) as relief from the seriousness of drama.[25]

---

23 "IWA-AIT Congress in Madrid 1931." The complement of the decorously clothed anarchist body is, of course, the nude body, central to anarchist practices of naturism and nudism, which enjoyed popularity among a substantial minority of the compañeros and compañeras in Europe (France, Germany, Spain) and the Americas (Cuba, the U.S.). Nudity—of a generally decorous, albeit not entirely desexualized kind—is also central to the world of anarchist images, as we shall see, from the woodcuts of Frans Masereel and Manuel Monléon's posters to the cinema of Armand Guerra.

24 Li qtd. in Tschanz, "Where East Meets West," 98n3.

25 Carlos Fos, "Anarquistas, libertarios, actores," in *Historia del actor: de la escena clásica al presente*, ed. Jorge Dubatti (Buenos Aires, Argentina: Edi-

White's survey of French anarchist theater before 1914, meanwhile, finds a fifty-fifty split between dramatic and comic productions.[26]

It is true, however, as Constance Bantman observes, that the spectrum of anarchist entertainments entirely excludes "the purely ludic": even when they take on playful forms, they are first and foremost *means of resistance*.[27] Increasingly, they constitute a defense against what will turn out to be an emerging "society of the spectacle" that will provide endless escapist substitutes for revolution, and which will gladly peddle images—for instance, in the minstrel show—pandering to the worst forms of hatred and contempt dividing the working classes.[28] Even the most harmless spectacles, those which appeal in a rudimentary way to social conscience, are desocialized, placed in a special "aesthetic" frame that insulates them from action and lived experience in a way that anarchists absolutely rejected. Edouard Rothen conjures up the image of the spectator who

---

ciones Colihue, 2008), 190; Wenqing Kang, *Obsession: Male Same-Sex Relations in China, 1900–1950* (Hong Kong: Hong Kong University Press, 2009), 139; Tschanz, "Where East Meets West," 95; Suriano, *Paradoxes of Utopia*, 107; Mariângela Alves de Lima and Maria Thereza Vargas, *Teatro operário na cidade de São Paulo* (São Paulo: Prefeitura do Município de São Paulo, Secretaria Municipal de Cultura, Departamento de Informação e Documentação Artísticas, Centro de Documentação e Informação sobre Arte Brasileira Contemporânea, 1980), 112, 29.

26 Robert White, "Anarchist Theatre in Paris Prior to 1914," in *Essays in Honour of Keith Val Sinclair: An Australian Collection of Modern Language Studies*, eds. Keith Val Sinclair and Bruce Merry (Townsville, Australia: University of North Queensland, 1991), 108.

27 Constance Bantman, "Sociabilités anarchistes: Le cas des anarchistes français d'Angleterre (1880–1914)" (Université de Paris-13: Centre de recherches interculturelles sur les domaines anglophones et francophones), 13.

28 This was by no means an issue confined to the U.S. One of Carlos Fos's interviewees, an Argentine ceramics worker named Juan Cortés, says: "We could not go to bourgeois shows. The Argentine authors insisted on servile, superficial melodramas or fell into xenophobia with their poor sketches. I remember that when one of them severely castigated the Turkish and the southern Italian families, Enrique Miguens decided along with the *compañeros* of the little theater group 'La Humanidad' to write and perform a play as compensation for the insult." Their dramaturgical retaliation came in the form of "El Bueno de Emir [Emir's Goodness]," depicting "the travails of an immigrant who first fought against a ruthless boss and then joined with others to form a cooperative" (qtd. in Fos, *En las tablas libertarias: Experiencias de teatro anarquista en Argentina a lo largo del siglo XX*, ed. Lorena Verzero [Ciudad Autónoma de Buenos Aires: Atuel, 2010], 109).

has wept at the sufferings of imaginary orphans—then, exiting the theater, walks coldly past the orphan who is hawking newspapers in the street.[29] When emotion itself is turned into a commodity by the commercial melodrama, the classic function of the stage—Aristotle's "catharsis," or the purging of emotions—takes on a newly grim aspect: the anarchist labor organizer and dramatist Hirasawa Keishichi (1889–1923) recounted with horror how, at a performance of a progressive melodrama, "The public, amused, entertained, watched the drama as mere spectators. The glittering gilt Imperial Theatre laughed at the dark misery represented."[30] By contrast, anarchist drama is almost never performed outside of a framework that grounds the scene in its politics, cementing it to a context: it is typically presented as just one of the elements of a *velada*, sandwiched between other entertainments (songs, poems, dances) and more directly political discourses (e.g., lectures and discussions).[31]

Finally, it is not at all clear that the anarchist theater corresponds to a simple sender/receiver model—the Marxist model of "interpellation," for instance—in which anarchist militants "hail" non-militant, non-anarchist workers, exhorting them to adopt anarchist identities. Consider, for instance, what appears to have been a not uncommon phenomenon at anarchist performances: the *audience* breaks the fourth wall. Thus, for instance, a writer for *La Luz* (1886) reporting on a theatrical *velada* held to commemorate the anniversary of the Paris Commune, notes that during a performance of Pedro Marquina's

29 Rothen, "Théâtre," 2756. Decades later, Paul Goodman makes a strikingly similar point about the limitations of cinema; see "Designing Pacifist Films," in *Utopian Essays and Practical Proposals* (New York: Vintage Books, 1964), 70–79.

30 Qtd. in Jean-Jacques Tschudin, "Hirasawa Keishichi et le théâtre ouvrier," *Ebisu* 28 (2002): 179.

31 Suriano, *Paradoxes of Utopia*, 97. Sometimes these may have been deliberately intended to guide spectators' interpretation of the spectacle: thus, Alvan Francis Sanborn relates how, before performances of his own *Barbapoux* at the Maison du Peuple, "Malato himself provided an introductory lecture" (*Paris and the Social Revolution: A Study of the Revolutionary Elements in the Various Classes of Parisian Society* [Small, Maynard & Co., 1905], 38). Likewise, Cecilia Beach notes that "Between the prologue and the first act" of Louise Michel's play, *La Grève*, "Leboucher, an anarchist orator, gave a speech"—ensuring that it would "not [be] performed in isolation" (*Staging Politics and Gender: French Women's Drama, 1880–1923* [New York: Palgrave Macmillan, 2005], 41).

one-act play, *El Arcediano de San Gil* (*The Archdeacon of San Gil*), the audience got so worked up at the sight of "that unworthy priest, who so faithfully represents his class, displaying the vile passions that necessarily develop in many when systematic celibacy violates the laws of nature" that they couldn't maintain their stance as detached observers any longer: "'Kill them,' screamed some outraged, recalcitrant viewer who could not endure such an exhibition of vileness."[32] "Steal a chicken!" shouts a horrified spectator at a performance, somewhere in the Argentine Pampas during the 1930s, of the social drama *Hambre* (possibly José Nakens's *El Hambre y la honra* or *Hunger and Honor*, 1884), unable to bear watching a woman *pretending* to be the starving mother of children.[33] The audience for a series of short anarchist plays at the Théâtre d'Art Social (1893) breaks out into cries of "Down with the Fatherland! Down with the Army! Long live dynamite! Long live Anarchy!"[34] And at the opening of Mirbeau's *Les Mauvais Bergers* at the Théâtre de la Renaissance (1897), observers heard frequent shouts: "Long live Anarchy! Death to the bourgeois!"[35] "Even the calmest show" at the Théâtre de l'Œuvre (ca. 1893–1899), according to Monique Surel-Tupin, is marked by similar outbursts: "Dirty bourgeois! Idiots! Brutes!... Long live Anarchy!"[36] At a Rōdō Gekidan performance, Akita Ujaku reports, "the spectators ... cried out 'yes!' 'that's it!' yelling as they watched the plays."[37] Incidents such as these do not seem to indicate an alienated, unengaged audience—on the contrary.

This sense of immediacy, confounding the pretend with the real, might not be unique to the anarchist theater (in the late-nineteenth century, rioting was not an uncommon response to new art), but it also might seem contrary to the interests of a radical dramaturgy like Bertolt Brecht's. For Brecht, the confusion of theater with

---

32 *La Luz* qtd. in Aisa, *La cultura anarquista*, 154.

33 Sandra McGee Deutsch, *Crossing Borders, Claiming a Nation: A History of Argentine Jewish Women, 1880–1955* (Durham: Duke University Press, 2010), 153.

34 As reported by Pouget's *Père Peinard*, qtd. in Durand, "L'art social au théâtre," 19.

35 Granier, *Les briseurs de formules*, 105.

36 Monique Surel-Tupin, "Scènes et publics," in *Au temps de l'anarchie: Un théâtre de combat, 1880–1914*, ed. Jonny Ebstein et al. (Paris: Séguier Archimbaud, 2001), 42.

37 Akita qtd. in J. Thomas Rimer, *The Collected Writings of J. Thomas Rimer* (Tokyo: Edition Synapse, 2004), 141.

life, of representation with reality, is an uncritical state of mind, one in which the spectator is likely to think: "Yes, I have felt like that too—Just like me—It's only natural—It'll never change—The sufferings of this man appall me, because they are inescapable.... I weep when they weep, I laugh when they laugh." Instead, "the theatre must alienate what it shows," so that the audience is puzzled, detached, skeptical.[38] This distancing is taken to be the hallmark of critical consciousness.

Against this rationalist image of thought, equating distancing and mastery with critical thinking, anarchist theater foregrounds intimacy, contact, empathy. Sergio Pereira Poza finds that the Chilean anarchists' theater, too, made use of techniques of "distanciation," but that these "acquired a different sense from the Brechtian mechanism" by operating only on "a rational level," while refusing to allow "emotional" distance.[39] Likewise, citing Erich Mühsam's 1912 essay on "Volksfestspiele," or plays staged at popular festivals, David Shepherd writes that despite his equally combative politics, "Mühsam's concept of theatre was the antithesis of Brecht's": he sought, in his works, to produce a "*Geist der Gemeinschaft* [spirit of community]," tantamount to the very "intoxicating evocation of empathy against which Brecht warns."[40] Apparently, his counterparts could sometimes be quite successful at doing just that.

At the same time, as Xavier Durand notes, anarchist drama is often markedly artificial: a play debuting at the Théâtre de l'Art Social, Auguste Linert's *La Cloche de Caïn* (*Cain's Bell*), is especially ostentatious in this respect. "Everything is fake in the theater," writes Linert; "I frankly construct my play in a fully conventional manner."[41] Durand summarizes the play:

38 Bertolt Brecht, *Brecht on Theatre*, ed. and trans. John Willett (London: Methuen, 1965), 71, 193.

39 Sergio Pereira Poza, *Antología crítica de la dramaturgia anarquista en Chile* (Santiago de Chile: Editorial Universidad de Santiago, 2005), 143.

40 David A. Shepherd, *From Bohemia to the Barricades* (New York: Peter Lang, 1993),125. The language Mühsam uses here is, in fact, highly reminiscent of Landauer's defense of the need for the positive delusion, the *Wahn*. See Charles B. Maurer, *Call to Revolution* (Detroit: Wayne State University, 1971), 92–93.

41 Durand, "L'art social au théâtre," 20; Auguste Linert, "Le socialisme au théâtre," *L'Art Social* (January 1892): 60.

The capitalists Ritch and Mangeor face the poet Rêve-Azur, a clerk in Mangeor's bank.... The décor [is] dominated by the massive presence of the bank-safe of Capital. The piece thus describes, by a succession of tableaus, the capitalists who rub their hands together and urge conscripts to die for their country (For the Motherland); who reject the complaints of workers whose wages have decreased (Vox Populi); who first repress the riot before the explosion of the safe. Cain's bell, the dynamite, rings out, and Rêve-Azur concludes: "Do the brothers of Mangeor understand?"[42]

In short, as Linert gleefully admits (in a brochure distributed at the performance): "The succession of tableaus in my play is illogical by preference, the plot is fantastic, the characters are vague, the incidents false, the development is contrary to nature, and the characters are puppets dancing on strings."[43] Here again is that use of a strong *impasto* effect, a caking-on of the paint to make the act of painting visible behind the picture—an effect not unlike Brecht's *Verfremdungseffekt* in reminding the audience that they are present at something that has been constructed, that could have been constructed otherwise, that is not the same as the merely given. Indeed, if an anarchist playwright like Linert deliberately "suppresses all the conventions meant to ensure the work's illusion of realism [*vraisemblance*],"[44] this may be part of *why* it would make sense to shout "Steal a chicken!" to the actress playing the starving mother: the situation calls for action, not passive spectatorship. Perhaps the working-class spectator at an anarchist play thinks: "I'd never have thought it—People shouldn't do things like that—That's extraordinary, hardly believable—It's got to stop—The sufferings of this man appall me, because they are unnecessary.... I laugh when they weep, I weep when they laugh."[45] Could this be, in fact, what the reports from *La Protesta* and *El Rebelde* indicate?

This does not answer the question, however, of whether the intended audience for anarchist plays *does* really consist primarily of workers who are not (yet) anarchists—something that bears very

---

42 Durand, "L'art social au théâtre," 20.
43 Auguste Linert, *Théâtre d'art social, spectacle d'essai du 12 mars 1893* (Paris: Charpentier, n.d.), 11.
44 Durand "L'art social au théâtre," 20.
45 Brecht, *Brecht on Theatre*, 71, modifications mine.

strongly on the question of whether the main function of anarchist theater is to recruit or persuade unaffiliated workers. Certainly, this was one of the things the performers sometimes hoped for.[46] Yet our data are limited and equivocal. For instance, when progressive dramatist Nakamura Kichizō first attended a performance of Hirasawa Keishichi's Rōdō Gekidan (Workers' Theater Company) in the rough-and-tumble Nankatsu neighborhood, he attested that "the audience assembled in this *yose* [a kind of cabaret] hall are all workers." However, as Jean-Jacques Tschudin points out, Nakamura and his middle-class intellectual friends only arrived at the hall after getting thoroughly lost, having never before set foot in this sketchy quarter—testifying to the fact that this represented "contact with a reality about which they indeed knew almost nothing."[47] How reliable are his demographics, then?

Hirasawa, himself a metalworker, certainly did aim to reach a broad working-class audience, and his aims were thwarted when new legal restrictions forced him to "choose between a legality that would prohibit any militancy and the semi-clandestinity of certain agitprop groups in the early 1930s—effective, but not reaching beyond already-convinced activists."[48] However, there are some strong indications that at least one core audience for anarchist plays consisted of the same anarchist militants who staged and, frequently, *wrote* those plays—small "philo-dramatic" companies of working-class anarchist militants, untrained in dramaturgy. Hirasawa's own Rōdō Gekidan was largely composed of amateurs ("Imagine," exclaimed Itō's friend Akita Ujaku, "making playwrights and actors out of laborers!").[49] This meant rejecting the

---

46 Thus, the manifesto of the "Théâtre en Camaraderie" initiative (Paris, 1907) optimistically proclaims that "the theater has the advantage drawing to of our gatherings a greater crowd of people than any other mode of action can reach." Moreover, this expectation influences their repertorial choices: "Obviously, we don't intend only to perform purely anarchist works. That has to be abandoned" ("Théâtre en Camaraderie," *L'Anarchie* 2.91 [Jan. 3, 1907]: 4).

47 Itō Matsuo qtd. in Tschudin, "Hirasawa Keishichi," 178; Tschudin, Ibid., 178.

48 Ibid 182.

49 Rimer, *The Collected Writings*, 141; Akita qtd. in Rimer, 141. See also Paul Avrich, *Sacco and Vanzetti: The Anarchist Background* (Princeton, NJ: Princeton University Press, 1991), 54–55; and Niccolò Baldari, "L'attentato a Mussolini," *Ricerche di S/Confine* 1.1 (2010): 86–87 on the importance of the *filodrammatiche* in the Italian anarchist movement.

hierarchy and specialization of the professional theater; in a group comprised of just "a handful of committed members," Robert White observes, "the role of actor, set-designer, stage-hand, publicist and ticket-seller might be filled successively or simultaneously by the one individual."[50] According to Maria Antonía Fernández, this was the case in Spain, at least during the crucial formative period of Spanish anarchism, and Juan Suriano asserts that the audience for the *filodramático* performances in Buenos Aires was made up of "individuals with a basic knowledge of anarchist ideas, probably activists and sympathizers who occasionally brought along a co-worker."[51]

What would it mean if the audience of the anarchist theater were people already thoroughly convinced of the ideas the plays seem designed to propagate? Addressing this unusual homogeneity between audience and performers, Eva Golluscio de Montoya claims that these performances represent "what Yuri Lotman called a 'communication of the second type,' one in which the message is directed at an audience whose prior knowledge is known, evaluated and, in our case, even shared by the sender." On the one hand, this concept of Lotman's, which he elsewhere calls "autocommunication," does seem to capture something about these plays: they *do* seem centered on "a basic message, always the same and known in advance by the public which shares its convictions and ideological principles," as Golluscio de Montoya has it, and they share some features of autocommunicative texts; e.g., they are short (one or two acts) just because they don't have to explain much to spectators who already know their content.[52]

All of this would be very much in keeping with the conception of anarchist theater as part of a resistance culture—a conception explicitly affirmed by the Argentine syndicalists, for example.[53] In *La força social i revolucionària del teatre* (1938), Manuel Valldeperes (1902–1970), translator of Octave Mirbeau into Catalan, wrote that the "mission of the theater" ought to be "to empower [*capacitar*] the

50 White, *Anarchist Theatre in Paris*, 105–106.

51 Antonía Fernández, "Evolucion de la propaganda," 73; Suriano, *Paradoxes of Utopia*, 108, 111.

52 Eva Golluscio de Montoya, "Pactos de representación en un teatro militante," in *De la Colonia a la postmodernidad*, eds. Peter Roster and Mario Rojas (Buenos Aires: Edit. Galerna, 1992), 110–111.

53 Fos, "Anarquistas, libertarios, actores," 190.

people to face the problems that directly affect them," a conception reminiscent of the Mujeres Libres' emphasis on *capacitación* (empowerment) over *captación* (recruitment).[54] The more stagey elements of anarchist drama often conduced to this effect: as a study of the workers' theater of São Paulo points out, "the allegorical characters who represent the libertarian idea are generally powerful in stature and possessed of a magnetic force, unlike the sickly and physically narrow bourgeoisie.... Workers are represented on a scale four or five times greater than that of their opponents (state, clergy, employers, etc.)"[55] This, perhaps, is what the audience of the Rōdō Gekidan experienced when they saw Hirasawa, dressed in a worker's clothes, "jump up on the stage without hesitation and rush at the wicked capitalist"—to the sound of their own "thunderous applause."[56] Rather than corresponding to an Althusserian or Brechtian model of theater as an ideologizing or critical apparatus, then, it might be more accurate to align it with Augusto Boal's Theatre of the Oppressed, centered on the concept of "rehearsal": much as syndicalists saw partial strikes as a kind of "revolutionary gymnastics," toning up the body politic for the final assault on capitalism, Boal advocates revolutionary drama as "a *rehearsal of revolution*": "No matter that the action is fictional; what matters is that it is action!"[57] Rather than transmitting a discourse from sender to receiver, both the Theatre of the Oppressed and the anarchist theater are spaces within which people who are at once actors *and* spectators enact moments of rebellion—"autocommunication" *par excellence*.

Or so it might seem. But something is amiss: the language of anarchist dramaturgy is not consistent with an autocommunicative discourse. Discourse produced for oneself, Lotman predicts, will use "elliptical constructions" and a "domestic," even "intimate" vocabulary—*exactly the opposite* of what we find in actual anarchist

54 Valldeperes qtd. in Robert Marrast, *El teatre durant la guerra civil espanyola* (Barcelona: Inst. del Teatre, 1978), 295.

55 Alves de Lima and Thereza Vargas, *Teatro operário*, 58. Likewise, Carlo Tresca's (1879–1943) *L'attentato a Mussolini ovvero Il segreto di Pulcinella* (*The Attack on Mussolini: Or, Punch's Secret, 1926*) depicts Il Duce's flunkies as "fearful," "bumbling," "quaking," "stupid," etc. (Nunzio Pernicone, *Carlo Tresca: Portrait of a Rebel* [New York: Palgrave Macmillan, 2005], 344–345).

56 Itō Matsuo and Osanai Kaoru qtd. in Tschudin, "Hirasawa Keishichi," 178.

57 Jacques Julliard, *Autonomie ouvriére: études sur le syndicalisme d'action directe* (Paris: Gallimard, 1988), 49; Boal, *Theatre of the Oppressed*, 155, 122.

dramaturgical practice. "The anarchist theatre," writes Granier, "is a direct, 'frontal' theatre ... in contrast to Brecht's oblique theatre"; accordingly, "there is nothing esoteric about the language of the anarchist authors: it is a means of agitation and communication."[58] Even the disruptive Living Theater dramaturges sided with Piscator's rationalism against Artaud's Surrealism: "Where Artaud cries out for Madness," writes Kenneth H. Brown, author of *The Brig*, "Piscator advocates Reason, Clarity, and Communication."[59] The emphasis on being "clear," "forceful," and "straightforward," in the words of *La Protesta*'s Eduardo Gilimón (birth and death dates unknown), seems to be almost universal, over time, in all corners of the anarchist diaspora.[60] In fact, one of the defining characteristics of these anarchist plays is their accessibility, their *transparency*. They are constructed according to the demands of persuasive oratory—namely, the demand for "brevity" (most are one or two acts at most), "economy" (reducing the universe of characters and symbols to a minimum), "clarity" (i.e., the avoidance of ambiguity), and "repetition" (of themes, of phrases, of symbols...).[61] Moreover, these plays were often wrapped in an extra layer of redundancy: in Argentina and Catalonia, for instance, it was common for anarchist newspapers to publish the plays, *in toto* or excerpted, in installments during the weeks preceding the opening. Thus, part of the audience would often arrive already knowing the lines.[62] All in all, everything is designed as if it were extremely important that the spectator not misunderstand the message.

Why should this be? What does it mean for autocommunicative texts to be constructed so as to be maximally open and accessible,

58 Granier, *Les Briseurs de formules*, 99.

59 Kenneth H. Brown, *The Brig: A Concept for Theatre or Film* (New York: Hill and Wang, 1965), 87. This is not to say that the anarchists embraced Piscator or vice versa, although they did cross paths: Erich Mühsam was on the board of Piscator's theater, which produced works by him (*Judas* and *Staatsräson*, 1928) and Ernst Toller (*Hoppla, wir leben*, 1925). "I did not refuse Piscator my cooperation," grumbles Mühsam, but "the Piscator Theater is no proletarian theater" ("Proletarische Theater," *Fanal* 2.1 [October 1927]: 23–24, trans. Chris Edmonston).

60 Gilimón qtd. in Eva Golluscio de Montoya, "Elementos para una 'teoría' teatral libertaria," *Latin American Theatre Review* 21.1 (Fall 1987): 85. One may note that these are also virtues shared by the middle-class playwrights favored by anarchists, e.g., Ibsen and Zola.

61 Golluscio de Montoya, "Pactos de representación," 110–111.

62 Golluscio de Montoya, *Teatro y folletines libertarios rioplatenses*, 9.

rather than closed and esoteric? The only reasonable explanation would seem to be that their spectators are neither purely initiates nor purely outsiders; they are a mixed multitude, a hybrid audience. If we distinguish, with the semiotician Eliseo Verón, between the "*contradestinatario*" of political discourse (the "*counter*-addressee," the political enemy), the "*paradestinatario*" (the "*para*-addressee," who is the target of persuasive speech: a potentially friendly "you") and the "*prodestinatario*" (the "*pro*-addressee," who, as Laura Fernández Cordero explains, "shares a collective identification with the speaker and is easily incorporated into the inclusive 'we'"), this hybridity becomes easier to understand. We can then see that just as an anarchist poetics aims, in the words of Iris M. Zavala, "to transgress all closure through heterogeneity and the force of signification," the mode of address favored by anarchist plays might well be plural, heterogeneous rather than homogeneous.[63]

What we seem to find—quite parallel to the case of anarchist poetry prior to the Second World War—is an anarchist theater situated within a porous, translucent counterpublic.[64] The staged speech of a

---

63 Fernández Cordero, "Queremos emanciparos," 8–9; Zavala, *Colonialism and Culture*, 135. Although it is never easy to be sure of the demographics of an sometimes clandestine global workers' movement, we can find some indirect evidence for this dual audience. In 1885, a St. Louis anarchist paper, Joseph Reifgraber's *Die Parole*, reports that a performance of Chicago anarchist August Spies's "agitational" drama, *Die Nihilisten* (1883) drew an audience of three thousand at a festival celebrating the anniversary of the Paris Commune, and the following year, an anarchist professor named Mezeroff estimates that perhaps just 150 anarchists call St. Louis home (Carol Poore, *German-American Socialist Literature: 1865–1900* [Bern: Lang, 1982], 105; Goyens, *Beer and Revolution*, 147). Now, it is possible that the audience numbers were inflated (it was Reifgraber's own Literarischen Club that published Spies's play!), just as it is possible that Mezeroff's estimate was low (and vice versa). However, the twenty-fold gap between the two numbers would seem to indicate that the audience for anarchist theater, even confined to an immigrant audience, could be substantially larger than the audience of active, committed, self-identified anarchists. See also Marcella Bencivenni on the high attendance estimates for Italian anarchist drama in West Hoboken, New Jersey, ca. 1892 (*Italian Immigrant Radical Culture: The Idealism of the Sovversivi in the United States, 1890–1940* [New York: New York University Press, 2011], 101).

64 Susan Hinely points out one source of evidence for this porosity: "Just as the anarchist women's journals included non-anarchist women within their constituency, non-anarchist women journalists like Henrietta Muller reported favorably on the activities of anarchist women.... See for example

Rêve-Azul, we might say, is not a voice of protest aimed at capitalists (the *contradestinatario*) but is primarily intended to be heard by an anarchist audience (its *prodestinatario*) whose desires it is meant to express, and at the same time to be overheard by a working-class audience (its *paradestinatario*) whose desires it is intended to capture.[65] In this complex web of expression and persuasion, the anarchist theater can fulfill several functions at once, varying according not only to the genre, but to the spectator and the situation.

Thus, comedic plays often seem designed to encourage the militant anarchist *prodestinatarios* by reducing the enemy (often a nebulous, abstract entity: the bourgeoisie, capitalism, "society") to particular persons (e.g., the pathetically hypocritical, cowardly governors in Mirbeau's *The Epidemic*, Linert's nefarious but easily defeated bankers, or Malato's ridiculous Barbapoux). If this seems to manifest a "Manichean" worldview, "lacking in nuance or originality in the depiction of [the] oppressor-oppressed relationship," as Juan Suriano charges, this reduction nonetheless helps dispel what Errico Malatesta called the "metaphysical" aura of established power, the sense that it is everywhere and nowhere, and that therefore it cannot be grasped and confronted; it simultaneously

---

Women's Penny Paper (8 March 1890), for a favorable review of [Louise] Michel's anarchist theater production" ("Charlotte Wilson, the 'Woman Question,' and the Meanings of Anarchist Socialism in Late Victorian Radicalism," *International Review of Social History* 57.1 [2012]: 27, 27n64).

65 It is also sometimes overheard by other audiences. "The public of the [Théâtre de] l'Œuvre is varied," Surel-Tupin claims: "One sees there petit bourgeois and shopkeepers, workers alongside men in rather more posh habits and evening dress." And some among them are Roger Farr's "hostile informatives": "The police are always present at performances" (*Scènes et publics*, 43). The interactions between these audiences—anarchist, non-anarchist, and anti-anarchist—could, at times, come to resemble Boal's or Deleuze's "theater of rehearsal": thus, police informants present at the opening of Louise Michel's *Nadine* (April 29, 1882) recorded with alarm that "as the armed struggle became more and more intense and violent on stage, the commotion in the hall grew to a point where the theater administration hesitated to raise the curtain for the final act. The anarchists in the audience actually began attacking the bourgeois [characters] with various projectiles, crying 'Vive le pétrole!' (Long live petrol!) ... The judicious bourgeois, who had come prepared for such audience participation, protected themselves with umbrellas, crying 'A bas le pétrole!' (Down with petrol!) in response. In the end it was necessary to turn off the lights in order to avoid a full-scale confrontation" (Beach, *Staging Politics*, 36–37).

magnifies the audience's sense of its own constituent power.[66] Anarchist comedies summon the force of a "we" against a "they."[67]

On the other hand, anarchist plays often appear as an attempt to work through the problems of the "we." Anarchist tragedians often confront the people's betrayal of itself in the form of strikebreakers (as in Alberto Ghiraldo's *Columna del Fuego*, 1913) and of the military (as in the 1906 adaptation of George Darien's novel *Biribi* or the Living Theater's *The Brig*, 1964), but also in the form of family strife. It often concerns the anguish of the ideologically mixed marriage, particularly as seen from the point of view of the male anarchist married to a counter-revolutionary woman, as in Rodolfo González Pacheco's *Hijos del Pueblo* (*Sons of the People*, 1921) and Antonio Penichet's *¡Salvemos el hogar!* (*Let's Save the Home!*, 1925). In these melodramas, the woman, who should be the "assistant" to the man's aspirations, seduced by the comforts of the Church and the attractions of commercial glamor, fails to support her *compañero* in the struggle, castigating him for wasting time at the *centro obrero*, pleading with him not to go on strike, or even dragging him back to the Church.[68] However, we sometimes see the scenario reversed, as in Ernst Toller's *Masse Mench* (*Masses Man*, 1921), where it is Sonia who is the radical and her husband the perfidious "state official" who tries to drag her away from her revolutionary calling. Nelly Roussel's one-act *Pourquoi elles vont à l'église: Comédie en un acte* (*Why*

---

66 Malatesta, *Anarchy*, 10.

67 Note that this distinguishes them radically from what Henry Jenkins calls "anarchistic comedy," a term he applies (with a minimal sense of its history) to the Marx Brothers (*What Made Pistachio Nuts?* [New York: Columbia University Press, 1992], 22–23). As Mark Edmundson observes, the Marx Brothers' comedies revolve around the anxieties of immigrants as "outsiders" vis-à-vis assimilation, aiming to reduce that anxiety by deflating the bourgeois images of propriety, authority, and rectitude to which the outsider cannot attain ("From Sweet Anarchy to Stupid Pet Tricks," *Civilization* 3.6 [December 1996–January 1997]: 35–49). However subversive this deflation may be, it ultimately underscores the centrality of the "insiders" who are still permitted to define the proper, the authoritative, the right. Anarchist resistance culture instead produces an entirely different sense of the "inside," a standpoint from which the bourgeois image-world merely appears bizarre and barbaric, not even worthy of the immanent critique of an Oscar Wilde.

68 Ana Ruth Giustachini, "La dimensión verbal en el teatro anarquista," *Espacio de crítica e investigación teatral* 4.8 (October 1990): 98–99; Shaffer, "The Radical Muse," 138–139.

They Go to Church: Comedy in One Act, 1911) revisits the scenario of
¡Salvemos el Hogar! from the perspective of a wife saddled with an anarchist husband, Bourdieu, who wants to discuss nothing more with
her than "what's for lunch?" and whose concept of companionship
is limited to "when you come home, it's to drink your soup in peace,
without bothering with anything else." The time comes when the gap
between the "fine words" about freedom he reserves for an all-male
audience and his "personal conduct" at home becomes too great, and
she will defy him by answering her friend Madame Rosier's invitation
to attend Vespers.[69] Accepting this invitation, ironically, will have
been *her* one act of freedom, just because *he* has forbidden it—an
irony that would not have been lost on the male *compagnons* in the
audience.[70] In this case, contrary to Suriano's claims, the *contradestinatario*, the accused, is the "us."[71] Despite the title, we have witnessed
not a comedy, but, from an anarchist perspective, a tragedy—a classical tragedy, even, as Bourdieu's hypocrisy also smacks of *hubris*.

If anarchist comedies let us taste victory, anarchist tragedies
such as *Pourquoi elles vont à l'église*, *Columna del Fuego*, and *Masse
Mensch* attempt to think through the reasons for failures of solidarity, historical defeats, the lack of revolutionary will, dilemmas,
and impasses of action. Alan Pearlman, translator of *Masse Mensch*,
likens the seventh act, a polemic between Sonia and her fellow prisoner, "The Nameless," to a "medieval psychomachia," i.e., "a war
in the soul" between the anarchist partisans of revolutionary violence (which included most anarchists then as now) and nonviolence (which included Toller's friend Landauer and, to some extent,
Toller himself).[72] Here, rather than remaining uncontested, mono-

---

69 Roussel, in *Au Temps de l'Anarchie*, 158–160.
70 According to Jo Burr Margadant, Roussel "recounted how she had shamed
    men in the audience—a tactic she would frequently use when talking to and
    about men—and how she had succeeded in making them repent: 'As for the
    male listeners, they avowed the next day that when I had looked at them ...
    during the course of the lecture, they felt ashamed and wished they could
    hide.... Many of the women workers are, it seems, abandoned single moth-
    ers.... And their seducers, who were also in the room, admitted responsibil-
    ity for their actions'" (*The New Biography: Performing Femininity in Nine-
    teenth-Century France* [Berkeley, University of California Press, 2000], 225).
71 See Fernández Cordero for an extended analysis of the difficulties encoun-
    tered by early anarchist feminists in effecting such a change of address.
72 Alan Raphael Pearlman, "Introduction," in *Ernst Toller Plays One*, ed.

logues in favor of both positions are allowed to contest one another, to produce a space of tension and ambiguity.

Tension and ambiguity also haunt Erich Mühsam's *Judas* (1921), Ernst Toller's *Hoppla, wir leben* (*Hoppla, We're Alive!*, 1927), and Jens Bjørneboe's *Fugleelskerne* (*The Bird Lovers*, 1966). None of these dark plays is intended to serve as propaganda for the cause, certainly, although all are defined by the rigors of anarchist ethics. Can it ever be right to sacrifice one man's life in the service of others, as Raffael Schenk attempts to sacrifice Matthias Seebald in *Judas*? What do we do when, like Karl Thomas in *Hoppla, We're Alive!*, our old comrades have all deserted us? Is it true, as the faithless Wilhelm tells Karl, that "violence is always reactionary"?[73] Do the victims of an oppressor, like Caruso and his old partisan comrades in *The Bird Lovers*, have a right to revenge, even through a judicial process, if this very process sets in motion a kind of miniature State apparatus? Or are we all equally guilty by our inevitable complicity with oppression, therefore unable to judge? If so, is this a relief (we can be done with trials, with verdicts, with executions, with obedience) or a catastrophe (all is pardoned, all is permissible, there is no justice)? No solutions are provided, and we are not invited to identify just with any one character; the production of an open space for discussion is the important thing.

Plays addressed primarily to a *paradestinatario*, on the other hand, are characterized by the presence of what Ana Ruth Giustachini calls "the Enlightened Character [*Personaje esclarecido*]," a hero-protagonist upon whom we are to model ourselves, and/or what Golluscio de Montoya calls the "mirror-character [*personaje-espejo*]," a secondary character, undergoing a process of evolution toward the ideal, in whom "flesh

Alan Raphael Pearlman (London: Oberon Books, 2000), 41. Sonia, in *Masses Man*, directly echoes Landauer in her replies to the pro-violence arguments of The Nameless; for instance, when The Nameless claims that "Masses are holy," she replies, "Masses are not holy. Violence made the Masses.... Masses are a trapped and buried people" (Toller, *Ernst Toller Plays One*, 182)—phrases that directly recall Landauer's assertion, in *Aufruf zum Sozialismus* (1911), that the poet's seemingly individual genius is in fact "smothered people ... living people that have collected in them, that are buried in them and will be resurrected out of them.... And these isolated few, into whom richness of spirit and power has fled, face the many isolated, atomized people who are left only with unspirit, desolation and misery: the masses, who are called the people, but who are only a heap of uprooted, betrayed men" (*For Socialism*, 33–34).

73 Toller, *Ernst Toller Plays One*, 231.

and blood spectators can see the image of their own evolution."[74] Quite often, these are heroines, such as the allegorical Eve of Nelly Roussel's *Par la révolte: scène symbolique* (1903). Here, having received no succor from Church or Society, Eve receives Revolt "as [her] savior":

> EVE (*standing, trembling, excited*)—Ah! Your powerful breath revives me, lifts me, carries me! ... I sense within me the raging flow of generous anger!...
>
> Treacherous Religion, infamous Society, monstrous and foolish prejudices, your slave is a rebel! ... The prisoner shakes the bars of her prison![75]

Put Roussel's Eve next to Elena, the martyred heroine of Adrián del Valle's often-performed *Fin de fiesta, cuadro dramático* (1898)—literally taking one in the chest for the workers[76]—and it is not hard to see an attempt at *captación* at work. In fact, the "social theatre" and the evenings of entertainment (*veladas, vetllades, soirées, festas*) in which it is usually embedded, during anarchism's second period, can be seen largely as an attempt to include and recruit women, particularly those who, like Madame Bourdieu, might otherwise go to the Church.[77]

---

74 Giustachini, "La dimensión verbal," 98; Golluscio de Montoya, "Pactos de representación," 116.

75 Nelly Roussel, *Par la révolte*, 4th edition (Paris: Imp. L. et A. Cresson, 1905), 12–13.

76 Shaffer, "The Radical Muse," 138.

77 Again, in spite of the inevitable difficulties that surround any demographic studies of the anarchist movement, there is a considerable amount of anecdotal evidence favoring this assertion—and once again, this seems to have been true globally. Thus, in the U.S. context, circa 1880–1914, Goyens notes that the German anarchists' festivals and picnics were intended to draw women's attendance (often successfully), while around the same time in Buenos Aires (circa 1890–1910), Suriano estimates that "a significant number of women—one-third of attendees—were present at such gatherings" (*Paradoxes of Utopia*, 93). See, for instance, Goyens, *Beer and Revolution*, 147, 158; José Moya, "Italians in Buenos Aires's Anarchist Movement" in *Women, Gender and Transnational Lives*, eds. Donna R. Gabaccia and Franca Iacovetta (Toronto: University of Toronto Press, 2002), 205–206; Kirwin R. Shaffer, "Prostitutes, Bad Seeds, and Revolutionary Mothers in Cuban Anarchism," *Studies in Latin American Popular Culture* 18 (1999): 2, 8. At the same time, play production was strongly masculinized; "The scarcity of women in what was principally a male environment," White remarks, "led to frequent appeals for female volunteers to play the parts of mothers, wives

For both its *prodestinatarios* and its *paradestinatarios*, the anarchist drama seeks not passive spectatorship but active agency, not consumption but "coparticipation" or "coproduction of meaning," as Pereira Poza describes it.[78] This invitation to participate takes place not only on the level of production, where actors are drawn from the same pool as the audience in the self-directed *grupo filodramático*, but at the level of reception. Here, the audience is confronted with what is not a "finalizing discourse" that purportedly "defines anything once and for ever," as in the supposedly "completed, conclusive and immutable" discourse of the Church, but a message that makes an open show of its cracks and gaps, analogous to the open wounds of history (Claramunt's *El mundo que muere*) as well as to the openness of the world waiting to be born (*El mundo que nace*). The anarchist play, unlike the "well-made play" of bourgeois convention, presents an "open conclusion," either in terms of the radical intolerability of the scene, which challenges the audience to construct an alternative to the reality it reflects, and/or in terms of the unresolved contradictions it stages, which challenge the audience to address them in reality.[79] "We want voices," said González Pacheco, "that *open up* streets, horizons, perspectives."[80] Perhaps only such a theater of radical openness could hope to reverse the spectacular logic of power, to revise the partition of the sensible.

---

and sweethearts, and imposed still further restrictions on the choice of repertory" ("Anarchist Theatre in Paris," 106). One wonders: if anarchists had given more effort to theater, and if, after the example of Nelly Roussel and the anarchist women's *filodramáticos* that sprung up here and there, more women had been involved in production, might not the movement have assumed a more genuinely feminist character? Would an anarchist movement equally of women and men, endowed with greater powers of social reproduction, have weathered the disruptions of the twentieth century better? It may not be too late to ask such a question in practice.

78 Pereira Poza, *Antología crítica*, 128.

79 Bakhtin, *Problems of Dostoevsky's Poetics*, trans. Caryl Emerson (Minneapolis: University of Minnesota Press, 1984), 251; and *The Dialogic Imagination*, trans. Caryl Emerson and Michael Holquist (Austin: University of Texas Press, 2006), 17; Pereira Poza, *Antología crítica*, 129.

80 Rodolfo González Pacheco, *Carteles* (Buenos Aires: Ediciones Anarquía, 2009), 52, italics mine.

9: THE MIRROR STAGE

"**TO** faithfully reproduce in a realistic manner all of this sad, gray existence is a kind of sadomasochism," declared members of the anarchist Compañía de Espectaculos Ibéricos, writing in the post-Franco anarchist journal *Bicicleta* (1977–1982).[1] This disastrously sterile reproduction of the real is a danger courted by novels of denunciation as bitter as Octave Mirbeau's, in which the bitterness threatens to spread, like an ink blot, to color everything.

Nor is anarchism necessarily founded in this bitterness. Rather than comprising a sum total of "antis" ("anti-capitalism, anti-clericalism, anti-statism, anti-militarism, anti-colonialism," etc.), Colson argues, anarchism can best be conceived as "an *affirmative* force that breaks the chains of *domination* through revolt only in order to better affirm, in the very movement of rupture, another *possibility*, another *composition* of the world."[2] And so it is that anarchist fiction, on the model of Lazare's "social art," seeks to evoke a sense of possible worlds worth fighting for—that is to say, to offer what Goodin aptly names "hope" and "clarity."

In his study of victim narratives, Goodin observes that the "problem of hope"—the forces of oppression and evil must not be depicted as so trivial that they are not worth fighting, nor as so dreadful that they cannot be fought at all—is matched by an equally serious "problem of clarity." On the one hand, unless the forces that oppress the victim are given a rationale and a logic of their own, they become simply

---

1   Compañía de Espectáculos Ibéricos, "del teatro a la anarquía," *Bicicleta* 1.8 (September 1978): 77.
2   Colson, *Petit lexique*, 33.

mysterious, arbitrary, ill-delimited, producing a confusion, one form of which is Mirbeau's misanthropy. On the other hand, as Goodin puts it, "As the presentation of antagonists becomes fuller, they almost inevitably turn into victims themselves and start to command sympathy"; we may even come to see the victim as complicit in his or her own victimization, collapsing the difference between protagonist and antagonists, and again rendering it impossible to determine an appropriate target for one's anger, outrage, derision, and blows. Thus, Ōsugi Sakae admonished novelist Miyajima Sukeo for "fall[ing] into the darkest despair and sentimentality, into self-destructive desperation."[3] To resist both resignation and confusion, then, anarchist narratives must provide sufficient hope (title of the French CNT-AIT journal, *L'Espoir*, 1960–1977 and 2005–present) and clarity (title of the Chilean student union's anarchist journal, *Claridad*, 1920–1926 and 1931–1932).

Nor is this hope to be found only in utopian or revolutionary narratives, important as those are. Rather, it is manifested in "some *living* quality [that] can be apprehended growing out of the ruins of tragedy and evil," as George Woodcock put it.[4] It is just this vitality that radiates from the pages of Jules Vallès's "Vingtras" trilogy, where we encounter a subject who consistently refuses to be "finalized," whose resources of subjectivation (verbal energy, imagination, even "stupidity") are never exhausted by the forces of subjectification that converge upon him (family, Church, State...). It is also manifested in Adrián del Valle's *Cuentos inverosímiles*, where feminine presences come to represent the possibilities for transcendence that are immanent in all that lives and the vitality within everything. Witness "Eterna Lucha [Eternal Struggle]," in which two disillusioned poets in a bar argue fruitlessly over the source of their "modern malady: mental distress" until their dialogue is interrupted:

> We suffer from mental distress, true, but because we lack an ideal
> to stir up our souls and shake up our minds. We are powerless

---

3 Ōsugi Sakae, "Mouvement ouvrier et littérature ouvrière [The Workers' Movement and Workers' Literature]," trans. Jean Jacques Tschudin, *Ebisu* 28.28 (2002): 164.

4 Woodcock, *The Writer and Politics*, 183, italics mine. This is never a small demand to make of literature, and he wrote this in the aftermath of World War II (in the year that gave birth to Orwell's *Nineteen-Eighty-Four*).

because we are cowards, ambitious worshipers of the conventions and lies of a money-obsessed society. And our illness can not be cured by drinking ...
—How, then? ...
—By struggling,—cried a voice behind them.

The interrupting voice, "a beautiful young woman with blonde hair, very pale skin, and bright, serene blue eyes," at first a subject of misrecognition. She refuses the wine offered her by the one who toasts her: "Ideal woman, illusion or reality, come, drink, speak, your presence sweetens our bitter hours of mortal anguish!" Asked her name, she answers only "a woman"; asked where she is from, she replies, "My country has no borders." " Your home is the Earth," the younger man offers; it is "the entire Universe." No, she replies; it is "bigger, bigger ... An ideal country, creation of good, generous, dreaming souls: the land of freedom, well-being, happiness"—a declaration that is dismissed as "craz[y]."[5] The nameless woman, unfazed, declines the toast to her as an "ideal woman" and refuses to assign herself a *place*: that is, she stands outside all the conventional frameworks readymade for her by masculinist fantasy or nationalism—her reality is "bigger" than any of the available realities—but she simultaneously refuses to place herself in some transcendent beyond ("the ideal," a realm "foreign" to the everyday reality within which the poets are suffering). What the cynic rejects as "craz[y]" is a paradox central to anarchism: the source of hope is at once transcendent (as in the slogan "another world is possible!") and entirely immanent to the world in which we find ourselves trapped. "In anarchism," Colson explains,

> the revolution is not initially the product of the contradictions of the existing order or system, the dialectical product of this system, its negation.... It is born from the outside of this system, from what this system does not manage to enclose, from the infinity of possibilities that this currently dominant system ignores, plunders, repels and denies, potential forces that always haunt it with the fact that it is itself merely one possibility among an infinity of other possibilities.... The libertarian movement is not born from the order that it refuses, even if this order

5   del Valle, *Cuentos inverosímiles*, 105–106.

is contradictory, but from the anarchic profusion of forces and possibilities that are alien to this order, or from those that this system dominates and distorts.[6]

It is in this sense that the woman whose watchword is "struggle!" can belong at once to this world (of bars, of men and women) and to a country greater than the universe itself.

Instead of simply staging "reality," then, an anarchist poetics aims, in the words of the manifesto issued by the Compañía de Espectáculos Ibéricos, "to distill and refine the quintessence of what is distillable and refinable in reality, thereby showing a different view of it, full of magic, new sensations, surprises, sensuality, offering something that makes us vibrate anew, awakening our sensibilities." Is this not also a description of the defamiliarizing, deformative style of Louise Michel's "delirious realism," aimed at disrupting the seemingly self-explanatory, static images we have been given of the "real" world?

At the same time, opposition to an oppressive *status quo* reality entails the need to name and know it. Even if, as Proudhon says, "everyone is complicit"—*especially* if this is the case—oppressors and forces of domination need to be carefully mapped and evaluated, in some cases imagined even before they can emerge (from that same "outside of the system," which is home to horrible as well as marvelous possibilities). From this need for radical clarity comes the frequently reiterated perception of anarchist poetry, fiction, and drama as "Manichean"[7]—as we shall see, not necessarily an accurate reflection of anarchists' vision of the world.

It is precisely because of these demands for hope and clarity that anarchists have a conflicted relationship with metaphors such as "accurate reflection," with the image of a thought and a writing that would be, in the words of Richard Rorty's famous work of

---

6   Colson, *Petit lexique*, 24–25.
7   Golluscio de Montoya, "Pactos de Representación," 111. See also, for instance, Suriano, *Paradoxes of Utopia*, 109; Litvak, *El cuento anarquista*, 54; Granier, *Les Briseurs de formules*, 120, 237; Salaün, *Romancero libertario*, 26; Lucienne Domergue and Marie Laffranque, "À propos des contes anarchistes," in Federico Urales, *Cuentos de amor y otros cuentos anarquistas en "La Revista Blanca" 1898–1905* (Toulouse: Presses Universitaires du Mirail, 2003), 242, 254.

philosophical demolition, "the Mirror of Nature."[8] On the one hand, this trope of mirroring *does* appear in anarchist theory, where it often seems to function just like the positivist representationalism skewered by Rorty and his colleagues. In anarchist dramaturgical and literary discourse, too, mirror-imagery is prolific: Emma Goldman praises modern drama for serving as "the reflex, the mirror of life," and Voltairine de Cleyre speaks of "Literature, the Mirror of Man," while Rudolf Rocker claims that the artist's very ego is a kind of mirror "in [which] is reflected the whole environment in which he [or she] lives and works."[9] On closer inspection, though, the trope turns in unexpected directions: thus, in Goldman's case, "Such literature, such drama, is at once the *reflex* and the *inspiration* of mankind in its eternal seeking for things higher and better." This is clearly no ordinary mirror, for it reflects not only what exists, as it is, but, impossibly, things as they should be, "higher and better." Rocker's artist-as-mirror, too, "does not simply give back what he [or she] sees," but creatively modifies it like the rest of his or her materials. De Cleyre's mirror is even less passive or neutral: it is "not ... a powerless reflection ...," but an active modifying agent, reacting on its environment and transforming circumstances, sometimes greatly, sometimes, though not often, entirely"—"as the image in the glass which should say to the body it reflects: '*I* shall shape *thee*.'"[10] This is not the "Mirror of Nature" dreamed of by Western thought; it is closer to the famous "mirror stage" of Jacques Lacan's psychoanalysis.

Something like Lacan's "misrecognition" is at work in the trope of art as mirror: the spectator gazes at his or her own image and fantasizes about being (like) that image. Whereas the real self is plural and fragmented, lacking autonomy, the mirror image, being external, appears self-contained, intact, unified. This is the analogy Lacanians make between what the experience of the infant who first "misrecognizes" itself in the mirror and the adult pleasure in identifying with

---

8   Richard Rorty, *Philosophy and the Mirror of Nature* (Princeton, NJ: Princeton University Press, 2009), 170.

9   Emma Goldman, *The Social Significance of the Modern Drama* (Boston: R.G. Badger, 1914), 3; Rudolf Rocker, *Nationalism and Culture*, trans. Ray E. Chase (New York: Covici-Friede, 1937), 474; de Cleyre, *Selected Works*, 359.

10 Goldman, *Social Significance*, 6; Rocker, *Nationalism and Culture*, 474; de Cleyre, *Selected Works*, 83, 80.

images occupying the impossible place of the "ideal-I." This, in turn, serves a disciplinary function, subordinating real people to abstract ideals, pushing us to strive towards socially approved goals.[11] This account of the social function of mirror-images might remind us uncomfortably of how many anarchist playwrights equipped their plays with "mirror-characters" and idealized heroes to inspire imitation; indeed, it sounds similar to what the anarchist Max Baginski (1864–1943) described as the social function of "the Old Drama," which presented itself as a "mirror of life" intended "to show the terrible consequences of uncontrolled human passion, and ... teach man to overcome himself": "Go ye, atone and make good." As the reflection of conventional social morality, an apparatus of "chastisement" and "resignation," this kind of narrative mirror naturally produces docile subjects, not rebels.[12]

However, rather than opting for a non-representational theater or a stage clear of *personajes-espejos*, Baginski praised the social dramas of playwrights like Gerhard Hauptmann for broadening the "scope" of dramatic reflection, violating the code of decorum governing what could be displayed on the stage ("The new drama means reproduction of nature in all its phases.... It rehabilitates the human body, establishes it in its proper place and dignity, and brings about the long deferred reconciliation between the mind and the body") and stealing focus from the tragic hero of the privileged classical type (the "persons of high position and standing" who then fall from their "heights") in favor of the neglected people ("the ordinary man, the man of the masses" and the whole social "ensemble").[13] Likewise, Gustav Landauer lamented modern playwrights' tendency to produce "family catastrophes" instead of genuine "social dramas." "Modern pieces sometimes offer us too much interiority," he opined:

> I wish our young poets to free themselves from the narrow
> bonds of the *family*; I wish them to go into the street and to

---

11 Jacques Lacan, *Écrits: The First Complete Collection in English*, trans. Bruce Fink (New York: W.W. Norton & Co., 2006), 76; Bruce Fink, *A Clinical Introduction to Lacanian Psychoanalysis* (Cambridge, MA: Harvard University Press, 1999), 87–88.

12 Max Baginski, "The Old and the New Drama," *Mother Earth* 1.2 (April 1906): 36.

13 Ibid., 38–39.

give themselves to the whole public, so that if the power of fate should nevertheless be at work, it will be not only in "family catastrophes" but also in the intervention of power, which is, after a well-known saying, the modern fate: i.e., politics and society.[14]

Again, the mirror is not to be destroyed but enlarged, broadened. Heroes may appear, but of a different kind: for Landauer, these are the characters out of Shakespeare (Hamlet, Prospero) as well as out of Georg Kaiser (Eustache de Saint-Pierre in *The Burghers of Calais*) who exemplify "the new deed," the renunciation of power that inaugurates a new ethics and a new community of equality (that which Rancière calls "politics" proper, rather than the order of "the police").[15]

Without reducing this new community to a utopian "blueprint," a static and finalized image, the anarchist stage nonetheless presents us, as Galili Shahar paraphrases Landauer, with "the shape of the revolution ... render[ing] revolutionary thought 'visible'": "The theatre is, in this sense, to be seen as a prefiguration [*Vorfeld*] of the political."[16] Here we see resolved one of the questions that more narrowly "reflectionist" theories of art have found irresolvable: How can art be simultaneously reabsorbed into the social while also leading society beyond itself? How can it become an agent of transcendence while remaining steadfastly immanent? For Landauer, a thoroughly social, immanent art *prefigures* possibilities, potentialities, which transcend the actuality in which they are anchored, precisely *because* reality already contains more than just what is immediately present and visible. The goal, for Landauer as well as Baginski, is to prefigure reality in its plenitude, its irreducible heterogeneity, its messy and mutable truth.

Anarchist narratives struggle against homogeneity and enclosure in so many ways—even against narrative closure as such. If the mark of the "well-made play" is its tight sense of closure, with all the loose ends of the plot tidily gathered up by the end, then the anarchist tradition of dramaturgy could perhaps be captured, on one

---

14 Gustav Landauer, *Zeit und Geist* (München: Boer, 1997), 21, 23.
15 Landauer, *Shakespeare*, 254; Galili Shahar, *Theatrum Jadaicum* (Bielefeld: Aisthesis Verlag, 2007), 107.
16 Jacoby, *Picture Imperfect*, xiv; Shahar, *Theatrum Jadaicum*, 107.

end, by the single-act sketch or *bozzetto* as exemplified by works like Roussel's *Par la révolte* and Capetillo's *Influencia de las ideas modernas*, and on the other end by Federico Urales's (a.k.a. Joan Montseny's) *El Castillo Maldito* (1903–1904), a work of "impossible theatre" ("impossible," as Eva Golluscio de Montoya specifies, by virtue of its sheer size—eighty-four pages of script, more than sixty actors *without counting* extras—as well as "by the violence of its protest").[17] Likewise, the "implacable unity" that marked the modern short story *à la* Poe and the rejection of the "loose baggy" plot by the modern novel *à la* Henry James can be contrasted to Félix Fénéon's flippant "Nouvelles en trois lignes" ("News/Novels in Three Lines"), which end almost before they begin, and to Louise Michel's sprawling, proliferating *Les Microbes Humains*, which threatens never to end.[18]

Le Guin's work also resists ends and endings, the "THOK!" of the spear-shaped masculinist narrative, in favor of that baggy middle: "I would go so far as to say that the natural, proper, fitting shape of the novel might be that of a sack, a bag." "The means are the end," a slogan espoused by the protagonists of *The Dispossessed*, also holds true of the novel itself, with its circular structure (ending where it began).[19] Derrick Jensen's *Lives Less Valuable* manifests an equally trenchant skepticism about beginnings, as Malia writes what would otherwise seem to be a classic expository letter to her ex-lover Anthony:

> You could say it started because one night I stayed downtown too late and got mugged coming home from work. Chance. Wrong place at the wrong time. But women are mugged and worse constantly, yet rarely does that lead to... What do I call it? Murder? Terrorism? Stupidity? Brilliance? One of the only sane things an environmentalist has ever done?

17 Marie Laffranque, "El Castillo Maldito: Urales et le théâtre," in Federico Urales, *El Castillo Maldito* (Toulouse: Presses universitaires du Mirail, 1992), 113.

18 Brander Matthews, *The Short-Story: Specimens Illustrating its Development* (New York: American Book Co., 1907), 24; Henry James, *The Tragic Muse* (London: Charles Scribner's Sons, 1908), 1.x.

19 Le Guin, *Dancing at the Edge of the World: Thoughts on Words, Women, Places* (New York: Grove Press, 1989), 168; *The Dispossessed*, 144.

> So where do I start? My parents? The muggers' parents? Why
> don't I cut to the chase and go all the way back to Columbus
> landing in America and the Indians not slitting his throat?... In
> any case it's much too complicated.[20]

Creating a sense that more is always lurking beyond the edge of the
narrative frame—that reality is "much too complicated" for a simple, unified representation—is one way in which, as Granier suggests,
anarchist narratives try to avoid "solidifying into dogma"—a dogma
that can then become the fetishized object of a new cult or the ritual
foundation for a new State.[21]

One way to avoid reifying one's story into a universalizing dogma
is to affirm it as one's own, to attest openly to its subjective nature,
owning up to its biases and limitations. Another is to prevent the
reader, as much as possible, from too quickly or too simply taking up
one's own subject position, blocking identification. "What is subjective," writes Han Ryner in the *Encyclopédie anarchiste*, "must remain
individual and never try to impose itself on others."[22] Often, this
subjectivity is affirmed by telling first-person "victim stories" (including the anarchist memoir, a terrifically important genre in its own
right), as anarchists from Vallès to Jensen have done: we are invited to
identify with an experience of pain, loss, and humiliation that never
ceases to represent a singular experience, never making the subject
into a model or an authority, so that subjectivity itself becomes, as
Granier puts it, a "pledge of truth."[23]

We have also seen how anarchist narratives can ward off their
own finalization by taking up "shifting enunciative positions," keeping the narrator on the move (temporally, spatially, or both), or by the
use of ambiguity to suspend the force of the authorial voice—both
techniques heavily favored by Lazare and Traven.[24] If the anarchist

---

20 Derrick Jensen, *Lives Less Valuable: A Novel* (Oakland, CA: PM Press,
    2010), 5–6.
21 Granier, *Les Briseurs de formules*, 65.
22 Ibid., 335; Ryner, "Subjectif, Subjectivisme, Subjectivité," *Encyclopédie an-
    archiste*, 2673–2674.
23 Granier, *Les briseurs de formules*, 227.
24 Donald Bruce, "Translating the Commune: Cultural Politics and the His-
    torical Specificity of the Anarchist Text," *TTR: Traduction, Terminologie,
    Rédaction* 7.1 (1994): 71.

narrative presents us with a mirror, then, it is more like Stendhal's "mirror which goes out on a highway" than the fixed mirror of narcissism.[25] This vagrant mirror is also a *fractured* mirror, reflecting not a unitary but a plural subject, a self that could say, with Walt Whitman: "Do I contradict myself? / Very well, then, I contradict myself; / (I am large—I contain multitudes.)"[26]

This internal heterogeneity is often embodied in a heterogeneity of the language used to narrate the self. In a study of Jules Vallès, for instance, Donald Bruce notes the coexistence of "foreign discursive elements," e.g., "Latin and Greek expressions, revolutionary slogans, bourgeois platitudes," all juxtaposed uncomfortably within the split consciousness of a boy caught between his bourgeois upbringing and education and the rebel desires arising from his body, refractory experiences his prejudices cannot assimilate, the radical currents he encounters and increasingly participates in.[27] This "interweaving of different discourse types by juxtaposition" or *"interdiscursive mixing"* can also be observed in Gilliland's *The Free*, where the narrative voice sometimes shifts unpredictably between discourses, each reflecting a distinct point of view. In the first version of the novel, this is especially notable in the chapter that is nominally focalized by Christo Reilly. Reilly, a onetime wheeler-dealer in the trade union, has been sidelined, first by massive deindustrialization and offshoring (leaving him with no more deals to cut), then by the rise of the Free Union and Co-Ops:

> It was Christo himself who negotiated the deal, whereby the Co-Ops took over the redundant North West Works and leased the plant there. *He had lost credibility* on that deal, for they had moved in and *never paid a penny* for rent or hire. Yet they had set up an *apparently* thriving business, repairing and adapting their fleet of alcohol powered lorries, branching into factory and farm machinery repairs, scrap metal and workshops of every description. It was *economic nonsense of course*, yet they still expanded....

---

25 Stendhal, *The Red and the Black: A Chronicle of 1830*, trans. Horace Barnett Samuel (London: K. Paul, Trench, Trubner & Co., 1922), 366.

26 Walt Whitman, *Leaves of Grass* (Philadelphia, PA: David McKay, 1900), 51.

27 Bruce, "Translating the Commune," 68.

Christo disliked them, this horde of new *tinkers*, the place had become *a warren*, whole families even lived there, amongst the great piles of scrap metal, wood and tyres. They took *what was not theirs* and there was not [sic] place for *the likes of Christo and their scheme*. Yet their ideas caught rapidly....

For Christo and the union these last years had been *a growing nightmare*, as *the screws tightened* and *his power faded away*. *The Works had been his life*, and *bureaucratic infighting* his breath. And now the Free Union, mushrooming suddenly within the works itself. *Demanding the impossible*, trebled wages! Refusing negotiation, building up to a strike, and putting enormous pressure on Christo to come up with the goods. *Cowboys, extremists*, Christo had determined to fight them all the way.[28]

We oscillate between Christo's own point of view (concerned for his "credibility," mourning the loss of "his life," and contemptuous of the "tinkers" squatting the works, outraged by their "impossible" and "extremist" positions, their disregard for property rights) and a point of view identifiable with that of the Free (contemptuous of "the likes of Christo and their scheme," seeing his career as one of "bureaucratic infighting," triumphant at the prospect of "his power fad[ing] away"). The phrase "demanding the impossible" occupies both registers at once: it is both a denunciation of anarchism from the perspective of bourgeois common sense and an old anarchist slogan ("demand the impossible!"). What we are reading, then, is the discursive face of a shift in relations of force. Christo is caught up in a transition: by the end of the chapter, Christo finds himself giving in to his granddaughter and, humbled, joining the Free.[29]

"A Mirror Maze is literature," writes Voltairine de Cleyre,

wherein Man sees all faces of himself, lengthened here, widened there, distorted in another place, restored again to due proportion, with every possible expression on his face, from abjectness to heroic daring, from starting terror to icy courage, from love to hate and back again to worship, from the almost sublime down to the altogether grotesque,—now giant, now

---

28 Gilliland, *The Free*, 3rd ed., 55–56, italics mine.
29 Ibid., 61.

dwarf,—but always with one persistent character,—his *superb curiosity to see himself.*[30]

It is easy to miss what is distinctive about anarchists' writing; the resort to commonplace genres often masks unexpected uses of those forms. Here, de Cleyre's use of the trope of reflection masks a less than commonplace epistemology—a way of thinking of the relations between reality and ideas, self and non-self, plurality and singularity, the changing and the persisting, that is nowhere better embodied than in the stories anarchists tell about themselves and their world.

---

30 de Cleyre, *Selected Works*, 380.

IV

BREAKING THE FRAME:
ANARCHIST IMAGES

In the theater or at the cinema or even watching TV ... because the frame or the proscenium arch is always the same, you usually block it out. You don't notice it, and you get sucked into the picture that much more quickly.

— Dave Gibbons, "Pebbles in a Landscape."

We believe in the hegemony of the image, in the visual preponderance of our time.

— Alfonso Longuet, *El Cinema y la realidad social.*

We're the smashers of images!

— Auguste Percheron, "Briseurs d'images."

1: VIRILE BODIES

IN the December 1, 1901 issue of the *Revista Blanca*, someone writing under the name "Uno del público [Someone in the audience]" complains of a recent play, *La Huelga (The Strike)*, by the Christian socialist Pablo Cases:

> The socialist [character] in *La Huelga* says: "Hunger makes martyrs." No socialist could pronounce such great nonsense. Hunger makes hungry people and nothing else. The great martyrs have been precisely the better fed, those who, endowed with health and energy, were healthy enough to defend to the martyrdom of great ideals. The hungry man is weak, anemic, and anemia and weakness are the main factors of slavery. In the revolution hunger can be the accessory, but the main thing is the *idea*, and it assumes a certain portion of energy that the hungry lack. No one revolts from hunger if not convinced that the pain in his stomach is a consequence of social injustice.[1]

This denunciation might surprise us: a line like "Hunger makes martyrs" might not be out of place in an anarchist play. Behind the bravado of the slogan, however, the reviewer detects a valorization of hunger as such, a sentimentalization of the hungry, weak body, which runs counter to a long-standing anarchist aesthetic of *virility*.

We have seen that even the bookishness of anarchist culture is often overcoded with appeals to masculine potency ("Read anarchist

---

1 Uno del público, "En el Teatro Martín," *La Revista Blanca* 4.83 (December 1, 1901): 340.

Fig. 1: Anarchist "virility" on display: José Planas Casas, cover for *Hombre de América: Fuerte y Libre* (January 1940).

books and become a man"). The titanic male figures from the illustration in *A Guerra Social* (Part I, ch. 1, fig. 6) and the iconic image of the "strong and free" *Hombre de América* (fig. 1, above) belong to this tradition. The concept of "*virilité*," according to Colson, "play[s] a great part in the discourse and imaginary of the revolutionary syndicalists and anarcho-syndicalists." Thus, in the strains of Joe Hill's "There Is Power In a Union," with its call to "do your share, like a man," Francis Shor hears echoes of a "virile syndicalism," a "masculine identity" constituted by images of physical strength, bravery, and boundlessly energetic activity.[2]

Some have suggested that in this respect, the aesthetics of anarchist images actually mirror those of their authoritarian socialist rivals. In his study of the culture of work in the Spanish Civil War, Michael Seidman notes the predilection shared by anarcho-syndicalists and Stalinists alike for "productivist" images of resolute, "virile," block-shouldered workers—never "tired, hungry, or ill," and

---

2   Francis Shor, "Masculine Power and Virile Syndicalism: A Gendered Analysis of the IWW in Australia," *Labour History* 63 (November 1992): 83–85.

Fig. 2 (L to R): Posters for the Trotskyite POUM militia (Carles Fontserre), the socialist PSOE (Arturo Ballester), and the CNT-FAI (Aleix Hinsberger).

"indistinguishable except by their implements and positions"—marching in unison toward a radiant future.[3] Both movements, at least in the 1930s, employed "persuasive and coercive images that were designed to convince [workers] to work harder," and they "reflected shared values—[namely,] a glorification of labor ... and the vision of the worker as producer" (fig. 2).[4] Liberation, seen through this optic, does not consist in the unification of art with life, a diffusion of aesthetic sensuality into the experience of the everyday; instead, it is located at the point of production, at the workplace.

This history of "workplace utopianism," with its combination of productivist and masculinist themes, runs from the patriarchal Proudhon, who warns that the "feminine" energies of art should be subordinated to the "virile" faculties of reason and labor, to CNT filmmaker Mateo Santos, who expresses a concern that "Spanish cinema" not be allowed to degenerate into a "female cinema [*cine hembra*]": "what we need here is a masculine cinema [*cine macho*], strong, vigorous, with impudence."[5] Likewise, writing from the humiliation of defeat and

---

3   Michael Seidman, *Workers against Work: Labor in Paris and Barcelona During the Popular Fronts* (Berkeley: University of California Press, 1991), 102–103.

4   Ibid., 105.

5   Ibid., 311–312; Proudhon qtd. in Paul B. Crapo, "The Anarchist as Critic," *Michigan Academican* 13.4 (Spring 1981): 462–463, translation mine; Proudhon, *De la Justice dans la Révolution et dans l'Église* (Paris: Lacroix, 1868), 4.216; Santos qtd. in Geoffrey B. Pingree, "Modern Anxiety and Documentary Cinema in Republican Spain," *Visualizing Spanish Modernity*, ed. Susan Larson (Oxford: Berg, 2005), 306.

exile, Felipe Alaíz advocates a style of writing that is close to "the clear language of the people" by contrasting it with the "abnormal" and "estravagan[t]" excesses of avant-garde writers such as André Gide by explicitly identifying the latter with French "homosexuality" and the former with a "virile Spain."[6] Nor is this necessarily a dead tradition. A flyer produced during the May–June '68 events in France featured a détourned photograph of a semi-nude model, flat on her back, in whose mouth have been inserted words declaring her disdain for the "little prick[s]" from the reformist and institutionalized left-wing factions: "these turds bore me stiff. / But tonight it's going to be different. Some comrades from the *council for maintaining the occupations* are going to come and fuck me violently. Judging by their practice, their theories must be truly radical."[7] Such emphatic advertisements of sexism (as if literalizing Stokely Carmichael's quip that the position for women in the movement was "prone"[8]) have become rarer anywhere on the radical left, let alone among anarchists. However, invocations of virility have not vanished from anarchism. Lara Montesinos Coleman and Serena A. Bassi note the persistence, within the British

---

6 Felipe Alaíz, *El Arte de escribir sin arte* (Toulouse: Editorial FIJL, 1946), 19, 13.

7 Peter Stansill and David Zane Mairowitz, eds., *BAMN (By Any Means Necessary): Outlaw Manifestos and Ephemera (1965–70)* (Harmondsworth, UK: Penguin, 1971), 141.

8 Sara Evans, *Personal Politics: The Roots of Women's Liberation in the Civil Rights Movement and the New Left* (New York: Vintage Books, 1979), 87. To be fair, radical feminists were entirely capable of turning the technique to their own ends, demonstrating not only a stronger grasp of the Situationist critique of commodity fetishism but also a sharper wit: one particularly incisive example, titled "Rex Macho, S.O.B.," simultaneously sends up the melodrama of soap-opera strips like *Rex Morgan, M.D.* and the sexism of macho male radicals. The visuals tell a coherent story of a romantic dinner date, while the word balloons undercut the "romance" between male and female activists: wistfully leaning over the dinner table set with wine glasses, "Gertie Guerilla" asks, "Could anyone as alienated as you ever make a revolution worthy of the name?" while her would-be beau grumbles, "Women are so illogical!" This strong-jawed male lead is no match for Gertie: from predicting that "If I can make her feel insecure enough she'll tell me their secrets and lay me too," he is reduced to wheedling, "Why don't you struggle with my chauvinism instead of just being castrating?"—finally stalking off with a resentful promise that "When we make our revolution, we won't invite any heavy chicks." Her cool reply: "Who will do your typing?" (Stansill and Mairowitz, *BAMN*, 206).

anarchist movement circa 2011 (although this is certainly also true of the North American scene as well), of "Anarchist Action Man," the idealized image of the anarchist, enshrined in countless *YouTube* videos, as enacting "physical and confrontational gestures, based on the destruction of a small, symbolic aspect of the existing order": "The 'system-smashing' nature of the actions, the focus on the individual and the clear affinity of direct action with war and its rhetoric, recalls an image that dominates the modern western imagery—that of the epic hero, singlehandedly fighting against enemy forces for the triumph of good over evil."[9] In short, the iconography of contemporary "riot porn" (photographs and video of direct actions) centers around "an ideal male body" that is typically young, white, nondisabled, and dressed in a veritable "anti-uniform" comprised of mixed elements from confrontational subcultures (punk, hippie, Rastafarian, etc.).[10] Virile anarchism, it would seem, is still alive.

However, the gender and sexual coding of this iconography may not always be as straightforward as it seems. Colson insists that traditional anarchist conceptions of *virilité* were "synonymous with *affirmation* and *force*, and thus with a power common to *all* collective beings, without exception."[11] The objection to imagery of "weakness" then would have less to do with sexism or productivism than with a certain strain of vitalism, an affirmation of "the joy of living," in Albert Libertad's words. The ideological heritage of these celebrations of "strength" and "vitality" (and, conversely, denigrations of "weakness") can be traced not only to Proudhon's theories of "collective being" and the origin of ideas in practice (a kind of "labor pragmatism" *avant la lettre*), but to thinkers standing outside the anarchist tradition who nevertheless influenced it deeply, such as Nietzsche and Bergson.[12] It owes a special debt to J. M. Guyau, author of an *Esquisse d'une morale sans obligation ni sanction* (*A Sketch of Morality Without Obligation or Sanction*, 1884) to which Nietzsche and Kropotkin

9   Lara Montesinos Coleman and Serena A. Bassi, "Deconstructing Militant Manhood," *International Feminist Journal of Politics* 13.2 (2011): 216.

10   Ibid., 215–216.

11   Colson, *Petit lexique*, 349–350.

12   Pereira Poza, *Antología crítica*, 227, 230; Daniel Colson, "Nietzsche and the Libertarian Workers' Movement," trans. Paul Hammond, in *I Am Not a Man, I Am Dynamite!* eds. John Moore and Spencer Sunshine (New York: Autonomedia, 2004), 19.

alike gave close attention. Kropotkin draws extensively on Guyau in his *Ethics: Origin and Development* (1924) and "Anarchist Morality" (1889)—notably, on the conception a "fecundity of will":

> This thirst for action ... this fertility in every direction is life; the only thing worthy the name. For one moment of this life, those who have obtained a glimpse of it give years of vegetative existence. Without this overflowing life, a man [sic] is old before his time, an impotent being, a plant that withers before it has ever flowered.... If you feel within you the strength of youth, if you wish to live, if you wish to enjoy a perfect, full and overflowing life—that is, know the highest pleasure which a living being can desire—be strong, be great, be vigorous in all you do.[13]

This "strength," "great[ness]," "vigor," "poten[cy]," even "pleasure," is never more present than in the heroic deed that incurs death for the doer: "The plant cannot prevent itself from flowering. Sometimes to flower means to die. Never mind, the sap mounts the same."[14] The language of virile heroism merges neatly with that of floral imagery and "fecundity," opening onto the feminine. Nor is this a local idiosyncrasy: here as elsewhere in the symbolic universe of anarchism, feminine iconography is capable of signaling force, activity, the creative. An ethics of superabundant life, of fecundity, is, as we have already seen, the ethics of the great tragic heroines of anarchist fiction. One thinks of the heroine of Adrián del Valle's "En El Mar: Narracion de un Viaje Trágico," collected in *Cuentos inverosímiles*. Among the survivors of a shipboard fire at sea, huddled in the lifeboat, are the decadent Lord Vilton and a noble, nameless woman, referred to merely as "La Rusa [the Russian]." "At sea," as Kirwin Shaffer writes,

> hunger sets in among the survivors, a fact made unbearable by the continuous cries of the starving infant. In a moment of true noble revolutionary motherhood, La Rusa bares her virgin breasts and offers her milkless nipples to the child. In contrast, Lord Vilton is so hungry that he pays a sailor five thousand pounds sterling

---

13 Peter Kropotkin, *Anarchism: A Collection of Revolutionary Writings* (Mineola, NY: Dover Publications, 2002), 110–113.
14 Ibid., 109–110.

Fig. 3: Frontispiece of Adrián del Valle's *Cuentos inverosímiles* (1903).

so that Vilton can make a gash in the sailor's arm and suck the sailor's blood. After three days at sea, the baby dies from hunger and dehydration. Lord Vilton tries to wrestle the infant from La Rusa's hands in order to eat it. In the ensuing struggle, La Rusa throws Vilton's suitcase full of money into the sea, shouting, "Get it.... Buy some shark's blood with it!" Then someone hits Vilton over the head and dumps him into the sea. Upon being rescued some time later, La Rusa is still holding the little corpse.[15]

Despite her appellation (something less than a private name), La Rusa does not stand for Russians generally, as she clarifies to the narrator. When he compliments her choice of reading (Tolstoy's *Resurrection*)—"the Russian soul, hungry for love and freedom, vibrates in its pages"—she rejects the flattery this entails: "No, no, the human soul,—she replied fervently.—In Russia, my poor Russia ... there is only a small part of the human soul."[16] Refusing a national identity as well as a private name, she becomes an allegorical figure, like the frontispiece to *Cuentos inverosímiles* (fig. 3), carrier of a force of signification greater than death itself.

Images of such women populate great swaths of the anarchist imaginary, their nude or draped bodies radiating power, at times in

---

15 Shaffer, "The Radical Muse," 145.
16 del Valle, *Cuentos inverosímiles*, 136.

La Revolución

Fig. 4: *La Revolución*: Illustration from *La Huelga General* (January 25,1903).

a manner strikingly parallel to their masculine counterparts; compare, for instance, the female figure from *La Huelga*, with torch and sword in hand (fig. 4), to the male figure on the cover of the 1912 *Almanaque de la Tierra y Libertad* (Part I, ch. 1, fig. 3), or the female and male figures on horseback appearing in *El Productor* and *La Tramontana* (fig. 5). In these neo-classical settings, both nudity and drapery, like the suppression of personal and national identity, tend to allegorize the body, to render it more universal and ideal, rather than rendering it up for the "visual pleasure" of heterosexual male viewers. As a perpetual motif of anarchist visual culture, then, we encounter these figures of men and especially of women in gestures that convey both *capacitación*—they shatter chains, trample columns and cannon-barrels, smash time-clocks, topple the statues of gods and masters (figs. 5 and 6)—and, at the same time, emanate a kind of joy, a sensuousness, a pleasure in their own forms.

It is not to be forgotten, in this connection, that a significant strand of the anarchist movement (primarily among the younger militants and the minority individualist tendencies) embraced nudism as part of its libertarian culture.[17] Whereas some forms of nudist ide-

17 Navarro Navarro, *A la revolución*, 362. Navarro Navarro is careful to add: "Many sectors of militancy did not accept these practices and criticized their defenders" (363). Max Nettlau, for instance, writing in 1932–1934,

Fig. 5a (left) Illustration from *Kain: Zeitschrift für Menschlichkeit* (February 15, 1919).
Fig. 5b (right) Illustration from *La Tramontana* (January 20, 1888).

Fig. 6: Cover of *Xin Shiji/La Novaj Tempoj* (*The New Era*) (June 27, 1908).

laments the interest of young anarchists in "the naturism which was based on diet, vegetarianism and so on, as well as the little centres of the simple life," which he considers "a diversion of energy and attention" (*A Short History of Anarchism*, ed. Heiner Becker [London: Freedom Press, 1996], 288–289). However, there was sufficient respect for these practices among anarchist and anarcho-syndicalist militants that the famous Zaragoza Conference of the CNT (May 8, 1936) at which libertarian communism was formally adopted as a goal also passed a resolution specifically reserving the rights of "naturists and nudists" within the new social order (José Peirats, *The CNT in the Spanish Revolution*, eds. Chris Ealham and Stuart Christie [Hastings, East Sussex: Meltzer Press, the Cañada Blanch Centre for Contemporary Spanish Studies, 2001], 1.106).

ology constructed the naked body as ascetically, asexually "pure"—an understandable defense against the conservative criticism to which they were subjected—anarchists embraced a "revolutionary nudism," as it was dubbed by the French individualist anarchist E. Armand (a.k.a. Ernest Lucien Juin, 1872–1963), which did not care to completely desexualize the experience of public nudity:

> The detractors of nudism—moralists or hygienists, conservatives of the State or Church—maintain that the sight of the naked, the relation between nudists of both sexes, arouses erotic desire. Contrary to what most nudist theoreticians argue, we do not deny it, but say that the erotic *exaltation* generated by nudist accomplishments, if it exists, is pure, natural, instinctive, and cannot be compared with the fictitious excitement produced by the half-naked, the gallant "deshabillé," and all the dressing table artifices.[18]

At the same time, anarchist nudism was constructed as an ethical practice, a proving ground for the new, egalitarian sexual morality advocated by anarchists in general: thus, Mariano Gallardo rebukes comrades who "assume that nudism means nothing more than taking off their underwear and throwing themselves, bellowing like a bull, on the first woman who passes and, whether she wants it or not, 'covering her.'"[19] The principle of mutual consent central to anarchist ethics was to govern the expression of desire.

By November 1936, four months into the Spanish Revolution, Armand's journal, *L'En-Dehors*, could publish a list of "Naturist and anarchist colonies in Spain"—Spanish anarchists having become some of the most avid readers of Armand's writings on lifestyle and sexuality, thanks to the translations of José Elizalde and others. As in France, which was home to a number of libertarian colonies or *milieux libres* ("free environments"), nudist camps, and "naturist" communities, the Spanish settlements combined a variety of alternative lifestyle elements, from diet to dress, reminiscent of J. William Lloyd's fantasy of "Vale Sunrise"—and a prologue to the communes that would emerge from the counterculture of the 1960s.

---

18 E. Armand, "El Nudismo," *Iniciales* 6 (June 1932): 5–6.

19 Gallardo qtd. in Xavier Díez, *Utopia sexual a la premsa anarquista de Catalunya* (Lleida: Pagès, 2001), 158.

Among the Spanish enthusiasts of *naturismo* was Manuel Monleón Burgos (1904–1976), illustrator of anarchist publications such as *Estudios* (1928–1937) and *Crisol* (1935–1936) and one of the foremost poster artists of revolutionary Spain. In his work—which he also gave to radical naturist publications such as *Helios* (1916–1939)—the nude body, male and female, is prominently displayed, always charged with desire and power, breaking bonds and smiting symbols of oppression (chains, snakes, swastikas). Their nudity is at once radical enough to be just a step away from the on-stage nudity of the Living Theater's *Paradise Now* (1969) and classical enough to retain ancient Greek standards of beauty (there is no room, among these bodies, for the balding, beaky physique of a Julian Beck).

Anarchist images of nude and semi-nude male bodies are also often sensual/sexual, invested with desire, even homoerotic desire. Granted, this was also sometimes true of Stalinist iconography, and anarchists were by no means consistently homophiles; on the contrary (even the contributions of Félix Martí-Ibáñez on the subject in journals like *Estudios*, while advocating tolerance for homosexuality, are pretty thoroughly laced with heteronormative assumptions).[20] And yet it is difficult to read an image like Monleón Burgos's antifascist poster (fig. 7) without thinking of the links between anarchism and some homophile associations of the late-nineteenth and early-twentieth centuries, particularly in the milieu of the German *Freikörperkultur* (Free Body Culture) and *Lebensreform* (Lifestyle Reform) movements.

In his entry on nudism for the *Encyclopédie anarchiste* of 1934, Charles-Auguste Bontemps (1893–1981) notes the link between the "libertarian spirit" and the "*free-culture* of the body, which is what the Germans call it."[21] Indeed, one of the animating spirits of both *Freikörperkultur* and the more diffuse *Lebensreform* movement was Adolf Brand (1874–1945), publisher of the repeatedly banned individualist anarchist journal *Der Eigene* (1896), which he proudly advertised as "the first homosexual publication in the world."[22] Although constituencies for nudism in Germany spanned the far left and the far right, anarchists such as Erich Mühsam and John Henry Mackay

---

20 See Cleminson, "Sexuality and the Revolution of Mentalities."

21 Charles-Auguste Bontemps, "Nudisme," *Encyclopédie anarchiste*, 1810.

22 Florence Tamagne, *A History of Homosexuality in Europe: Berlin, London, Paris, 1919–1939* (New York: Algora, 2006), 69.

Fig. 7: Poster by Manuel Monleón Burgos, CNT-AIT (1937)

persistently linked opposition to compulsory heterosexuality with "the right to live naked, to take off our clothes, to walk naked, to form alliances with other nudists" as part of "a protest against all dogmas, laws and customs, establishing a hierarchy of body parts"—and ultimately against the hierarchical organization of the body politic itself.[23]

Control over one's own body was a central anarchist concern. "The question of souls is old," wrote Voltairine de Cleyre; "we demand our bodies, now." "Your body is your own" (*Ton corps est à toi*), the title of a novel by Victor Margueritte (1927), became an anarchist slogan, repeated in the titles of pamphlets, articles, and lectures, synonymous with the fight for "conscious maternity" (birth control), free love, anti-militarism, and self-determination.[24] Even the German anarcho-syndicalist Frei Arbeiter Union Deutschlands (FAUD) enlisted in the fight, with the Verlag Der Syndikalist (1919–1933) publishing works like sexologist Wilhelm Schöffer's *Das Recht auf den eigenen Körper* (*The Right to One's Own Body*, 1926).

---

23 E. Armand, "Nudisme révolutionnaire," *Encyclopédie anarchiste*, 1811–1812; Richard D. Sonn, *Sex, Violence, and the Avant-Garde: Anarchism in Interwar France* (University Park, PA: Pennsylvania State University Press, 2010), 111.

24 de Cleyre, *Selected Works*, 350; Sonn, *Sex, Violence, and the Avant-Garde*, 12.

Sovereignty over one's body was asserted, in turn, by a variety of corporeal practices, by turns hedonistic and ascetic: nudism and free love, to be sure, but also gymnastics, therapeutic air- and sun-baths, the refusal of meat, alcohol, and tobacco. These elements of discipline, therapy, and refusal are never conceived as a chastisement of the recalcitrant, deviant, or impure body on behalf of a governing soul, but as *intensifications* of embodiment.[25] In this way, anarchists practiced what Michel Foucault calls—after the Greek—*askēsis*, or "[the] practice of the self by the self, of the self on the self": whereas "in Christianity asceticism always refers to a certain renunciation of the self ... [Stoic] *askēsis* means not renunciation but the progressive consideration of self, or mastery over oneself."[26] The common ideological thread binding together these many varieties of libertarian body culture is, in the first place, a belief that discipline exercised over the body from the outside (e.g., sexual repression, compulsory clothing, compulsory heterosexuality) is *physically* as well as psychologically unhealthy. On a symbolic register, this anarchist *askēsis* expressed itself in a political vision of the naked body, male and female, as both a *sign* and a *source* of strength and vitality.

We can see an anarchist politics of the body at work in one of the great lost films of revolutionary Spain, *Carne de Fieras*, directed by Armand Guerra (a.k.a. José María Estivalis Calvo, 1886–1939), former collaborator in the Cinéma du Peuple cooperative in Paris, which began filming mere days before the outbreak of the July 19th revolution (figs. 8–13).[27] The plot of *Carne de Fieras* (a title which can be translated as *Savage Flesh*, but also as *Meat for the Beasts*) turns

---

25 Thus, for instance, Jules Méline's entry on vegetarianism in the *Encyclopédie anarchiste* speaks of "excluding all that is likely to compromise the physiological and mental balance and, consequently, the strength of man, i.e., meat, fish, spirits, fermented beverages (incorrectly called hygienic), chocolate, coffee, etc., etc." (2852); Sophie Zaïkowska's entry on the same subject defines it as "not indicating specifically what we should eat, but ensuring that what we eat is 'invigorating'" (2850).

26 Michel Foucault, *The Hermeneutics of the Subject: Lectures at the Collège De France, 1981–1982*, ed. Frédéric Gros, trans. Graham Burchell (New York: Picador, 2005), 317; *Technologies of the Self: A Seminar with Michel Foucault*, ed. Luther H. Martin et al. (Amherst: University of Massachusetts Press, 1988), 35.

27 Eric Jarry, "Armand Guerra, cineasta e pioniere del cinema militante," trans. Marco Camenish, *Bolletino Archivio G. Pinelli* 18 (December 2001): 37.

around the failure of possessive marriages and patriarchal families, on the one hand, and the construction of an alternative family based on generosity and respect, on the other.

The events of the story are precipitated by an orphaned boy named Perragorda, a "gutter rat," whose name means "fat dog"; when he is teased about this "cheap name," Perragorda replies, matter-of-factly, "Maybe my life isn't worth more ..." One day, Perragorda falls into the pond in the park and nearly drowns but is saved by Pablo. Pablo, a prizefighter, is upbraided by his wife, Aurora, for jumping to the rescue of a mere street urchin. "A heart of gold," exults Pablo's friend and trainer, Picatoste. Aurora is not impressed. "A nice mess you've made of your suit," she sniffs. "A ruined suit can be replaced by another," he retorts. "A lost life has no substitute." "How can you let your woman treat you like that?" Picatoste scoffs. "The first woman who treated me like that ... I'd KO her for a whole season." Pablo demurs. He is already coming unglued from a culture in which love is paired with brutality.

Aurora's emotional stinginess, we can see, is a displacement of her frustrated love for another man, Antonio, and her guilt over cheating on a husband who "idolizes" her. Events come to a head when Pablo, missing a train in downtown Madrid, comes home early to find Aurora and Antonio together. And why does he miss the train? Cross-cutting reveals: his watch is no longer in sync with the time kept by the clock in the square (fig. 8). It stopped when he jumped in the pond to save Perragorda. And what does he do in town with this wasted time? He has a drink with Picatoste; he is accosted by a beggar girl who limply thrusts forth a sheaf of flowers, mumbling, "I haven't had any supper..." "You will eat like a princess," he tells her gently, and buys the flowers. In the street behind them, we see *milicianos* walking by (fig. 9)—a testament to the new reality that has erupted in the middle of filming. It is not part of the script, and no reference is made to the revolutionary situation (although, oddly, we see Pablo and Picatoste getting out of a car driven by a uniformed *cenetista* and exchanging a cheery raised-fist salute). Time is really out of joint, here: the diegetic time of the story does not align with historical time, and Pablo's time, a time of waste, loss, and generous expenditure, does not accord with a rational, utilitarian, official time—the economic time that is being

Stills from *Carne de Fieras*, clockwise from top left. Fig. 8: time is out of joint. Fig. 9: Picatoste and Pablo in town, with *milicianos* in the background. Fig. 10: lioness, dancer and domador. Fig. 11: Marck hits Marlène. Fig. 12: Marlène dances with Pablo. Fig. 13: Marlène, Perragordo, Pablo, and Picatoste as new family.

shattered by the revolution, the stoppage of ordinary routine, the break with history.[28]

Pablo's initial rage at Aurora gives way to depression, and he lets himself be beaten mercilessly in the ring by his opponent, "El Tigre." You might say that his timing is off, that he has stopped keeping score. Losing as an ostensibly "virile" boxer and husband, he finds himself again when he sees Marlène and Marck perform. Marck, the lion-tamer, keeps four hungry lions at bay with chair and whip while Marlène dances nude in their midst. (The lions really *are* hungry: the

28 Colson, *Petit lexique*, 39–40.

outbreak of war has made meat scarce, and "carne de fieras" is hard enough to come by that every time they film this scene, the artists, Marlène Grey and Georges Marck—"both French and partisan to our cause," Guerra recalls—are really in danger of being eaten. Some compañeros from the Madrid Sindicato Único de la Gastronomía come to the rescue, though, and the beasts are fed—the film itself is a product of life-giving generosity.)[29] Unafraid, strong, graceful, sensuous, Marlène passes through the lion's den unharmed (fig. 10).

What are we to make of Marlene's nude dancing? Carmen Peña Ardid dismisses this as yet another example of "more or less chaste exhibition of the female body," invoking Laura Mulvey's critique of "the spectacle and erotic forms of looking."[30] A cartoon in the *Almanaque de Tierra y Libertad para 1911* likewise satirizes the "artistico-bourgeois sensualism" that licenses the ostensibly cultured gentleman to leer at a nude sculpture's rear (fig. 14). However, as I have said, nude figures (male as well as female) also stand as figures of liberation in the anarchist imaginary, where they are figures for subjective identification, powerfully active, rather than passive objects for the spectator's enjoyment. Marlène's self-display in *Carne de Fieras* is somewhat unique in that it is both aestheticized and eroticized.[31]

Pablo falls for Marlène, who admires him but is watched jealously by her possessive lover, Marck, whose job title, "domador," implies

---

29 Armand Guerra, *A través de la metralla: escenas vividas en los frentes y en la retaguardia* (Valencia: Talleres Editorial Guerri, 1938), 9.

30 Carmen Peña Ardid, "La representación de lo diferente: mujer y personajes femeninos en el cine español," *Teatro Antzerki: Revista de la Escuela Navarra de Teatro* 8 (June 1997): 25.

31 At the same time, we can't read the Spanish libertarian culture of these periods through the lens of a contemporary American pop culture in which the spectacular display of female bodies is often taken to be self-evidently a sign of freedom and empowerment. On the contrary, here is where the other side of Proudhon's aesthetic seems to have had particular salience for Spain. For Proudhon the moralist, there is such a thing as decadence in the negative sense—and in this respect, he was congenial not only to patriarchal elements within the Spanish anarchist movement, but also to the feminists who sought to apply libertarian critique to the family. For these, there could be no simple choice between the official culture of virginity and abstemious purity and the equally sexist culture of drinking and debauchery, the carnival tradition that is always the obverse side of officialdom (Umberto Eco, *Travels in Hyperreality: Essays*, trans. William Weaver [San Diego: Harcourt Brace Jovanovich, 1986], 275).

something more than "lion-tamer": he is a dominator, dressed in a mock naval officer's uniform, bristling with aggression (fig. 11). Of course they will end up together (figs. 12 and 13); *Carne de Fieras* follows the narrative logic of the Hollywood film for which, as Mateo Santos writes, the "formula for commercial success" is nearly as precise as a chemistry or math: "such a dose, or such a percentage, of emotion: such-and-such an amount of conventionalism, X doses, or even X hundred, of eroticism, etc., etc." However, Guerra's film does not obey the limitations of Hollywood commercialism, which dictate a "happy outcome, with the obligatory moral that virtue is rewarded in the end ... and that bad deeds never go unpunished"—in other words, that "in the plot there is to be no place for any ... theory which conflicts with the general moral norms governing in the countries where the bank, the church, or the army rules."[32] On the contrary, the romantic problems of Guerra's film play out in miniature the problems of overcoming a society structured by the bank, the church, and the army, and the poverty they superintend: "if all Spaniards did as we," Pablo reflects wistfully, "there would be no more children of the gutter." At the same time, *Carne de Fieras* avoids the trap of the social realist films that discourage and alienate audiences in the attempt to proselytize them.[33] Indeed, apart from the nudity, transgressive even by the standards of pre-Hays Code cinema, Guerra's filmmaking resembles that of Charlie Chaplin (of whom we shall hear more) in its linkage of a romantic plot to an ethic of generosity, a certain will to innocence, and a vaudevillean structure, with interludes of song and dance. Like Chaplin, like commercial cinema, it gives audiences something they want: pleasure, fantasy, escape, transcendence of the actual. But it does so in the act of making something that is possible visible, and using this possibility to critique the actual.

Moreover, it does this in a way that is at once "popular"—working at the level of explicit statement, so that it cannot be easily recuperated for conservative interpretations—and subtle, working through implicit identifications of images and ideas via juxtaposition

32 Mateo Santos, "Del cine burgués al cinema social," *Timón: Síntesis de orientación políticosocial* (November 1938):135–136.

33 José Cabeza San Deogracias, "Vendiendo un sueño equivocado: Cine de ficción republicano durante la Guerra Civil Español," in *El cine cambia la historia*, ed. Julio Montero et al. (Madrid: Ediciones Rialp, 2005), 117.

Fig. 14: Cartoon from the *Almanaque de Tierra y Libertad para 1911*, titled "ANARCHIST CRITIQUE OF BOURGEOIS AESTHETICS: Artistico-bourgeois sensualism, or art as appetize" (Image courtesy of Rare Books and Special Collections, McGill University Library.)

and association (particularly through the strategic use of dissolves and match cuts). It does not hide its politics, but it also expresses them through a series of associations, what Proudhon might have called the "serial dialectic" of film. Marlène's beautiful body is seriated not only with the feminine and the erotic but also with the lions, with fierceness, with a power that is barely held within restraint. Marck's whip, his cap and buttons, his scowl, his possessiveness, form another series with the court, the law, punitive violence, fear, miserliness. Pablo's losing a watch, losing a match, and losing a wife are seriated with his saving a life, giving a gift, and falling in love. Ultimately, Pablo, Marlène, Perragorda, and Picatoste are made to form a single series (fig. 13). *Carne de Fieras* plays out this dialectic, transforming rather than merely reinforcing the meanings of things; it mobilizes a feminine economy of the *fiera*, the sensual, the libidinal, the excessive, and also of generosity, the gift, against a masculine economy of efficiency, rationality, discipline, utility, exchange, possessiveness, and competition. Not a bad example, perhaps, of an egalitarian vision of superabundant life—if not of another kind of virile body.

2: "HE PEDDLES SIGNS": WORDS AND IMAGES

IT cannot be said that anarchists welcomed the cultural prospects of what Benjamin called "the Age of Mechanical Reproduction" uncritically. They brooded about the proliferation of popular amusements and distractions—café-concerts, sports competitions, movies, radio, television—well before Debord raised the specter of a "Society of the Spectacle." These spectacles required not "active collaboration" but spectatorship, accustoming us to consuming representations of ourselves, to allowing ourselves to be represented. A politics of the radical subject, which, in Pouget's words, "teaches her will-power, instead of mere obedience, and to embrace her sovereignty instead of conferring her part upon a representative," could not content itself with merely appropriating the existing means of representation.[1]

Nonetheless, a "euphoria of human self-creation," as Robert Damien calls it, is visible not only in the anarchist iconography of the body, but in anarchist publications' experimentation with visual form. Despite the disconnect between anarchist "social art" and the formalism of the artistic avant-gardes, working-class anarchists in the second period were often bold in their exploration of visual styles, producing an aesthetic of the sensuous, of the affective, of imaginative excess. A disproportionate number of anarchists, starting with Proudhon himself, worked as typesetters, and advances in print technologies at the end of the nineteenth century permitted

---

1 Émile Pouget, *Direct Action* (London: Kate Sharpley Library, 2003), 11, modifications mine.

Fig. 1: Banner of *La Protesta* (Cadíz, 1901).

a terrific expansion of the means of graphic expression that could be incorporated, leading them to experiment broadly and lavishly with layout, illustration, and typography.[2] Accordingly, unlike their scruffier descendants, anarchist journals of the second period are often tour-de-forces of design, flaunting Art Nouveau and Art Deco stylistic traits that signal their modernity far more than their honest poverty. Look at the banner design (*portada*) of the Cadíz *La Protesta*, a typical Spanish anarchist journal around the turn of the century: here, print is not merely the utilitarian container of the intelligible word, it is a sensible experience in itself, baroque, sinuous (fig. 1). Anarchist newspapers routinely make use of what had become, in the modern period, one of the least common word-picture relations: the fusion of both into a single experience. The technology of early printing presses (displacing the illuminated manuscript, which integrated word and picture, in favor of solid blocks of text with occasional illustrations) and the elaboration of increasingly realistic forms of visual art (culminating in the rich tradition of oil painting) had tended to drive images and words apart, and certainly text predominates over images in some anarchist newspapers and journals—New York's *Le Libertaire* (1858–1861), Boston's *Liberty* (1881–1908), or Buenos Aires's *Timón* (1938–1940), for instance.[3] Nonetheless, the typesetters, artists, and editors of anarchist periodicals like the Parisian *Père Peinard* (1889–1902), Barcelona's *Tierra y Libertad* (1904–1919), Berlin's *Der Syndikalist* (1918–1932), San Francisco's *The Blast* (1916–1917), or the Valencian photo-journal *Umbral* (1936–1938) sometimes achieved a striking, evocative integration of the said and

2   Kathy E. Ferguson, *Emma Goldman: Political Thinking in the Streets* (Lanham, MD: Rowman and Littlefield, 2011), 101–105; Litvak, *La Mirada Roja*, 51–55.

3   Scott McCloud, *Understanding Comics: The Invisible Art* (New York: HarperPerennial, 1994), 143–148.

Fig. 2: Typographical schemes from *La Revue Anarchiste* 1.1 (1922).

the seen. This was sometimes achieved, as Litvak points out, through the creative use of typography:

> Contrary to the uniform layout identified with conservative news-papers ... they display many different contrasts between headers and headlines, paragraphs and even whole sections printed on different typographical models.... By these means, the reader is conditioned to understand the messages on two levels, one com-municative and logical, and other typographical and emotional.[4]

We can see something of this typographical diversity in a typical page from the October 1, 1929 issue of the Argentine anarchist journal *La Batalla* (1910–1935), where not only "La Poesia Selec-ta [Selected Poetry]," and "El Cuento Breve [The Short Story]" and "Fabulas de Esopo [Aesop's Fables]" receive differently-styled head-ers, but the title of each poem and story appears in a distinctive typeface of its own. The header for the poetry section, set in what appears to be a hand-drawn ultra-modern typeface, seems to em-phasize the modernity of the featured poet, Armando Vasseur, and the sheer diversity of scripts may indicate the will to form a plural-istic, anarchic society.[5]

---

4   Litvak, "La Buena Nueva," 14, trans. mine.

5   Crispin Sartwell points out, conversely, that "Almost every attempt to

Fig. 3: Seamless integration of words and pictures: *Der Syndikalist* (1927).

Another device by which anarchists sought to engage readers was, of course, the inclusion of illustrations and other forms of pictorial expression—engravings, lithographs, aquatints, engravings, and photography—that serve to underscore, to echo, and to amplify the textual information, sometimes crudely, sometimes in a fairly sophisticated and subtle fashion. Notice, for instance, the cover of the April 23, 1927 *Syndikalist* (fig. 3): the banner title is literally a banner, a black flag waved by the virile worker, echoed underneath by the illustration of marchers carrying an antifascist protest banner. Not only does the verbal (the title) become the visual, while the visual (the illustration) becomes the verbal; the boundary between words (the text of the banners) and deeds (the act of defiant flag-waving, of protest) is effaced, very much in the spirit of "propaganda by the deed." Or take the page from the September 1, 1933 *Acción Libertaria* (fig. 4), on which the verbal imperative—"¡Detened la reacción! [Stop the Reaction!]"—finds an immediate, literally *arresting*, visual echo in the photograph of a hand. In these ways, as Litvak observes, anarchist journals and

standardize scripts has been accomplished under the auspices of political authority, from Alexander to the Roman emperors, Charlemagne to the French monarchy, Stalin and Hitler" (*Political Aesthetics* [Ithaca: Cornell University Press, 2010], 211).

Fig. 4: A page from *Acción Libertaria* (Sept. 1, 1933).

newspapers "sought at once to draw attention and to promote more emotive and dramatic reading ... emphasiz[ing] a reading of the newspaper that is not passive, but one of solicitation and discovery."[6]

Another significant visual genre to which Andrew Hoyt has called attention is the martyrological portrait—images of fallen revolutionary heroes, often with accompanying biographies, presented as living embodiments of the Idea, ideal for decorating the mantelpiece of an anarchist home (fig. 5). Here, perhaps, is the print counterpart to the "mirror-character" in the anarchist drama.[7] The term "martyrology" is native to anarchism in the sense that anarchist culture is marked by ritual commemorations of acts of martyrdom (e.g., May 1 and November 11 for the "Haymarket martyrs"). Thus, for instance, in 1904, an Italian anarchist writing for the *Cronaca Sovversiva* observes sadly that "1903 had passed without giving the martyrology [*martirologio*] of the international proletariat even one executioner."[8] Clearly, this refers

---

6   Litvak, "La Buena Nueva," 14.

7   Andrew D. Hoyt, "Carlo Abate, Luigi Galleani and the Art of *La Cronaca Sovversiva*" (unpublished paper, 2011), 5; Litvak, *La Mirada Roja*, 53–54, 61, 70–71.

8   G. Pimpino, "Facciamoci Frati!," *Cronaca Sovversiva* 2.15 (April 9, 1904): 3.

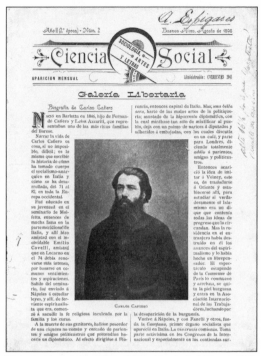

Fig. 5: Portrait of Carlo Cafiero (1846–1892) in *Ciencia Social* (August 1898).

to a non-Christian conception of martyrdom, but other examples are more parallel. The journal *Lucifer, the Light-Bearer*, for example, dated its issues not only according to the "Common Era" (C.E.) system, dating from the death of Jesus, but in years "E.M."—the "Era of Man" inaugurated in 1600 by Giordano Bruno's execution for heresy. All of this aroused discomfort among some anarchists, who warned against the formation of a "hagiography ... just like the Catholics."[9] In practice, however, this may have pulled against the spiritualistic traditions of the Church by concretizing and personalizing anarchist ideology.[10]

Nor was anarchist "pedagogy through the image" limited to heroic portraiture; "*retratos difamatorias* [defamatory portraits]" were also popular.[11] Caricature—part of "a parodic tradition, a mode that moti-

---

9   Altair (Mariano Cortés) qtd. in Suriano, *Paradoxes of Utopia*, 213.
10   Litvak, *La Mirada Roja*, 70–71.
11   Enric Olivé i Serret, *La Pedagogía Obrerista de la Imagen* (Barcelona: José J. de Olañeta, 1978); Litvak, *La Mirada Roja*.

vates extreme departures from concerns of verisimilitude," according to Hans-Christian Christiansen[12]—formed another highly important anarchist genre, right from the first period. Proudhon wrote *Du Principe de l'Art* as an extended defense of a satirical painting by his protégé Gustave Courbet, titled *Le Retour de la conférence* (also known as *Les Curés*)—a scabrous caricature of the clergy, refused even by the Salon des Refusés.[13] Courbet, in turn, tutored the young Louis-Alexandre Gosset de Guines, better remembered as André Gill (1840–1885), who quickly "mastered" the art of "the *portrait-charge*, the practice of drawing a large caricatural head on a squat comic torso."[14] Gill, a Communard, a member of Courbet's Federation des Artistes, and a sometime contributor to Jules Vallès's *La Rue*, came to edit a series of influential (and frequently censored) satirical journals, mentoring a new generation of caricaturists. Patrice Terrone emphasizes the inverse relationship between "the institutional art of the portrait which embellishes, solidifies, mythifies and idealizes the beauty of a character" and "the caricature [which] uglifies, exaggerates and demythifies its subject";[15] however, the subject of anarchist caricature is less often a particular, living individual than a *type* (like "the priest") or even a *force* (like "capital"), placing it on the side of allegory. Like Louise Michel's grotesques, the enemy is visualized as a monster to be slain (fig. 6).[16]

But not always. Sometimes, as in the anarchist lyric and the anarchist melodrama, the critical gaze of the anarchist caricature turns to the working class itself. *Anarchisant* cartoonists of the time draw

---

12 Hans-Christian Christiansen, "Comics and Film: A Narrative Perspective," in *Comics & Culture: Analytical and Theoretical Approaches to Comics*, eds. Anne Magnussen and Hans-Christian Christiansen (Copenhagen: Museum Tusculanum P, 2000), 118.

13 Chakè Matossian, *Saturne et le Sphinx: Proudhon, Courbet et l'art justicier* (Genève: Droz, 2002), 115–116; Proudhon, *Du Principe de l'Art*, 38–39

14 Donald Crafton, *Émile Cohl: Caricature and Film* (Princeton, NJ: Princeton University Press, 1990), 11.

15 Patrice Terrone, "'Chargez!' La caricature dans l'optique d'une strategie et d'une culture libertaires," in *La culture libertaire*, 308–309.

16 Litvak, *La Mirada Roja*, 74. There are exceptions to this rule as well, however; Hoyt notes the publication of portraits of "oppressors" and "nemeses" in *Cronaca Sovversiva*, for instance ("Carlo Abate, Luigi Galleani and the Art of *La Cronaca Sovversiva*," 18), and Aristide Delannoy (1874–1911) faced prison time for a caricature of General d'Amade, butcher of Morocco, in 1908 (Robert Justin Goldstein, *Censorship of Political Caricature in Nineteenth-Century France* [Kent, OH: Kent State University Press, 1988], 255).

Fig. 6a: Monstering the enemy (from Félix Dubois, *Le Péril Anarchiste*): Lucien Pissarro, "Le Capital et la Charité," *Père Peinard* (March 8, 1891). Fig. 6b: Maximilien Luce, "Abominable, insatiable Ghoul! A tough bitch, Madame Patrie: she devours her children!" (Almanach du Père Peinard, 1894).

similar images of the deracinated, indeed, *decapitated* working class: Frans Masereel's stark engraving, in Zo d'Axa's *La Feuille*, of an "ideal worker of the future," whose head has been neatly replaced by a clock (October 27, 1919), and Albert Daenens's "L'Homme-Machine [Man-Machine]" (ca. 1922) reveal the worker as mutilated by capitalism, the person deprived of personality, the subject deprived of subjectivity (fig. 7).[17] Mechanized, robotized, how will this worker rebel? Regarding the baleful figure astride the Man-Machine's back, Eugen Relgis writes: "This is the omnipotence of capital."[18]

A similar motif appears in the revolutionary syndicalist Ernest Riebe's (birth and death dates unknown) comic strip, "Mr. Block," which ran in the publications of the IWW. Wobbly organizer Walker C. Smith's introduction to a collection of "Mr. Block" strips hails it as a vital attempt "to catch the eye and mould the mind of any Block into whose hands it might fall":

This pamphlet may enable the readers to see their reflection on a printed page without the aid of glass or quicksilver. Right off

17 This trope of the headless proletarian can also be seen in Frans Masereel's *Debout les morts, Résurrection infernale* (1917), as well as in Robert Minor's cartoons for *The Blast* ("Intolerance," cover of the January 1, 1917 issue) and *Golos Truda* ("At Last I've Found the Ideal Soldier Who'll Carry Out Orders without Arguing!" October 27, 1917).

18 Eugen Relgis, "Peregrinaciones Europeas: Un día en Bruselas," trans. E. Muñiz, *La Revista Blanca* 2.10.213 (Sept. 1, 1932): 198, trans. mine.

Fig. 7: Albert Daenens, "L'Homme-Machine" (ca. 1922).

the reel we wish to state that these cartoons that please you are portraits of the other fellow, while the ones that arouse your ire are exactly as though you had looked in a mirror.[19]

Rather than following the narcissistic procedures of the culture industry, then, the anarchist comic strip is intended to confuse and disrupt the reader's self-image. It is, in short, a method of sabotage (a subject on which Smith had literally written the book) directed at the image- and identity-making apparatus of modern capitalism, aimed at producing moments of self-consciousness in the form of an uncomfortable laughter.

Riebe's Mr. Block never sees anything funny in his own person and behavior. He resolutely refuses subjectivity, resists seeing the world from the standpoint of his own material interests and conditions, thus impersonating the inanimate object that capital requires him to be—the producer mimicking his own alienated product: "As a human being," in Riebe's words, "he is only an imitation, a nature faker."[20]

19 Walker C. Smith, "Introduction," in *Mr. Block: Twenty-Four IWW Cartoons*, ed. Franklin Rosemont (Chicago: Charles H. Kerr Publishers Company, 1984), 1.

20 Ernest Riebe, *Mr. Block and the Profiteers* (Chicago: All-American Publishing Co., 1919), 4.

Fig. 8: Ernest Riebe, "Mr. Block: He Peddles Signs" (*The Industrial Worker* 4.46 [Feb. 6, 1913]).

Mr. Block could have been developed as a single-panel, one-time image, a send-up of the American worker as wooden-headed "willing slave."[21] Instead, he becomes the protagonist of a series of verbal as well as physical misadventures. How Block "thinks" is only partially manifested in his appearance—his literal block-headedness;

21 Ibid., 2

it is made even more manifest by the word balloons which tumble abjectly out of his slack cartoon mouth. "This here paper is honest," he reasons (in an episode titled "He Peddles Signs"), "because it is so very popular, everybody is reading it" (fig. 8).[22] Another unboxed caption indicates that the ideas enunciated by Block's wooden head are "solid oak philosophy"—objectified, perhaps even too "material" to *be* ideas. Yet the job he takes is an exercise in idealism: he literally "peddles signs" for goods and services rather than the things themselves. Indeed, he is not "material" enough in his identity as consumer either: "For his recreation," Riebe comments, "he meekly accepts imitations of the good things of life."[23] He has been swindled out of his own material interests by a savvier sign-peddler—the very newspaper whose representations he has taken for real on the basis of its popularity. The reproduction of capitalism lies in the selling of selling ("The success of our salesmen is phenomenal," trumpets the next advertisement he falls for)—an endless proliferation of signs without referents, valueless tokens presented as the touchstone of value.[24]

Riebe's comics consistently exploit one of the primary resources afforded by the comics—*the* primary resource, according to Robert C. Harvey: the duality and interplay of words and pictures. For Harvey, "comics are a hybrid form: words and pictures," and thus resist reduction to cinematic, painterly, or literary models.[25] Riebe's work seems to demonstrate that the power of the image to present a critical vision is often enhanced, rather than undermined, by playing on the disparity as well as the coincidence between visual and verbal codes: one code can be used to criticize the other. Here, perhaps, is a source for Smith's relative optimism about the potential of comics in contrast with other anarchists' pessimism about cinema. *Mr. Block* indeed passes Harvey's "litmus test of good comics art": rather than presenting us either with a predominantly visual narrative accompanied by essentially redundant captions (as in the model of the silent film) or a predominantly verbal narrative accompanied by decorative images (as in the model of the illustrated novel), Riebe plays off the visual against the verbal, "using to

---

22 Riebe, *Twenty-Four IWW Cartoons*, 4.

23 Riebe, *Mr. Block and the Profiteers*, 4.

24 Ibid., 5.

25 Robert C. Harvey, *The Art of the Comic Book: An Aesthetic History* (Jackson, MS: University Press of Mississippi, 1996), 3.

the fullest the resources the medium offers him."[26] In this interplay, it is the visual register that most consistently tells the truth, the material truth of situations and actions; the verbal register is that in which lies and propaganda crowd out truth, in which empty "signs" proliferate.

Some commentators have argued from this predominance of the visual that the "wordless comic" is the most prototypically anarchist genre. Undeniably, Frans Masereel's wordless *romans in beelden*, such as *Mon Livre d'Heures* (*Passionate Journey*, 1919), *Die Sonne* (*The Sun*, 1920), *Die Idee* (*The Idea*, 1924), *La Ville* (*The City*, 1925), and *Geschichte ohne Worte* (*Story Without Words*, 1927), have formed a particularly powerful example for latter-day anarchist comics writers such as Peter Kuper and Eric Drooker, who learned from them how one might create art as, in Masereel's words, "communication addressed to all men," while at the same time avoiding the "traps" of the dominant language, its tendency to hypostasize social conventions as the categories and structures of "reality" as such, putting in its place the bodily language of "gesture."[27] Thus, Kunzle writes, what is *drawn* presents a more materialist "truth" than the textual caption. Adding captions to Steinlen's wordless comic "would only vulgarize and banalize," reducing the complex meaning of the images to an "official line" or "received truth." Instead, Steinlen allows the "conventional morality, expressed by captions that traditionally functioned as a kind of censorious social super-ego" to "[fall] mute," leaving the reader to "visualize the social struggle ... as it really is, rather than as we have been taught to read it." The adventures of Steinlen's black cat—the *Chat Noir* that was also the emblem of the satirical journal and Montmartrois cabaret of the same name—play out scenarios of desire, danger, and death without verbal commentary, in a "morally indifferent" atmosphere that leaves the determination of their meaning to the reader's sense of sympathy or irony.[28]

---

26 Ibid., 4.

27 Perry Willett, *The Silent Shout: Frans Masereel, Lynd Ward, and the Novel in Woodcuts* (Bloomington, IN: Indiana University Libraries, 1997), 15; Masereel qtd. in Roger Avermaete, *Frans Masereel* (Antwerp: Fonds Mercator, 1976), 84; Colson, *Petit lexique*, 127, 131–132.

28 David Kunzle, "Willette, Steinlen, and the Silent Strip in the *Chat Noir*," in *The Language of Comics*, eds. Robin Varnum and Christina T. Gibbons (Jackson, MI: University of Mississippi Press, 2001), 15, 12

Fig. 9: Detail from André Bernard, *Le Retour de la Colonne Durutti* (1967).

We will see whether this interpretation of the virtues of word-lessness holds up. However, one of the most recognizable and memorable styles of anarchist comics comes from the tradition of *détournement*, the creative appropriation of cultural commodities for subversive purposes. Blending left Marxism with anarchism, the "friends of Marx and Ravachol," who produced the détourned comic book *Le Retour de la colonne Durutti* (*The Return of the Durutti Column*, 1966)—the title of which represented an homage (albeit misspelled) to one of the Spanish Revolution's most intransigent heroes[29]—consistently reversed Kunzle's formula. Instead of supplying the voice of convention, returning the unruly image to order, here the text represents the invasion of an unlicensed narrative, the irruption of *unofficial truths* ("public secrets," in Ken Knabb's fertile phrase) into the domain of conventional lies.

Most of the images in André Bernard's *The Return of the Durutti Column* (fig. 9), apart from just a few crude hand-drawn pictures, are stolen from commercial product, an act of cultural *reprise individuelle* facilitated—really made possible—by the liberal addition of captions and word balloons that radically alter their meanings. Tough-talking American cowboys spout French radical theory; a glamorous model smilingly denounces "two thousand years of Christianity"; a pair of toothbrushes mock every political faction from the right ("the fascists," "the Gaullists") to the sectarian left ("the J.C.R.

29 Steef Davidson, ed., *The Penguin Book of Political Comics*, trans. Hester and Marianne Velmans (London: Penguin Books, 1982), 56.

[*Jeunesses Communistes Révolutionnaires*]" and "the anarchists of '*Le Monde Libertaire*'"); the doomed king in Delacroix's famous canvas, *The Death of Sardanapalus*, pronounces on the "critique of everyday life."[30] Without Bernard's text, the images merely refer us back to their original contexts—entertainment, commerce, the institutions of official art; with the words, they become stolen artifacts, pregnant with new meanings. "Ultimately," as Guy Debord and Gil J. Wolman boasted, "any sign or word is susceptible to being converted into something else, even into its opposite."

At the same time, it is worth noting what comics constructed through *détournement* (and particularly détourned comics) do *not* do. Although the panels of *The Return of the Durutti Column* indeed must be read in a sequence (following the traditional top-to-bottom, left-to-right order of the Western printed page), the sequentiality of the comic is maintained entirely by the text. That is to say, the *visual* transition from panel to panel is always in the form of a non sequitur;[31] each segment of *text* follows the last more or less in the manner of paragraphs in an argumentative prose essay. This is perhaps due to Bertrand's over reliance on what Debord and Wolman called "*minor* détournement," i.e., "the détournement of an element which has no importance in itself and which thus draws *all* its meaning from the new context in which it has been placed," rather than "the détournement of an intrinsically significant element, which derives a *different* scope from the new context."[32] Bertrand's *written* argument becomes the context that overcodes and determines the otherwise trivial or meaningless *images* he has appropriated. Although Debord and Wolman trace the technique back to the inspiration of Lautréamont's *Poésies*, "minor détournement" hardly resembles Lautréamont's "chance juxtaposition of a sewing machine and an umbrella on a dissecting table";[33] on the contrary, it can assume a unilateral, arbitrary character, an appropriation of one discourse by another— putting one's own words into somebody else's mouth.

---

30 André Bernard, *Le Retour de la Colonne Durutti* (Strasbourg: Association fédérative générale des étudiants de Strasbourg, 1966), 3, 1, 4.

31 McCloud, *Understanding Comics*, 72.

32 Guy Debord and Gil J. Wolman, "A User's Guide to Détournement," trans. Ken Knabb, *Bureau of Public Secrets* (web), emphases mine.

33 Comte de Lautréamont (Isidore Ducasse), *Maldoror and Poems*, trans. Paul Knight (Harmondsworth, UK: Penguin, 1978), 216.

Fig. 10: Detail from "Contradiction," *Wildcat Comics* (1971). (Image courtesy of the Beinecke Collection, Yale University.)

Indeed, the potential for authoritarian or vanguardist uses of *détournement* is a perpetual danger. Thus, *Wildcat Comics*, a comic-strip "intervention in a San Francisco wildcat strike of cable-car drivers" produced by Knabb's group, "Contradiction," in 1971 (fig. 10) superimposes word balloons—written by white radicals?—over photographs of black strikers, one lamenting that "we let someone represent us," another agreeing that "we never did grasp the significance of our action." Did not the artist (perhaps Knabb himself) take on a similar privilege, here, of representing the strikers to themselves?[34] Another 1971 strip, "The Sexuality of Dialectics" (a reversal—*détournement*?—of Shulamith Firestone's *The Dialectic of Sex*) by Chris Winks's group Point-Blank!, using détourned panels from romance comics, stages dialogues between women over the feminist movement: "Love isn't possible in this society," one opines; "All men want is your body." The reply: "To say that love isn't possible is to be counter-revolutionary." The conclusion, placed in the mouth of a determined-looking woman: "Remember, sister, don't let all the bosses, cops, priests, teachers, and militants fuck with you. MAKE LOVE WITH REVOLUTIONARIES!"[35] Evidently, women are to achieve the status of revolutionary subjects by mouthing the right "revolutionary" lines and spreading their legs for their authors. The unstated assumption behind this discourse would seem

34 Davidson, *The Penguin Book of Political Comics*, 69.
35 Ibid., 73.

to be that liberation means sexual liberation, which is to be understood as the liberty of (active) men to "fuck" (passive) women; a
deeper subtext is the notion that women who refuse this role are
bourgeois "bitches," "frigid," and/or counter-revolutionary, with the
further implication that men who are insufficiently "radical," conversely, are impotent, weak, effete, "feminine."

In the end, one may well ask, with Richard J. F. Day, whether the
détourned comic is destined, by its form, to carry a radical content,
or whether it is always in danger of "failing to adequately distance
itself" from the "spectacular representations" on which it is parasit-
ic.[36] At the same time, however, one of the more intriguing aspects
of détourned comics is their occasional suggestion that they are *not*
merely imposing a predetermined political script upon a passive-
receptive surface of images but discovering a latent or unconscious
content *within the images themselves*—that they constitute "a certain
utopian extrapolation," to borrow a phrase from Graeber, a method
of "teasing out the tacit logic."[37] Deprived of their textual alibis, children's humor strips like *Desperate Dan* and *Beano* reveal a universe of
anti-authoritarian slapstick and absurdity, refusals of the politics of
everyday life; comics like *Superboy* divulge fantasies of escape, struggle, contestation; in other genres, too, there are scenarios of crimi-
nality, romance, enjoyment ... In short, détourned comics appeal to
the essentialist hope that "our ideas are in everyone's heads"[38]—that
the reason the otherness of the comics can exist within a capitalist
framework is because we in fact *already* desire something other than
capitalism.

---

36 Richard J. F. Day, *Gramsci is Dead: Anarchist Currents in the Newest Social
    Movements* (London: Pluto Press, 2005), 22.

37 David Graeber, *Fragments of an Anarchist Anthropology* (Chicago: Prickly
    Paradigm Press, 2011), 32.

38 René Vienet, "Les situationnistes et les nouvelles formes d'action contre la
    politique et l'art," *Internationale situationniste* 11 (1967): 4.

3: "EVOLUTION IS NOT OVER YET": VISUAL NARRATIVE

"COMICS, as a medium, [are] not conducive to expressions of democracy," complains Phil Nugent; "what comics are really, really good at expressing and embodying is *anarchy* ... wild-eyed, raving satirical fantasies." For critics such as Nugent, it is the very openness of the comics medium to expressions of anarchism that is the mark of its essential immaturity, its affinity for unilateral declarations and position-takings (as opposed, presumably, to the more nuanced expressions of anguished liberalism in novels such as Ian McEwan's *Saturday* or Jonathan Franzen's *Freedom*). At the same time, one of the very features of comics that gives it its formal identity as a medium—the *division* of images into panels—presents the inherent possibility of multiple points of view.

Fig. 1: Detail, Clifford Harper, *Class War Comix* (1973)

Fig. 2: Cartoon from *Le Père Peinard*, reproduced in Félix Dubois, *Le Péril Anarchiste*: "THE MINE / Those who live on the mine / Those who die from it."

Indeed, one of the most common devices of the polarizing comics published in Émile Pouget's *Le Père Peinard* was the contrast between how things appear *"Chez eux!"* and *"Chez nous!"*: from their point of view, and from ours.[1] Often these two panels seem to be organized by a logic not of time but of space, the transition from *chez eux* to *chez nous* being a matter of "place," both geographically and socially: a bourgeois dining at his leisure appears to be spatially perched above a squalid scene of death, so that his dinner is seen to literally depend upon the misery of others (fig. 2).[2]

Nonetheless, it can be said that this juxtaposition of scenes does not amount to a juxtaposition of perspectives. And as we have already seen, while the détourned comic demonstrates the presence of subversive fantasy within the most banal forms of entertainment, it often does so at the cost of the *dialogic* dimension of sequential art: a single voice speaks from these pages, no matter how many balloons and boxes it may appear in. However, like the novel, comics are capable of representing more than one perspective at once. J. Daniels's *The Adventures of Tintin: Breaking Free* (1989) attempts to combine this kind of polyvocality with the subversive fun of *détournement* (fig. 3).

1 Dieter Scholz, *Pinsel und Dolch: Anarchistische Ideen in Kunst und Kunsttheorie 1840–1920* (Berlin: Reimer, 1999), 120.
2 Dubois, *Le péril anarchiste*, 271.

Fig. 3: J. Daniels, *Breaking Free* (1988)

Daniels steals not only a few particular images, but an entire graphic vocabulary, from one of the most famous and lucrative comic-book series in the world: Hergé's *Tintin*. For the first few pages, the reader is invited to laugh at the spectacle of the erstwhile inhabitants of Marlinspike Manor—Tintin the "boy adventurer" and campaigner for good Catholic values against godless Communism, and his faithful pal Captain Haddock, memorable for his euphemistic, made-up oaths ("blistering blue barnacles!" etc.)—spouting a sometimes gleefully foul Cockney English: "Tintin, me old mate, how's it going?" "Well things ain't that hot to tell you the truth ... you see, they cut me dole last week!"[3] Soon, however, the fact that these characters inhabit the bodies of Hergé's creations fades in importance in the face of the larger situation inhabited by these bodies: the frustration of proletarian life in Thatcher's Britain, juxtaposing labor precarity with a rollback of the welfare state, the squalor of decaying council flats with yuppie gentrification, race riots, and the rise of neo-nazism. Daniels's real preoccupation is with finding the radical potential hidden in this landscape: the possibility of solidarity.

This solidarity is conceived, on fairly traditional anarcho-syndicalist terms, primarily through class identity.[4] However, the story does attempt to grapple with some of the other identity politics and new social realities that have emerged since the heyday of Ernest

3   Jack Daniels, *The Adventures of Tintin: Breaking Free* (London: Attack International, 1989), 1.
4   Ibid., 67.

Riebe's IWW, and a few of the best scenes play out in miniature the conflicts between these emphases and priorities, simulating the kinds of dialogues through which they might be resolved: "I mean it's all this women's liberation stuff ... it's *crap*!" Tintin fulminates to his friends Nicky and Mary. "Y'know ... *lesbian feminists* in *woolly hats* ... *middle-class wankers*!"[5] Here we are back with Mr. Block, the object who cannot recognize his own subjective interests in those of his kind—but whereas Riebe was content to satirize, Daniels pushes his objects toward ever-greater subjecthood, toward the mutual recognition that makes a pluralistic revolution possible. "That's *bollocks*, Tintin, and you know it!" Nicky counters. In the end, "there ain't no contradiction" between her struggle and his.[6] The status quo is effectively preserved by strategies of "divide and rule," and ultimately, as the Captain puts it, "we're all in the same boat."[7] Struggles against sexism, racism, heterosexism, ecocide, and exploitation converge in a general uprising—strongly reminiscent of Gilliland's *The Free*, from the same Brixton publisher—that pits a reassembled working class against the increasingly isolated managing elites.

Clifford Harper's remarkable early work, *Class War Comix*, also attempts to explore this perspectivist potential (fig. 4): in one page after another, we watch a group of revolutionary "communards" attempt to sort out their considerable differences. Here, once again, is an "ambiguous utopia," a utopia-in-process or -in-tension. The ratio of words to panels in Harper's comic is quite high, with considerable attention given to the hand lettering, done in a incongruously pretty art nouveau font, while the images are done in an extremely photo-realistic style (which gives each panel a curiously static appearance). From the first panel on the first page, the images announce that their subjects will be stripped bare, that they will be seen, as Bakhtin puts it, not in heroic attitudes, frontally, but "disrespectfully," from "the *back* and *rear*."[8] The heroic gestures and kooky capers selected for visual attention in the comics of Point-Blank! or Contradiction are absent here; instead, we see figures standing in public space deliberating together, occasionally bickering. "So ... should we widen the existing

---

5 Ibid., 25.
6 Ibid., 26, 104.
7 Ibid., 125, 44.
8 Bakhtin, *The Dialogical Imagination*, 23.

Fig. 4: Clifford Harper, *Class War Comix* 1 (1973)

bridge ...? Or can we build another bridge somewhere else?" one asks. "Or leave things as they are," interjects another. "I've thought about it a lot and I think Jim's overestimated the dangers. It seems to me we can't afford to spend time and energy ... on dismantling the bridge—when there are so many other more important jobs to be done in the commune like—" "*Bullshit!*" breaks in a voice from off-panel.[9]

The sentences that clutter these frames are relatively free from stammers, hesitations, and phatic particles, and some of them have a certain dramatic closure or wholeness that smacks of speech-making—"If we sit back and let them get away with this," a woman warns, "one day we will wake up to find our freedom has *passed away like a dream!*"[10] Nonetheless, the total effect tends to foreground something quite different

9   Clifford Harper, *Class War Comix* 1 (Princeton, WI: Kitchen Sink Enterprises, 1973): 1.
10   Ibid., 3.

from the defiant declarations and scenarios of rebellion advanced by détourned comics: the density and disorder of actual argument, the process of negotiating the use of power among free and equal people.

The reliance of *Class War Comix* on the word balloon to carry the weight of narrative may obscure other modes which other anarchists have exploited. Thus, Paul Glover's eco-utopian *Los Angeles: A History of the Future* (1983) uses sequential images and caption boxes to narrate the process of "a Santa Monica neighborhood ... evolving toward self-sufficiency" in seven stages, showing how a square mile of "car-clogged road grid" in Boyle Heights "gradually becomes orchard looped with bikeways and solar rail" (figs. 5 and 6). Glover's choice of visual angles, however—the god's-eye view of the cartographer, rendering everything "legible from above and outside"—seems strangely inappropriate to the anarchist vision; this is transformation envisioned from the vertical perspective of a planner, not the horizontal perspective of citizens on the ground.[11] Here, perhaps, illustrations recently added to the original work—panoramic paintings of the process by Thomas Slagle (1993)—not only flesh out this urbanist vision in color and depth, but do more to invite us to imagine ourselves as potential participants in the process.

Chad McCail, too, "narrates the attempts of a small, urban community to create its own 'utopian' society" in a series of drawings titled "Evolution is Not Over Yet" (1999), in which we watch as "roads are dug up," "money is destroyed," "people build homes and grow food," "soldiers leave the armed forces," "armour dissolves," "land is shared," and ultimately "everything is shared."[12] While "Evolution Is Not Over Yet" lacks the strong sense of chronology manifested by *Los Angeles: A History of the Future*—in McCail's vision, "evolution" seems to erupt spontaneously in every area of life, all at once—it, too, is clearly narrating a process of revolutionary transformation, the force and profundity of which is also conveyed by the recurrence of erotic body imagery (men and women in business suits stripping down and plunging into a pond) and surreal motifs (a banquet of skeletons). This libidinal

---

11 James C. Scott, *Seeing Like a State: How Certain Schemes to Improve the Human Condition Have Failed* (New Haven, CT: Yale University Press, 1998), 43.

12 The website for McCail's project is archived at https://web.archive.org/web/20000917092436/http://www.spring-alpha.org/pages.php?content=story.

Fig. 5: *Los Angeles: A History of the Future* (Paul Glover, 1983)

content is nonetheless also strangely at odds with its form: the drawings use a kind of *ligne claire* style that flattens out color values and
erases depth, effectively closing us out of the frame, distancing us from
what we are looking at rather than pulling us in: "a better world is set
out, one by which we may judge our own," critics complained, "but
there is no longer any sense that any political action we might take
(revolutionary or reformist) could ever bring us closer to this utopian state ... it is all impossibly idealistic." Yet like Glover, McCail uses
the rhetoric of the schematic, the diagram, the very form of contemporary technological "realism." Indeed, in McCail's object world, the cars,
buildings, machines, and articles of clothing stand out in crisp, outline,
as if traced from photographs—reminiscent of the corporate clip-art
appropriated by David Rees in *Get Your War On*—while his subjects
are left weirdly faceless, as if equality has left individuals interchange-
able. This may be why McCail's drawings have been compared to "Chinese propaganda cartoons from the Mao era."[13] Once again, subjects
seem reduced to objects.

13 Ralph Rumney et al., *The Map is Not the Territory* (Manchester: Manchester University Press, 2001), 25; Richard Cork, *Annus Mirabilis?: Art in the
Year 2000* (New Haven, CT: Yale University Press, 2003), 31.

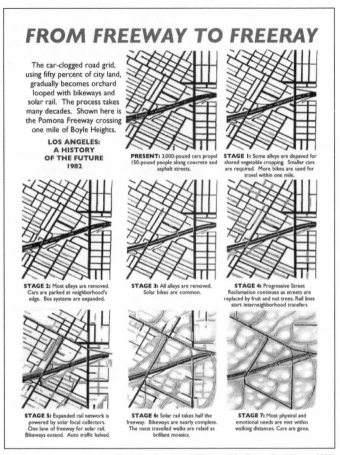

Fig. 6: Los Angeles: *A History of the Future* (Paul Glover, 1983)

Perhaps, however, this impression is misleading. In the vocabulary of the history of art, abstraction is often taken to signify this kind of objectification or distancing; the flattened, stiffened lines of a Byzantine Madonna-and-child, for instance, are commonly said to represent the compromise reached with iconoclasm, an attempt to observe (even in the breach) the commandment against making likenesses and thereby reducing the sacred difference or distance between the spiritual and material worlds, whereas a Renaissance treatment of the same subject in terms of codes of verisimilitude (depth, texture, light and shadow, etc.) signifies a humanization of the divine, and so on. Theories of graphic narrative, however, have often inverted this scheme, as per McCloud's dictum of the "masking effect," wherein the placement of "very iconic [i.e., abstract] characters" set against "unusually *realistic* backgrounds" is said to enhance, rather than diminish, "the degree to which the audience *identifies* with a story's *characters*."[14] Just as the extended use of "subjective" camera angles is unusual in cinema—it quickly becomes both disorienting and "claustrophobic," as Slavoj Žižek points out, inhibiting rather than facilitating audience involvement—its use in graphic narrative is relatively restricted; "viewer-identification" tends to be facilitated instead by inviting viewers "to *mask* themselves in a character."[15] By leaving his revolutionary protagonists blank, open, McCail allows us to project ourselves onto them, to inhabit them. Indeed, it is interesting, in this context, to note that one of McCloud's first examples of the masking effect is the *Tintin* series appropriated by Daniels, and that another is the work of Jacques Tardi, a French graphic novelist with markedly libertarian tendencies.[16] Indeed, Tardi's most politically engaged work—his antimilitarist *C'était la guerre des tranchées* (1993) and his four-volume graphic realization of Jean Vautrin's novel of the Paris Commune, *Le Cri du peuple* (2001–2004)—make abundant use of this principle.

Within the anarchist tradition, the trope of the "mask" has a range of connotations. In the nineteenth century, while "the theme of the mask is important," according to Caroline Granier, it is generally a negative theme, associated with the lies and hypocrisies of bourgeois society. In recent years, however, with the intensification of surveillance and "societies of control," masks appear to have been recoded, in the figure of the Black Bloc, in conjunction with another traditional motif of anarchist culture. The manifest taste of nineteenth-century anarchism for "the internal, the private, and the secret, as opposed to the external, the explicit, and the public," Colson argues, beyond merely reflecting the exigencies of politics in a time when worker organization was almost entirely illegal, embodies a certain critique of "the person," the unified subject produced by a

---

14 McCloud, *Understanding Comics*, 43, 42.
15 Slavoj Žižek, *Looking Awry: An Introduction to Jacques Lacan Through Popular Culture* (Cambridge, MA: MIT Press, 1991), 41–42; McCloud, *Understanding Comics*, 43.
16 Ibid., 42, 43.

dominatory social order—self-identical, identifiable, representable, and "docile."[17] It is interesting to see, in this connection, how Alan Moore and David Lloyd's *V For Vendetta* revives the appeal of *propagande par le fait* in the figure of "V," the masked anarchist superhero. V's Guy Fawkes mask protects not only against the "Leader" and his omnipresent security cameras (another apparatus of identification), but against the tendency of the oppressed to identify their own emancipation with a single person, to find a new "leader."

Anarchists have always been wary, as Mitchell Verter points out, of the danger of "*personalismo*"—of "identifying the struggle for human liberation with a certain leader"—but Eve, V's protegé, is all too tempted to hypostasize V into a personal savior, a replacement for her lost father (and for the patriarchal authority whose downfall he has helped to engineer). When V is mortally wounded, in what appears to be a kind of "suicide by proxy," he boasts that "There's no flesh or blood within this cloak to kill. There's only an *idea*. Ideas are *bullet-proof*."[18] As the Mexican anarchist saying has it, "*las personas mueran, pero los ideales buenas son eternos* [persons die, but noble ideals are eternal]": by eliminating the fiction of the "person," demonstrating "the limits of personhood," V extends his freedom to infinity, eternalizing himself as a "hope" in others.[19] Eve takes up the mask—a gesture that has since become a ritual of popular dissent, thanks to the Wachowski brothers' 2006 film treatment—and appears before the people of London to demonstrate that V survives; the reader, by extension, is invited to imagine himself or herself as V—a creature of "preternatural strength and speed," "superhuman feats and perceptions," possessed of a "prescience" which "verges on the prophetic," capable of embodying all of history's unrealized revolutionary fantasies.[20]

Here, however, objections can be raised, once again from an anarchist perspective. Josh Lukin takes Moore to task for essentially ignoring his own critique of "the superhero." In *Watchmen* (1986), indeed, Moore unmasks the superhero as not only a kind of

17 Colson, *Petit lexique*, 165, 231–233.

18 Josh Lukin, "I'm Not Your Boss: The Paradox of the Anarchist Superhero," *Anarchist Studies* 5.2 (1997): 139; Alan Moore, David Lloyd, et al., *V for Vendetta* (New York: Vertigo/DC Comics), 236.

19 Qtd. in Mitchell C. Verter, "Persons Die but Noble Ideals are Eternal," *Waste.org*, March 29, 2007, trans. Verter.

20 Lukin, "I'm Not Your Boss," 137.

vanguardist (acting on behalf of society, in place of others, standing in for us, representing us) but a closet fascist—a vigilante who decides what is right and wrong for the rest of us, setting himself up as the sovereign exception over and outside of humanity. Ultimately, Lukin argues, despite his final self-canceling gesture, "V is in fact as much a monitory figure as the Fascist Leader."[21] As a vehicle for intrinsically irresponsible fantasies, fantasies of power over others, superhero narratives align our desires with domination.

If we are flattered by our reflections in the mirror of the comics page, Lukin seems to worry that—in a striking echo of the terms set by Smith's 1913 preface to *Mr. Block*—we may fall in love with them, losing our ethics in the trance of mediated narcissism. Much as anarchist dramaturgy shows an awareness of the problems entailed in what Emma Goldman called "the impossible figure of the hero, with a gesticulating crowd in the background,"[22] preferring sometimes to bestow agency on that crowd rather than on an individual, a number of anarchist comics likewise favor ensemble casts: thus Tardi's *Le Cri du Peuple* and Daniels's *Breaking Free*, for instance—and, once again, *Watchmen*, which perpetually pulls our attention away from the would-be "heroes" (all but one of them entirely ineffectual) to probe the significance of the intersecting lives of "minor" characters: a newspaper vendor, a butch lesbian cabbie and her punk girlfriend, a psychiatrist and his wife, a black kid engrossed in reading a comic book. No perspectives are privileged (not even the panoptical perspective of Adrian Veidt, the self-appointed *Übermensch*, "watching" over the world from his Antarctic castle); all are partial, all are limited, all are ultimately dependent on one another ("inna final analysis," as the vendor's refrain has it).[23] Indeed, it is perhaps here that *V For Vendetta* falls short: to the extent that V *is* "superhuman"—a status reinforced by the way in which his face (and body) are masked, kept hidden from our inspection—we are in fact *barred* from entering and occupying V's subject position. As Seth Tobocman complains, "V is not a real person."[24] He is, finally,

---

21 Ibid., 143.

22 Emma Goldman, "Observations and Comments," *Mother Earth* 1.1 (March 1906); 5.

23 Moore and Gibbons, *Watchmen*, 3.25.9.

24 Tobocman qtd. in Lukin, "I'm Not Your Boss," 137.

another example of "the impossible figure of the hero"; he resists authority so that we don't have to.[25] The figures created by Tobocman, Eric Drooker, and other artists for *World War 3 Illustrated* (1980–present)—an ecumenically left-wing publication which nonetheless finds its imagery widely appropriated and reprinted across anarchist media—are the opposite of V; they are the rioting "mass of people" in Tobocman's "Spatial Deconcentration" (1985), or Drooker's iconic tableau of a dark crowd facing down tanks armed only with fantastical musical instruments (1992).[26]

V does *not* share one trait of the classic comic book superhero, however: he is not unambiguous. More so than Stan Lee's neurotic Spider-Man, more so even than Bob Kane's remarkably dark Batman, V is posited *as* problematic from the very first. Standing over the bodies of dead policemen, Detective Eric Finch confiscates whatever enjoyment we might have taken from watching them fall to V's flashing knife: "Whatever their faults, those were two human beings—and he slaughtered them like cattle!"[27] While their confrontation is still chapters away, the detective has already begun to interrogate V's morality, the ethics of "vendetta," of violent revolt against a violent regime. In a parallel movement, as Finch gets closer and closer to his target, he and V move closer and closer together morally and mentally, so that in the end, their two perspectives annihilate one another: V allows Finch to destroy him, and Finch internalizes V's insights so entirely that he can no longer see any purpose in the "order" he is supposed to be defending.[28] In the end, Eve, too, declines to follow V's path, accepting his ends but rejecting his means as radically inconsistent with them: "I won't do any more killing, V.... Not even for you."[29] Moreover, it is by no means certain

25 This criticism, however, ignores the increasingly important roles played by other, non-superhuman characters in the later chapters of the book: Ally Harper, the gangster who inevitably becomes the law's left hand; Rose Almond, the victimized and humiliated widow who ultimately becomes the Leader's assassin; and Valerie Page, the prisoner who teaches freedom in the face of death.

26 Seth Tobocman, *You Don't Have to Fuck People Over to Survive* (San Francisco: Pressure Drop Press, 1990), 70–73; Eric Drooker, *Flood!: A Novel in Pictures* (New York: Four Walls Eight Windows, 1992), 149–150.

27 Moore and Lloyd, *V For Vendetta*, 24.

28 Ibid., 252.

29 Ibid., 64, 66.

that "V" stands for "victory"; perhaps the villainous Helen Heyer will not find another Juan Perón to sponsor her will to power, but no guarantee is given that another oppressive order will not emerge from the ruins of the old.[30] All that wins out over fascist absolutism, finally, is existential ambiguity.

Is narrative ambiguity per se anarchist, however? David Kunzle raises this question in his analysis of one of Steinlen's signature pieces, "Idylle," a one-page narrative told in twelve borderless panels ("a grey world deprived of spatial coordinates," as Kunzle remarks), which appeared in an 1885 issue of *Le Chat Noir*. We watch the black cat yowl his cry of love from his rooftop lair across the foggy nighttime street to a white cat ("surely a female") in the window opposite, who, in attempting the impossible leap, "drops to her death below": "She dies for following a fatal, instinctual signal, and for her enticer's unwillingness or inability to help." Which is it?—callous indifference or innocent helplessness? Is this a tragedy lightly drawn or a rather dark comedy? Is this an "idyll" in the sense of a (failed) romantic episode or in the sense of a vision of peace? Nature, as an evolutionary motor driven by forces of sex and violence, admits of both interpretations, and so we are left with "a kind of social-Darwinist anarchist" world-hypothesis.[31]

The very phrase "social-Darwinist anarchist," however, is a contradiction in terms, as Steinlen surely would have known from his broad association with the actual anarchist movement in *fin-de-siècle* Paris. Elisée Reclus's *Evolution et Révolution* (1891), to which Steinlen supplied the rather less ambiguous cover illustration—an allegorical woman with a torch leads prisoners striving to breach the walls of their cell (fig. 7)—repudiates *laissez-faire* notions of natural "survival of the fittest" as "the rude struggle of conflicting egoisms" in capitalist society. Steinlen also published far more pointedly radical illustrations in such *anarchisant* publications as *L'Assiette au Beurre*, *Les Temps Nouveaux*, and *La Feuille*. If he remained of necessity a commercial artist, if he was sometimes prey to patriotic and racist impulses, if he was at times fascinated with violence itself as a kind of natural spectacle, these are not evidence of his anarchist commitments, nor do they constitute a contribution

---

30 Ibid., 265.
31 Kunzle, "Willette, Steinlen, and the Silent Strip."

Fig. 7: Steinlen, cover illustration for Elisée Reclus, *Evolution et Révolution* (1891). (Image courtesy of the Rubenstein Library, Duke University.)

to the history of anarchist visual culture. The question concerns the lessons Kunzle draws from these observations. Rather than see these two sides of Steinlen as simply contradictory, he interprets them as two phases in the development of artist's politics and that of the art form itself:

In 1890 Steinlen abandoned narrative, and the *Chat Noir*, to dedicate himself to that rich iconography of the poor and oppressed for which he has achieved lasting renown.... Now, as a contributor to politically engaged socialist and anarchist magazines, Steinlen could no longer treat human struggle, suffering, and exploitation, or its animal analogues, with the moral ambivalence or relative detachment of his *Chat Noir* period. The serious philosophical undertow of his narrative strips surfaced openly in large, powerful, self-sufficient images, the humanitarian purpose of which would only be undermined by the whimsical and anecdotal or by formalistic overconcern with movement for its own sake. At this point in its development, then, by the fin de siècle, the comic strip form had become an impediment to serious, radical political commitment.[32]

In short, for Kunzle, single-panel caricature is *the* anarchist genre; the attempt to narrate, to add time and motion to the image, leads to formalism and the abandonment of political content. A political content, an *ideal*, is static, not mobile, fluid, or living. Once again, nothing could be further from the anarchist tradition, which conceives of the "Idea" as "neither an *ideal*, nor a *utopia*, nor an abstraction," but as "a living force"—witness Masereel's depiction of "l'Idée" as a woman in struggle with the world, as if literalizing Brousse's insistence on the *embodiment* of thought in action, so that "the idea ... shall walk in flesh and blood and bone;" or Déjacque's description of "the idea" as a "lover"—and demands of art that it provide "forms which, if they are not living in the sense of real life none the less excite in our imagination the memory and sentiment of ... the living, real individualities that appear and disappear under our eyes."[33] If Steinlen fails to find these forms, it is not proof against the content.

The work of Frans Masereel, stemming from strong Flemish and Belgian traditions of social art, makes an even more vigorous attempt than did Steinlen to wed form and content, aesthetics and ethics.[34] While Masereel is more frequently remembered as a "pacifist," his anarchist credentials are firmly established: as Joris van Parys points out, his commitment to a "radical conception of liberty and solidarity" was lifelong, and even as an old man, he believed in "an anarchist communism, a communism without coercion,"[35] and he never ceased to associate himself with other anarchists, contributing illustrations to Joseph Ishill's (1888–1966) *Free Vistas* and Zo d'Axa's (1864–1930) *La Feuille*, and as well as drawing satirical cartoons against fascism and militarism for the local anarchist

---

32 David Kunzle, *History of the Comic Strip: The Nineteenth Century* (Berkeley and Los Angeles: University of California Press, 1990), 212.

33 Colson, *Petit lexique*, 152; Brousse and Déjacque qtd. in Ibid., 152; Bakunin, *God and the State*, 57.

34 Joris van Parys, *Masereel: ein biografie*, trans. Siegfried Theiseen (Zurich: Edition 8, 1999), 28.

35 Ibid., 28–29; Masereel qtd. in Ibid., 29.

federation.[36] "As a young bloke," in his own words, Masereel had picked up his aunt's Flemish translations of Peter Kropotkin's *Idealen en werkelijkheid in de Russische literatuur* (*Ideals and Realities in Russian Literature*, 1915) and *Wederkeerig dienstbetoon: Een factor der evolutie* (*Mutual Aid: A Factor of Evolution*, 1904).[37] In the first, he would have read the anarchist's admonition that "realistic description" in literature must be coupled with "an idealistic aim."[38] The latter book, however, exemplifies this strategy, locating the anarchist ideal within the material processes of nature, wherein, demonstrably, "mutual support not mutual struggle ... has had the leading part."[39] These two ideas seem to recur in Masereel's woodcut novel, *Mon Livre d'Heures* (literally, "My Book of Hours").

A "book of hours" is, of course, a medieval religious genre, an illuminated prayerbook for lay worshippers, and Masereel does testify in a letter of 1922 to being "deeply gothic and more religious than you seem to believe."[40] Nonetheless, the book's title seems to testify less to his affinity with "gothic" spirituality than to the kind of gothicism espoused by Kropotkin (along with Morris, Ruskin, and the Pre-Raphaelites), tied to an emphasis on craft and populism: the medieval artist, wrote Kropotkin, "spoke to his fellow-citizens, and in return he received inspiration."[41] At the same time, the possessive *My* modifies the sense of a *Book of Hours*: the choice of a quotation from Walt Whitman's *Song of Myself* as an epigraph ("Behold! I do not give lectures, or a little charity: When I give, I give myself") suggests that this book too is—if not a "genuine autobiography"—then "a 'Song of Myself' on Whitman's model, a picture-poem in which dreams and fantasies merge with the memory of everything that he really experienced."[42] It is indeed possible to read *Mon Livre d'Heures* as a kind of *Kunstlerroman* tracing the artist's journey from youthful innocence, through the joys and sorrows of experience, toward a kind of self-transcendence. The gestures of transcendence, however,

---

36 Ibid., 61, 64, 179; Pierre Vorms, *Gespräche mit Frans Masereel* (Zurich: Limat-Verlag, 1967), 42.

37 Parys, *Masereel*, 27.

38 Kropotkin, *Ideals and Realities*, 86.

39 Kropotkin, *Mutual Aid*, 300.

40 Qtd. in Parys, *Masereel*, 93.

41 Peter Kropotkin, *The Conquest of Bread* (New York: Putnam, 1907), 139.

42 Parys, *Masereel*, 91.

are also directed at the society against which this journey unfolds—a radical content that is frequently disavowed by commentators intent on confining Masereel's narrative to a mystique of the inward.

When he wrote his preface to Masereel's *Mon Livre d'Heures*, in 1926, Thomas Mann had just published his portrait of the radical as utopian fanatic in the *Magic Mountain*, and was in the process of redefining himself as the man who would be an ideological hero for post-Nazi Germany: the "'nonpolitical' modernist" as liberal humanist for whom irony is a both a call to sobriety and a prophylactic against all forms of political idealism.[43] It is telling that in his sympathetic portrayal of Masereel, he resists calling Masereel "subversive" or "a revolutionary": while acknowledging that his work "accuses and condemns our civilization," he insists that Masereel "has no intention of teaching or exhorting," for the protagonist's journey is

> really too planless to be considered a virtuous life, the life of a revolutionary. It does not involve principles. So it is not incongruous to see our hero burst with laughter at the sight of a bejewelled priest and then, one day when his anguish and disgust are great, to encounter him in a church, bowing his head and kneeling in the mystic atmosphere of muted sorrow.[44]

Thus Mann reads *Mon Livre d'Heures*, after the manner of his own work, as a "human-moral" rather than an engaged novel—at the cost of distorting it almost entirely. In order to do so, he must supply the novel with its missing captions, explicating its inarticulate conclusions. "Do you understand?" Mann asks the reader, in a pedagogical tone—adding quickly, in case we do not, that "its meaning is clearly conveyed: the catharsis of human suffering…. His heart, not Socialism, made a revolutionary of him, even when he indulged in pranks and follies. For the true revolution is not 'in principle,' not in 'The Idea,' but in the human heart."[45] The final lesson of the

---

43 Weir, *Anarchy and Culture*, 262, 85.

44 Thomas Mann, "Introduction to Frans Masereel, *Passionate Journey: A Novel Told in 165 Woodcuts*," trans. Joseph M. Bernstein, in *Arguing Comics: Literary Masters on a Popular Genre*, eds. Jeet Heer and Kent Worcester (Jackson, MS: University Press of Mississippi, 2004), 17–19.

45 Ibid., 19.

wordless novel, then, is to be oneself wordless, inwardly free and outwardly quiet.

It would seem, however, that the meaning is not "clearly conveyed" enough by the visual narrative, since it requires this exegesis, which seems particularly preoccupied with asserting that "Socialism" has no place in such a "human" story except as part of a young man's "experiences and follies": "Four of the one hundred sixty-five pictures present him listening to a speaker at a mass meeting, studying social problems in a library, even making a revolutionary speech himself and stirring a crowd of men to revolt. Then come other adventures, showing that he has also sown his Socialist wild oats."[46] In fact, despite his apparent disillusionment with "mass" politics, the protagonist returns repeatedly to acts of political defiance, snatching the whip from a father beating his daughter, knocking down a slavemaster in colonial Africa, mocking the bourgeois citizen, refusing to go to war, laughing before the courtroom and its "law," and, amid a popular riot, climbing the statue of a medieval hero in the town square to crown it with the bourgeois bowler hat.[47] Mann has even gotten the sequence of panels wrong, inverting the order and hence the meaning of events: whereas an earlier "episode" of rejection and despair drives the protagonist to fall on his knees in a church, by the *end* of the book, he has regained himself and shows his contempt for its consolations by lifting his coattails to fart at a priest.[48]

Anti-clerical, anti-militarist, anti-capitalist, anti-patriarchal, anti-colonial—at every opportunity, this book gestures toward the negation of dominatory order, the overturning of every kind of hierarchy and its transcendence in the direction of nature, a living order. It is perilously open to Mann's kind of reading, however, not only because of its muteness (which opens a space for the critic to become its "representative" by default), but because of its *mise en page*. Since we encounter just one image per page, juxtaposition is enacted only by a page turn. This separation of panel from panel tends to inhibit "closure," the meaning-making process that allows us to leap the abyss between one moment and another, to see them as images in action,

---

46 Ibid.

47 Frans Masereel, *Mon Livre d'Heures* (Geneva: Albert Kundig, 1919), 84, 99, 134, 140, 160–161, 167.

48 Ibid., 97, 159.

forming a sequence—e.g., arriving in the city by train, *then* disembarking onto the platform, *then* bending down to peer curiously at the great wheels of the engine.[49] It is relatively easy to look at each image in isolation, as a fixed and separate composition (a problem perhaps compounded by the woodcut technique Masereel uses, which encourages both the artist and the viewer to perceive the image as a unified "block" of space), rather than as *narrative* at all.

Here, once again, for all the disruptive and unruly forces present in anarchist culture, we have to strongly question theorizations of it that ask us to read it as intrinsically anti-narrative (seeking, as Uri Eisenzweig has it, "to unhinge narration *as narration*").[50] While Kunzle argues that the trajectory taken by Steinlen signals a more decisive turn in anarchist aesthetics *toward* "radical political commitment" and *away from* "the comic strip form," it would appear that anarchist work in the visual field actually may *require* the force of narrative if it is to prevent its own recuperation. Far from simply constituting a "trap," as Colson suggests (following Louis Marin),[51] narrative may constitute a way to avoid the traps laid for expressions of the anarchist Idea by recuperative forces—those of liberalism no less than those of fascism or authoritarian communism. Joan Ramon Resina seems to reach similar conclusions in his analyses of anarchist and fascist filmmaking during the Spanish Civil War, suggesting that whereas fascist film "denarrativizes" documentary images, reducing them to "the static and the iconic" and then milking them for their "purely emotive" shock value, documentaries produced by the anarchist Confederación Nacional del Trabajo rely on "sequence" and "chronology"; while each image is in many respects simply "permitted to tell its own story," the editing provides a "metanarrative" framework for the ensemble of images, giving "a teleological ... center of gravity to the visual content."[52] This, in turn, suggests that an authentically anarchist sequential art would be characterized by an aesthetic aiming to produce a participatory, dialectical play of forces between the producers

49 Ibid., 23–25.

50 Eisenzweig, "Représentations Illégitimes," 79.

51 Colson, *Petit lexique*, 317.

52 Joan Ramon Resina, "Historical Discourse and the Propaganda Film: Reporting the Revolution in Barcelona," *New Literary History* 29.1 (1997): 78–79, 82.

and consumers of images—one in which otherwise ambiguous *visual contents* are invested with unambiguously contestatory meaning by the *narrative form* into which they are inserted. Narrative form, in turn, is a matter of the spatial representation of time. Such considerations of spatiality deserve further consideration, and it is to these that we now turn.

In Ursula K. Le Guin's *The Dispossessed*, Takver, an amateur sculptor, creates a series of mobiles that she names *The Occupations of Uninhabited Space.*[53] The title is fitting: there is a rather long tradition of anarchist thought concerning space, its inhabitation, its occupation (as testified, more recently, by the anarchist presence in the Occupy Wall Street movement). Kropotkin and Reclus were geographers, and their work exerted considerable influence on the regionalism of Patrick Geddes and the urbanism of Ebenezer Howard, whose conception of the "Garden City" attracted the interest of anarchists such as Landauer and Martínez Rizo.[54] This preoccupation with occupation continues into the twentieth century with the writings of thinkers such as Paul and Percival Goodman (*Communitas*, 1947), Michel Ragon (*Où vivrons-nous demain?*, 1963), and James C. Scott (*Seeing Like a State*, 1998), and in journals like *Black and Green* (1981–1982) and the radical office-workers' zine, *Processed World* (1981–2005).[55]

For Marxists of a certain stripe, the spatial focus of anarchism is evidence of its inability to come to grips with the temporal, hence its ahistorical character.[56] On the contrary: anarchist geographers and urbanists have generally been convinced that the only way to really understand spatial relationships is in terms of time, as structures

---

53 Le Guin, *The Dispossessed*, 183.

54 Peter Geoffrey Hall, *Cities of Tomorrow: An Intellectual History of Urban Planning and Design in the Twentieth Century* (Oxford: Blackwell, 1988), 143–152; Eugene D. Lunn, *Prophet of Community: The Romantic Socialism of Gustav Landauer* (Berkeley: University of California Press, 1973), 148–150; Aisa, *La cultura anarquista*, 149–150.

55 See Dan Chodorkoff and Matthew Seig, "Loisaida: Community Self-Reliance in New York City," *Black and Green* 2/3 (Fall/Winter 1982); Bradley Rose, "The Walling of Awareness," *Processed World* 9 (1983); and Tom Wetzel, "San Francisco's Space Wars," *Processed World* (2001).

56 See Nicholas Spencer for one version of this trope (*After Utopia: The Rise of Critical Space in Twentieth-Century American Fiction* [Lincoln, NE: University of Nebraska Press, 2006]).

that arise historically, and that then condition the unfolding of future social relations—from the plan of New Delhi (as discussed by the Goodman brothers), bearing the imprint of British colonialism, to the classroom structured so as to organize students by "ranks," training their attention upon the teacher, the subject-presumed-to-know (as discussed by Paul Goodman).[57] In both cases, an entire ideology, a set of social relationships, has been encoded in spatial relationships, in layout.

Layout, what the French call *mise en page*, is perhaps the dimension of comics (apart from caricatural abstraction) that most distinguishes it from cinema. It is true that the very phrase, as applied to the study of comics, is modeled after *mise en scène*, a cinematic term borrowed from theater, where it refers to the disposition of light, color, line, and shape on stage. However, unlike the fixed proscenium arch or movie screen, the comics *frame* can change shape. Moreover, the spatial relations of panels on a page can be experienced in terms of simultaneity (viewing the page or multiple panels as a single design unit), sequential repetition (reading left to right and top to bottom, but backtracking to reread), or nonsequential meandering (roaming around the page, jumping back and forth between regions of "relative visual salience").[58] In other words, the comics page offers a degree of freedom that other art forms do not.

Given this range of options, it is surprising to discover that the form of *mise en page* favored by anarchist comics has historically been what Benoît Peeters calls "conventional," that is, determined by "a strongly codified system in which the arrangement of the panels on the page, by repeating itself, tends to become transparent."[59] In short, the formal possibility most explored by anarchist comics artists has been the one that *obscures* form in favor of content. This is perhaps in keeping with the pedagogical function of much anarchist culture, which places a priority on accessibility; the grid is the easiest layout to find one's way through, so it makes sense that comics addressed

---

57 Goodman and Goodman, *Communitas*, 3–5; Goodman, *Utopian Essays*, 156–181.

58 Gunther R. Kress and Theo van Leeuwen, *Reading Images: The Grammar of Visual Design* (London: Routledge, 1996), 139.

59 Benoît Peeters, *Case, planche, récit: lire la bande dessinée* (Paris: Casterman, 1998), 42.

Fig. 8: "L'Histoire vraie de Croc-Mitaine," Paul Robin and Félix Lochard (1906).

to a broad public—such as Paul Robin and Félix Lochard's flyer advocating birth control (fig. 8) or Paul Glover and Jim Houghton's pamphlet explaining the way a local currency works (fig. 9)—would arrange themselves into geometrical tiers of more or less identical panels. Both examples deviate from the strict "waffle iron" pattern to a minor degree—Lochard gives the upper left and upper right panels a decorative shape, giving the ensemble the look of panels in a church window, and Houghton staggers the frames a bit, alternating closed with borderless panels, and violating gutter boundaries occasionally to suggest exchange—but both allow the reader's eyes few decisions about where to begin, how to proceed, what to rest on, and when to stop. In French, the phrase *sens unique* can indicate a "single meaning" or a "one-way street"; to closely determine the direction (*sens*) of reading is to exercise maximum control over the reader's production

Fig. 9: "Five Months in the Life of an Hour: An Actual Ithaca HOUR Trading Path,"
Paul Glover and Jim Houghton (1997).

of meaning (*sens*). Is this compatible with an anti-authoritarian ethos? Peeters himself is quick to point out that conventional form doesn't necessarily spell conventional content.[60] Indeed, anarchist uses of the "conventional" mode for unconventional ends—like those employed to such subversive effect in Moore and Gibbons's *Watchmen*—might seem to undermine Peeters's entire taxonomy of *mise en page*.[61]

60 Ibid.
61 Jan Baetens and Pascal Lefèvre, *Pour une lecture moderne de la bande*

Without departing from the pedagogical tradition, however, Harper suggests another model for anarchist *mise en page*: once again, the *diagram* (fig. 10). In the diagram, the reader encounters a field of images juxtaposed so as to suggest certain relations between them without dictating the order in which they are to be read. As Gunther Kress and Theo van Leeuwen remark, on such pages, we find only "semi-linear" structures to guide the reader's eyes, so that "where the eye will move ... is difficult to predict" and "there is neither chronology ... nor a clear hierarchy of salience." It is perhaps rightly that they call this an "anarchic" scheme of *mise en page*: a decentered, paratactic, nonlinear page that enables multiple reading paths.[62] Might this not be the kind of space that corresponds to an anarchist temporality—"a multiple and qualitative time," as Colson puts it, which is determined not by any universal clock, but by the "relations of composition, recomposition, and decomposition" among a plurality of beings?[63] The diagram, distanced from its techno-bureaucratic uses, links formal experimentation to pedagogical populism. It presents not fantasy "persons" with imaginary agency, but networks of relationship, social structures, *systems*. They can be rhizomatic, spreading in all directions without a root, presenting a world in which "the center, the origin of force" is "scattered and disseminated," simultaneously "everywhere and nowhere."[64]

The dichotomy between grid and diagram, however, can be overstated. As can be seen from McCail's work, diagrams often incorporate little linear strips of panels, and grids can be manipulated to enable multiple reading paths as well. Short of abandoning the strip-and-tier form altogether, some anarchists have found ways to use it to approximate the virtues of diagrammatic *mise en page*. Glover and Houghton's "Five Months in the Life of an Hour" (fig. 9), tracing the circulation of alternative labor-note currency from hand to hand—there are no Invisible Hands here—pushes conventional layout in the direction of the diagram, dislodging the *character* from the center of narrative and allowing us to see lives in terms of their interconnectedness.[65]

dessinée (Brussels: Centre belge de la bande dessinée, 1993), 60; Thierry Groensteen, *Système de la bande dessinée* (Paris: Presses universitaires de France, 1999), 116–117.

62 Kress and van Leeuwen, *Reading Images*, 220.

63 Colson, *Petit lexique*, 230.

64 Kropotkin, *Anarchism*, 117.

65 In this respect, it is strangely reminiscent of Peter Kuper's wordless graphic

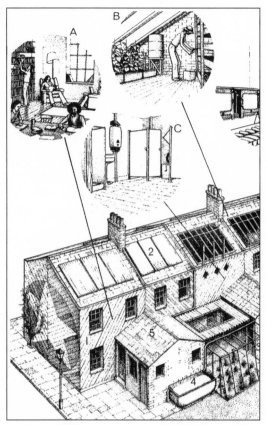

Fig. 10: Detail, Clifford Harper, "Vision #1: Autonomous Terrace" (1975).

novella, *The System* (1997). Here, too, we "follow the money" as it travels from hand to hand, from cabbie to prostitute to pusher to cop to suit, weaving together enterprises licit and illicit, establishing "the system" in which they all have their place (*The System* [New York: DC Comics, 1997], 34–35). Where the HOUR links labor-power to labor-power, neighbor to neighbor, economy to community, community to itself, the dollar links work to hunger, hunger to crime, crime to law, law to wealth. In both cases, frames are repeatedly broken.

4: THE STUTTERING IMAGE: ANARCHIST CINEMA

IS the great age of cinema over, in the era of *YouTube*? For anarchists, it might seem as if it had barely begun; as Andrew Hedden points out, "the anarchist movement was weakest during the years of film's ascendancy as a medium."[1] Perhaps this ascendancy itself was a sign of doom for anarchism, a harbinger of the "society of the spectacle" as well as of the "society of control." Even now, the camera eye that at once confers celebrity and exercises surveillance holds a baleful look for those who would change the world. Thus, in June 2010, the old Toronto Film Studios became the closed set of another kind of production when it served as a jail for about a thousand protesters of the G8 Summit: divided into "large cages," it was fitted with "video cameras ... placed on the ceiling about every five metres to monitor prisoners from the time they entered to the time they left."[2]

The studio as prison: here, ironically, is one of the dominant anarchist conceptions of cinema. In 1913, long before the Frankfurt School arrived on the scene with its critique of the "culture industry," anarcho-syndicalists such as Gustave Cauvin (1886–1951) denounced film as a toxic swamp of "tasteless, crude and militaristic views," an "incessant propaganda" in favor of capitalism and its police forces,[3] while

---

1   Andrew Hedden, "Videotaping a New World: Anarchist Video at the Beginning of the 21st Century," *Arena* 1 (2009): 148.
2   "Police give tour of G20 prison site," *CBC News Toronto*, June 29, 2010.
3   Gustave Cauvin, "Le Cinéma de Peuple," *Le Combat: organe hebdomadaire de défense et d'éducation ouvrière* 2.37 (September 13, 1913): 2.

Victor Roudine lamented the growing "success of the cinema" in *La Bataille Syndicaliste*: sapped of their vitality by industrial labor and urban life, the working classes were all too eager for "a spectacle that does not require any sustained attention" and that activates "the two most developed feelings of our time: sentimentality and brutality."[4] Of course, only *some* forms of sentimentality and brutality were permitted to pass through the double filter of the profit motive and the Hays Code, as Mateo Santos darkly observed: in effect, Hollywood film (the "bourgeois cinema") was subject to a law dictating that

> in the plot there is to be no place for any philosophical, metaphysical, scientific, religious, political, or social theory which conflicts with the general moral norms governing in the countries where the bank, the church, or the army predominates.

Thus, "the black 'pogroms,' though they exist in the United States of America, are not an object for the screen." On the contrary, cinema was a marketing device for Americanism and its "general moral norms," a hegemonic long-range weapon.[5] For Henry Poulaille, cinemas were the vendors *par excellence* of modern capitalism's big lie, the "fantasy of a redistribution of wealth," of upward mobility, and Jackson Mac Low saw popular films as "vicious fictions which are made to appear by every device of burocratized [sic] art to be 'the real thing'—'this is real life!' Hollywood tells us—& millions of men & women *believe* this lie!"[6]

Nor were anarchist criticisms of film confined to its failure to provide an accurate reflection of proletarian reality. As early as 1909, in an essay on "The Cinema as Educator," Franz Pfemfert, a prominent German radical close to the anarchists, protested that "cinema destroys fantasy."[7] Writing more than two decades later in the Valencian journal *Estudios*, Alberto Mar concurred: while "falsehood" was rampant, "it is hard to find any decent fantasy film title among the few masterpieces of

4 Victor Roudine, "L'art pour le peuple? (Le cinéma calomniateur)," web.
5 Santos, "Del cine burgués al cinema social," 136, 132, 135.
6 Henry Poulaille, "Le cinéma a failli à sa mission," *Mon Ciné* 4.346 (October 1928): 6; Jackson Mac Low, "The Movies: A Note on Falsification," *Why? An Anarchist Bulletin* 5.5 (October 1946): 9.
7 Franz Pfemfert, "Kino als Erzieher," in *Kino-Debatte: Literatur und Film, 1909–1929*, ed. Anton Kaes (Tübingen: Niemeyer, 1978), 62, 61.

this new art."[8] "My objection," Mac Low specified, writing in the wake of World War II, "is not to the lack of *realism*," although he found its pretension to realism especially repugnant; rather, it was the utter poverty of the cinematic *imagination* that struck him.[9] "The Hollywood movies are essentially imitations of vast, ambiguous, quasi-conscious consensual psychosexual types and life-attitudes," his friend Paul Goodman wrote, "subsequently doctor[ed] ... into inconsistent and threadbare works of art."[10]

The rigidity of genres was particularly repulsive. "The film of today pretends to present us with Life. How conventional, this Life which it presents!," wrote Léo Claude in *La Revue Anarchiste* (1930).[11] In *El Cinema y la realidad social* (1934), Alfonso "Alfo" Longuet denounced the manufacture of "'standard' characters" as "molds for the personality": the "hero," the "vamp," the "villain," and so forth.[12] Worse still, for José Peirats, was the cult of the movie star, which invited the working class to interest itself in "sterile disquisitions concerning the folds and ornaments of Jeanette MacDonald's morning robe."[13] Anarchist critics such as Santos and Longuet generally saw commercial cinema as sexually exploitative as well.[14]

The difficulty of mounting an effective response to the challenge posed by cinema was twofold. On the one hand, in an emphatically visual age, the era of "the hegemony of the image," in Longuet's words, to simply shun the new technology as the bosses' tool would mean surrendering space to the images of hegemony, and to no avail, as the anarchists had discovered early on: just as bourgeois newspapers failed to list anarchist theater productions in their "Entertainments" columns, Isabelle Marinone observes, the movie theaters' offerings were not to be found among the listings in French anarchist

8   Alberto Mar, "La pantalla: La fantasía en el Cinema," *Estudios* 14.150 (February 1936): 26–27.

9   Mac Low, *The Movies*, 8–9.

10   Paul Goodman, *Five Years: Thoughts During a Useless Time* (New York: Brussel and Brussel, 1966), 57.

11   Léo Claude, "L'avenir du cinéma," *La Revue Anarchiste* 3 (February 1930): 47.

12   Alfonso Longuet, *El Cinema y la realidad social* (Buenos Aires: Ediciones IMÁN, 1934), 30, 19, 24, 25, 36.

13   Peirats, *Para una Nueva Concepción del Arte* (Barcelona: Ediciones de "La Revista Blanca," 1934), 10.

14   Longuet, *El Cinema*, 38–40; Santos, "Del cine burgués," 136.

newspapers between 1895 and 1908, while workers' attendance at these spectacles grew apace.[15] Within two decades, the once-thriving anarchist community of São Paulo found that the same theaters that had once provided both a meeting space for workers and a stage for anarchist plays were being converted en masse into movie theaters screening the latest entries from Hollywood—"a process that further reduced the strength of the anarchists, who failed to deal with it," according to Gabriel Passetti.[16] On the other hand, to compete on the same technological terrain required an investment of capital that an already hard-pressed movement could ill afford.[17] Whereas anarchists had, in certain times and places, been able to field a journalistic apparatus capable of competing with the official presses, the advantage of increasing technological efficiency—state-of-the-art printing presses just fourteen years after Proudhon's death, for instance, were capable of producing at forty times the rate of the machines he had apprenticed on—did not apply to this new realm, where expensive equipment was required to mass-produce an entertainment that was remarkably cheap to attend.[18] Nor was the technical capability anarchists brought to the production of newspapers (labor provided by skilled typographers) readily available for cinematic production: while a few militants worked in the new industry,[19] these were not

---

15 Gabriel Passetti, "Cultura no Brás no início do século XX: teatro anarquista e cinema burguês," *Klepsidra: Revista Virtual de Historia* (2000): 18 (web). Francisco Foot Hardman notes that the anarchist newspaper *A Folha do Povo* regularly included "announcements of film spectacles and new movie theaters" from 1908, the year it first appeared in the port city of Santos, Brazil (*Nem Pátria, Nem Patrão*, 65).

16 Passetti, "Cultura no Brás," 7.

17 As far away as Bahia, Eric Gordon notes, the Cinéma du Peuple venture drew attention and enthusiasm: "A page-one article in July 1914 in *A Voz do Trabalhador* announced 'A Project We Urge You to Support! Cinema for the People.'" However, there was no question of replicating the experiment locally: "In Brazil the resources available to the anarchist movement would have made filmmaking impossible at that time" (*Anarchism in Brazil*, 224).

18 George W. S. Trow, *Within the Context of No Context* (New York: Atlantic Monthly Press, 1997), 8n; Passetti, "Cultura no Brás," 7.

19 For instance, Paul Delesalle (1870–1948), a steelworker who served as official in the syndicalist Bourses du Travail, worked as a mechanic for the first entrepreneurs of cinema in France, the Lumière brothers (Isabelle Marinone, "Educational Cinema: A Libertarian Invention," *Arena* 1 [2009]: 15), while Jules Scarceriaux (1872–1963), a Belgian potter and sometime anar-

many in comparison to the veritable army of technicians fielded by Capital (and by the State Capital of the eastern *apparatchiks*).

Nevertheless, anarchists did contest the reigning cinemas of Hollywood and Moscow alike, and not only by the rejectionist route. Anarchists like Rafael Barrett saw "stutter[ing]" flickers of poetic potential in the new medium, which lets us "see what we have never seen."[20] Cauvin, too, felt that if commercial film was "a poison in the brains of the people," then it could also furnish the "antidote."[21] Even in his horror at the "bourgeois cinema" (and, even worse, the fascist cinema of which he was perhaps the first to write a study, *El cine bajo la svastica* [1937]), Mateo Santos dreamed of an "educational" cinema, a "teacher of masses, of multitudes" possessed of "an effectiveness lacked by other pedagogical systems ... because its lessons profit the cultivated and the unlearned equally." Since, as Poulaille put it, "the cinema says realities with reality," educational film could present "lessons gathered directly from life, with the multiplicity and variety of its everyday events," bypassing the mediation of teachers.[22] Claude dreamed of a cinema freed from the constraints of Capital and State that could present "scenario and technique elevated to the same height"—a vision close to that expressed by Henry Poulaille in his plea for a "human cinema."[23] Peirats spoke for this tendency in titling his 1934 pamphlet on the subject *Para una Nueva Concepción del Arte: Lo que Podría Ser un Cinema Social (For a New Conception of Art: The Possibility of a Social Cinema)* (fig. 1).

Increasingly, particularly as the era of the "talkies" opened, one means of struggle was film criticism, conducted both within anarchist publications (such as *La Revue Anarchiste* and *Umbral*) and in broader public forums (such as *Popular Film*, a Spanish journal that drew participation from several prominent anarchist intellectuals).

---

chist educator, worked on the sets of Cecil B. DeMille himself ("Scarceriaux, Jules," *Dictionnaire International des Militantes Anarchistes*, web).

20 Rafael Barrett, "El cinematógrafo," *Moralidades actuales* (Madrid: Editorial-América, 1919), 25.

21 Cauvin, "Le Cinéma du Peuple," 2.

22 Santos, "Del cine burgués," 138; Poulaille qtd. in Isbaelle Marinone, "Henry Poulaille, défenseur du cinéma humain," *R.A. Forum*, April 7, 2007 (web).

23 Léo Claude, "Pour prendre langue," *La Revue Anarchiste* 1 (1929): 48; Claude, "Films," *La Revue Anarchiste* 5 (1930): 39; Poulaille, "Le cinéma a failli," 6.

Fig. 1: A thirty-two-page pamphlet on cinema by José Peirats, published by
La Revista Blanca (1934).

"The prevalence of the cinema that we find detestable," argued Peirats, "rests less on government censorship and the materialism of the companies than on the apathy and ignorance of the public."[24] Santos agreed: "The public that does not exercise its right to be critical debases itself socially."[25] Subjecting film to rigorous scrutiny, anarchist critics sought to educate audiences against too easy an acceptance of what they were being given to watch. Here, too, was room for praise as well as censure. What many anarchists called a "social cinema"— conceived, as Isabelle Marinone notes, along lines markedly similar to those of Bernard Lazare's conception of "social art"[26]—could be glimpsed *in potentia* in just a few of the films thrown up by statist and capitalist production systems.

Anarchist film critics were highly ambivalent toward Soviet film

24 Peirats, *Para una Nueva Concepción*, 31–32.
25 Santos qtd. in Gerard Pedret Otero, "Grups libertaris i cinema a Barcelona: El paper de Mateo Santos (1930–1936)," *Cercles: Revista d'història cultural* 11 (January 2008): 172.
26 Isabelle Marinone, "Qu'est-ce que le cinéma « Humain »? Retour sur une conception du cinéma défendue par Henry Poulaille," *Mille huit cent quatre-vingt-quinze* 43 (2004): 8–9.

before the era of Stalin; Eisenstein's *The Battleship Potemkin* and *The General Line* were widely admired, and it was conceded that at least the Russians had shown that it was possible to make films free from "the preoccupation with the 'star'" and the romantic plot.[27] Clearly, however, Soviet production had been pressed into service as State propaganda.[28] Others saw moments of radical consciousness in the "poetic realism" of René Clair and Marcel Carné or in American films such as Paul Muni's *I Am a Fugitive From a Chain Gang* (1932) and King Vidor's *Our Daily Bread* (1934), just as some contemporary anarchists have critically endorsed films such as the Wachowski brothers' *The Matrix* (1999).[29] Charlie Chaplin, in particular, drew anarchists' praise for his subversive humor, his embrace of the pariah (and particularly of that favorite anarchist protagonist, the tramp), and his ability to communicate these social values to a wide audience.[30] Not only was Chaplin "the real creator of modern cinema," to one reviewer for the Chilean anarchist journal *Claridad*, but he was "a unique being in the Stirnerian sense of the word; he is the owner of his spirit.... He is the cinema's madman of La Mancha ... defy[ing] the representatives of common sense."[31] Nevertheless, a tremendous gap lay between the "bourgeois cinema," even at its best, and "the possibility of a social cinema."

27 Alfo (Alfonso Longuet), "La Línea general de S.M. Eisenstein," *Nervio* 1.1 (May 1931): 40–42; Santos, "Del cine burgués," 137–139.

28 Ibid., 137; Longuet, *El Cinema*, 41–43; Léo Claude, "Le cinéma soviétique," *La Revue Anarchiste* 5 (1930): 47–48; J. T. (José Torres), "La Toma de Berlín," *Ruta* 7.324 (December 15, 1951): 2.

29 Alberto Mar, "La pantalla: Anverso y reverso de la cinta de celuloide," *Estudios* 14.149 (January 1936): 60; Peirats, *Para una Nueva Concepción*, 22; Luis Veramón, "Revision de films: Revolución y antirrevolución en dos films de Paul Muni," *Umbral* 44 (September 17, 1938): 12; Mar, "La pantalla: La fantasía en el Cinema," 27; Sandra Jeppesen, "*The Matrix*: Revolution or Simulacrum in Hollywood?," *Social Anarchism* 36 (Spring 2004): 45–62.

30 Henry Poulaille, *Charles Chaplin* (Paris: Bernard Grasset, 1927); Alfo (Alfonso Longuet), "Cinema: Concepto standard del séptimo arte," Nervio 1.1 (May 1931): 40; José Peirats, "La Ironía hilarante y la sátira social," *Anthropos* 18 (1990): 118; Roger Toussenot, "Charles Spencer Chaplin: poèt et homme libre," *Défense de l'Homme* 2 (November 1948); Paul Goodman, "Chaplin Again, Again, and Again," *Partisan Review* 7.6 (1940): 456–60.

31 Eugenio Silva Espejo, "Problemas Cinematográficos," *Claridad* 9.140 (January 21, 1932): 2.

Another phase of struggle entailed organizing screenings of the few films that were deemed worthy. Cauvin's first effort to administer a cinematic "antidote" came in 1910 in the form of a "Cinéma Social" film series he offered via the Bourses du Travail, combining comedy, documentary, and drama, all with an educational aim—a format directly borrowed from the old *soirée*, the evening of entertainments and lectures.[32] In March 1930, Claude proposes "the foundation of an Anarchist Ciné-Club projecting those repertory films which hold so much hope for the future of the cinema"; two summers later, in Spain, Peirats and Santos create "an extensive series of lectures and cultural events ... with the title 'Projections of Social Art,' which aimed to contribute, in the words of its organizers, 'without evasions or accommodations,... to the rise of a contemporary art with a social orientation.'"[33]

Finally, anarchists did succeed a few times in making films of their own. In a French film archive, we find the work of a cooperative studio, the Cinéma du Peuple, established in 1913 by a group of French anarchists, syndicalists, and socialists.[34] Despite its ecumenical character, this organization, based in a CGT union hall in Paris, was founded on anarchist principles (its statutes forbade "electoral action and propaganda") and was staffed and underwritten by some leading lights of French anarchism, from its secretary, railway workers' union organizer Yves-Marie Bidamant, to its subscribers and supporters, among whom numbered Sébastien Faure and Jean Grave.[35] With an initial capital of 1,000 francs raised from the sale of forty shares, growing to 3,000 francs and some six hundred shares by 1914, the Cinéma du Peuple produced at least six films.[36]

If public memory has not been kind to the 4,895 meters of film reportedly shot by the Cinéma du Peuple, memory's official

---

32 Tangui Perron, "'Le contrepoison est entre vos mains, comrades': CGT et cinéma au début du siècle," *Le Mouvement social* 172 (July–September, 1995): 27.

33 Claude, "Films," 39; Pedret Otero, "Grups libertaris," 177.

34 Laurent Mannoni, "28 Octobre 1913: Création de la Société 'Le Cinema du Peuple,'" in *L'Année 1913 en France*, eds. Thierry Lefebvre and Laurent Mannoni (Paris: Association Française de Recherche sur l'Histoire du Cinéma), 100.

35 Ibid., 100; Eric Jarry, "The Cinema du Peuple Cooperative Venture," trans. Paul Sharkey, *Arena* 1 (2009): 3.

36 Ibid., 3–4.

custodians have at least made available a small sample of this production by which we may imagine the rest. And so a 1995 restoration sets before us the flickering images of director Armand Guerra's *La Commune* (1914).

Before the image, there is the word: the film is punctuated by prolix intertitles, apparently produced not by Guerra and his assistants but by the French archivists. The first announces:

> After the defeat at Sedan and the fall of the Second Empire, Adolphe Thiers was named chief executive. In Paris, the populace is on the brink of insurrection. On March 18, 1871, Thiers summons General Lecomte to the Quai d'Orsay. He orders him to retrieve the cannons held by the National Guard. In spite of his reservations, Lecomte obeys.

Were these intertitles a recreation of what the film's original audiences would have seen, or are they for the benefit of a contemporary audience that does not remember what the Commune was, that does not arrive already knowing the significance of March 18th, already reputing Thiers a treacherous murderer and Lecomte a bumbling thug? On opening night—March 18th, 1914—these scenes unfolded before a house seating many men and women as old then as my parents are now, who would have remembered these events as clearly as my mother and father remember the March on the Pentagon or Kent State. "What touching figures they make, these old Communards filling the seats in the front rows of the hall," Guerra writes in an account of the event. "Their names circulate by word of mouth through the huddled crowd of spectators and when the first round of applause echoes through the hall, these heroes of the revolution express to us their gratitude, their eyes filled with tears, tears of consolation at seeing how, even today, the people of Paris remember those who fought for freedom."[37] Some of them appear in the film's last frames—footage from a forty-year reunion of surviving Communards.

The first thing we see, following this lengthy advertisement, is a full shot of Thiers behind his desk. An officer enters the room, salutes, and ushers in Lecomte (fig. 2). The two men then pantomime precisely the conversation we have just read about. There is no camera

37 Qtd. in Ibid., 6, modifications mine.

Fig. 2: *La Commune* (dir. Armand Guerra, 1914): power securely located behind a desk.

movement, no editing together of shots, just one fixed perspective, as if we were viewing a stage set from a seat in a theater. After a minute and a half, the action complete, the scene ends.

Subsequent scenes reveal a camera eye made lighter and more mobile by the power of the editor. Splicing together seer and seen, interiors and exteriors, the filmmakers rapidly narrate the downfall of that other infamous general, Clément Thomas ("one of the leaders of the repression of June 1848," the intertitles explain, "and, according to many Parisians, the one to blame for the disaster of Buzenval"—a key battle lost during the siege of Paris, weeks earlier). We are no longer seated in the middle distance before individual men of power, watching them make decisions; the visual field expands to allow crowds to become the actors, assailing Thomas and Lecomte, mingling uniformed soldiers with a proletarian multitude.

What is this crowd-agency? Is it a mob? A contemporary viewer might read the scene as uncomfortably close to a lynching, watching this dark mass swarm around the solitary old man in a frock coat and top hat who is General Thomas (fig. 3). What is Thomas doing, peering out over a wall, when the soldiers spot him? Here, the intertitles do not supply enough information to fill in the gaps: it is the fateful 18th of March, and Thomas, in civilian disguise, is surveying the preparations for what will become an uprising. In this light, we might read his movements as furtive, suggesting that he is a spy. When he is apprehended, we might read his gestures not as pathetically warding off menace but as blustering, as the attempts of a man who is used to being obeyed to make himself obeyed once again. And then we

Fig. 3: *La Commune*: Général Thomas accosted by National Guardsmen and civilians.

might read the climactic execution of Lecomte and Thomas not as a horrible murder or as the madness of a crowd but as rough justice.

In short, especially without the benefit of the intertitles, *La Commune* is a very efficient device for reconcentrating the preexisting prejudices of the audience. For those already inclined to remember the Paris Commune as "the festival of the oppressed," annually and reverently commemorated, the film is another reenactment, another tribute to a lost moment of radical hope, perhaps especially exciting in its technological newness. For those predisposed to view the Commune as a lapse into moral depravity—the kind of audience, for instance, that had seen fit to sponsor the erection of the Basilica of Sacré-Coeur atop the butte of Montmartre, begun in 1875 and completed the same year as the film, as expiation for the Communards' sins—Guerra's images would have confirmed the essential horror of that history, with its faceless masses overwhelming the figures of individual authorities, stripping them of their dignity. Perhaps this is a distant ancestor of the genre that is currently dubbed "riot porn."

"Sensational images of activists fighting cops," "graphic images of masked crowds doing property destruction," "images of ... the uncommon breakdown of the social order," riot porn forms part of the iconography of contemporary anarchism.[38] According to Michael Truscello,

38 Jeff Shantz, *Constructive Anarchy: Building Infrastructures of Resistance* (Farnham, UK: Ashgate, 2010), 47; Jim Straub qtd. in Barbara Epstein and Chris Dixon, "A Politics and a Sensibility: The Anarchist Current in the U.S. Left," in *Toward a New Socialism*, eds. Anatole Anton and Richard Schmitt (Lanham, MD: Lexington Books, 2007), 456; Gary Patrick Norris, "[An-

The riot porn trend began with the emergence of Indymedia in Seattle in 1999, and video incorporated into documentaries such as *This Is What Democracy Looks Like* (2000) and *Breaking The Spell* (1999), the latter distributed by the anarchist group CrimethInc.... With the appearance of YouTube in 2005, and other video-sharing sites, however, riot porn found new life, and the visage of the riot cop, what Richard Day calls "the death-mask of the social," took on an iconic presence in radical visual communication.[39]

Clearly, though, the genre has roots in a much older anarchist imaginary—older, even, than the "Hospitalised Copper" photos in the anarchist newspaper *Class War* (1983–1997), in parody of the softcore-porn "Page 3 girls" of the mainstream British newspaper the *Sun*. One of the genre's identifying traits, for Truscello, is not the anarchist audience's reception of it as titillating and/or excessive (to which it owes its name) but its presentation of "decontextualized" images of confrontation.[40] Anarchist filmmaker Kyle Harris agrees: "Far too often, activist media producers presume viewers are familiar with the social and historical context of their story ... the anarchist narrative we live and believe in, in which we are the protagonists and the capitalists are the antagonists."[41] What might otherwise seem inexplicable—how could anarchist filmmakers fail to understand that the general public will not share the same narrative, that it will read these images as mere confirmation of anarchists' violent irrationality?—is in fact a structural principle: it is *because* the context is assumed rather than given, *because* it is not aimed at an external audience, that the riot-porn video confirms and strengthens internal bonds among an anarchist audience that knows the context and shares the narrative.

We can recognize this structure at work not only in *La Commune*

---

swer to question:] Will you elaborate on why Riot Porn blows? I'm Curious," *DagSeoul: Positions, Populations, Punk, Poetics*, July 13, 2011 (web).

39 Michael Truscello, "Social Media and the Representation of Summit Protests: *YouTube*, Riot Porn, and the Anarchist Tradition," in *Transgression 2.0: Media, Culture and the Politics of a Digital Age*, eds. Ted Gournelos and David J. Gunkel (London: Continuum, 2011), 277–278.

40 Ibid., 276.

41 Kyle Harris, "Beyond Authenticity: Aesthetic Strategies and Anarchist Media," in *Realizing the Impossible: Art Against Authority*, eds. Josh MacPhee and Erik Reuland (Oakland, CA: AK Press, 2007), 214.

Fig. 4: Still from *Reportaje del movimiento revolucionario en Barcelona* (dir. Mateo Santos, 1936).

but in the first anarchist documentary film to emerge from the Spanish Revolution: Mateo Santos's *Reportaje del movimiento revolucionario en Barcelona* (1936). Hastily composed of footage shot in the first week of the revolution (July 19–23), it presents us with, in the words of Joan Ramon Resina, "an enthusiastic, almost ecstatic witnessing" of "the event that had been [the anarchists'] ideological horizon for over half a century," rendered as a series of iconic images: the construction of barricades in the streets, cheering crowds with clenched fists held high, trucks painted with the insignia of the CNT-FAI, burned-out and shattered church windows.[42] All of this improvised reportage is held together by an almost equally improvisatory narration, a voiceover that carries the fervor of denunciation and triumph, but that generally does nothing to situate the images in terms of time, place, and persons.[43] Thus, in the course of this breathless testimony, the camera places us before a Salesian convent that has been raided by the revolutionaries, exhumed mummies propped up in the atrium (fig. 4). The voiceover announces:

> In this convent of the Salesian nuns have been found mummies of nuns and monks tortured by their religious brethren. The sight of these tortured mummies has provoked the indignation

42 Ramon Resina, "Historical Discourse," 78.
43 Vicente Sánchez-Biosca, "Propaganda y mitografía en le cine de la guerra civil española (1936–1939)," *Cuadernos de Información y Comunicación* 12 (2007): 88.

of the people. The Catholic Church, in this and in other aspects, has bared its rotten soul, revealing in the course of a few hours the message of twenty centuries. These corpses, petrified in their coffins, constitute the harshest accusation ever made against Catholicism.[44]

What the Nazi propagandists could do with this footage highlights the problems Truscello and Harris identify in riot porn: "In the Babelsberg studios," as Resina recounts, "the pictures of mummies and burnt churches ... lifted from Santos's documentary, subjected to clever montage and supplied with a new soundtrack," became an iconography of violation and outrage (how many taboos are stronger than those surrounding the treatment of the dead?), instant symbols of left-wing depravity, visual "proof" that Franco's rebellion against the elected government of Spain was really a defense of all that is sacred.[45]

How to prevent the recuperation of anarchist cinema into an authoritarian spectacle that is all too ready to supply its own narrative "soundtrack"? For Harris, there is no choice but to compete with this spectacle on its own terms: "we [should] clarify our heroism through narrative conventions," e.g., "character development," "the organization of events into a beginning, middle and end, containing moments of recognition, reversal and suffering," and—drawing on Aristotle's classical poetics—"pertinent and appropriate arguments."[46] This, too, has precedent in the history of anarchist film production efforts, particularly in those mounted by the Spanish studios collectivized by the CNT during the first phase of the 1936 revolution—a second historic attempt not only to project an anarchist vision of the world in a popular form but to democratize the medium itself, to place the cinematic production apparatus under worker control.

Organized under the auspices of the CNT unions—the Sindicato Único de la Industria de Espectáculos Públicos (SUIEP), Federación Regional de la Industria de Espectáculos Públicos (FRIEP), and finally the Sindicato de la Industria del Espectáculo (SIE)—the Spanish film industry produced numerous documentaries (of which

---

44 Qtd. in Ramon Resina, "Historical Discourse," 74, trans. Ramon Resina.
45 Ibid., 75–76.
46 Harris, "Beyond Authenticity," 214, 217; Aristotle qtd. in Ibid., 217.

Reportaje del movimiento revolucionario was only the first—and one of just half to survive Franco's victory), but also a few feature-length fiction films. All of these films, condemned by critics for combining "clunky" cinematography and "hackneyed plot" with "mawkish" and "doctrinaire sentimentality,"[47] enlist the kinds of genre conventions to which Harris appeals in the service of anarchist ideals, from Antonio Sau's use of melodrama in *Aurora de Esperanza* (1936) to Pedro Puche's crime film, *Barrios Bajos* (1937), and Fernando Mignoni's satirical musical comedy, *Nuestro culpable* (1937).

Here, as we have seen so many times before, the education of our taste can limit our perception. A long-standing critical bias has it that the goal of every art form is to purify itself, to develop what is most intrinsic to its means and materials, thereby becoming "autonomous" of all that is extraneous to it. Thus, the goal of painting, rather than to imitate visual reality (the virtue of photography), would be to exhibit flat planes of color; the goal of poetry, rather than to make sense or persuade (the virtue of rhetoric), would be to make sounds; the goal of cinema, therefore, rather than to record a performed narrative (the virtue of drama and prose fiction), would be to juxtapose images in motion. In short, as Giorgio Agamben puts it, "The specific character of cinema stems from montage."[48] An autonomous cinema, on this account, would have to be organized around montage rather than around the staging of a story, i.e., the tradition film historians sometimes refer to—borrowing the term from drama—as *mise-en-scène*. Film genres, by contrast, are sometimes held to be intrinsically conservative: "Genres hold the world in place," for Michael Ryan and Douglas Kellner, "establishing and enforcing a sense of propriety, of proper boundaries which demarcate appropriate thought, feeling, and behavior."[49] The authentically anti-authoritarian film, then, would be anti-generic, *sui generis*. On this account, then, the prototype for anarchist film might be something like the early Soviet

---

47 Richard Porton, *Film and the Anarchist Imagination* (New York: Verso, 1999), 79; Ramon Resina, "Historical Discourse," 71, 83n12.

48 Giorgio Agamben, "Difference and Repetition: On Guy Debord's Films," trans. Brian Holmes, in *Guy Debord and the Situationist International*, ed. Tom McDonough (Cambridge, MA: MIT Press, 2002), 315.

49 Michael Ryan and Douglas Kellner, *Camera Politica: The Politics and Ideology of Contemporary Hollywood Film* (Bloomington, IN: Indiana University Press, 1991), 77.

filmmaking of Dziga Vertov (who, intriguingly, once placed himself among the "anarchists-individualists").[50]

So the theory goes. However, as Vittorio Frigerio points out apropos of the anarchist narrative traditions we have examined,

> sentimental romance, swashbuckling adventure, and melodrama form an important part of the fictional arsenal with which nineteenth-century anarchists viewed themselves and their situation. These "recycled genre conventions" were arguably felt as providing a better representation of the living conditions of the people and of the struggle of the militants than the "high brow," modern fragmentary aesthetic of the avant-garde.[51]

And so, for all the lack of avant-garde subtlety in *Aurora de Esperanza*, the story of Juan and Marta draws us into its representation of the pre-July 19th world by melodramatic means—primarily by enlisting our sense of indignation.

Juan (Félix de Pomés), father of the family, is thrown into unemployment by the economic crisis, forcing Marta (Enriqueta Soler) to seek work—a reversal of the gendered order that we are made to experience as uniquely humiliating for both parties, culminating in a scene in which we find out, with the husband, what his wife has been hired to do. A crowd of men bustles in front of a shop display window, hooting and catcalling. When he pushes through the throng, Juan is suddenly brought face to face with a cowed Marta, who is modeling lingerie. Bursting into the shop, Juan lets loose one of a series of memorably sharp, deep-throated tirades against the predatory employer who has thus exploited women's desperation. Further humiliations follow as Juan tramps the city seeking work, ending up one night, in a state of drunken despair, having pity taken on him by a bourgeois who pays for his dinner. Not only has Juan failed the primary test of working-class masculinity; now he is in danger of becoming nothing better than a kept man. Forced to send Marta and

---

50 Vertov qtd. in Vlada Petric, "Vetrov's Cinematic Transportation of Reality," in *Beyond Document: Essays on Nonfiction Film*, ed. Charles Warren (Hanover, NH: University Press of New England, 1996), 287.

51 Vittorio Frigerio, "Aesthetic Contradictions and Ideological Representations," *Film-Philosophy* 7.53 (December 2003), web.

the children back to live on the farm with her parents, Juan finds himself on a soup line, listening to one of the volunteers grousing about how the unemployed men in the queue "ought to be thankful to eat without working.... But still they aren't grateful. I don't know what they want." "Imbeciles!" Juan thunders, stalking away.

The remainder of the film is a process—not unlike that other masculinist working-class melodrama, *Rocky* (1976)—whereby Juan turns his humiliation into indignation and rebellion, finding a new masculine identity as he organizes with others and ultimately takes up arms, joining the revolution. Where the process of Rocky Balboa's redemption is captured in his run up the steps of the Philadelphia Museum of Art to stand in triumph before the statue of George Washington, the force of re-masculinization in *Aurora de Esperanza* is carried by the image of a ragged, unshaven Juan haranguing a crowd of his fellow unemployed from the pedestal of a massively muscled male nude—an emblem of virility whose qualities he takes on by association.

Of course, this very dependence on the ideology of *machismo* saddles *Aurora de Esperanza* with another kind of poverty—a poverty of the egalitarian imagination. If Sau's script remains captive to a masculine ideology, however, it may also be worth remembering that, as Kenneth Burke put it, "an ideology is ... the nodus of beliefs and judgments which the artist can exploit for his effects."[52] To some extent, we might see the film as simply taking advantage of the ready-to-hand rhetorical resources of the Spanish social imaginary, turning it in the direction of an anarchist conception of empowerment as virility. The obvious, serious limitations of this strategy are easier for us to assess, from our historical distance, than its efficacy.

A less apparently masculinist example is to be found in Puche's *Barrios Bajos*, where the men on display are almost all in various states of dereliction. Here, again, is a vision of a pre-July 19th Barcelona—"a society that is to disappear," in the words of a reviewer for the SIE's house organ, *Espectáculo*.[53] Loosely transposing Gorky's *Lower Depths* into the Barcelona setting of his own 1935 satire, *No me mates o Los misterios del Barrio Chino*, Puche takes us to its notorious Barri

---

52 Kenneth Burke, *Counter-Statement* (Berkeley: University of California Press, 1968), 161.

53 Qtd. in José María Caparrós Lera, *Arte y política en el cine de la República (1931–1939)* (Barcelona: Edit. 7½, 1981), 187.

Xinès or "Chinese" neighborhood (the "Chinese," in Spain's Orientalist imaginary, signifying sleaze), where women are prey for exploiters, pimps and madams in the employ of a decadent bourgeoisie.[54]
An atmosphere of decadence and despair prevails over Barri Xinès,
bracketed by heavily canted establishing shots (the "Dutch tilt" later
popularized by film noir, connoting a world out of kilter), gloomily
lit alleys strung with laundry lines, and the hard faces of bar patrons
listening to what turns out to be the theme song, a melodramatic tan-
go: "Slums ... your eternal madrigal / is rhymed by pimps and whores
/ with the point of a dagger."

The shades of film noir, that space from which, as Paul Schrader
says, "No character can speak authoritatively," are not far off.[55] The action begins with a murder: Ricardo, a young lawyer, having caught his
wife *in flagrante* with her lover, has shot him, fleeing into the depths of
Barri Xinès. There, El Valencia, a stevedore he once saved from a murder charge, hides him in his room above Paco's bar, down by the docks.
Meanwhile, the wealthy pimp, Floreal, and his accomplices are ma-
neuvering to entrap a young domestic worker, Rosa, into prostitution.
Watching Floreal do business down by the docks, we gather that he's
no small-time operator—he supplies the so-called white slave trade.
The big-hearted El Valencia notices Rosa, who reminds him of his
wife, eight years dead; he gets her a place at Paco's, drawing the wrath
of Floreal and his thugs. Romantic tension emerges as Ricardo also
falls for Rosa; will El Valencia betray him? But no: after a final street
fight, the dying stevedore says that he saw Rosa as a kind of daughter,
not an object of romantic love, and gives his blessing to them both
before expiring. Meanwhile, we meet other denizens of the Barri, such
as the alcoholic ex-opera singer, Catuso ("*El gran Catuso, borracho,*"
laughs one of the street buskers—"*Pituso,*" her partner corrects her),
who finds his voice once again, for just a moment, outside the bar,
winning the respect of the buskers, who eagerly include him in their
act—only to watch him relapse into abject, drunken muteness.

Criticism of *Barrios Bajos*—appealing, once again, to the standards of what Erich Mühsam and Adrián del Valle might have called

---

54 M. Porter Moix, *Història del Cinema a Catalunya: 1895–1990* (Barcelona: Generalitat de Catalunya, Dep. de Cultura, 1992), 202.

55 Paul Schrader, "Notes on Film Noir," in *Film Genre Reader III*, ed. Barry
Grant (Austin: University of Texas Press, 2003), 235.

"bourgeois realism"—has tended to complain of the lack of "human nuance" in the characterization and plot, the use of "histrionics" in place of more naturalistic acting.[56] Santiago Juan-Navarro, however, suggests that this places *Barrios Bajos* partially in the tradition of Expressionist films like Fritz Lang's *M* (1931) and *Das Testament des Dr. Mabuse* (1933), which also partake of the melodrama (as well as the crime film).[57] Here, too, are the hallmarks of anarchist visual culture as such—deformation (caricature, grotesque, polarization), defamiliarization (the elevation of the "low," the debasing of the "high"), narrative decentering (multiple plotlines, a social cross-section), and perhaps even a form of *détournement* (textual "poaching," the subversive appropriation of narrative resources). Melodrama is a resource, a reserve of popular spirit, on which anarchists are poaching—freely, now that the game wardens of popular narrative have been chased out of the country.

But to poach on another's narratives, as the anarchists administering the SIE found, is still to be beholden to that other. Experience was teaching the anarchists a bitter lesson in the politics of mass culture. For instance, when Madrid was under siege, in November 1936, the only three movie theaters remaining open—the Actualidades, the Capitol, and the Monumental, under the auspices of the CNT, the socialist UGT trade union, and the Ministry of Education—showed almost exclusively "political" and "educational" films, including many borrowed from the Soviet propaganda repertoire, e.g. *Los Marinos de Cronstadt* (*The Kronstadt Sailors*, Yefim Dzigam, 1936) and *La Patria os Llama* (*Men On Wings*, Yuli Raizman and Grigori Levkoyev, 1935). Very quickly, the movie houses turned back to Gary Cooper, Greta Garbo, and Laurel and Hardy. Similarly, in Badalona, where some eight movie houses had been taken over by the CNT, their marquees, predominantly featuring American films in October 1936, briefly gave way, in November, to a strange mixture of left-friendly American films (like Charlie Chaplin's *Modern Times*) and Soviet propaganda epics (Georgi and Sergei Vasilyev's biopic of *Chapaev*),

---

56 Caparrós Lera, *Arte y política*, 192; Santiago Juan-Navarro, "Un pequeño Hollywood proletario: el cine anarcosindicalista durante la revolución española (Barcelona, 1936–1937)," *Bulletin of Spanish Studies* 88.4 (2011): 538.

57 Ibid., 538. Indeed, in his study of the genre, Peter Brooks defines melodrama as "the expressionism of the moral imagination" (*The Melodramatic Imagination* [New Haven, CT: Yale University Press, 1995], 55).

before reverting to a mainly American diet (Frank Capra's *Lady For a Day*, Henry King's *The Country Doctor*, Edward Ludwig's *Age of Indiscretion*).[58] Public tastes had been shaped by Hollywood. Even in the virtual absence of any alternative entertainments, with no effective competition, non-Hollywood films fared so poorly as to frighten the Spanish anarchists away from their earlier aspirations to a more purely "political" and "educational" cinema.[59] The workers' movie houses showed the bosses' films: according to Emeterio Díez, "80 per cent of the 69 films screened in Barcelona during the 1936–1937 season were US productions from the likes of Warner, MGM, Columbia, Paramount, Universal, Fox, United Artists and RKO Films."[60]

A decision had to be made. Just as the CNT-FAI, after its quick initial victory on July 19th, 1936, had to choose between trying to go it alone without a sufficiently large popular base or accepting an alliance of convenience with the other antifascist forces (in the stark formulation of Juan García Oliver: "Either we collaborate, or we impose a dictatorship"[61]), so the SIE, finding itself in control of an entire apparatus of production and distribution, had to decide whether to screen only films that met its political criteria, thus "going against the tastes of the public," as Cabeza San Deogracias notes, or to cater to those tastes, at the risk of abandoning its political mission.[62] Thus, Enrique Sánchez Oliveira observes, just as the CNT-FAI entered the Republican government and dissolved its own militias into the Republican army, the SIE decided to "promote a film production that would be competitive and economically profitable" by shunning "partisan and doctrinaire approaches" and embracing Hollywood.[63] By the summer of 1937, we find anarchist artist and filmmaker Gil Bel Mesonada arguing, in *Espectáculo*, for "[making] commercial movies with an eye to the outside

---

58 Emeterio Díez, "Anarchist Cinema During the Spanish Civil War," trans. Paul Sharkey, *Arena* 1 (2009): 39, 93n4; "Espectaculos Públicos," *Via Libre* (October 3, 1936; November 21, 1936; May 1, 1937).

59 José Cabeza San Deogracias, *El descanso del guerrero: Cine en Madrid Durant la Guerra Civil Española (1936–1939)* (Madrid: Rialp, 2005), 139.

60 Emeterio Díez, "Anarchist Cinema," 91.

61 García Oliver qtd. in Alexandre Skirda, *Facing the Enemy: A History of Anarchist Organisation*, trans. Paul Sharkey (Edinburgh: AK Press, 2000), 156.

62 Cabeza San Deogracias, *El descanso del guerrero*, 139.

63 Enrique Sánchez Oliveira, *Aproximación histórica al cineasta Francisco Elías Riquelme (1890–1977)* (Seville: Universidad de Sevilla, Secretariado de Publicaciones, 2003), 120.

world."[64] This was the direction taken by the Consejo Superior Técnico de Cinematografía, inaugurated in August of the same year.[65]

It would be inaccurate to assume a naïveté about the politics of the dream factory on the part of anarchists who knew its less-than-glamorous workings pretty well inside and out—Barcelona's Comité de Producción Cinematográfica, for instance, was directed by studio workers like Anselmo Sastre, an electrician, and the SUIEP was headed by a former usher and ticket-taker, Miguel Espinar Martínez. Nonetheless, in the final period of the Spanish Civil War, the Consejo Superior Técnico de Cinematografía, with a less working-class and more politically diverse staff—the CNT delegate, Juan Saña, had solid anarchist credentials but no experience in the film industry, while artistic director Francisco Elías was secretly a member of a Falangist organization[66]—oversaw a further transition away from the kind of politically committed fiction film that the SIE had produced in its brief stewardship of the studios. Elías's own contribution, ¡No Quiero... No Quiero!, which took the place of films whose production was abruptly canceled (such as Cain, with its overtly anti-clerical screenplay), was only lightly endowed with anti-authoritarian themes (in a manner somewhat reminiscent of Vigo's Zéro de Conduite), and was ironically completed in 1940, under fascist rule, with government approval.

Was it a predictable betrayal? Many, then and since, thought so. For many militants in the CNT and FAI, the attempt to preserve political commitment in filmmaking while compromising with popular tastes had resulted in films that were neither fish nor fowl, failing as partisan propaganda and failing as popular cinema.[67] "The lack of acceptance of this film [Aurora de Esperanza] by the Hispanic audience," Sau complained, "was due to the fact that [it] was a departure, a renewal of the cinema that had been made until then, and the audience did not connect with this change—as it was used to another

---

64 Bel [Mesonada] qtd. in Emeterio Díez, "Anarchist Cinema," 64.
65 Ibid., 61.
66 Ibid., 52, 44, 61, 88–89.
67 Juan-Navarro, "Un pequeño," 537; Manuel Cortés Blanco and Mariano Lázaro Arbués, "Anarquismo y lucha antialcohólica en la Guerra Civil Española (1936–1939)," Proyecto Hombre: revista de la Asociación Proyecto Hombre 56 (2005): 20.

type of cinema."[68] Here, once again, we find anarchists confronting what Paul Goodman described as the fundamental dilemma of "radical art": it seems to require an audience that, by definition, is defunct or absent.[69]

Faced with such a dilemma, some anarchists have insisted on a more intransigent, agitational, and avant-garde/vanguardist approach. More than a decade after the ashes of Guernica and Teruel had settled over the aspirations of the CNT-FAI in Spain, its exiled partisans revisited the question of an anarchist cinema. Writing in *Ruta*, the journal of the Federación Ibérica de los Juventudes Libertarios (the Iberian Anarchist Youth Federation, FIJL) based in Toulouse, José Torres declared that as "the seventh art," film is "a synthesis, not of the various arts, but of all the discontents, of all the 'hungers' that are aroused in our senses by contact with life, which can only be realized in a burst of annihilation of the conventional world."[70] The most powerful examples of this "annihilation," for Torres, were to be found in the Surrealist cinema of filmmakers like Luis Buñuel—a director who, while declaring that "I have never been ... an anarchist," and having never carried an SIE union card (leaving Spain mere weeks after the outbreak of the revolution), had nonetheless been close to the anarchists before the war.[71] Ironically, Buñuel's closest collaboration with the anarchists was perhaps his least surreal venture, *Las Hurdes: Tierra Sin Pan* (1933), a gritty documentary about rural poverty, which he made during a period when he had distanced himself from the Surrealist movement.[72] Another reviewer for *Ruta*, under the signature "L. N.," lauded Buñuel's *Los*

---

68 Sau qtd. in Núria Triana-Toribio, *Spanish National Cinema* (London: Routledge, 2003), 34.

69 Paul Goodman, *Creator Spirit Come!: The Literary Essays of Paul Goodman*, ed. Taylor Stoehr (New York: Free Life Editions, 1977), 77.

70 José Torres, "El Cine: Arte Anarquista?," *Ruta: Órgano de la FIJL en Francia* 8.329 (January 17, 1952): 2.

71 Luis Buñuel, *An Unspeakable Betrayal: Selected Writings of Luis Buñuel*, trans. Garrett White (Berkeley: University of California Press, 2002), 259; Weir, *Anarchy and Culture*, 256; Luis Buñuel et al., *Objects of Desire: Conversations with Luis Buñuel* (New York: Marsilio Publishers, 1992), 7.

72 Gwynne Edwards, *A Companion to Luis Buñuel* (Rochester, NY: Tamesis, 2005), 39; Magí Crusells, "Cinema as Political Propaganda During the Spanish Civil War: España 1936," *Ebre 38: Revista Internacional de la Guerra Civil, 1936–1939* 2 (December 2004): 158.

Olvidados (1950), another venture into quasi-documentary realism, for having gone "beyond realism and surrealism": the film's importance, the reviewer argued, was in its "reflection" of "social cruelty," however distorted.[73] For Torres, however, authentically revolutionary film would break entirely with the conventions of realism: "this revolution is only possible ... when the form is not conditioned by circumstantial fact, but comes from the intimate contradictions inherent in the nature of man."

It is not hard to draw a line between this shift away from the objective (the world of "circumstantial fact") and toward the subjective (the inner, "intimate" world) and the "valley time" of a movement that, having experienced its peak, had gone into eclipse. We have already seen how this descent into valley times played out in anarchist poetry, which shifts from a more public mode of address toward a more private, hermetic style. Anarchist poets, writing from the valley, are stricken with a self-consciousness, an awareness of the already-used character of the tropes of social poetry, that inhibits them from using that language in any direct, naïve manner; they are, in Bloom's term, conscious of their poetic and political "belatedness." A similar problem confronts anarchist filmmakers arriving too late to film the "circumstantial facts" of revolution, and swamped by the creations of an entertainment industry that has thoroughly colonized even the "intimate" world of dreams and desires.[74] "The world," declares an intertitle in Guy Debord's *Société du Spectacle* (1973), "has already been filmed." In this spectacular society, all radical cinema is placed under the sign of the belated, the untimely, the repetitive.

For both Marx and Freud, repetition itself is a sign of pathology. It is in his exasperation with France's relapse into autocracy after its brief experiment with democracy that Marx writes: "Hegel remarks somewhere that all facts and personages of great importance in world history occur, as it were, twice. He forgot to add: the first time as tragedy, the second as farce."[75] In psychoanalytic terms, the compulsion to repeat the past ("repetition compulsion") is strongly linked to trauma; the neurotic helplessly "*repeats*

---

73 L. N., "El Cine: 'Los Olvidados,'" *Ruta* 8.325 (December 22, 1951): 2.
74 Bloom, *The Anxiety of Influence*, xxv. I borrow the term "valley times" from Andrew Cornell, who in turn borrows it from Myles Horton.
75 Marx, in Marx and Engels, *Collected Works*, 11.103.

attitudes and emotional impulses from his early life," as if the clock had stopped in childhood.[76] For anarchists, however, repetition has other possibilities: mimicry and mockery are forms of repetition that undermine the authority of what they repeat, showing it to be at odds with itself. A subversive mode of repetition, in the words of J. Hillis Miller, "posits a world based on difference," a world in which we can never step in the same river twice.[77] Daniel Colson avers that it is the very "repetitive character of revolts or insurrections"—e.g., the way that the May 1968 riots in Paris seemed to mysteriously recreate the circumstances of the Paris Commune of 1871—that allows them to "radically escape … from a linear conception of time" such as Marx's theory of history.[78] Thus, as untimely visionaries, filmmakers such as Debord, René Vienet, Isaac Cronin, or Terrel Seltzer (who did not place themselves in the anarchist movement, but who drew on and contributed to the anarchist tradition) take up the challenge of an already-filmed world by recourse to *détournement*, reappropriating the stolen product of our collective dream-labor. It is in this sense that Debord echoes Marx's famous thesis: "The world has already been filmed; now it is a matter of transforming it." This, for Agamben, is what constitutes Debord's "epoch-making innovation": by "de-creating" films of the world, the filmmaker also "decreate[s]" ready-made images of life, restoring a sense of possibility to the already-filmed world.[79]

Vienet's *La Dialectique peut-elle casser des briques? (Can Dialectics Break Bricks?*, 1973), advertised as "The first entirely détourned film in the history of cinema" with "V. O. subtitles by the Association for the Development of Class Struggles and the Propagation of Dialectical Materialism," stands as a striking example of the possibilities of "de-creative" repetition (fig. 5). Recycling almost the entirety of Guangqi Tu's martial-arts film *Crush (Tang shou tai quan dao*, 1972), about a group of Korean villagers who band together to resist their Japanese oppressors through the Chinese-inspired discipline of

---

76 Sigmund Freud, *Beyond the Pleasure Principle*, trans. James Strachey (New York: W.W. Norton, 1989), 359.

77 J. Hillis Miller, *Fiction and Repetition: Seven English Novels* (Cambridge, MA: Harvard University Press, 1982), 6.

78 Colson, *Petit lexique*, 280.

79 Agamben, *Difference and Repetition*, 315, 318.

L'OISEAU DE MINERVE et TÉLÉMONDIAL présentent

LA DIALECTIQUE PEUT-ELLE CASSER DES BRIQUES?

LE PREMIER FILM ENTIÈREMENT DÉTOURNÉ DE L'HISTOIRE DU CINÉMA
V.O. SOUS-TITRES PAR L'ASSOCIATION POUR LE DÉVELOPPEMENT DES LUTTES
DE CLASSES ET LA PROPAGATION DU MATÉRIALISME DIALECTIQUE.

Fig. 5: Flyer for René Vienet's *La Dialectique peut-elle casser des briques?*
(*Can Dialectics Break Bricks?*) (1973)

Taekwondo, Vienet and his collaborators overdub it with another narrative, a story of proletarians' resistance to co-optation by their would-be leaders and interpreters, from the Communist Party and the trade unions to the Trotskyist and Maoist factions and the entire army of liberal intellectuals that attempts to discipline and repress them. "You can't conquer alienation with alienated means," the hero is admonished by his frustrated girlfriend, in what could be the ultimate slogan of the film.

What does Vienet intend by putting these words in the mouths of Guangqi's characters? "France in the 1950s and early 1960s saw the emergence of a particularly rich body of alienation theory," David Graeber recalls, including that of the Situationists, who

> saw modern consumer society as a gigantic "spectacle," a vast apparatus composed of not only media images but market logic, the rule of experts, and the nature of the commodity form, all combining together to render individuals passive and isolated spectators of their own lives.[80]

The Situationist critique of alienation drew heavily on the young Marx, for whom the worker, "estranged from himself," faces "his own creation as an alien power," experiencing "his production as the production of his nullity."[81] In the film, we witness a sorrowful gathering of the villagers around the body of the gangsters' most recent victim:

---

80 Graeber, "Alienation," *New Dictionary of the History of Ideas*, ed. Maryanne Cline Horowitz (New York: Charles Scribner's Sons, 2005), 1.49.

81 Marx, in Marx and Engels, *Collected Works*, 3.217.

VILLAGER #1: They've alienated yet another proletarian.

VILLAGER #2: Another one lost.

HERO: What's going on?

VILLAGER #1: This one just became a union rep.

VILLAGER #2: As soon as he did, he repressed a wildcat strike, just before buying a TV on credit.

Here, as Debord says, détourned images present a "double meaning," the "coexistence ... within them of their old senses and their new, immediate senses."[82] The scene's old sense overlaps with the new to form an allegory, an extended analogy: "bureaucrats" are a bunch of thugs, "proletarians" are like villagers terrorized by bandits, "alienation" is a kind of death.

But this is not the end of it; since the original film offers a heroic plot—a fantasy of empowerment, which of course ordinarily substitutes for real action on the part of the passive, powerless spectator—the détourned film is able to take advantage of this plot while reversing its ideological signs. Tapping his forehead, a villager defies one of the head gangsters: "Ideology can only shatter to pieces on contact with radical subjectivity." As if in response, the gangster's henchman promptly picks up a bottle, raises it, and shatters it on the head of the entirely unfazed villager. Clearly, "radical subjectivity" is not mere verbalism—it is more solid than mere "ideology." (As the hero later tells his enemies: "The illusion of your power is only the power of your illusion.") And so we are given hope: just as the villager has made the gangster's attempted show of force into a demonstration of the force of resistance, so we can turn the very weapons of the spectacle against themselves via the jiu-jitsu of *détournement*. "It seems their latest discovery is to detourn the mass media," one of the arch-gangsters observes nervously. "These détournements disturb me." During the opening credits, as we watch the hero-protagonist rehearse his martial-arts moves against an empty black background (almost literally an exercise in powerlessness, of potential isolated in nothingness), a voiceover remarks: "He looks like a jerk, true, but it's not his fault. It's the producer's. He's alienated and he knows it. He has no control over the use of his life. In short, he's a proletarian.

---

82 Debord in Ken Knabb, ed. and trans., *Situationist International Anthology* (Berkeley: Bureau of Public Secrets, 1981), 55.

But that's going to change." The spectacle of individual heroism is de-created, transformed into a fantasy of collective liberation.

In addition to working on this allegorical level, Vienet's film also uses the images as a kind of ideological crowbar to pry away the authority of certain words. "From the start of this détourned film," complains one of the villains with a sheepish smile, "they've had me say a bunch of stupid shit." Much of the film is designed to reveal the stupidity of the stupid—in particular, to unmask the stupidity of pseudo-revolutionary Left discourse. Despite advertising the film as a "dialectical materialist" production, Vienet wants to get past the Bakunin-Marx split of the First International, blending bits of Marxist theory with a generous helping of specifically anarchist references (e.g., to Déjacque, Coeuderoy, Bakunin, Catalonia, Durruti, Ravachol, etc.). When the self-appointed "Marxist" representatives of the proletariat in Moscow or Beijing preach a gospel of productivity—"Work! Family! Fatherland! Just stick to that," bark the smirking gangsters—then they have become another ruling class (either in power or in waiting for power), and the very vocabulary Marx had created as a tool of subversive critique, has become another instrument of ruling-class ideology. The very truth-content of Marxism, reduced to a set of frozen clichés and falsehoods ("bricks" in an ideological wall, indeed), stands in need of an anarchist emancipation from its official guardians. And so Vienet sets his sights, first and foremost, on de-creating that ossified vocabulary of critique, deploying a dubbed-over dialogue that at once mimics and mocks the rhetoric of the sectarian left—"reducing our own wooden language to shavings if not to sawdust," as the leader of the "bureaucrat" villains complains.

At the same time, *Can Dialectics Break Bricks?* also leverages the power of subversive words against the authority of images. The power of kung-fu narrative to enlist our desires, to persuade us to suspend our disbelief and rest our critical faculties, is subjected to a dislocation, what Walter Benjamin might have called a "shock," dislodged by disobedient words that turn the images against themselves.[83] One of

---

83 Benjamin, *Illuminations*, 242. A somewhat obscure martial-arts film like *Crush*, as a minor form of popular entertainment, might not seem to have much "authority" to begin with, at least if the authority of film is conceived in terms of cultural capital. However, *Crush* does produce some of the effects of authority, both in the way that the stunts and fight choreog-

the simplest ways to do this is to break the fourth wall, to call attention to the artifice of the art, and Vienet does this repeatedly. Near
the beginning of the film, as the hero listens to the people's woes,
he comforts them: "Don't worry, the film's just starting." When one
of the toughs draws his sword, he's met with a taunt: "Go put away
your phallic symbol." A shot cluttered with the grisly spectacle of
dead bodies is undercut by the explanation offered by one of the oppressed villagers: "They're sick of dubbing dialogue tracks, so they're
pretending to be dead. It's hard work, and doesn't even pay cab fare."

Where this procedure is successful, *Can Dialectics Break Bricks?*
is at its funniest and most subversive. However, it often seems
to backfire, to produce its own negation, in a manner that has become familiar to us in our exploration of other forms of visual-ver-
bal *détournement*. That is to say, the dubbed-over dialogue tends to
present itself as a battery of Hegelian-Marxist abstractions, a series of
stock phrases, lines from previous revolts recited in ways that make
them seem curiously empty, alienated from the contexts in which they
originated, drained of whatever power they once had to elicit belief.
At times, even when the actual semantic content is absolutely anti-
authoritarian, it is not unlike listening to a young Red Guard spouting quotations from Mao's *Little Red Book*. "Our tactics," declares a
villager, in a line lifted from Raoul Vaneigem's situationist tract, *The
Revolution of Everyday Life*, "must be indissolubly founded on the
practice of individual realization." "We must annihilate forever what
could one day destroy our work," says another, strangely apropos of
nothing, plagiarizing from the Marquis de Sade's *Philosophy in the
Bedroom*.[84] In a climactic battle scene, without any diegetic motiva-
tion (nobody in the frame is speaking), the voiceover spouts length-
ier quotations: "Those who speak of revolution and of class struggle
without explicitly referring to everyday life, without understanding

---

raphy lay claim to "authenticity"—Guangqi frequently uses wider shots
and longer takes to showcase the actors' performative prowess—and in
the way that, in keeping with its generic code, it locates spiritual truth,
righteousness, and virtue in a humble but inevitably patriarchal "master."
Cf. Leon Hunt, *Kung Fu Cult Masters: From Bruce Lee to Crouching Tiger*
(London: Wallflower Press, 2003), 22, 46.

84 Donatien Alphonse François de Sade, *Justine, Philosophy in the Bedroom,
and Other Writings*, eds. and trans. Richard Seaver and Austryn Wain-
house (New York: Grove Weidenfeld, 1990), 297.

what is subversive in love and positive in the refusal of constraints, have a corpse in their mouths" (again, reciting from Vaneigem).[85] At points, the writers even joke about this bookishness: during another fight scene, a voiceover announces, "For this sequence, consult [René Vienet's] 'Enrages and Situs in the Occupations Movement,' in the Gallimard edition, pages 207 and 231." But even as Left rhetoric is strenuously disavowed, this doesn't dispel the hectoring, rhetorical tone. It is as if the sawdust of ideology is reconstituted as a pressboard imitation of the original—a not-so-de-creative kind of repetition, a corpse in the mouth.

Contemporary anarchist filmmakers can make a subtler and perhaps more effective use of *détournement*. A notable example might be Franklin López's presentation of a talk by Derrick Jensen (based on Jensen's book, *Endgame*) as a five-minute short, *Star Nonviolent Civil Disobedience*. Playing with the iconography of the Death Star—"an unspeakably powerful and horrific weapon developed by the Empire ... capable of destroying entire planets"—Jensen and López détourn it into a ready-made metaphor for the forces currently destroying our planet, while parodying the narrative as a saga of incredibly ineffectual resistance to those forces:

> In this version, the rebels do not of course blow up the Death Star, but instead prefer to use other tactics to slow the intergalactic march of Empire. For example, they set up programs for people on planets about to be destroyed to produce luxury items like hemp hacky sacks and gourmet coffee for sale to inhabitants of the Death Star. Audience members will also discover that there are plans afoot to encourage loads of troopers and other citizens of the Empire to take ecotours of doomed planets. The purpose will be to show to one and all that these planets are economically important to the Empire and so should not be destroyed. In a surprise move that will rivet viewers to the edges of their seats, other groups of rebels file lawsuits against the Empire, attempting to show that the Environmental Impact Statement Darth Vader was required to file failed to adequately support its decision that blowing up this planet would cause "no significant

---

85 cf. Raoul Vaneigem, *The Revolution of Everyday Life*, trans. Donald Nicholson-Smith (Oakland, CA: PM Press, 2012), 11.

impact." Viewers will thrill to learn of plans to boycott items produced by corporations that have Darth Vader on the board of directors, and will leap to their feet in theaters worldwide when they see bags full of letters written directly to Mr. Vader himself asking that he please not blow up any more planets.... Other plans include sending petitions and filing lawsuits.[86]

The increasing extravagance of Jensen's send-up of reformist and pacifist environmental politics is powered, of course, by our foreknowledge of the way the *real* narrative of *Star Wars* is *supposed* to go: Luke Skywalker is supposed to shoot the damn thing with a torpedo and blow it up. What looks silly, useless, and ridiculous by contrast is doing *anything else*: "Some few rebels sneak aboard the Death Star and lock themselves down to various pieces of equipment.... Stirring debates are held onscreen among these rebels as to whether they should voluntarily surrender on approach of the troopers, or whether they should remain locked down to the end. In a brilliant and brave touch of authenticity, the rebels are never able to come to consensus." We behold banner drops on the Imperial flagship, rebels linking arms and chanting, Darth Vader pied by a prankster. To no avail: "the planet"—the famous image of a whole Earth shot by *Apollo 8*—comes into view, and as it must, the Death Star destroys it. The moral of the détourned story, clearly, is that anything short of violent direct action is a criminal waste of time.

There is a bullying tone to this bit of film that is not quite like that of *Can Dialectics Break Bricks?*, but that is strongly reminiscent of a story written by Theodore Kaczynski, also known as "FC" or "the Unabomber," from prison, published in *OFF!* in 1999. This allegory compares society to a ship sailing slowly toward icebergs while its crew bickers amongst themselves: one man is incensed at his low pay, another complains that he's treated unfairly because of his race, another is angry about being oppressed as a gay man, a woman passenger is incensed at how she's treated by the men, and so on. The only thing they seem able to agree on is to shout down the cabin boy who warns them: "You all have good reasons to complain. But it seems to me that what we really have to do is get this ship turned around and headed back south,

86 Derrick Jensen, *Endgame, Vol. II: Resistance* (New York: Seven Stories Press, 2006), 449.

because if we keep going north we're sure to be wrecked sooner or later, and then your wages, [equal rights, and so on] ... won't do you any good, because we'll all drown." Nobody listens. "The ship," Kaczynski drily recounts, "kept sailing north, and after a while it was crushed between two icebergs and everyone drowned."[87] The point, obviously, is that the environmental struggle should take *absolute* priority over *every other struggle*—nothing else matters; no other issues, no experiences of oppression are remotely important in the face of the apocalypse.

This is, of course, not Jensen's brief. On the contrary: Jensen routinely makes linkages between different struggles, viscerally identifying the destruction of ecosystems with the experiences of rape victims and of tribal peoples facing invasion and eviction, and so on.[88] However, Jensen's rhetoric of urgency, of apocalypse imminent, operates in much the same way as Kaczynski's. This is especially strange in light of the dominant uses of apocalyptic rhetoric, which operates, in our time, largely as an instrument of the U.S. radical right: talk of the End Times, of "[the] death of whole worlds, whole political orders, whole systems of human values," as historian Richard Hofstadter noted in his famous Cold War essay on "The Paranoid Style in American Politics," is once again closely associated with the "extreme right wing."[89] If the election of Barack Obama became the occasion for a spike in the sale of guns, underground survival bunkers, and TV and film franchises centering on zombie swarms and giant killer waves, this was not in any way conducive to a public rethinking of our civilization on the order of Jensen's *Endgame*. On the contrary, these were panicked ideological defenses of a civilization supposed to be fundamentally threatened by the supposed ascent of left-wing policies and ideas. Readiness for the apocalypse, in this context, generally functions to occlude the thought of any alternative to our accustomed way of life. The specter of ecological apocalypse is evoked far more weakly by liberal productions

---

87 Ted Kaczynski, "Ship of Fools," *theanarchistlibrary.org*, 2010, http://theanarchistlibrary.org/library/ted-kaczynski-ship-of-fools.pdf.

88 See, for instance, Derrick Jensen, *The Culture of Make Believe* (New York: Context Books, 2002).

89 Richard Hofstadter, "The Paranoid Style in American Politics," in *The Fear of Conspiracy: Images of Un-American Subversion from the Revolution to the Present*, ed. David Brion Davis (Ithaca, NY: Cornell University Press, 1971), 6.

such as Al Gore's *An Inconvenient Truth* (2006), Annie Leonard's *The Story of Stuff* (2007), and Mark Achbar and Jennifer Abbott's *The Corporation* (2003), which round off warnings of danger with vague promises that this accustomed way of life can be somehow rescued by better technologies in the service of an enlightened self-interest.

Jensen's larger collaboration with López, the feature-length *End:Civ* (2011), is equally apocalyptic, indicting reformist and pacifist co-optation of radical movements against a fundamentally lethal civilization. Creative and carnivalistic protest tactics, of the kind associated with Reclaim The Streets and the Pink Blocs, are caricatured as mere clowning: while activists literally painted and dressed as clowns parade by, Peter Gelderloos, author of *How Nonviolence Protects the State*, opines that "the Left, to a large extent subconsciously, has as its primary role to make resistance harmless." Conversely, riot-porn images of burning police cars and smashed windows are coded as exemplary actions—concrete, immediate, physical.

End:Civ avoids the parodic route taken by *Star Nonviolent Civil Disobedience*, favoring a tragic mode. An especially disturbing sequence uses a split screen and overlapping soundtracks to produce an effect of estrangement. The first shot presents us with two images—one of them, inverted, occupying the top half of the screen; the other, correctly oriented, on the bottom: while the lower half of the screen is a helicopter shot—a sunset flyover of a big city in the industrialized world, featuring tall and gleaming skyscrapers— the top half gives us a dark, unreadable landscape, filled with orange clouds and floating lights. At the same time, we are hearing voices from a TV cooking show, happily chattering about how to make the nicest smoothies—punctuated, bizarrely, by the sounds of enormous explosions, which correspond to the eruption of brighter orange lights and new clouds in the topmost field. Suddenly, we recognize the inverted landscape: it is Baghdad at night, lit by the flashes of incoming bombs and missiles, probably during the "shock and awe" phase of the U.S. invasion in 2003. The television chatter goes blithely on, underscoring the gulf separating the two scenes before our eyes, while the visual juxtaposition and auditory overlap underscores their simultaneity. How to make sense of this? We have already been cued by Jensen's voice, duplicated by a supertitle: "Our way of living—industrial civilization—is based on, requires, and would collapse very quickly without persistent and widespread violence." The visual fulfills the verbal: here is industrial civilization, there is violence. A quick montage of other split-screen shots, dividing the screen vertically, drive home the message: a QVC ad for diamond jewelry is juxtaposed with images of hungry, bloodied, and militarily oppressed Africans; sordid scenes of factory farming juxtaposed with commercials featuring ecstatic white people consuming fried chicken; and so on. The technique here, while emphasizing simultaneity via the split screen, is not much different than the montage of contrasts favored by Soviet filmmakers in the early days (e.g., juxtaposing shots of hungry workers with shots of a well-fed bourgoisie), and likewise, it explicitly avows the aim of propaganda bluntly announced by the title (a curt imperative aimed squarely at the viewer).[90]

Another approach is represented by López's *Join the Resistance, Fall in Love* (2003), a seventeen-minute short inspired by a like-titled pamphlet produced by the CrimethInc. Ex-Workers Collective (collected in their book, *Days of War, Nights of Love*). As the CrimethInc. writers themselves note, "One might say that it is ridiculous to implore others to fall in love."[91] Nonetheless, *Join the Resistance, Fall in Love* makes an extended plea to "fall in love," and thereby to resist capitalism. Here, rather than presenting the appalling spectacle of ecological destruction and economic brutality that form the focus of *End:Civ*, López makes an appeal to the forces of desire. After a sequence framing the title against an exterior shot of a prison, the first scene opens on an extreme close-up of an alarm clock sounding off. The image is almost reminiscent of the opening shot of Spike Lee's *Do the Right Thing* (1989), but whereas Lee uses this to signal the viewer that it is time to "wake up," López presents us with another response. In an array of split screens, we watch different couples somewhere in Atlanta awaken to their alarms, quickly focusing in on just two: one a "Yuppie Couple" (Scott

90 David Bordwell, *Narration in the Fiction Film* (Madison, WI: University of Wisconsin Press, 1985), 234–235.
91 CrimethInc. Workers' Collective, *Days of War, Nights of Love: Crimethink for Beginners* (Atlanta, GA: CrimethInc, 2001), 156.

Poyntress and Claire Bronson) fumbling through their morning preparations for work in a haze of anomie (a wide shot underscores their emotional distance from one another), the other a bohemi-an "Working-Class Couple" (Toniet Gallego and Alex Rambaud) who awaken, notice that "it's a beautiful day outside," call in sick to work, and begin fucking, careless of the time. Suddenly, to the accompaniment of a sententious voiceover ("Falling in love," we are told, "is the ultimate act of revolution, of resistance to today's tedious, socially restrictive, culturally constrictive, patently ridicu-lous world"), we are watching what ironically appears to be softcore porn.[92] We, the audience, apparently assumed to be heterosexual, are meant to be turned on by this sex scene, rather than to read it as part of the "tedious, socially restrictive, culturally constrictive, pa-tently ridiculous world" that is being verbally denounced—but in spite of the very mild rebellion involved in faking sickness to avoid work, it is not clear why this sexual idyll is not just another facet of the tedium and ridiculousness.

López makes considerable use of split and inset screens here, frames within frames, contrasting the humdrum, subservient life of the respectable Yuppie (we specifically follow the woman through her day as a real estate agent, consumed with real-estate minutiae, intermittently fantasizing about sex) with the thrilling, carefree life of the rebel (kissing passionately outside a church, having sex in a graveyard in broad daylight). A cop harasses a homeless man look-ing for something to eat in the garbage; our rebel couple greets him warmly, offering him some food pilfered from the local Starbucks by a friend working there. Through it all, a relentless voiceover in-sists that "love is a wild flower that can never grow within the con-fines prepared for it," rather than a set of clichés, "the stereotyped images used in the media to sell toothpaste and honeymoon suites"; that "modern Western culture" is a continual "assault upon the in-dividual" (not, say, an engine of individualization that keeps us from organizing collectively); that since love gives this threatened

---

92 It follows what David Andrews describes as the "constraints and conven-tions" of softcore: namely, "erection and ejaculation" cannot be shown, and the male partner is positioned as "relatively quiescent during the act" ("Convention and Ideology in the Contemporary Softcore Feature," *The Journal of Popular Culture* 38.1 [2004]: 20).

individual "a lot to live for," lovers will not be "willing to fight and die for an abstraction such as the state" (personified by the policeman, presumably not a lover); and so on. The verbal track devours the visuals, chews up the time we spend watching these split realities, synthesizing them for us, processing them into pre-established conclusions.

As avant-gardists like Torres warned, ironically, the dependence of the filmed on the written seems to inhibit its meaning-making potentials, steering the spectator's interpretation down specific avenues. However, it does so even in the relative absence of a dramatic narrative: for most of its running time, *Join the Resistance, Fall in Love* is content to merely illustrate the pamphlet titled "Join the Resistance, Fall in Love." The closest it comes to drama is in the last two minutes, where we watch as the policeman, determined to beat up the bum, is ambushed by our male rebel protagonist, whom he brutally guns down, accidentally wounding a bystander who happens to be the bourgeois woman, driving past in her car. The scene obeys the conventions of drama (slow motion conveys the message that something important and violent is happening) without bothering to supply dramatic motives (has our protagonist gone mad from "true love," that he thinks, unarmed, he can assault a cop without getting himself killed?). Ultimately, because it defers so much to its text, the film ends up sharing the defects of the text itself. In a review of *Days of War, Nights of Love*, anarchist Ramor Ryan complains: "Having disassembled the world, CrimethInc. leaves the rebel outside the system, isolated and alone in personal revolt, further from the general population without the social formation or tools to start building collective projects or the ability to organize concretely." All that is left are isolating fantasies of isolated revolt, fantasies no less passing than Yuppie Woman's daydreams, and no less subject to the brutal negation of the reality-check: "Eating out of garbage cans is not the answer ... [and] making feral love in a graveyard under the stars is no fun with really smelly people."[93]

This is not to negate the power of fantasies, of images—or, to borrow López's useful device, of *frames*. Works of art provide frames—visual, narrative, social—through which we are invited to

93 Ramor Ryan, "Days of Crime and Nights of Horror," *Perspectives on Anarchist Theory* 8.2 (Fall 2004): 19.

see the world, ways of seeing that suggest ways of being: "An artist," as Le Guin says, not only "makes the world her world," but "makes her world *the* world"—if only "for a little while."[94] The trick, for a radical artist, is to demonstrate, somehow, that this substitution of *a* world for *the* world, of a limited "worldview" for the "unspeakable" plenitude and plurality of things as they are, is the stuff of everyday life under domination.[95]

We are always seeing the world through frames, a world as seen through "enframing."[96] The anarchist project demands that we find ways to break with the framework of conventional perception, to make the means of perception into its own object, calling attention to the frame as frame, to make ourselves aware that it *is* a frame—and not the limits of the world itself.

---

94 Le Guin, *Dancing at the Edge of the World*, 47, emphasis mine.

95 Gustav Landauer, *Skepsis und Mystik* (Berlin: F. Fontane & Co., 1903), 6.

96 Martin Heidegger, *The Question Concerning Technology and Other Essays*, trans. William Lovitt (New York: Harper and Row, 1977), 36–37.

CONCLUSION: LINES OF FLIGHT

WHAT can a history of anarchist resistance culture teach us about the future of anarchism? Perhaps we should ask rather what it is that anarchists might have to learn from it: to *repeat* it (seeking to retrieve what was lost, to recreate what was destroyed), or to *supercede* it (seeking to shed what has become an embarrassment, to get free of what is now an encumbrance)? In a series of thoughtful interventions in the anarchist journal *Fifth Estate* ("Anarchist Poetics," Fall 2006; "The Strategy of Concealment: Towards an Anarchist Critique of Communication," Spring 2007; "The Intimacies of Noise," Fall 2007) and elsewhere ("Protest Genres and the Pragmatics of Dissent," a presentation at the Kootenay School of Writing, May 26, 2002), the Canadian poet and activist Roger Farr makes a case for something like the latter option. "Many of the forms of oppositional speech ... that have emerged in the West over the last century," Farr laments, "have lost much of the power and force they once enjoyed"—not because of official repression, but because these "protest genres" have been so effectively neutralized and co-opted by statist and capitalist forces.[1] Casting the anarchism of the first and second periods as "a rational, if somewhat wayward child of the Enlightenment," Farr suggests that its modes of cultural resistance were limited by what he calls "open-communicative concepts," bounded by "the old world of

---

1 Roger Farr, "Protest Genres and the Pragmatics of Dissent: A Talk Prepared for the series 'Studies in Practical Negation,' at the Kootenay School of Writing, for the 2002 Mayworks Festival," Emily Carr University of Art and Design, 4 (web).

political representation."[2] In an era when practically *all* communication has been thoroughly colonized by capitalism, the very insistence that anarchists need to "try to get [their] point across more effectively," or "express [their] ideas in a clearer form" threatens to reduce our thoughts and acts to "a reified instrument of exchange."[3] Moreover, clarity is a demand made of us by the authorities—the "hostile informatives" who form the unthought-of third corner in simplistic sender/receiver models of political communication.[4] The only path open to the new anarchism, Farr argues, is to invent tactics that reject established protest genres *in toto*, instead creating "indecipherable" and "unreadable" acts that resist the very efforts of the authorities to make sense of them at all.

I find little to dispute in Farr's diagnosis, insofar as the protest genres he takes issue with are comprised by "marches, rallies, sit-ins, leaflets," and the like. I've always found something about these practices to be more an-aesthetic than aesthetic—boring, insofar as they repeat the same slogans and gestures again and again, and then depressing and disempowering to boot, insofar as they largely "demonstrate" how ineffectual these slogans and gestures are. They address a phantasmatic "audience" that is supposed to possess power—an audience who would, by definition, be in a position of authority over the people who are "speaking" to them, and who benefit from holding on to that power, but who are somehow imagined to be just waiting to be persuaded to give up that power voluntarily, as if it wearied them. Sociologist Richard Day calls this "the politics of demand"—a politics that, no matter how it wears the guise of defiance, ever positions us as humble petitioners waiting to be acknowledged, recognized, included by "the state as a neutral arbiter, a monological consciousness that, upon request, dispenses rights and privileges in the form of a gift."[5]

---

2   Farr, "Anarchist Poetics," 36, 38.
3   Ibid., 36.
4   Farr, "Protest Genres," 4; "Anarchist Poetics," 36.
5   Day, *Gramsci is Dead*, 81. The genealogy of Day's fruitful term stems from Lacan's definition of "demand" as marked by an interminable quest for symbolic fulfillment, marked by relations of radical dependency: "every demand is a demand for love, regardless of what is requested" (Alfredo Eidelsztein, *The Graph of Desire: Using the Work of Jacques Lacan* [London: Karnac, 2009], 63).

But the modes of anarchist resistance culture rarely intersect with these protest genres, or with "protest" as a genre of action per se; anarchists have never waited for this subject in power to listen to demands, not even when waging struggles around their own freedoms of speech and assembly. They created counterpublic spaces, taking the risk of being overheard by "hostile informatives" for the potential reward of being overheard by sympathetic ears. And that risk was frequently rewarded; anarchism became, in many times and places, a dangerously attractive proposition for working-class men and women as well as for a considerable string of middle-class, professional allies.

It is always perilous to draw implications from the past for the present, even if we are also always doing just that. For example, the social conditions that made it possible for so many to respond to the kinds of identities with which they were presented by anarchist discourse—to wish to see themselves in lines from songs like Joe Hill's ballad, "The Rebel Girl," in which his idealized resistant proletarian subject is described as "true to her class and her kind"—may be irretrievable. Yet it seems that even now, it is possible for a conjunction of social forces to produce new mass rebellions such as North America's Occupy movement, which, while inspired by examples ranging from trade-union activism in Wisconsin to the Spanish *indignados* and the demonstrations in Egypt's Tahrir Square, have also drawn conspicuously on anarchist ideas and practices. Once again, anarchists of diverse stripes find themselves rubbing shoulders with disgruntled trade unionists, disenfranchised liberals, workers thrown out of work, and students struggling under debilitating debt loads, participants in what is not so much a "protest" aimed at persuading the powerful to accept concrete proposals—significantly, Occupy has refused to phrase itself in the "thetic" language of "demands"—but a strange new public forum for the discussion and construction of a new way of life. Once again, a crack has opened up in the social compact that was established in the *trente glorieuses*, as the French call them, the "glorious thirty years" that marked the economically expansive period of 1945–1973, when the working classes of the wealthier nations were so effectively co-opted. In this crack, a new kind of counter-public space has emerged, the space of the Occupations, through which anarchism can percolate.

Deprived of audience, excluded from public life, anarchist resistance culture increasingly began to borrow from the styles that had developed in the bohemian countercultures of the late-nineteenth and early-twentieth centuries, which had themselves grown up in the shadow of the anarchist movements—a proliferation of artistic *avant-gardes* (Symbolism, Expressionism, Dadaism, Futurism, Constructivism, Surrealism, etc.), with their manifestos, cadres, and sectarian squabbles, populated by élite writers and artists who had one foot planted in the world of the radical proletariat. The poetics created by their fusion of modernism with anarchism is characterized by:

- *Noncommunication:* a special affinity to the "destructive gesture" of the anarchist bomber, to "propaganda by the deed" as an alternative to propaganda by the word;

- *Nonsense:* a "resistance to representation" via absurdity or abstraction, the negation or emptying-out of meaning;

- *Nonutility:* a contempt for conceptions of art as having a use or purpose outside itself, rejected in favor of aesthetic "autonomy";

- *Noncollectivity:* a basic credo (despite the apparent diversity of the sects) of "aesthetic individualism," especially inspired by Max Stirner's egoism; and

- *Nonpopularity:* a repudiation of the popular and the accessible as hopelessly bourgeois and "corrupt."

With the waning of the period of propaganda by the deed, with the rise of practices of organization and direct-action unionism, the ever-fragile threads of connection between aesthetes and the anarchist movement were largely severed, but once organizations like the FAI and unions like the CNT had been broken and dispersed, anarchist poets like Robert Duncan and anarchist dramaturges like Judith Malina recovered the tradition of the aesthetes, claiming it for their own. In so doing, they constructed a more self-contained, hermetic, opaque counterculture.

What remains to be seen is whether an anarchist resistance culture, which has adapted itself to the "valley times" of those *trente glorieuses*, clothed in the symbolism of subcultures like punk and hippie, speaking the language of a bohemia that has lived on the margins of public life, can evolve once again to provide the symbolic framework for a new anarchist movement that would stand in the public square, that would have broad popular appeal and institutional staying power. If it is to do that, it seems to me, it will have to abandon some of the themes and devices that served it in anarchism's eclipse.

Take, for instance, the aesthetics of the punk subculture with which anarchism has been conflated for more than three decades now. Punk shows, much as I have loved them, tend, in my experience, to be so loud and crudely amped, the songs shouted so quickly (with minimum redundancy—i.e., little in the way of refrains or repetition) that the lyrics, whatever their political content, are often effectively drowned out.[6] Something is communicated anyway, and the sense of community may be strong, but the scene, permitting mainly the sharing of simple signs among people who know what to expect, tends to favor homogeneity, what Jello Biafra derides as the "safe little punk womb."[7] Do-It-Yourself culture can easily devolve into Talk-To-Yourself culture.

Anna Poletti points out the similar way in which autobiographical punk zines counter their own confessional impulses by a variety of visual, textual, and distributive tactics—limited circulation, pages crammed with teeny-tiny handwriting, fragmentary narratives, deliberately crude photocopying, words crossed out, corrupted, blurred, misspelled—that render them partially "illegible" and "inaccessible."[8] The zinester thus has his or her cake and eats it too, achieving both

---

6   Neil Nehring strenuously protests suggestions that the specificity of a song's meaning vanishes when the lyrics become "incomprehensible," arguing that "emotion supplies a missing link ... between tactile vocality and meaning, the body and language, biology and society" (*Popular Music, Gender, and Postmodernism: Anger is an Energy* [Thousand Oaks, CA: Sage Publications, 1997], 101). However, Deena Weinstein points out that at least one major reason why there are, in effect, so few protest songs is that even "protest songs that *are* heard aren't understood as protest songs" ("Rock Protest Songs: So Many and So Few," in *The Resting Muse: Popular Music and Social Protest,* ed. Ian Peddie [Aldershot, UK: Ashgate, 2006], 8, italics mine).

7   Jello Biafra, interview with David Grad, in *We Owe You Nothing: Punk Planet, The Collected Interviews,* ed. Daniel Sinker (Chicago: Punk Planet Books, 2008), 31.

8   Anna Poletti, "Auto/Assemblage," *Biography* 31.1 (Winter 2008): 91.

self-exposure and self-protection. No doubt much of this has to do precisely with the need to avoid the scrutiny of "hostile informatives"—conservative parents, gaybashing peers, teachers, cops, etc. Yet how often might this contrived illegibility and inaccessibility turn out to be yet another attempt to make oneself cool, to construct an image of oneself as glamorously secretive, available only to those similarly cool and in the know? How often might it amount to canceling the gesture of rebellious, defiant self-exposure—*here I am; if you don't like it, fuck you!*—by ensuring that it is effectively performed only within one's own clique, inside the safe bounds of one's extended self? Maybe, particularly for teen zinesters, this serves as a kind of rehearsal for bolder acts in the future, empowerment by degrees—but I have my doubts.

An anarchist poetics that amounts to "a form of self-imposed exile," as Ramor Ryan describes the CrimethInc. project, is in danger of becoming an end in itself, a dead end, rather than a way towards any broader social transformation. The conclusion Ryan draws from his reading of CrimethInc.'s *Days of War and Nights of Love*—"It's not enough to merely identify with the dispossessed; the task is to find common voice and organize with them"—might be read, I would argue, as having wide significance for the rest of the U.S. anarchist movement.[9] It might be read as a call for other strategies of communication.

Confusing the authorities can be fun. Sometimes it can even be an effective resistance tactic: for instance, Anja Kanngieser points out that groups such as Hamburg and Berlin Umsonst were able to defuse police responses to their events by making it unclear whether they were "protest" or "art," "real" or "play."[10] But resorting to pure Dada, creating confusion for the sake of confusion, can be a dead end as well: by presenting our politics as "indecipherable," we risk rendering it also incommunicable, and by making it "unreadable," we risk rendering it also unintelligible. We just end up looking crazy, confirming the ideological assumption that *any* alternative to the status quo is crazy. And so we're confronted again with the problem

9   Ramor Ryan, "Days of Crime," 21.
10 Anja Kanngieser, "Gestures of Everyday Resistance: The Significance of Play and Desire in the Umsonst Politics of Collective Appropriation," *Transversal* (February 2007), web.

Proudhon outlined so plainly a century and a half ago: i.e., "to live without government, to abolish all authority, absolutely and unreservedly, to set up pure *anarchy*, seems to [ordinary people] ridiculous and inconceivable."[11]

As long as anarchy continues to appear ridiculous, inconceivable, unintelligible, nonsensical, we haven't a chance. Conversely, we know we're getting somewhere when our ways of doing things— mutual aid, direct action, participatory democracy, cooperation, etc.—start to look like common sense and feel like second nature. Often this becomes possible in crisis situations, e.g., when your national economy collapses (hence the sudden growth of the "solidarity economy" in Argentina, 2001) or when the government sits on its hands while a hurricane wipes out your city (hence the chance for the Common Ground Collective to shine in the wake of Hurricane Katrina). Short of such extremes, however, we're stuck with the task of trying to convince others that there is some better way to live than what they're used to. A key function of radical art is to facilitate this shift of perspective not only by making the status quo order of things look odd, counter-intuitive, nonsensical, bizarre— defamiliarizing it—but also by representing the radically unfamiliar in familiar, recognizable, and comprehensible terms, reducing the quantity of anxiety intrinsic to all change and uncertainty. Thus, in the Shakespearean phrase that gave Herbert Read another one of his book titles, "as imagination bodies forth / The forms of things unknown, the poet's pen / Turns them to shapes, and gives to airy nothing / A local habitation and a name."[12] It has, in this sense, a deeply rational function.

While rejecting as excessive the definition of the artist as "a sort of consecrated person, whose values and accomplishments are too refined to be appreciated by the vulgar, philistine majority," Holley Cantine spoke for many anarchists of the postwar generations when he cast a skeptical eye on "concepts of utility" in art, regarding as disastrous "forced attempt[s] to make art into a species of

11 Proudhon, *General Idea*, 245.
12 William Shakespeare, *A Midsummer Night's Dream* in *The Riverside Shakespeare*, eds. G.B. Evans and J.J.M. Tobin (Boston: Houghton Mifflin, 1997), 5.1; Herbert Read, *The Forms of Things Unknown: Essays Towards an Aesthetic Philosophy* (New York: Horizon Press, 1960).

useful work."[13] This defense of artistic "autonomy" was taken to one kind of extreme, at least, by Abstract Expressionist artists such as Mark Rothko, who came of age as an IWW sympathizer and a self-defined anarchist, but whose formalist paintings reflected not a glimmer of the anarchist or syndicalist graphic traditions; seemingly removed from the sphere of articles-for-use, ironically, they accumulated enormous monetary value, reaching six figures before his suicide in 1970.[14] Here as elsewhere, the "disavowal of commercial interests and profits," as Pierre Bourdieu argues, has come to function as a means for the "*accumulation of symbolic capital*"—cultural cachet that can later be converted to cash.[15]

Anarchist traditions of narration and depiction are often strongly collectivist, favoring protagonists either representing entire groups (the allegorical figures of the anarchist imaginary) or who actually *are* groups (e.g., the crowds in Armand Guerra's *La Commune*). To some extent, that has remained a constant of anarchist resistance culture, even in the period of eclipse. However, we can also see the emergence of a more individualistic, subjectivist aesthetic typified by the early works of CrimethInc. and perhaps foreshadowed by the fantastic narratives of authors such as Martí-Ibáñez. Josh Lukin points to the work of Grant Morrison on the comics series *The Invisibles*—powerfully influenced by avant-garde aesthetics such as Surrealism—as an example of a subjectivist tendency, recasting anarchist ideals, once firmly linked to a mass movement and organizations, as "the quietist belief that freedom is a state of mind."[16]

One sign that anarchist resistance culture might have a future is the renewed interest, particularly notable since the 1990s, in shared pleasure, playfulness, and collective joy. Groups organized around tactics such as Reclaim The Streets (RTS)—which, as an offshoot of the British anti-roads movement, began throwing massive dance parties in the street to shut down traffic as early as 1991—have tried to bridge the gap between individualism and collectivism by making collective action a byproduct of individual enjoyment. Rather than

---

13 Cantine, "Art," 10, 12, 15.
14 James E. B. Breslin, *Mark Rothko: A Biography* (Chicago, University of Chicago Press, 1988), 35, 677.
15 Bourdieu, *The Field of Cultural Production*, 74–75.
16 Lukin, "I'm Not Your Boss," 153.

earnestly propagandizing a proletarian audience with messages that call upon their sense of duty (cf. the old Spanish anarchist anthem, "A Las Barricadas," with its appeal to the *duty* to resist, "*el deber*"), RTS actions attempt to render an *experience* of anarchy attractive, seductive, sexy, fun. Moreover, anticipating the Occupy movement, RTS staged resistance as an event unfolding in public space—indeed, as a collective act *creating* public space.

Of course, the emphasis on "experience" as such gives RTS something of a subjectivist tinge, despite its public staging and populist aspirations; as many have pointed out, an RTS street party is an example of Hakim Bey's "Temporary Autonomous Zone," a transitory event, designed to avoid confrontation with the State and to remain only as a shared memory. Many other anarchist institutions, extending into the contemporary period, have aimed to create permanent spaces for anarchist counterculture, e.g., in the 1970s, the "infoshops" originating among the West German Autonomen and the Italian "*centro sociale*" phenomenon, and in the 1980s, the Swiss *Autonomes Jugendzentrum* ("autonomous youth centers," the cause and product of an extended struggle with the State) and the squatter movements of the Netherlands, Britain, and the U.S. To some extent, these institutions recreated the populist spaces of the anarchist movement in its second period: *ateneos*, *centros de estudios sociales*, Ferrer schools, and so on. However, the community spaces created by anarchists in "valley times" do not always successfully open out onto a wider, more diverse public sphere. Unable or unwilling to reach beyond a homogeneous counter-community, they risk becoming self-contained, exclusive.

What happens when anarchist politics get hitched to a culturally limited (white bohemian) aesthetic? During the antiwar protests of 2003, a debate broke out on a St. Louis Indymedia forum over what some perceived as the "internalized racism" demonstrated by "some of the anarchist community" at a protest. After several indignant denials from local black-blocers, an activist contributed another example:

> On the march back to the park, both [local civil rights activists] Percy Green and Zaki Baruti (who are black) tried to get people to walk on sidewalks. One young white male shouted to Percy Green "get back on the street, motherfucker!" not that he

represents the ideology of all of the young white anarchist kids, though. But he probably does not know who Percy Green is, nor do many of his comrades.[17]

That kind of arrogance probably stems in part from inexperience, ignorance, and hotheadedness, but it must also owe something to spending a whole lot of time around other "young white anarchist kids." And at least some of the practices that encourage that kind of insularity and isolation might be considered a poetics of the anti-aesthetic, of the unreadable and indecipherable, a refusal to engage in the difficult work of representing oneself to others, preferring instead the erratic, individual eruption of desire and aggression. It is little wonder that the fastest-growing varieties of anarchism in the period of punk's cultural hegemony—e.g., primitivism and insurrectionary anarchy—have been so strongly anti-organizational.

If, as we have already seen (in Part IV, ch. 4), for Marx, "The tradition of all the dead generations weighs like a nightmare on the brain of the living," this theoretical anxiety about "tradition" made itself felt in the temporary Communist Party support (prior to Stalin's definitive veto in 1932) for the avant-garde aesthetics of the Russian Futurists and Constructivists—artistic efforts to shed the entire "weight" of the past—as well as in Pol Pot's Cambodia, in the aspiration to make a blank slate of history, to begin again in a Year Zero.[18]

To be fair, anarchists have also frequently seen tradition as essentially mindless, robotic reiteration, a sign of human self-enslavement; for instance, Kropotkin condemned the conventional schools of his day for inculcating "slavishness and inertia of mind" through "parrot-like repetition," and worried about the tendency of human societies to slip into self-imitation.[19] However, as Colson points out, anarchists such as Gustav Landauer were also willing to declare that "we need tradition." "There are no more dead causes ... for us," Landauer remarked in 1901, since "what works, is present; what works,

---

17 Anonymous post, *St. Louis Indymedia*, March 2003.
18 Marx, *Collected Works*, 11.103.
19 Peter Kropotkin, *Fields, Factories and Workshops: Or, Industry Combined with Agriculture and Brain Work with Manual Work* (New York: G.P. Putnam's sons, 1913), 382; *Anarchism*, 203–204.

pushes and exercises a certain power; and what exercises a certain power, exists, is that which is alive."[20] Similarly, for Colson,

> As opposed to what a superficial interpretation might lead us to believe, anarchism is not opposed to tradition, since tradition is not only a past to which one refers in an extrinsic way. History, in unfolding, accumulates a multitude of experiences that, like everything that constitutes the real, continue to act within the life that constitutes us at a given moment—experiences both good and bad, emancipatory and dominatory; libertarian action selects from among these and redescribes them.[21]

Indeed, this perpetual work of selection and redescription takes place, for Colson, under the sign of "repetition" and "eternal return"—not interpreted in any fatalistic or ahistorical manner, but from a standpoint that is indeed "foreign to the linear conception of time." From such a perspective, the resemblance of the May 1968 revolt in Paris to the Paris Commune of 1871, for example, is not merely a matter of the relation between a model and an imitation; rather, in such moments, the past "becomes real again; it ceases to be past; it can be lived for a second time, a third, an infinite number of times, therefore remade, modified ... making [us] the contemporary and recipient of a reality which never ceases to be present." Moreover, the meaning of the past is never fixed for once and for all, but always subject to our "infinite capacity to interpret and reinterpret the signification of events and facts ... everything is always to be resumed, repeated and revalued anew."[22] Thus, Colson argues,

> Anarchism is not indifferent, indeed, to the "poetry of the past," the singularity and magic of the hats, pickaxe handles, long dresses, and moustaches, but precisely because it is not a matter of "poetry" in the sense Marx intends, because every present situation, stemming from the details and conditions of past situations—singular in every case ... has the possibility of acceding to worlds, movements, and possibilities that it carries in itself here

---

20 Landauer, *Revolution*, 100–101.
21 Landauer qtd. in Colson, *Petit lexique*, 333; Colson, Ibid., 333–334.
22 Colson, *Petit lexique*, 100, 104, 106.

and now, and that these past details, conditions, and situations divulge in turn.[23]

What is repeated is a tradition's "possibilities": "Each conflict, each moment of revolt, repeats all the others from a new perspective, through new circumstances and with a new intensity."[24]

What would it mean, in this sense, to *repeat* the past of anarchist resistance culture? It could not mean mechanically copying the style of Monleon Burgos's graphics or Han Ryner's narratives—nor, for that matter, Dalí's imagery or Debord's phraseology. Nor could it assume that all the old tactics retain their relevance under "new circumstances." Instead, it would have to mean somehow retrieving the *possibilities* that have been lost or obscured by the passage of time.

For example, we have seen that in many cases, anarchists were quite able to make use of popular genres for their own purposes—*chanson*, melodrama, romance, science fiction, heroic portraiture—even when these genres were, in their popular forms, thoroughly imbricated with noxious ideologies of all kinds. Certain prejudices have perhaps made this seem more difficult than it was; in practice, genres are rather more plastic and less restrictive than certain theories, from high modernism (with its emphasis on the importance of stylistic innovation) to structuralism (with its emphasis on the meaning-regulating powers of structure), have made them seem. Genres sustain fantasies that not only enhance our ability to project alternatives to the mundane, given world—to say and believe that, in the words of the slogan, "another world is possible"—but that connect people, producing *shared* imaginaries.[25] Would the Guy Fawkes mask have become such a powerful symbol of resistance to our own "society of control" if it had not been previously embedded in Alan Moore's comic-book resistance narrative, *V For Vendetta*—even (or especially) when it had been converted into a Hollywood film spectacle?

We might also attend to the possibilities that were *never* fully realized. For example, despite all of its ethnic diversity and dynamism,

---

23 Colson, "L'Ange de l'histoire."
24 Colson, *Petit lexique*, 280.
25 See Stephen Duncombe's *Dream: Re-Imagining Progressive Politics in an Age of Fantasy* (New York: New Press, 2007).

anarchism in multiracial locales like the U.S. and Brazil never managed to formulate an adequate response to the race question, tending to rely instead on concepts such as class or hierarchy.[26] If there were obstacles to organizing across race lines, it seems nonetheless that anarchist resistance culture has sometimes produced obstacles of its own, producing subcultural worlds that excluded racial pariahs just as effectively.[27] But as we have seen, anarchist resistance culture was also a product of *movement*, of migrations and deterritorializations. The specific waves of immigration that brought Italians or Jews to Buenos Aires or New York might have ended, and those populations assimilated, but the currents that produced them have not finished flowing; new populations of immigrants from the global peripheries crowd the metropolitan capitals. How many workers in Chicago or Los Angeles might have brought anarchist experiences with them from Oaxaca or Chiapas? What might be some ways in which these migratory energies could once again be tapped to create newly fluid, inclusive, trans-racial as well as transnational cultural forms?

The current global economic crisis, some have remarked, is above all a crisis of imagination.[28] In the absence of popular radical narratives, the media sphere has filled up with scenarios of disaster. From Glenn Beck's scenarios of socialist takeover to zombie-survival soap operas, from Cormac McCarthy's *The Road* to Tim LaHaye's chiliastic potboilers, and from Christian Dispensationalist tracts to blockbuster films of asteroid impacts, floods, twisters, and quakes, we inhabit an apocalyptic imaginary. And yet, apart from the desperate aspirations of those expecting the Rapture—and the grimmer plans of survivalists stocking up for the collapse of civilization—there is a relative absence of plausible scenarios for the day after. Barack

---

26 See Joel Olson, "The Problem with Infoshops and Insurrection: U.S. Anarchism, Movement Building, and the Racial Order," in *Contemporary Anarchist Studies: An Introductory Anthology of Anarchy in the Academy*, ed. Randall Amster et al. (London: Routledge, 2009), 35–45 and George Reid Andrews, *Blacks & Whites in São Paulo, Brazil: 1988–1988* (Madison, WI: University of Wisconsin Press, 1991), 62–65.

27 See Stephen Duncombe and Maxwell Tremblay, eds., *White Riot: Punk Rock and the Politics of Race* (London: Verso, 2011) and Portwood-Stacer, *Lifestyle Politics*, especially chapter 4, "'You Gotta Check Yourself: Lifestyle as a Site of Identification and Discipline."

28 David Graeber, *Debt: The First 5,000 Years* (Brooklyn: Melville House, 2011), 381–382.

Obama's remarkably successful one-word campaign slogans, cannily vague, now seem signs not only of an unfulfilled craving for "Hope" and "Change," but of the bankruptcy of liberalism. No revolution is threatening to irrupt upon the scene, this time, and no New Deals are forthcoming.

As early as the waning days of the second Bush Administration, a special issue of *Fifth Estate* addressed what the editors aptly perceived as a strain of "End of the Worldism." It is in this context that Ron Sakolsky, a longtime anarchist cultural activist now based in Canada, penned a brief but noteworthy manifesto. "Reality," he writes, "is a tunnel constructed between the realm of the possible and all that is deemed impossible." As long as we remain within it, accommodating ourselves to the narrow space, we are subject not only to bodily constraint and cramping but to a poverty of perception. Instead of looking for the exits, we dread the tunnel's "collapse"; we suffer from "tunnel vision," an incapacity to imagine a life occupied with anything besides maintaining our unsustainable and unbearable way of living. In a bit of inspired wordplay, Sakolsky suggests that the alternative is to become "tunnel visionaries":

> Instead of merely decorating the walls with our creativity to make tunnel life more tolerable to those of us confined within, why not use our creativity to refuse enclosure? We can choose the poetic adventure of the unknown over the security of the tunnel....
>
> There is no crushing hail of rocks raining down on our heads, no insurmountable waves of water waiting to engulf us as the tunnel crumbles. Awaiting us is an autonomous life to be lived with all its upsetting pitfalls, welcome challenges, exhilarating moments, and ludic joys.[29]

What this otherwise salutary perspective seems to overlook, however, is that the artificial narrowing of reality, the obscuring of possibility, is an effect produced precisely by the constant evocation of the terror of the "insurmountable," the "upsetting," the "unknown." It is, as Paul Goodman observed, "a chronic low-grade emergency" in which "there is no thinkable alternative, and any suggestion of one

---

29 Ron Sakolsky, "A Call for Tunnel Visionaries," *Fifth Estate* 42.2 (2007): 55.

rouses anxiety"—the word itself deriving from *angustia*, "narrowness."[30] In this condition, to propose a "poetic adventure" is to invite an incredulous, angry response. In just such a context, the appearance of anarchists at demonstrations against the G20 or at Occupy Wall Street have been instantly, easily incorporated into a media imaginary of "dirt," "disorder," and "danger," stereotyped as filthy hippies in drum circles, masked window-breakers, or, ultimately, stigmatized as "domestic terrorists," a "cancer" on society.[31]

Anxiety, Goodman shrewdly observed, is produced by the new—aesthetically no less than politically. As "the neurotic symptom par excellence," anxiety is peculiarly resistant to conversion into the sense of "excitement" that is the sure sign of an authentic revolutionary moment. Only a careful approach could work around the intrinsic resistances:

> The cure of anxiety is necessarily indirect. One must find out *what* excitements one cannot at present accept as one's own. Since they arise spontaneously, they must be related to genuine needs of the organism. Ways must be discovered to fulfill these needs without jeopardizing other functions of the organism.[32]

The language may be dated, the science suspect—but the suggestion seems valid: in our current phase of chronic low-grade emergency, more than ever, resistance cultures are bound to flourish best wherever they meet real and deeply felt needs, including the needs

---

30 Paul Goodman, *Utopian Essays*, 229; *Decentralizing Power*, 5; Frederick S. Perls, Paul Goodman, and Ralph Hefferline, *Gestalt Therapy: Excitement and Growth in the Human Personality* (New York: Julian Press, 1951), 128.

31 The "domestic terrorist" appellation comes both from the Fox News apparatus and from paranoid government agencies—not long after 9/11, the FBI identified organizations such as Reclaim The Streets and Carnival Against Capital, as well as "anarchists" generally, as "domestic terrorist" threats; leftwing pundit Chris Hedges, notably, referred to "Black Bloc anarchists" as "the cancer of the Occupy movement" (Watson, "Testimony Before the Senate Select Committee on Intelligence, Washington, D.C."; Hedges, "Black Bloc: The Cancer in Occupy"). Cf. Dwight Conquergood's observation, apropos of Chicago city officials' response to tenement residents: "Anxiety about dirt and disorder sets the stage for the elimination of difference and mobilizes efforts to patrol boundaries and purge the environment" (135).

32 Perls, Goodman, and Hefferline, *Gestalt Therapy*, 131.

for security and excitement, tradition and novelty, community and autonomy.

In place of industrial capitalism's inescapable prison, electronic finance capitalism has built an inescapable mall, which does as poor a job of meeting people's needs as it is good at arousing people's wants. It is no wonder that the worker-shoppers are so frustrated, so bored, so embittered. If they could not only find the exit but know that it opened onto a better place, onto a real city of women and men, how many would leave?

INDEX

A

A Folha do Povo (periodical), 346n15
A Guerra Social (periodical), 59, 284
A Lanterna (periodical), 52–3
A Plebe (periodical), 76, 83
Abbott, Jennifer, 374
Abbott, Leonard D., 75, 112–13
Abstract Expressionism (*see also*
   abstraction, aesthetic), 107, 386
abstraction, aesthetic, 15–6, 107, 115,
   117, 324–25, 337, 382, 386
Acción Libertaria (periodical), 304–5
Achbar, Mark, 374
Acracia (periodical), 252
Adeane, Louis, 113
Adorno, Theodor W., 76, 130
Aestheticism, 51
affinity (*see also* grupos de afinidad),
   10, 12, 179, 287, 332, 382
affinity groups: *see* grupos de afinidad
Africa (*see also* South Africa), 240,
   334, 375
African-Americans, 6–7, 20, 108n11,
   209, 315, 327, 344
Agamben, Giorgio, 357, 366
agency, 6, 57, 140, 153, 190, 260, 268,
   273, 275, 327, 340, 352
Agraz, Antonio, 84
Agrupación Mujeres Libres: *see*
   Mujeres Libres (group)
Aka to Kuro (periodical), 73
Akira Tanzawa, 94
Akiyama Kiyoshi, 51
Alaíz, Felipe, 286
Alfo: *see* Longuet, Alfonso
alienation effect: *see*
   Verfremdungseffekt
alienation of artists from audience, 80,
   115, 124, 127, 160, 247–48, 299
alienation effect: *see*
   Verfremdungseffekt
alienation, social, 12–15, 47–48, 160,
   163, 164n8, 223, 286, 309, 367–70

allegory (*see also* women, allegorical
   representations of), 159, 168–70,
   177, 260, 267, 288–90, 307, 329–
   30, 368–69, 372–73, 386
Almanach du Père Peinard, 308
Almanaque de Tierra y Libertad, 42,
   298, 300
Alsberg, Henry G., 112
Altair (Mariano Cortés), 306n9
Althusser, Louis, 254, 260
ana-boru ronso (anarchist-bolshevik
   controversy), 111
anakisuto no bungaku (literature
   of anarchism/literature of
   opposition), 51
anakizumu bungaku (literature by
   anarchists), 51
anarcha-feminism (*see also* feminism,
   Mujeres Libres), 25, 68, 73,
   265n71, 298n31
anarchism, "lifestyle": *see* lifestylism
anarchism as fatalistic/optimistic (*see
   also* revolution), 17–9
anarchism, anti-organizationalist, 251
anarchism as tradition, 10, 109, 247,
   287, 325, 331, 366
anarchism, classical, 23–4
anarchism, ethics of (*see also* ethico-
   aesthetic paradox; ethics; ethics,
   sexual; vocation, dilemma of),
   11–15, 266, 287–89, 292, 326–28
anarchism, new, 22–3, 25
anarchism, periods of development,
   23–26, 46, 247, 233n2, 267,
   301–2, 307, 379, 387
anarchism, pro-organization, 251
anarcho-communism, 13, 33, 84
anarcho-syndicalism (*see also*
   revolutionary syndicalism), 16,
   16n39, 54, 84, 99, 182, 191, 252,
   284–85, 291n17, 294, 319–320,
   343–44
Anarchy: A Journal of Desire Armed
   (periodical), 39, 175n36

anatropism: *see* representation,
  anatropic
Andalusia, 37
Anderson, Benedict, 3n3
Anderson, Margaret, 81
Andrews, Bruce, 140–41
Andreyev, Leonid, 50
animals, 164–65n9, 200, 221, 235,
  295–96, 298, 330
anonymity; *see also* clandestinity,
  intimacy, masking, pseudonyms,
  40–1, 52, 77, 84, 88, 94, 226
anthem, 62, 91, 94, 97, 99–101, 387
anticlericalism (*see also* Church,
  religion), 8, 52, 198, 269, 334,
  363, 376
anticolonialism, 72–3, 165–66, 169,
  234, 237–44, 269, 334, 337
anti-intellectualism (*see also* education),
  84–86, 247–49
anti-militarism, 142, 144–47, 165, 180,
  264, 269, 294, 325, 331–32, 334,
  343–44, 375
Antoninus, Brother: *see* Everson,
  William
anxiety, 46, 62, 264n67, 365, 385, 388,
  392–394
apocalypse, 373–74, 391–93
Arabian Nights, 172
Aragon, Louis, 110
Argentina (*see also* Buenos Aires,
  Rosario), 3, 10, 25, 35n23, 40, 60,
  84, 88, 94, 110, 123, 154, 166, 189,
  250–52, 255, 259, 261, 303, 385
Argentina, anarchists in (*see also*
  Bayer, Osvaldo; de Maturana,
  José; Ghiraldo, Alberto; Gilimón,
  Eduardo; González, J. D.;
  González Pacheco, Rodolfo;
  Longuet, Alfonso; M. R. Martínez,
  Josefa; Rouco Buela, Juana), 3,
  22, 25, 35n23, 36, 40, 60, 84, 88,
  94, 110, 123n8, 154, 166, 189,
  250–52, 253n28, 255, 259, 261,
  264, 303
argot, 89–90, 96, 165n9
Aristotle, 127, 147, 254, 356
Armand, E. (Ernest-Lucien Juin), 159,
  292, 294

Aronowitz, Stanley, 5–6
asa'pili, 229–231
asceticism, 98, 172–74, 252, 290–292,
  295
askēsis (*see also* asceticism,
  body, subjectivation versus
  subjectification), 294–295
assassinations: *see* attentats
Association des Écrivains et des
  Artistes Révolutionnaires (AEAR),
  109–10
ateneos, 60, 387
attentats (*see also* propaganda by the
  deed), 25, 61
Auden, W. H., 116
audience (*see also* alienation of artists
  from audience, contradestinatario,
  counterpublics, hostile
  informatives, paradestinatario,
  Personaje esclarecido, personaje-
  espejo, prodestinatario, public
  sphere, reading, spectatorship),
  15, 32, 34, 36, 52–5, 79, 85–6, 98,
  100–11, 119, 123–24, 127–28,
  134–35, 140–41, 183, 230, 235,
  245–46, 250–51, 253–65, 268,
  283, 299, 325, 348–49, 351, 353–
  54, 363–64, 376, 380–82, 387
Austen, Jane, 153
Australia, 81–2, 125
authoritarianism, 5, 12, 20, 29, 31, 51,
  55–6, 68, 85, 92, 134, 167, 205–6,
  217, 249, 284, 303–4n5, 315,
  356–57
authors and authorship (*see also*
  anonymity; meaning and
  authorial intention; pseudonyms;
  subjectivity), 29n7, 31–3, 39,
  41, 48, 50–54, 57–8, 63, 71, 80,
  111, 129, 136–40, 153–55, 160,
  181–85, 277–78, 382
autobiography, ix, 10–11, 48, 129,
  133–35, 139, 177, 277, 383–84
autocommunication, 259–62
Autonomes Jugendzentrum (AJZ), 387
Autonomists, 20, 25
autonomous movements, 22–3, 387
autonomy of art, 116n42, 123, 357–
  58, 382, 386

Index

autonomy, political, 68, 138, 168n18, 222, 273, 392, 394

Avant-gardes (*see also* Abstract Expressionism, Avant-Pop, Constructivism, Cubism, Dada, Expressionism, Futurism, Imagism, Mavo, modernism, Neo-Impressionists, Surrealism, Symbolism, Ultraísmo), 15–6, 50–1, 67–71, 73–4, 77, 107, 115, 121–24, 127, 136, 138, 153–55, 286, 301, 358, 364, 382, 386, 388

avant-pop, 153

B

Ba Jin (Li Feigan), 73, 164n9, 166, 210–11

Baginski, Max, 274–75

baihua, 72

Bakhtin, Mikhail M., 86, 98, 249, 268, 321

Bakunin, Mikhail, 4, 11n27, 14, 19, 23–4, 67, 89, 101, 155, 163–64n7, 331, 369

Baldelli, Giovanni, 81–2, 137

Ball, Hugo, 68–9, 135

ballad, 73, 77, 117, 129, 381

barbarism and barbarization; *see also* civilization, 204, 233–44, 264n67

Barcelona, 24–5, 32, 37, 88, 101–2, 183, 226–27, 302, 355–56, 359–60, 362–63

Barrett, Rafael, 347

Barthes, Roland, 55, 182, 225

Baruti, Zaki, 387

Bayer, Osvaldo, 3, 22

Beat poets (*see also* di Prima, Diane; Lamantia, Philip; Ferlinghetti, Lawrence; Rexroth, Kenneth; Snyder, Gary; Whalen, Philip), 86, 113, 121–24, 128–29, 133–35, 142

Beck, Glenn, 391

Beck, Julian, 245–47, 293

Bel Mesonada, Gil, 362–63

Belgium, 331, 346–47n19

Bell, Thomas Hastie, 74, 113

Benjamin, Walter, 20n54, 62, 116, 164n8, 236, 301, 369

Bennet, Clif, 117n45

Béra, Victoire Léodile: *see* André Léo

Berkman, Alexander, ix, 36, 88, 112

Bernard, André, 313–14

Berneri, Camillo, 47, 85n66

Bevington, Louisa S., 196–97, 204–5

Bey, Hakim (*see also* Wilson, Peter Lamborn), 387

Biafra, Jello, 383

Biblioteca Estudios, 185

Biblioteca Pro-Vida, 161

Bicicleta (periodical), 154n9, 269

Bildungsroman, 133, 210

birth control, 294, 338

Bjørneboe, Jens, 82, 94, 141, 266

Black and Green (periodical), 336

Black Blocs, 325, 387, 393n31

Black Mountain College, 125, 129

Blake, William, 75n25

Blaser, Robin, 113, 133, 137

Blast (periodical), 302, 308n17

Bloch, Joseph S., 12

Bloom, Harold, 62, 67–8, 71, 365

Boal, Augusto, 83, 260, 263n65

body, concepts and practices of (*see also* asceticism, hedonism, nudism, naturism, sexuality, vegetarianism, veganism, virility), 36–7, 57, 98, 142–43, 159, 216–17, 251–52, 273–74, 278, 283–300, 301, 322, 326–27, 383n6, 331, 336

bohemia, 16, 71, 85, 115, 125, 195, 376, 382–83, 387

Bontemps, Charles-Auguste, 293

book culture, anarchist (*see also* literacy; periodicals, anarchist; print culture; reading), 28, 35–6, 45–6, 61, 283–84

Bookchin, Murray, 190–92

Bourdieu, Pierre (*see also* capital, cultural; capital, social; capital, symbolic), 15, 386

bourgeoisie, 47, 59, 68–9, 77, 124, 180, 198, 200, 216, 222, 242, 248 255, 257, 260, 263, 264n67, 298, 300, 318, 334, 358, 360, 369, 377

Bourses du Travail, 346n19, 350

Bovshover, Joseph (Basil Dahl), 75, 84

bozzetti, 155–56, 276

Brand, Adolf, 293
Brandão, Octavio, 83, 110
Brazil (see also Rio de Janeiro, Santos, São Paulo), 22, 37, 40, 52n71, 59–60, 76, 82–3, 94, 110, 155–56, 175n37, 180n2, 181, 188–89, 196–97, 222, 251, 346, 390–91
Brazil, anarchists in (see also Brandão, Octavio; Damiani, Gigi; Fóscolo, Avelino; Gonçalves, Ricardo; Gori, Pietro; Lacerda de Moura, Maria; Lanceta; Luz, Fábio; Oiticica, José; Ribeiro Filho, Domingos; Scala, Angelo; Vasco, Neno), 22, 25, 37, 40, 46, 52n71, 59–60, 76, 82–3, 94, 110, 155–56, 167n16, 175n37, 180n2, 181, 188–89, 196–97, 222, 251, 346, 390–91
Brecht, Bertolt, 21, 255–57, 260–61
Breton, André, 70–1, 121–22
Brill, John, 98–9
Britain (see also London), 26, 82, 97, 107, 112–13, 145, 211, 238, 240, 287, 318–20, 337, 354, 386
Britain, anarchists in (see also Adeane, Louis; Baldelli, Giovanni; Bell, Thomas Hastie; Bevington, Louisa S.; Christie, Stuart; Comfort, Alex; Daniels, Jack; Gilliland, Mike; Harper, Clifford; Mannin, Ethel; McCail, Chad; Moore, Alan; Read, Herbert; Rocker, Rudolf; Savage, Derek; Symons, Julian; Woodcock, George), 12, 47–8, 59–60, 74, 77, 81–2, 106, 113, 115, 119–20, 134, 196–97, 204–5, 210–12, 219, 223, 228, 278–79, 317–25, 325–29, 327, 339–41, 385, 390
Brousse, Paul, 36, 331
Browne, Lillian, 170
Bruno, Giordano, 306
Brustein, Robert, 245–46
Buenos Aires, 3, 37, 251–52, 259, 267–68n77, 302, 391
Bungei sensen (periodical), 111
Buñuel, Luis, 364–65
Burke, Kenneth, 81, 101, 147, 359

C

Cabeza San Deogracias, José, 299, 362
Caminita, Ludovico, 43
Canada, 343, 379, 392
Cantine, Holley R., 113–14, 116–17, 385–86
Canudos, 188–89
Caos (periodical), 123n8
capacitación (empowerment) (see also captación), 57–8, 259–60, 290
Capetillo, Luisa, 35–6, 40, 52, 169–70, 222–23, 276
capital, cultural, 369–70n83
capital, economic (see also capitalism), 346–47, 350, 386
capital, social, 130
capital, symbolic, 15, 21, 50n67, 386
capitalism, 8, 13–15, 17, 22, 30, 37, 39, 47, 55–6, 105–6, 116n42, 140, 153, 162–63, 188, 190–1, 197, 200–1, 203–5, 216, 225, 227, 230, 257, 260, 263, 307–9, 311, 316, 329, 343–45, 347–48, 354, 375, 379–80, 394
Capra, Frank, 362
captación (recruitment) (see also capacitación), 58, 260, 267
care for the self: see body, subject
caricature, 62, 194, 234n3, 306–7, 331, 337, 361, 374
Carné, Marcel, 349
Carnival Against Capital, 393n31
carnivalization, 98, 298n31, 374
Caro Crespo, Ferdinando, 155
Carpeña, Pepita, 61
Carreras, Vicente, 196, 221
Carruth, Hayden, 127–31, 142
Castelnuovo, Elías, 110
Catalan anarchists (see also del Valle, Adrián; Guerra, Armand; Valldeperes, Manuel), 3, 25, 37, 84–5n66
Catalonia (see also Barcelona), 24–5, 32, 37, 88, 101–2, 161, 183–85, 224, 226–28, 250n16, 259, 261, 302, 355–56, 359–60, 362–63, 369
Cauvin, Gustave, 343, 347, 350
Cavelier, Madeleine Eugènie: see

Index

Vernet, Madeleine
centri sociali, 387
centros de estudios, 60, 251, 387
Chan, Ming K., 51
Chapelier, Émile, 252
Chaplin, Charlie, 299, 349, 361
Chaplin, Ralph, 99
Chengdu, 156
Cherney, Darryl, 97
Cheyney, Ralph, 108–9
Chicago, 10, 105, 115–16, 156, 178,
   182n9, 262n63, 391, 393n31
Chicago, Free Society Group of, 105
Chile, 110, 168, 189–90, 256, 270, 349
Chinese anarchists (see also Ba Jin; Li
   Shizeng; Liu Shifu; Ou Shengbai;
   Wu Zhihui), 28, 37, 72–4, 99n19,
   164n9, 165–66, 210–11, 250, 252
Chinese literature, 48, 51, 72–3, 166
Christie, Stuart, 47–8
Church (see also anticlericalism,
   religion), 7, 11, 35, 55–6, 92, 97,
   117, 138, 170–71, 175, 197n5,
   198, 233n2, 264–65, 267–68, 270,
   292, 295, 299, 306, 313, 333–34,
   338, 344, 355–56
Ciencia Social (periodical), 54, 306
Cimine, 45–6
Cinéma du Peuple, Le, 26, 295, 346,
   350–54
cinema social: see social art, film,
   Cinéma du Peuple
cinema: see film
civilization; see also barbarism and
   barbarization, 188, 194, 199–200,
   211, 221, 224, 230, 233–244, 251,
   333, 373–75, 391–92
Clair, René, 349
clandestinity: see also anonymity,
   masking, 53–4, 89–90, 258,
   262n63
Claramunt, Teresa, 40, 160, 268
Claridad (periodical), 270, 349
Class War (periodical), 354
class: see bourgeoisie, class struggle,
   lumpenproletariat, middle class,
   petit bourgeoisie, working class
class composition of audience: see
   audience

class composition of anarchist
   movements, 16, 37–8
class, intersection of with other
   struggles, 8, 165, 208–9, 264–65,
   286–87, 319–20, 334, 358–59,
   372–73, 390–91
class struggle (see also revolution,
   strikes), 16n39, 222, 250, 370–71,
   391
classicism, 48, 72, 76–7, 86, 129, 145,
   274, 290, 293, 356
Claude, Léo, 345, 347, 349–50
closure, narrative, 43, 130–31, 172–75,
   179, 244, 262, 268, 270, 275–277,
   299, 321, 334–35, 377
Coeuderoy, Ernest, 24, 369
Colônia Cecília, 188
colonialism: see anticolonialism
Colson, Daniel, 8, 10n24, 23–5, 33,
   36, 62n96, 79n47, 85, 100n22,
   139, 158, 225–26, 269, 271–72,
   284, 287, 296–97, 312, 325–26,
   331, 335, 340, 366, 388–90
comedy (see also caricature, parody,
   parasong, satire), 252–53, 263–65,
   329, 350, 357
Comfort, Alex, 113
comics (see also caricature):, 210, 219,
   308–41, 386, 390
comics: détourned, 313–16, 318,
   321–22
Comité de Producción
   Cinematográfica, 363
commitment, 51–3, 68, 71, 77, 111,
   154, 329–31, 335, 363
Communist Party (see also Marxism),
   16n39, 24–5, 89, 91–2, 108–12,
   114, 118, 121, 319, 335, 367, 388
community (see also counter-
   community, counterpublics,
   individualism), 5, 19–20, 34,
   73, 78, 92, 107, 116–17, 119,
   124–25, 127, 129–30, 136–38,
   140, 147, 204n27, 256, 275, 322,
   340–41n65, 383, 394
Compañía de Espectáculos Ibéricos,
   269, 272
Confederación Nacional del Trabajo
   (CNT), 16, 41, 84, 184, 188, 226,

251, 270, 285, 291n17, 294, 335, 355–57, 361–64, 382

Confédération Générale du Travail (CGT), 109, 350

Connell, James, 91

Conrad, Joseph, 239–40

Conroy, Jack, 108–9, 112

consecration, 51–2

Consejo Superior Técnico de Cinematografía, 363

constatives: see performativity

Constructivism, 382, 388

contradestinatario (counter-addressee), 83–4, 86, 262–63, 265

Contradiction (group), 315, 320

Cooper, Gary, 361

Cornford, Adam, 121

Cortés, Mariano: see Altair

Cortéz, Carlos, 121

counter-addressee: see contradestinatario

counter-community (see also community), 11, 16, 38, 56n81, 71–2, 129, 154, 292, 346, 383, 387

counterpublics (see also intimacy, public sphere), 88–9, 106, 114, 119, 127, 262–63, 381

Courbet, Gustave, 156, 307

Couté, Gaston, 175

Creeley, Robert, 125

Cri du Peuple (graphic novel), 325, 327

Cri du Peuple (novel), 325

CrimethInc, 177, 191–92, 354, 375–377, 384, 386

Crisol (periodical), 293

Cronaca Sovversiva (periodical), 305, 307n16

Crosby, Harry, 108–9

Crowder, George, 23

Cuba, 21n56, 34–5, 161–64, 252n23, 267n77

Cubism, 16, 143

cultural studies, 153

culture of resistance: see resistance culture

D

D'Andrea, Virgilia, 40, 65

d'Axa, Zo, 157n17, 308, 331

Dada, 67–8, 71, 73, 135–36, 156, 382, 384

Daenens, Albert, 308–9

Dahl, Basil: see Bovshover, Joseph

Damiani, Gigi, 52, 196

Daniels, Jack, 318–20, 325, 327

Darwinism, 329

David-Néel, Alexandra (Alexandra Myrial), 13n32

Day, Richard J. F., 316, 380

de Cleyre, Voltairine, 43n46, 58–60, 75, 83, 115–16, 154n9, 158–60, 168n18, 171–72, 273, 279–80, 294

de Maturana, José, 36

de Pomés, Félix, 358–59

de Sade, Marquis, 370

Debord, Guy, 139, 236, 301, 314, 365–66, 368, 390

decadence, 47, 73, 76, 155, 191, 198, 200, 241–43, 288–89, 298n31, 360

Decadents, 72

decreation, 366, 369, 371

DeDeo, Simon, 87–8, 141–42

defamiliarization, 76, 197, 236, 240, 272, 361, 385

deformation, 62, 171, 272, 361

Déjacque, Joseph, 24, 77, 198–99, 213, 233n2, 234–35, 331, 369

del Valle, Adrián, 45. 161–64, 166, 198, 267, 270–71, 288–89, 360–61

Delesalle, Paul, 346n19

Deleuze, Gilles, 19, 21n55, 23, 79n47, 180, 263n65

demand, politics of, 380–81

deportation, 37, 94, 107

Der Eigene (periodical), 293

Der Syndikalist (periodical) (see also Verlag Der Syndikalist), 180, 302

Der Ziegelbrenner (periodical), 182

Derrida, Jacques, 31

deterritorialization (see also defamiliarization; Deleuze, Gilles; détournement; displacement, narrative; nomadism), 180, 391

détournement, 62, 98, 171, 286, 313–16, 318, 321–22, 361, 366–73

Index

di Prima, Diane, 86, 124
diagrams, 323–24, 340
dialogue (*see also* monologue), 31, 41,
    52, 56–7, 60–1, 162, 164n8, 205–
    7, 216, 226–28, 248–49, 270–71,
    315, 318, 320
Díaz Soto y Gama, Antonio, 175
Dickens, Charles, 153, 201
didacticism (*see also* education; theater,
    frontal vs. oblique), 28, 75, 154,
    170–71, 251
Diderot, Denis, 188
Die Freie Generation (periodical), 41
Die Parole (periodical), 262n63
Dirlik, Arif, 28, 51
displacement, narrative (*see also*
    deterritorialization), 76, 177–92,
    197, 237
displacement, social (*see also*
    deterritorialization, nomadism),
    37–8, 88, 164n8,
diversity of tactics, 141–42
Documentos Históricos (periodical), 49
Dolgoff, Sam, 118
Donne, John, 79
Dos Passos, John, 153–54
Dostoevsky, Fyodor, 228
Douwes Dekker, Eduard: *see* Multatuli
Drooker, Eric, 312, 328
Ducasse, Isidore: *see* Lautréamont,
    Comte de
Duncan, Robert, 113, 122–27, 135,
    382
Durruti, Buenaventura, 121, 313–14,
    369
dystopia (*see also* utopia), 160, 197–98,
    202, 229
Dzigam, Yefim, 361

E

Eco, Umberto, 54, 298n31
Ecology, 106, 129–31, 211, 276–77,
    320, 329, 332, 371–75
Edelstadt, David, 84–5, 94
Edmundson, Mark, 264n67
education (*see also* ateneos, centros
    de estudios, didacticism, Ferrer
    Schools, Modern Schools,

National Labor University,
    tertulias literarias, universités
    populaires), 35–6, 38, 45, 48–9,
    48, 51, 55–6, 58, 60–1, 70, 73,
    77, 165, 170–73, 209–11, 247n8,
    250–51, 278, 306, 337–38, 340,
    347–48, 350, 361–62
Ehrlich, Howard J., 17, 20, 174
Eisenstein, Sergei, 349
El Látigo (periodical), 193–94
El Rebelde (periodical), 251, 257
Elías, Francisco, 363
Eliot, T. S., 74, 80, 127. 130, 145
Elizalde, José, 292
enclosure, 181, 271–72, 275, 392
Encyclopédie anarchiste (Faure), 7, 45,
    48, 86, 100, 157, 277, 293–295
Engel, George (*see also* Haymarket
    Martyrs), 115
Engels, Friedrich, 10n23
Enlightened Character: *see* Personaje
    esclarecido
Enlightenment, 58, 172, 188, 379–80
Espectáculo (peridiocal), 359, 362–63
Esperanto, 72, 74
Espinar Martínez, Miguel, 363
essentialism: *see* nature; nature, human
Estivalis Calvo, José María: *see* Guerra,
    Armand
Estudios (periodical), 185, 293, 344
ethico-aesthetic paradox, 28–9, 331
ethics (*see also* anarchism, ethics of;
    ethico-aesthetic paradox; vocation,
    dilemma of):, 11–15, 46–8, 129–
    30, 133, 171–74, 190, 212, 218,
    266, 272–75, 287–89, 298–99,
    312, 326–28, 330–31, 344–45,
    361, 371–74
ethics, sexual (*see also* free love, union
    libre), 43–4, 59–60, 213, 216–18,
    292
Everson, William (Brother Antoninus),
    139
exile (*see also* deportation, nomadism),
    12, 37, 75, 81–2, 105, 137, 165,
    179, 183–85, 188–89, 221, 286,
    364
exodus, 20
Expressionism, 361, 382

F

Fabbri, Luigi, 69n8,
fables, 170–74, 183, 303
Falangists, 121, 184, 356–57, 363
family (see also free love, marriage,
 union libre):
family: anarchist theories and practices
 of, 95, 185, 209–13, 217–19,
 296–300
family: patriarchal, anarchist critiques
 of, 73, 134, 165, 264–65, 270,
 274–75, 296–300, 369
fantastic, the (see also folklore; realism;
 realism, magic; science fiction;
 Surrealism), 161–70, 186–88,
 344–45, 386, 390
Farr, Roger, 89, 263n65, 379–80
fascism (see also Falangists, Nazi Party,
 neo-nazism), 8, 46, 49, 81, 102,
 108–10, 112–14, 184, 228, 293–
 94, 304, 313, 327–29, 331, 333,
 335, 347, 356, 362–63
Faure, Sébastien, 45, 222, 350
FC: see Kaczynski, Theodore
Federación Anarquista Ibérica (FAI),
 184–85, 188, 226, 285, 355,
 362–64, 382
Federación de Estudiantes de Chile
 (FECh), 110
Federación Ibérica de los Juventudes
 Libertarios (FIJL), 185, 364
Federación Regional de la Industria de
 Espectáculos Públicos (FRIEP),
 356
Federal Writers' Project, 112–13
Fédération Anarchiste, 123
Fédération des Artistes, 307
Fédération du Théâtre Ouvrier de
 France (FTOF), 110
femininity (see also masculinism;
 masculinity; women,
 representations of), 44, 46n49,
 270–71, 285–86, 288, 300, 316
feminism (see also anarcha-feminism,
 family, gender, marriage, women),
 36n29, 111, 267–68n77, 286n8,
 286–87, 315, 320
Fénéon, Félix, 165n9, 276

Ferguson, Kathy E., 25, 88
Ferlinghetti, Lawrence, 128
Ferm, Elisabeth Burns, 113–14
Ferrer Center (New York), 75n25
Ferrer Schools: see Modern Schools
Ferrer y Guardia, Francisco, 56, 171,
 209,
feuilletons: see serial narratives
fiction: see fables, feuilletons, folktales,
 folletines, novel, nouvelles, serial
 narratives
Fifth Estate (periodical), 379–80, 392
film noir, 360
film:, 6, 9, 26, 47, 182n9, 251–52,
 254n29, 281, 285, 295–300, 311,
 325, 335, 337, 343–378, 390–91
film: anarchist critiques of, 47, 254n29,
 301, 311, 343–45, 347–49, 356,
 363–65
film: détourned, 366–73
film: documentary, 251–52, 335, 350,
 354–57, 364–65, 373–75
film: fiction, 182n9, 295–300, 326,
 344–45, 349, 353–64, 366–67,
 371–72, 390–91
film: Soviet, 348–49, 357–58, 361, 375
filodramático: see theater,
 philodramatic
filodrammatiche: see theater,
 philodramatic
Firestone, Shulamith, 315
First International, the: see
 International Workingmen's
 Association
Fischer, Adolph (see also Haymarket
 Martyrs), 115
Flores Magón, Ricardo, 24, 100n25,
 164n8, 170
folktale (see also ballad, fable, orality),
 34, 62, 73, 77, 86, 167–69, 172–73
folletines: see serial narratives
Fos, Carlos, 252–53, 259
Fóscolo, Avelino, 51
Foucault, Michel, 41, 295
Fourier, Charles, 158, 187
France (see also Lyon; May '68
 Revolt; Montmartre; Paris; Paris
 Commune; Revolution of 1789;
 French; Revolutions of 1848,

Index

European; French anarchists), 4n5,
8, 10n23, 12, 22–24, 37, 46–7,
53, 60, 67–8, 72, 96, 109–10, 184,
198–99, 204, 222, 234–36, 243,
253–57, 258n46, 267–68n77,
295, 302, 312, 329, 333, 346n19,
350, 365–66, 367, 389
France, Anatole, 50
free love (*see also* ethics, sexual;
marriage; sexuality), 42, 185,
195–96, 199, 213–18, 294–95
Free Society Group of Chicago, 105
Freeden, Michael, 204n27
Frei Arbeiter Union Deutschlands
(FAUD), 294
Freie Jugend (periodical), 114
Freikörperkultur, 293
French anarchists (*see also* Armand,
E.; Bontemps, Charles-Auguste;
Cauvin, Gustave; Chapelier,
Émile; Claude, Léo; Coeuderoy,
Ernest; Colson, Daniel; d'Axa,
Zo; Darien, Georges; de Cleyre,
Voltairine; Déjacque, Joseph;
Delesalle, Paul; Faure, Sébastien;
Grave, Jean; Jouy, Jules; Lacaze-
Duthiers, Gérard; Lazare, Bernard;
Léo, André; Lermina, Jules;
Libertad, Albert; Linert, Auguste;
Lochard, Félix; Luce, Maximilien;
Malato, Charles; Méric, Victor;
Michel, Louise; Mirbeau, Octave;
Pouget, Émile; Poulaille, Henry;
Proudhon, Pierre-Joseph; Quillard,
Pierre; Reclus, Elisée; Robin, Paul;
Rothen, Edouard; Roussel, Nelly;
Ryner, Han; Soulilou, Albert;
Steinlen, Théophile; Tolain, Henri;
Trieux, Jean; Vallès, Jules; Vernet,
Madeleine; Vienet, René; Yvetot,
Georges; Zévaco, Michel; Zisly,
Henry; Zaïkowska, Sophie), 12,
16n39, 21n56, 22, 25–6, 39–40,
46–53, 58, 60–62, 68, 72–3, 76–8,
81–2, 84–5n66, 86, 89, 92–6,
100–1, 109–10, 116n43, 121–23,
156–59, 165, 168, 170–71, 175,
180–81, 198–204, 210–11, 221–
22, 234–36, 242–43, 249–50,

252n23, 253–57, 264–65, 267,
270, 286, 292–94, 298, 303–4,
307, 313–14, 325, 338, 345–46,
349–53, 365–66, 367, 389
Freud, Sigmund, 25, 102–3, 157,
186–87, 239–40, 365–66
Frigerio, Vittorio, 50n67, 156, 170,
215n15, 358
Frumkin, Abraham, 10–11
Funü sheng (periodical), 111
Futurism, 71, 73, 154, 156, 382, 388

G

Gallardo López, Mariano, 213–16, 292
Galleani, Luigi, 13
Garbo, Greta, 361
García Lorca, Federico, 121
García Muñoz, Luis: *see* Zoais
García Oliver, Juan, 362
Garden City, 336
Gatti, Armand, 8–10, 21
Gatti, Auguste, 9–10
Gatti, Gino (José Baldi), 1–4, 8–10
Geddes, Patrick, 336
Gelderloos, Peter, 374
gender (*see also* anarcha-feminism,
femininity, feminism, masculinism,
masculinity, sexism, women), 42,
50, 52–3, 56n81, 185, 191–92,
210, 213, 229, 284–300, 358
genre (*see also* anthem; ballad;
Bildungsroman; bozzetti;
caricature; comedy; comics;
fable; folktale; film; film, fiction;
film, documentary; film noir;
hokku; hymn; Kunstlerroman;
melodrama; novel; nouvelle;
parody; parasong; portraiture,
heroic; kanshi; minyo; minyosi;
poetry; poetry, lyric; poetry,
occasional; pornography; protest
genres; protest song; romance;
satire; science fiction; serial
narratives; songs; sonnet; theater;
tragedy; uchronia; utopia;
vaudeville; victim stories; waka),
44, 52–4, 72–3, 86, 116–17, 124,
129, 151–53, 170–71, 213–14,

403

223, 252, 263, 277, 280, 304–7, 312, 316, 331–32, 345, 353–54, 357–58, 361, 390

German anarchists (*see also* Halfbrodt, Michael; immigration; Landauer, Gustav; Mackay, John Henry; Mühsam, Erich; Oerter, Fritz; Reifgraber, Joseph; Reitzel, Robert; Rocker, Rudolf; Schwab, Michael; Souchy, Augustin; Spies, August; Toller, Ernst; Traven, B.), 12, 18–20, 21n56, 22–3, 37, 39, 41, 59, 74–6, 77, 95, 99, 101, 105, 114, 126n12, 136–37, 154–55, 168, 177, 181–83, 237–40, 250n16, 252n23, 262n63, 267n77, 293–94

Germinal (periodicals), 156

Ghiraldo, Alberto, 36, 94, 264

Gibbons, Dave, 281, 327, 339

Gilimón, Eduardo, 261

Gill, André (Louis-Alexandre Gosset de Guines), 307

Gilliland, Mike, 210–12, 223, 278–79, 320

Gilman, Charlotte Perkins, 221

Glover, Paul, 322–24, 338–40

Godwin, William, 23–4

Goethe, Johann Wolfgang von, 37, 87, 124–25

goguettes, 93, 110

Golberg, Mécislas, 157

Goldman, Emma, 17, 25, 30–4, 36, 49, 75, 79, 88, 90, 112–13, 115, 127, 163, 247, 273, 327

Golluscio de Montoya, Eva, 249–51, 259, 261, 266–67, 272, 276

Golos Truda (periodical), 89, 398n17

Gonçalves, Ricardo, 83

González, J. D., 216

González Pacheco, Rodolfo, 264, 268

González Prada, Manuel, 110, 238n14

Goodin, George, 201–3, 269–70

Goodman, Paul, ix, 39, 47n54, 48–9, 59–60, 63, 85, 87, 115, 118, 119, 124–25, 127–29, 147, 149, 158, 181, 196n2, 221, 231, 245–47, 254n29, 336–37, 345, 349, 364, 391–93

Goodman, Percival, 39, 221, 336–37

Gore, Al, 374

Gori, Pietro, 25, 167n16

Gorky, Maxim, 50

Gosset de Guines, Louis-Alexandre: see Gill, André

Gothic, 158–59, 199–200, 332

Goyens, Tom, 21n56, 267n77

Graeber, David, 23n57, 316, 367, 391

Graham, Marcus, 76, 79, 81, 108–9

Granier, Caroline, 21n56, 33, 71–2, 87, 95, 165, 171, 174, 175n37, 198, 200–1, 210, 225, 235n6, 236n8, 241–42, 261, 272, 277, 325

graswurzelrevolution (periodical), 39, 126n12

Graul, Rosa, 57, 212–13, 216–17

Grave, Jean, 12, 158, 221–22, 350

Green, Percy, 387

Grey, Marlène, 297–300

grotesque, 200–1, 307, 361

grupos de afinidad, 60–1, 226

Guangqi Tu, 366–67, 369–70n83

Guerra Sociale (periodical), 196

Guerra, Armand (José María Estivalis Calvo), 252n23, 295–300, 351–53

H

Ha Ki Rak, 111

Hägglund, Joel Emmanuel: see Hill, Joe

Halfbrodt, Michael, 136

Hardy, Oliver, 361

Harman, Moses, 43n46, 212

Harper, Clifford, 317, 320–22, 340–41

Hauptmann, Gerhart, 50, 274

Haymarket Martyrs (*see also* Engel, George; Fischer, Adolph; Parsons, Albert; Schwab, Michael; Spies, August), 75, 115, 305

heckling (*see also* spectatorship, decorous), 31–2, 246–49, 251

Hedges, Chris, 393n31

hedonism, 55, 295

Hegel, G. W. F., 4, 169, 202, 365, 370

Heidegger, Martin, 378

Heine, Heinrich, 50, 75, 95, 119

Helios (periodical), 293

hermeneutics of recollection, 58, 172

hermeneutics of suspicion, 58, 172

Index

hermeticism (*see also* mysticism),
121–23, 127, 365, 382
Herrera, Ernesto, 165
heterogeneity, 3, 38, 262, 275, 278,
390–91
heterosexism, 286, 293–95, 320, 376
heterotopia (*see also* utopia), 152, 160
Heukdo Hoe (Black Wave Society)
(group), 70n9
Hill, Joe, 16, 97–8, 128, 284, 381
Hillström, Joseph: *see* Hill, Joe
hip-hop, 6
Hirasawa Keishichi (*see also* Rōdō
Gekidan), 254. 258, 260
Hobbes, Thomas, 194
hobos (*see also* nomadism, tramps), 37,
96, 177–79, 190, 192
Hobsbawm, Eric J., 11n27, 31
hokku, 129
Holmes, Lizzie, 43
Hombre de América (periodical), 284
homoeroticism (*see also* body,
sexuality), 293–94
homogeneity, 34, 259, 262, 275, 383,
387–88, 391
homosexuality (*see also* sexuality), 113,
286, 293–94, 320, 327, 372–73,
384
Hooton, Harry, 125
hostile informatives (*see also*
surveillance), 89, 263n65, 380–81,
384
Hotz, Charles (*see also* Rothen,
Edouard), 47
Houghton, Jim, 338–40
Howard, Ebenezer, 336
Hoyt, Andrew, 305
huaju, 250
Hugo, Victor, 50, 75, 77, 119
Huneker, James, 75n25
Huntley, May: *see* Holmes, Lizzie
Huret, Jules, 51n68, 67n1
Hwang Seok-Woo, 69
hymns (*see also* songs), 62, 87, 92, 94,
97–9, 101n25, 116–17

I

Ibsen, Henrik, 37, 42, 50, 52, 247,
261n60
identification, narrative/rhetorical (*see
also* audience, autocommunication,
community, homogeneity,
interpellation, masking, Personaje
esclarecido, personaje-espejo,
personalismo, subjectivity), 32–3,
39, 68, 79, 92–3, 100, 109–10,
134, 140n22, 147, 190, 207,
216, 233, 262, 266–67, 273–75,
277–80, 298–300, 303, 325–328,
373, 384
identity:
identity: personal (*see also* anonymity,
individualism, subjectivity,
surveillance), 10, 24, 38, 159,
181–90, 289–90, 309, 326
identity: political/social (*see also*
anarchism; class; consecration;
feminism; gender; identification,
narrative/rhetorical; liberalism;
Marxism; race; sexuality;
workerism), 2–3, 52–4, 56n81,
71, 84, 84–5n66, 92–3, 109–10,
116, 142, 146, 154, 181–90, 225,
254, 262, 284, 289–90, 309, 311,
319–20, 354, 359, 381, 391
ideology
ideology as false consciousness (*see
also* capitalism, heterosexism,
masculinism, Orientalism,
personalismo, racism, religion,
sexism), 30–1, 54, 56, 73, 180,
204n27, 233–34, 260, 337, 357,
359, 368–69, 373, 384–85, 390
ideology as political belief (*see also*
anarchism; Communist Party;
Falangists; fascism; feminism;
identity, political/social;
liberalism; Marxism; Nazi Party;
neo-nazism), 2–3, 16n39, 24–6,
29n7, 30, 38, 44–5, 54, 61, 73,
84–5n66, 99–101, 204n27, 207,
251, 259, 264, 287, 295, 306, 333,
355, 368–69, 371
Il Piccone (periodical), 70
Imagism, 71, 80–1, 115
immigration, 1, 3, 9–10, 22, 37–8,
81–2, 88, 107, 118, 179, 189,

253n28, 262n63, 264n67, 391
indignados, 381
individualism (*see also* community,
    anonymity)
Industrial Workers of the World
    (IWW), 16, 90–1, 94, 97–9, 100,
    101n25, 105, 112, 118, 127–28,
    153, 237, 284, 308–12, 386
infoshops, 39, 387, 391n26
insurrectionism, 190, 388, 391n26
Inter-América (periodical), 164n7
International Workingmen's Association
    (IWA), 23–4, 116n43, 369
internationalism (*see also* Esperanto,
    International Workingmen's
    Association, nationalism,
    transnationality), 16, 16n39, 95–6,
    195, 230
interpellation, 254, 260
intimacy (*see also* community), 32–3,
    87–8, 100, 125, 127, 129–30, 143,
    147, 214, 239, 256, 260, 365
Ireland, 81, 223
irrationality (*see also* rationalism), 127,
    169, 197, 241, 354
Ishikawa Sanshirō, 73–4, 228
Italian anarchists (*see also* d'Andrea,
    Virgilia; Berneri, Camillo;
    Caminita, Ludovico; di Prima,
    Diane; Damiani, Gigi; Fabbri,
    Luigi; immigration; Galleani,
    Luigi; Gatti, Gino; Gatti, Armand;
    Gatti, Auguste; Gori, Pietro;
    Lamantia, Philip; Malatesta,
    Errico; Pimpino, G.; Rafanelli,
    Leda; Romano, Primina; Sacco,
    Nicola; Tresca, Carlo), 1, 3, 9–10,
    13, 26, 37, 40, 52, 70, 81–2,
    84–5n66, 94–6, 101, 107, 155–56,
    179, 258n49, 260n55, 262n63,
    267n77, 305–6, 307n16, 391
Italy, 20, 23, 40, 241, 260n55

J

James, Henry, 276
Jameson, Frederic, 106, 151–53
Jangmichon (periodical), 70n9
Japan (*see also* Tokyo), 42, 51, 53, 69n9,
72–4, 91–2, 111, 156, 250n16,
    366–67
Japanese anarchists (*see also* Akira
    Tanzawa, Akiyama Kiyoshi,
    Hirasawa Keishichi, Ishikawa
    Sanshirō, Kaneko Fumiko, Kaneko
    Mitsuharu, Kanno Suga, Kōtoku
    Shūsui, Miyajima Sukeo, Nii Itaru,
    Ōsugi Sakae, Takamure Itsue,
    Tsuboi Shigeji, Tsuji Jun, Uemura
    Tai), 72–4, 91–2, 111, 155, 169,
    201, 247–49, 228, 250n16, 270
Jarry, Alfred, 123
Jensen, Derrick, 56, 276–77, 371–75
Jeppesen, Sandra, 3, 39, 51, 349
Jewish anarchists (*see also* Berkman,
    Alexander; Bookchin, Murray;
    Bovshover, Joseph; Edelstadt,
    David; Frumkin, Abraham;
    Golberg, Mécislas; Goldman,
    Emma; Goodman, Paul; Graham,
    Marcus; immigration; Kupferberg,
    Tuli; Landauer, Gustav; Lazare,
    Bernard; Milstein, Cindy;
    Mühsam, Erich; Nomad, Max;
    Roller, Arnold; Toller, Ernst;
    Yiddish language), 10–12, 37,
    59–60, 75, 77, 84–5, 101n25, 107,
    255, 391
journalism, 24, 38–9, 46, 52–3, 71, 155
Jouy, Jules, 222
Joyce, James, 34, 153–54
Juin, Ernest-Lucien: *see* Armand, E.
Jung, Carl Gustav, 102

K

Kabbalah, 137–38
Kabouters, 25
Kaczynski, Theodore, 372–73
Kafka, Franz, 154, 166
Kain: Zeitschrift für Menschlichkeit
    (periodical), 291
Kampflyrik, 77
Kanaks, 77, 168
Kaneko Fumiko, 73
Kaneko Mitsuharu, 15
Kanno Suga, 73
kanshi, 73

Kaufman, Bob, 121
Khleb i Volia (periodical), 89
Kim Hwa-san (Bang Jun-gyeong), 111
Kindai shisō (periodical), 42, 169
King, Henry, 362
Knabb, Ken, 133–35, 139, 313, 315
Kol Nidrei, 12, 101n25
Korea, 22, 72–3
Korea Artista Proletaria Federacio
   (KAPF) (*see also* proletarian
   literature), 111
Korean anarchists (*see also* Ha Ki Rak,
   Hwang Seok-Woo, Kim Hwa-san,
   Kwon Ku-hyeon, Shin Chae-ho, Yu
   Seo), 22, 37, 47–8, 69–70n9, 72–3
Kornegger, Peggy, 11n27
Kōtoku Denjirō: *see* Kōtoku Shūsui
Kōtoku Shūsui (Kōtoku Denjirō), 73
Kress, Gunther, 337, 340
Kristeva, Julia, 68, 115, 133, 135, 200
Kronstadt revolt, 115
Kropotkin, Peter, 10n23, 11, 17n43,
   23–5, 35, 45, 48 63n97, 112, 157,
   171, 233n1, 287–88, 332, 336,
   340, 388
Kundera, Milan, 188
Kunstlerroman, 332
Kunzle, David, 312–13, 329–31, 335
Kuper, Peter, 312, 340–41n65
Kupferberg, Tuli, 97
Kwon Ku-hyeon, 70n9, 216

L

L'Anarchie (periodical), 258n46
L'Art Social (periodical), 198, 256
l'art social: *see* social art
L'Assiette au Beurre (periodical), 234,
   329
*L'Atelier: organe spécial de la classe
   laborieuse* (periodical), 77
L'Endehors (periodical), 75
L'En-Dehors (periodical), 157n17, 292
L'Espoir (periodical), 270
La Autonomía (periodical), 39–40
La Batalla (periodical), 303
La Battaglia (periodical), 156
La Feuille (periodical), 308, 329, 331
La Lotta Proletaria (periodical), 94

La Muse Rouge, 93–4, 110
La Protesta (Buenos Aires)
   (periodical), 251, 257, 261
La Protesta (Cadíz) (periodical), 302
La Protesta Humana (periodical), 166
La Revista Blanca (periodical) (*see also*
   Novela Ideal, Novela Libre), 28,
   44–5, 53–4, 57, 154–56, 160, 196,
   218, 283, 308, 345
La Revue Anarchiste (periodical), 303,
   345, 347, 349
La Rue (periodical), 307
La Tramontana (periodical), 290–91
La Tribune Ouvrière (periodical), 46
La Voz del Esclavo (periodical), 34
La Voz de la Mujer (periodical), 84
Labadie, Joseph, 87, 109
Labor Literature, 51
labor, migrant, 38, 237
Lacan, Jacques, 23, 273–74, 380n5
Lacaze-Duthiers, Gérard, 235
Lacerda de Moura, Maria, 40, 46n49
LaHaye, Tim, 391
Lamantia, Philip, 113, 121–23
Lanceta, 196–97
Landauer, Gustav, 11n27, 18–20,
   36–7, 48, 59, 60n88, 75–6, 113,
   137, 139, 168, 204n27, 217,
   247n8, 250n16, 256n40, 265–66,
   274–75, 336, 378, 388–89
Lang, Fritz, 361
language, 9, 49, 78, 81, 95–6, 145n9,
   227–28
language, crises of, 106–7, 114–15,
   121, 124, 141, 228
language, egalitarian, 227–29
language, dominant, 312
language, invented, 107, 125, 129, 133,
   228–31
language, poetic, 78, 85–7, 119, 143,
   145, 194
language, secret: *see* clandestinity,
   hermeticism, intimacy
language, vernacular, 22, 78, 129, 286
language versus images: *see* word-
   picture relations
Laranjeira, Manuel, 154
Laurel, Stan, 361
Lautréamont, Comte de (Isidore

Ducasse), 122, 125, 139, 314
Lazare, Bernard, 48, 51, 62, 69n8, 109,
    151, 157, 168, 170–74, 234, 269,
    277, 348
Le Ça Ira (periodical), 86
Le Chat Noir (cabaret), 312
Le Chat Noir (periodical), 312, 330
Le Combat (periodical), 343
Le Communiste: Organe du propagande
    libertaire (periodical), 69
Le Libertaire (New York) (periodical),
    198, 302
Le Libertaire (Paris) (periodical), 46,
    121–22, 165
Le Monde Libertaire (periodical), 39,
    100, 314
Le Père Peinard (periodical) (see also
    Almanach du Père Peinard), 89,
    255, 302, 308, 318
Le Peuple (periodical), 109
Lebensreform movement, 293
Lecomte, General (Claude-Martin
    Lecomte), 351–53
lectors and lectoras (see also reading),
    34–5, 37
Le Guin, Ursula K., 149, 158n25, 167,
    218–19, 221–22, 228–30, 276,
    336, 378
Lenin, V. I., 33, 112
Léo, André (Victoire Léodile Béra),
    168
Leonard, Annie, 374
Lermina, Jules, 166–67, 215n15
Les Temps Nouveaux (periodical), 329
Levertov, Denise, 107, 128
Levine, Philip, 121, 128
Levkoyev, Grigori, 361
Li Feigan: see Ba Jin
Li Shizeng, 72, 250, 252
liberalism, 95n11, 97, 108, 114, 247,
    317, 333, 335, 367, 373–74, 381,
    391–92
Liberation (periodical), 140
Libertad, Albert, 13, 235–36, 287
Liberty (periodical), 75, 84, 302
Lida, Clara E., 50n66, 50n67
lifestylism, 177, 190–92, 391
Lindsay, Vachel, 128
Linert, Auguste, 198, 256–57, 263

lines of flight, 19, 23, 379–94
literacy (see also book culture,
    anarchist; education; orality; print
    culture; reading), 30–6, 38, 46, 87
Literarischen Club, 262n63
Litvak, Lily, 38–40, 216, 272, 302–7
Liu Shifu, 46, 74
Living Theater, The, 245–7, 261, 264,
    293
Lloyd, David, 326–29
Lloyd, John William, 94, 167, 214,
    221, 292
Lochard, Félix, 93, 338
London, 12, 24, 37, 115, 124, 182, 326
Longuet, Alfonso (Alfo), 281, 345, 349
López, Franklin, 371–72, 374–77
Lorenzo, Anselmo, 40, 164n9
Los Nuevos Caminos (periodical), 154
Lotman, Yuri, 259–61
love (see also ethics, sexual; free love;
    marriage; sexuality; union libre),
    13, 36, 43, 136, 144–47, 158–59,
    162–63, 166, 172–74, 178–79,
    186–87, 193–94, 199, 211–12,
    209–19, 243, 249, 279, 289,
    296–300, 315, 327, 329, 331, 360,
    370–71, 375–77, 380n5
Lu Xun, 166
Luce, Maximilien, 308
Lucifer, the Light-Bearer (periodical),
    42–3, 57, 167, 306
Ludwig, Edward, 362
Lukin, Josh, 326–27, 386
lumpenproletariat (see also hobos,
    marginality, tramps, trimardeurs),
    38, 96, 189
Luz, Fábio, 52n71
Luzana, Letizia, 10
Lyon, 10n23, 24
Lyrical Left, 81

M

M. R. Martínez, Josefa, 84
Mac Low, Jackson, 116, 118–20,
    138–42, 344–45
Macdonald, Dwight, 113
machismo: see masculinism
Mack, 177, 190–92

Mackay, John Henry (Sagitta), 293–94
MacLeish, Archibald, 78
Madrid, 115, 183, 185, 251–52, 296, 298, 361
Maison du Peuple, 254n31
Maitron, Jean, 38n33
Malatesta, Errico, 17–8, 55, 58, 263
Malato, Charles, 35, 164–65n9, 168, 196, 252, 254n31, 263
Malevich, Kasimir, 15
Malina, Judith, 245–47, 382
Mallarmé, Stéphane, 67–8, 78, 106, 120, 123
Mann, Thomas, 333–34
Mannheim, Karl, 11n27, 31n14
Mannin, Ethel, 59–60, 228
Maoism, 321, 367, 370
Mar, Alberto, 344–45, 349
Marck, Georges, 297–300
Marcus, Shmuel: see Graham, Marcus
marginality (see also lumpenproletariat, nomadism, victim stories), 37–8, 156, 189
Margueritte, Victor, 294
Marrast, Armand, 92, 146
marriage (see also free love, union libre), 165, 218, 264–65, 296–300
Martí Ibáñez, Félix, 49, 101–3, 168n18, 183–89, 196, 293, 386
Martín, José, 160
Martínez Carrasco, Alfonso, 155
Martínez Rizo, Alfonso, 223–24, 226–28, 336
martyrology, 18, 91, 115–16, 175, 252, 267, 283, 305–6
Marut, Ret: see Traven, B.
Marx, Karl, 4n5, 10n23, 19, 62, 100, 144, 162, 164n8, 313, 365–67, 369, 388–89
Marxism (see also ana-boru ronso; Communist Party; International Workingmen's Association; Korea Artista Proletaria Federacio; Lenin, V. I.; Maoism; Nippona Artista Proleta Federacio; socialist realism; Situationist International; Stalinism; Trotskyism), 10n23, 14, 25, 111–12, 154, 204n27, 254, 313, 336, 369–71

masculinism (see also sexism, virility):, 45–6, 271, 276, 285, 296, 358–59
masculinism, narrative and, 276, 359
masculinity (see also femininity, gender, sexuality, virility), 80, 283–300, 358
Masereel, Frans, 252n23, 308, 312, 331–35
masking (see also unmasking), 133, 137, 242, 325–27, 353, 390, 393
mass culture (see also popular culture), 57, 124, 153, 253, 281, 291, 301, 343–47, 361, 368, 376, 383–84
Masters, Edgar Lee, 128
maternity, conscious: see also birth control, 294
Matthews, Brander, 276
Mavo (group), 73
May '68 revolt (Paris), 23, 366, 389
May, Todd, 19
Maymón, Antonia, 45n47
McCail, Chad, 322–25, 340
McCarthy, Cormac, 391
McCloud, Scott, 302, 314, 325
meanings, authorial intention and, 52n71, 97, 136–7, 236, 254n31, 257–58, 263, 333, 367
meanings, control of, 55, 312, 333–36, 338–39, 377
meanings, coproduction of, 136, 138, 146, 312–14
meanings, decontestation of, 204n
meanings as function, 97
meanings, loss of, 117, 382, 383n6
meanings, plurality of, 5, 368
meanings, structural determination of, 21, 390
meanings, structure of, 227
meanings, transformation of, 31, 63, 98, 145, 172, 262, 231, 300, 389
medievalism, 76, 332
Mella, Ricardo, 55–6, 203–5
melodrama, 46–7, 54, 170, 200, 250, 253n28, 254, 264, 286n8, 307, 357–361, 390
memoirs: see autobiography
Méric, Victor, 86–7
Mexico, 24, 37, 100n25, 164n8, 170, 175, 182–83, 237–40, 326

Michel, Louise, 40, 75, 77–8, 168, 199–202, 216, 235n6, 254n31, 262–63n64, 263n65, 272, 276, 307
middle class, 51–2, 54, 77, 258, 261n60, 320, 381
Mignoni, Fernando, 357
milieux libres, 292
Miller, Henry, 153–54
Miller, J. Hillis, 366
Milstein, Cindy, 22n57
minyo, 73
minyosi, 73
Mirbeau, Octave, 51, 164n9, 236n8, 240–44, 249–50, 252, 255, 259, 263, 269–70
mirror-character: see personaje-espejo
mirror metaphors in anarchist discourse, 272–75, 278–80, 305, 309, 327
mise en page, 334, 337, 339–40
mise en scène, 337
Miyajima Sukeo, 45, 155, 270
Modern Schools, 56, 75n25, 79, 387
modernism (see also avant-gardes), 15–6, 50–1, 67–71, 73–80, 107, 115–24, 136, 138, 141, 144, 152–55, 286, 301, 333, 358, 364, 382, 386, 388
modernism, biases of (see also ethico-aesthetic paradox), 128–29, 144, 357–58, 390
modernism, engagement of with anarchism, 15–6, 50, 67–73, 115, 121–24, 261n59
Molotov-Ribbentropp Pact, 112, 115
Monleón Burgos, Manuel, 16, 252n23, 293–94
monologue, 41, 56–7, 133–34, 138, 248–51, 314–16, 380
montage, 375
Montmartre, 312, 353
Montseny, Federica, 40, 43–5, 154–55
Montseny, Joan: see Urales, Federico
Moore, Alan, 219, 326–29, 339, 390
Moore, John, 23, 233n2
More, Thomas, 151
Morris, William, 50, 95, 332
Morrison, Grant, 210, 386
Mother Earth (periodical), 75, 113–14, 118, 156, 170, 175, 274, 327
movie theaters (see also film), 344–46, 361–62
Mr. Block (Riebe), 308–11, 320, 327
Mühsam, Erich, 77, 94, 101n25, 256, 261n59, 266, 293–94, 360–61
Mujeres Libres (group), 44–5, 57–8, 61, 68, 260
Mujeres Libres: Novela sexual (novel), 213–16
Muller, Henrietta, 262–63n64
Multatuli (Eduard Douwes Dekker), 170
Mulvey, Laura, 298
mutual aid, 10n23, 188, 385
Mutual Aid: A Factor of Evolution (book), 45, 233n1, 332
Mutualism, 10n23, 24
Myrial, Alexandra: see David-Néel, Alexandra
mysticism (see also hermeticism, Kabbalah), 123–24, 126–27, 173, 185

N

Nafe, Gertrude, 170
Nakamura Kichizō, 258
National Labor University, 51
nationalism, 3, 20, 99, 101, 196, 271
Natura (periodical), 54
Naturalism (aesthetics), 50, 156, 200–1
naturalistic acting (see also realism, theater, Verfremdungseffekt), 361
nature (see also ecology, naturism):, 106, 118, 158–59, 186, 203, 229, 236, 244, 273–74, 329, 332, 334
nature, human, 8, 14, 195–96, 203, 229, 243, 255–57. 292, 365
nature, state of, 194–95, 233
nature fakers, 309
naturians (anarchist sect), 233n2
naturism (lifestyle practice), 161, 252n23, 291n17, 292–93
Nazi Party, 8, 49, 333, 356
neo-nazism, 319
Negri, Ada, 50
Nehring, Neil, 383n6
Neruda, Pablo, 110

Index

Nervio (periodical), 349
Netherlands, 25, 387
New Deal, 109, 112–13, 392
New Masses (periodical), 118
New York City, 37, 75n25, 81, 86,
    101n25, 125, 198, 238, 245–47,
    302, 391
Newman, Saul, 23
Newman, Sylvia: *see* Rainer, Dachine
Nietzsche, Friedrich, 25, 33–4, 50–1,
    100n22, 163, 287–88
Nii Itaru, 111
Ninn, Serge, 122–24
Nippona Artista Proleta Federacio
    (NAPF) (*see also* proletarian
    literature), 111
Nomad, Max (Max Nacht), 95
nomadism (*see also* hobos;
    immigration; labor, migrant;
    tramps; trimardeurs), 1, 3, 9–10,
    22, 37–8, 81–2, 88, 94, 96–7, 107,
    118, 151, 175, 177–80, 189–90,
    192, 194–95, 237, 247n8, 253n28,
    262n63, 264n67, 349, 391
nonviolence (*see also* anti-militarism,
    attentats, propaganda by the deed,
    violence), 80, 113, 117, 142n26,
    143–44, 265, 331, 371–72, 374
nouvelles, 170, 235–36, 276
novelas: *see* Novela Ideal, Novela Libre,
    Novela Proletaria
Novela Ideal, 28, 54
Novela Libre, 54, 213–14
Novela Proletaria, 28n4–5, 155
novels, adventure, 46–7, 200, 215n15,
    358
novels, anarchist (*see also* Novela Ideal,
    Novela Libre, Novela Proletaria),
    27–8, 30, 33, 43–6, 48, 51–2, 54,
    57, 73, 151, 155, 160, 165, 167,
    178–81, 185, 199–202, 209–19,
    221–229, 240–44, 269–70, 276–79
novels, serial: *see* serial narratives
novels, utopian: *see* utopias
Novo Rumo (periodical), 155
Now (periodical), 112–15, 119, 122,
    134
nudism, 161, 252n23, 290–95, 299
Nuestra Tribuna (periodical), 40

Nyonin geijutsu (periodical), 111

O

O Baluarte (periodical), 40
O Sindicalista (periodical), 76, 82
O'Hara. Frank, 125, 129
Obama, Barack, 373, 391–92
obrerismo: *see* workerism
obrerisme: *see* workerism
Occupy, 336, 381, 387, 393
Oerter, Fritz, 180
Oiticica, José, 76, 82–4
Olerich, Henry, 167
Olson, Charles, 125
Olson, Joel, 391n26
opera, 47, 360
opera, Chinese, 211n5, 250, 252
opera, comic, 252
operaismo: *see* workerism
orality (*see also* folklore, literacy,
    songs), 30–6, 38, 73, 86–7, 100,
    116–17, 167–68, 172,
Orientalism, 129, 172–74, 240–43,
    360
Orobón Fernández, Valeriano, 99
Orwell, George, 227, 229, 270n4
Ōsugi Sakae, 111, 169, 201, 247–49,
    270
Ou Shengbai (Qu Shengbai), 111
ouvrierisme: *see* workerism

P

p.m. (Hans Widmer), 107, 224–25,
    228–231
pacifism: *see* nonviolence, violence
para-addressee: *see* paradestinatario
paradestinatario (para-addressee),
    262–63, 266, 268
parasong, 97–9, 101n25
Parazols, Denis, 221
Paris (*see also* May '68 revolt; Paris
    Commune; Revolutions of 1848,
    European), 12, 37, 72, 184, 198–
    99, 222, 234–36, 243, 253–57,
    258n46, 267–68n77, 295, 302,
    329, 350
Paris Commune, 254, 262n63, 325,
    351–53, 366, 389

parody (*see also* détournement, parasong), 62–3, 94, 171, 196–97n5, 306–7, 354, 371–72, 374
Parsons, Albert (*see also* Haymarket Martyrs), 115
Parsons, Lucy, 40
Pataud, Émile, 203–4, 222–23, 225–26
Patchen, Kenneth, 113, 121
patriarchy (*see also* gender, masculinism, sexism), 8, 72–3, 102, 153, 165, 180, 209, 285, 296, 298n31, 326, 334, 370n83
pedagogy: *see* education
Peeters, Benoît, 337, 339
Peirats Valls, José, 154n9, 345, 347–50
Pellegrini, Aldo, 123
Pelloutier, Fernand, 69n8
Penichet, Antonio, 216–17, 284
Percheron, Auguste, 281
Péret, Benjamin, 121–22
performativity, 97, 138–39, 183
periodicals, anarchist (*see also A Folha do Povo, A Guerra Social, A Lanterna, A Plebe, Acción Libertaria, Acracia, Aka to Kuro, Anarchy: A Journal of Desire Armed, Bicicleta, Black and Green, Blast, Caos, Ciencia Social, Claridad, Class War, Crisol, Cronaca Sovversiva, Der Eigene, Der Syndikalist, Der Ziegelbrenner, Die Freie Generation, Die Parole, Documentos Históricos, El Látigo, El Rebelde, Espectáculo, Estudios, Fifth Estate, Freie Jugend, Germinal, Golos Truda, graswurzelrevolution, Guerra Sociale, Hombre de América, Il Piccone, Kain: Zeitschrift für Menschlichkeit, Khleb i Volia, Kindai shisō, L'Anarchie, L'Art Social, L'Assiette au Beurre, L'Atelier: organe spécial de la classe laborieuse, L'Endehors, L'En-Dehors, L'Espoir, La Autonomía, La Batalla, La Battaglia, La Feuille, La Lotta Proletaria, La Protesta* [Buenos Aires/Cadíz], *La Protesta Humana, La Revista Blanca, La Revue Anarchiste, La Rue, La Tramontana, La Tribune Ouvrière, La Voz de la Mujer, La Voz del Esclavo, Le Ça Ira, Le Chat Noir, Le Combat, Le Communiste: Organe du propagande libertaire, Le Libertaire* [New York/Paris], *Le Monde Libertaire, Le Père Peinard, Le Peuple, Les Temps Nouveaux, Liberty, Los Nuevos Caminos, Lucifer, the Light-Bearer, Mother Earth, Natura, Nervio, Novo Rumo, Now, Nuestra Tribuna, O Baluarte, O Sindicalista, Plus Loin, Processed World, Regeneración, Resistance, Retort: An Anarchist Quarterly of Social Philosophy and the Arts, Revista Pro-Vida, Road to Freedom, Ruta, The Ark, The Blast, The Firebrand, The Libertarian, Tianyi Bao, Tierra Libre, Tierra y Libertad, Timón: Síntesis de orientación políticosocial, Umbral, View, Why? An Anarchist Bulletin, Win: Peace and Freedom Thru Non-Violent Action, Wingnut Anarchist Collective Newsletter, Wohlstand für Alle, Xin Shiji, Xinmin Congbao, zines*), 28, 32, 34, 36, 84, 89, 39–45, 52–4, 57, 71, 94, 114, 155, 182, 205, 208, 261, 302–7, 336, 344–47, 364
Perlman, Fredy, 233n2
Personaje esclarecido (Enlightened Character), 266
personaje-espejo (mirror-character), 266–67, 274
Personalismo, 326
Peru, 110
Pestaña, Ángel, 251
petit bourgeoisie, 163, 263n65
Pfemfert, Franz, 344
Phillips, Utah, 100, 105, 128
photography (*see also* détournement, riot porn), 286–87, 302, 304–5, 315, 354, 357
photography as metaphor, 155, 157
Pi y Arsuaga, Francisco, 164, 170

Index

Picasso, Pablo, 16
Pimpino, G., 305
Pink Blocs, 374
Piscator, Erwin, 21n55, 261
Pissarro, Lucien, 308
Plato, 31, 152, 157n17
Plus Loin (periodical), 124
poaching, textual (*see also*
    détournement, parasongs, stealing
    back and forth of symbols), 361
Poe, Edgar Allan, 50, 159, 166, 276
poetry (*see also* genre), 67–90, 94–96,
    100, 103–147, 151–52, 177–79,
    209, 247n8, 254, 257, 262,
    266n72, 270–72, 274, 303, 332,
    357, 365, 382, 385, 389
poetry, aleatory, 134–40
poetry, coterie, 70n9, 125, 129
poetry, Language, 140
poetry, lyric (*see also* sijo), 73–4,
    78–84, 117, 129, 133, 136, 143,
    145, 307
poetry, occasional, 87, 116, 124–25
Point-Blank! (group), 315, 320
polarization, 318. 361
police, 2, 10, 31–2, 46–7, 55, 89,
    189–90, 205, 209, 222, 226–27,
    235, 238, 263n65, 275, 315, 328,
    340–41n65, 343, 353–54, 374,
    376–77, 384
Polinow, Samuel, 107–8
politics (periodical), 113, 119
Pope, Alexander, 119
popular culture (*see also* mass culture),
    153
Popular Film (periodical), 347
Popular Front, 108, 112–14
populism, 51, 77, 113–14, 123, 127–
    28, 137, 248, 266n72, 286, 332,
    340, 358, 387
Populistes (aesthetics), 109
pornography, 298, 300, 354, 376
portraiture, heroic, 305–6, 390
Portwood-Stacer, Laura, 13n31, 192,
    391n27
Pottier, Eugène, 95, 116n43
Pouget, Émile, 26, 83, 89, 165n9, 203–
    4, 222–23, 225–26, 301, 318
Poulaille, Henry, 53, 109–10, 344,
    347–49
Pound, Ezra, 72, 80, 115, 127, 129, 145
Prat, José, 157, 216
prefiguration, 13, 17–8, 190, 275
print culture, 38, 45, 86–7
prisons and imprisonment, ix, 1–4,
    8–10, 22, 23n58, 26, 37, 82–3,
    92, 99, 117–18, 146, 156, 168,
    187, 189–90, 210, 242, 265, 267,
    307n16, 328n25, 329–30, 343,
    362, 375, 394
pro-addressee: *see* prodestinatario
Processed World (periodical), 336
prodestinatario (pro-addressee),
    262–63, 268
progress (*see also* avant-gardes,
    barbarism, civilization, time,
    vanguardism), 7, 29, 38, 78, 101,
    180, 197n5, 198–99, 233, 236
proletarian literature (*see also* Labor
    Literature, *Le Peuple* [periodical],
    Nippona Artista Proleta Federacio
    [NAPF], Korea Artista Proletaria
    Federacio [KAPF], puroretaria
    bungaku, Rebel Poet [group],
    Rebel Poet [periodical]), 27, 53,
    70n9, 77, 108–12, 155, 261n59
propaganda, 27–32, 35, 45, 54–8, 78,
    92, 114, 185, 218, 252, 266, 312,
    323, 343, 349–50, 356, 361, 363,
    375, 382
propaganda, ethics of (*see also*
    anarchism, ethics of; education),
    33, 56–7, 146, 157–58
propaganda by the deed (*see also*
    attentats, violence), 25, 36n27, 60,
    304, 326, 382, 387,
protest genres, 379–81
protest song, 94, 96–7, 105, 383n6
Proudhon, Pierre-Joseph, 10n23, 14,
    18, 23–4, 46, 61, 77, 87, 92, 109,
    146, 156–58, 188, 209, 223, 226,
    233n1, 272, 285, 287, 298n31,
    300–1, 307, 346, 385
Proust, Marcel, 154
Provos, 25
pseudonyms (*see also* anonymity,
    clandestinity, intimacy, masking),
    13n32, 41, 43, 47, 72–4, 76, 84,

95, 97, 99, 111, 113, 116, 123, 154,
165n9, 167–69, 171, 177, 182–83,
193, 210, 224, 243n30, 276, 292,
295
psychoanalysis (see also Freud,
Sigmund; Lacan, Jacques), 23,
25, 102–3, 127, 134, 157, 162,
186–87, 239–40, 273–4, 365–66,
380n5
psychomachia, 265
public sphere (see also anonymity,
audience, clandestinity,
community, counterpublics.
intimacy), 26, 31–2, 34, 39, 70–1,
78, 82–3, 88–90, 92, 94–5, 106,
114–15, 119, 124–30, 141, 147,
212–13, 215, 275, 292, 313, 320,
325, 338, 347, 350, 365, 381, 383,
387
Puche, Pedro, 357, 359–61
Puerto Rico, 34–7, 222
punk, 26, 39, 97, 105, 287, 383–84,
388, 391
Punta Carretas, 1–4, 10, 26
puroretaria bungaku: see Nippona
Artista Proleta Federacio (NAPF),
proletarian literature
Pynchon, Thomas, 153–54

Q

Quanzhou, 250
Quillard, Pierre, 49
quilombos, 188

R

Rabelais, François, 48
race, 6, 20, 319–20, 372–73, 390–91
racism, 6, 8, 191–92, 209, 315, 319–
20, 329, 344, 372–73, 387–88,
391
Rafanelli, Leda, 155–56
Ragon, Michel, 53, 336
Rainer, Dachine (Sylvia Newman),
116–17
Raizman, Yuli, 361
Rancière, Jacques, 245, 275
rationalism (see also irrationality,
science), 103, 168n18, 169, 205,

224–25, 256, 261, 300
Read, Herbert, 59–60, 77, 106, 113,
115, 119–20, 134, 385
reading (see also audience, lectors and
lectoras, meanings, spectatorship),
32–37, 45–6, 58–9, 138, 142, 171–
74, 217, 305, 334–35, 337–40
realism (aesthetics) (see also
abstraction, aesthetic; allegory;
fantastic, the; science fiction; social
art; Verfremdungseffekt; verismo),
30, 50, 92, 143, 152, 155–57,
160–61, 167–70, 233, 257, 269,
299, 302, 307, 320, 323–24, 325,
332, 345, 349, 360–61, 365
realism, delirious, 198, 272
realism, magic, 186–88
realism, poetic, 349
realism, social, 152, 299
realism, socialist, 154
reason, collective, 61, 226
Rebel Poet (periodical), 109
Rebel Poets (group), 108–9
Reclaim The Streets (RTS), 374,
386–87, 393n31
Reclus, Elisée, 18, 34, 45, 329–30, 336
refugees, 37, 126, 188–89, 200
Regeneración (periodical), 43, 154,
164, 170
Reifgraber, Joseph, 262n63
Reitman, Ben, 177, 196
Reitzel, Robert, 177
Relgis, Eugen, 308
religion (see also Church,
anticlericalism), 7–8, 11–12, 35,
48–9, 52–3, 55–6, 79, 94, 97,
99, 101n25, 117, 138, 156, 165,
168n18, 170–71, 175, 197n5, 198,
204, 208, 218, 233n2, 264–65,
267–69, 270, 283, 292, 295,
299, 306, 313, 332–34, 338, 344,
355–56, 363, 376, 391
repetition, 62, 144, 173, 261, 365–66,
371, 383, 388–89
representation (see also abstraction,
mirror metaphors, realism,
spectacle), 8, 16, 60, 159–60,
256, 272–74, 277, 301, 311, 316,
379–80, 382

Index

representation, anatropic (*see also* realism, delirious), 166n13
Resistance (periodical) (*see also Why? An Anarchist Bulletin*), 113, 118
resistance culture, 4–7. 17, 20–1, 58, 89, 101, 116, 127, 136, 160, 190, 251, 259, 264, 379, 381–82, 386, 390–91, 393–94
Retort: An Anarchist Quarterly of Social Philosophy and the Arts (periodical), 113–18
Revista de Filosofía (periodical), 164n7
Revista Pro-Vida, 161
revolution, 4, 15, 17–19, 36, 76, 79, 83, 102–3, 130, 135, 137, 158, 190, 196, 249–50, 252–53, 260, 270–71, 275, 283, 286n8, 333, 365. 370–71, 376, 392–93
revolution as event (*see also* uchronia), 17–18, 137, 203, 205–8, 209, 222, 228, 233n2, 393
revolution as process (*see also* uchronia), 17–18, 137, 157, 203, 222–28, 320–24
revolution of 1919, Bavarian, 18, 114, 182
revolution of 1789, French, 116n43, 62, 100–1, 194
revolutions of 1848, European, 24, 100, 194, 198
revolution of 1917, Russian, 91, 112, 194
revolution of 1936, Spanish (*see also* Spanish Civil War), 102, 188, 227, 292–93, 295–97, 313, 356–362, 364
revolutionary gymnastics, 83, 260
revolutionary syndicalism (*see also* anarcho-syndicalism), 16, 16n39, 25, 38, 83, 225–27, 251, 259–60, 284, 308, 344, 346n19, 350, 386
Rexroth, Kenneth, 112–13, 115–16, 122, 129
rhetoric (*see also* audience; identification, narrative/rhetorical; public sphere), 26, 77–8, 83, 114, 116, 118, 124, 126, 141, 143, 145, 147, 165n9, 181, 202, 204, 207, 236, 287, 323, 357, 359, 369, 371, 373

Ribeiro Filho, Domingos, 46, 52n71
Richter, Hans, 136
Ridge, Lola, 79–81, 84
Riebe, Ernst, 308–11, 320
Rimbaud, Arthur, 120, 133, 137
Rio de Janeiro, 40, 82
riot porn, 287, 353–54, 356, 374
Rivkin, Boruch, 59–60
Road to Freedom (periodical), 107–8
Robin, Paul, 94, 171, 338
Rocker, Rudolf, 12, 59, 62, 251, 273
Rōdō Gekidan, 255, 258, 260
Rojas Sepúlveda, Manuel, 168, 179, 189–90
Rolland, Romain, 50
Roller, Arnold (Siegfried Nacht), 95
Romano, Primina, 1, 10
romanticism (*see also* Gothic), 14, 50, 74, 77, 172–73, 185–86
romanticism, social, 77
Rorty, Richard, 272–73
Rosario, 37, 84
Rosemont, Franklin P., 121
Rothen, Edouard (*see also* Hotz, Charles), 47–8, 76, 253
Rothko, Mark, 386
Rouco Buela, Juana, 40
Roudine, Victor, 344
Rousseau, Jean-Jacques, 14
Roussel, Nelly, 264–65, 267–68, 276
Russia (*see also* revolution of 1917, Russian), 22, 49, 88–91, 112, 194, 233n2, 241, 288–89, 348–49, 357–58, 361, 375, 388
Russian anarchists (*see also* Bakunin, Mikhail; immigration; Kropotkin, Peter), 4, 10n23, 11, 14, 17n43, 19, 22–5, 35, 45, 48, 55, 63n97, 67, 89–90, 95, 101, 105, 107, 112, 155, 157, 163–64n7, 171, 233n1, 287–88, 331–32, 336, 340, 369, 388
Ruta (periodical), 185, 349, 364–65
Ryan, Ramor, 377, 384
Ryner, Han, 164–65n9, 167–68, 175, 177, 180–81, 221, 235, 277, 390

S

sabotage, 309

Sacco, Nicola, 170
Sachs, Albie, 7
Sagitta: *see* MacKay, John Henry
Sagristá, Fermín, 42
Saint-Simon, Henri de, 158
Sakai Toshihiko, 42
San Francisco, 112–13, 125, 302, 315
Saña, Juan, 363
Sánchez Saornil, Lucía, 68
Sánchez, Florencio, 51, 243n30
Sandburg, Carl, 128
Santos, 37, 346n15
Santos, Mateo, 285, 299, 344–45,
    347–50, 355–56
São Paulo, 83, 94, 196, 252, 260, 346
Sappho, 144–45, 170
Sastre, Anselmo, 363
satire, 16, 42, 48, 92, 154–55. 166, 175,
    235, 252, 298, 307, 312, 320, 331,
    357, 359, 372–73
Sau, Antonio, 357–59, 363–64
Savage, Derek, 113
Scala, Angelo, 94
Scarceriaux, Jules, 346–47n19
Schöffer, Wilhelm, 294
Scholem, Gershom, 138
Schrader, Paul, 360
Schwab, Michael (*see also* Haymarket
    Martyrs), 75
science (*see also* irrationality, mysticism,
    nature, progress, rationalism), 19,
    34–5, 38, 45, 50n67, 53, 127, 167,
    183–84, 224–25, 230, 233, 242,
    250, 344
science fiction (*see also* fantastic, the,
    realism, uchronia, utopia), 166–
    68, 186–88, 218–19, 228–31,
    349, 390
Scott, James C., 5, 89, 322, 336
self: *see* subject, subjectivity
sensible, partition of the, 245, 268
serial dialectic, 300
serial narratives, 42, 45–7, 52, 62, 198,
    200, 216
sexism (*see also* masculinism), 8, 50n67,
    72–3, 102, 153, 165, 180, 209,
    264, 285–87, 292, 296, 298n31,
    315–16, 320, 326, 334, 370n83
sexuality (*see also* ethics, sexual;

free love; homoeroticism;
    homosexuality), 32, 42–4, 49,
    59–60, 75, 113, 165, 185, 195–96,
    199, 212–19, 286, 292–95, 320,
    327, 372–73, 384
Shaffer, Kirwin, 21n56, 95, 288–89
Shakespeare, William, 4n5, 47–9, 62,
    63n97, 246, 247n8, 275, 385
Shanghai, 51, 166
Shaw, Bernard, 42
Shelley, Percy Bysshe, 31, 50, 74, 85,
    106, 168
Shin Chae-ho, 47–8, 169
sijo, 73
Sinclair, Upton, 153, 200–1, 250n16
Sindicato de la Industria del
    Espectáculo (SIE), 356–57, 359,
    361–64
Sindicato Único de la Industria de
    Espectáculos Públicos (SUIEP),
    356, 363
Situationist International, 62, 98, 133–
    34, 139, 171, 236, 253, 286, 301,
    313–16, 318, 321–22, 343–46,
    356, 361, 365–68, 390
Slabs, Zeak, 205–8
Slagle, Thomas, 322
Slim, T-Bone (Matti Valentine Huhta),
    99
Smith, Walker C., 308–9
Snyder, Gary, 129, 133–35, 142
social art (*see also* L'Art Social
    [periodical], Théâtre de l'Art
    Social), 48, 92, 154, 157, 269, 301,
    341, 348, 350
Soler, Enriqueta, 358–59
solidarity, 32, 99, 107, 130, 137, 147,
    218, 265, 319, 331
songs, 12, 16, 30, 36, 61–2, 73, 77,
    91–104, 299, 360, 381, 383
sonnet (*see also* poetry), 76, 82, 129
Souchy, Augustin, 251
Soulilou, Albert, 53
South Africa, 7
space (*see also* deterritorialization;
    mise en page; nomadism; prisons;
    sensible, partition of the; public
    sphere; time; utopia), 3–4, 20,
    31, 38, 51–2, 62, 81, 102, 129,

137–38, 143, 152, 159–60, 180, 188–89, 212, 237, 245, 260, 277, 318, 320–21, 329, 335–37, 340, 346, 381, 387

Spahr, Juliana, 138, 142–47

Spain (*see also* Andalusia; Barcelona; Catalan anarchists; Catalonia; indignados; Madrid; Revolution of 1936, Spanish; Spanish anarchists; Spanish Civil War), 24–5, 31–2, 35n23, 37–8, 40, 53, 60, 88, 95, 99, 101–2, 115, 156, 161, 183–85, 224, 226–28, 241–42, 250n16, 251–52, 259, 261, 285–86, 292–93, 295–300, 302, 355–65, 369, 381, 387

Spanish anarchists (*see also* Agraz, Antonio; Alaíz, Felipe; Bel Mesonada, Gil; Caro Crespo, Ferdinando; Carpeña, Pepita; Carreras, Vicente; Catalan anarchists; Cimine; Durruti, Buenaventura; Elizalde, José; Espinar Martínez, Miguel; Gallardo López, Mariano; García Oliver, Juan; Guerra, Armand; Laranjeira, Manuel; Lorenzo, Anselmo; Mar, Alberto; Martí Ibáñez, Félix; Martín, José; Martínez Carrasco, Alfonso; Martínez Rizo, Alfonso; Maymón, Antonia; Mella, Ricardo; Montseny, Federica; Orobón Fernández, Valeriano; Peirats Valls, José; Pestaña, Ángel; Saña, Juan; Sánchez Saornil, Lucía; Santos, Mateo; Sastre, Anselmo; Sau, Antonio; Urales, Federico; Veramón, Luis; Zoais), 3, 16, 23, 25, 28, 37, 40–6, 49, 53–8, 61–2, 68, 84, 84–5n66, 86, 99, 101–3, 121, 154–56, 160, 164n9, 168n18, 170, 183–89, 193–94, 196, 203–5, 213–16, 218, 221, 223–24, 226–28, 251–52, 260, 270, 276, 283–86, 291n17, 292–300, 308, 313–14, 335–36, 344–45, 347–53, 355–64, 369, 382, 386

Spanish Civil War, 23, 28, 45, 61, 86, 102, 121, 184, 284, 335, 362–364

Spanos, William V., 152

spatiality: *see* space

spectacle, society of the (*see also* capital, cultural; capital, symbolic; capitalism; détournement; ideology as false consciousness; mass culture), 133–34, 253, 298, 301, 343–46, 356, 367–68, 390

spectatorship (*see also* audience, heckling), 100, 134, 219, 245, 249–68, 273, 298, 301, 348, 351, 354, 362, 377

spectatorship, decorous, 251–52

Spicer, Jack, 65, 113, 124–25, 127–28, 137

Spies, August (*see also* Haymarket Martyrs), 115, 262n63

Spivak, Joseph, 107–8

St. Louis, 37, 262n63, 387–88

Stalinism, 85n66, 105, 112, 228, 284–85, 303–4n5, 348–49, 388

State, the (*see also* prisons, police), 7, 14n33, 17, 22, 24–5, 102, 130, 168, 171, 190, 203, 218, 223, 225, 233, 266, 270, 277, 298, 347, 349, 374, 387

state capitalism, 347, 349

Statio, E., 46–7

Stein, Gertrude, 118, 124

Steinlen, Théophile, 234, 312, 329–31, 335

Stelton Colony, 118

Stendhal, 278

Stirner, Max, 10n23, 24, 34, 349, 382

Strindberg, August, 50

subject, the (*see also* identity, personal), 71, 78, 123, 133, 137, 139–40, 270, 273–74, 277–78, 320, 325–26, 381

subject, the, as plural, 137, 273–74, 278, 340

subject, the, as unified, 273–74, 325–26

subject, versus/as object, 139–40, 163–64, 308–9, 320, 323–24

subject position (*see also* identification, narrative/rhetorical; subjectivity), 277, 327

subject-formation: *see* subjectivation versus subjectification
subject-presumed-to-know, 337
subjectivation versus subjectification (*see also* askēsis), 159, 270, 295, 301, 325–26
subjectivity, 19, 123, 128, 277, 298, 308–9, 325, 365, 368, 386–87
subjectivity, avowal of, 277
subjects, revolutionary, 315, 320, 381
Sue, Eugène, 200
Sun Lianggong, 51
Suriano, Juan, 60, 251–52, 259, 263, 265, 267n77, 272n7
Surrealism, 70–1, 77, 110, 115, 121–24, 261, 364–65, 382, 386
surveillance (*see also* hostile informatives), 89, 263n65, 325, 343
Swift, Jonathan, 188
Switzerland, 107, 224–25, 228–231, 387
Symbolists, 49, 69–70n9, 78, 106, 115, 120–21, 123, 154, 382
symbols (*see also* allegory; capital, symbolic; symbols, stealing back and forth of), 15–6, 24, 54–5, 71, 78, 85, 92, 170, 261, 287–88, 293, 295, 356, 370, 380n5, 383, 390
symbols, stealing back and forth of (*see also* détournement; parasongs; poaching; capital, symbolic), 92, 101–3
Symons, Julian, 122

T

Tahrir Square, 381
Takamure Itsue, 73, 111
Talamo: *see* Malato, Charles
Tanjae: *see* Shin Chaeho
tanka, 73
Tardi, Jacques,
Tarrida del Mármol, Fernando, 45
temporality: *see* time
Tendenzlyrik, 77
tertulías, 60–1
tertulías literarias, 61
The Anvil: Stories For Workers (periodical), 109

The Ark (periodical), 122
The Blast (periodical), 302–3, 308n17
The Dial (periodical), 79–81
The Firebrand (periodical), 205–8
The Libertarian (periodical), 75
The Open Court (periodical), 158–59
theater (*see also* velada), 7–9, 21, 30, 35, 42, 45, 83, 88, 95, 106, 185, 198, 245–269, 274–76, 281, 293, 345–46, 382
theater, frontal vs. oblique, 261
theater, philodramatic, 258–59, 268
Theater of the Oppressed, the, 83, 260, 263n65
Théâtre en Camaraderie (group), 258n46
Théâtre d'Art Social, 255–57
Théâtre de l'Œuvre, 255
Thiers, Adolphe, 351–52
Thomas, General (Jacques Léon Clément-Thomas), 352–53
Tianyi Bao (periodical), 28, 156
Tierra Libre (periodical), 32
Tierra y Libertad (periodical) (*see also* *Almanaque de Tierra y Libertad*), 102, 170, 193–94, 302
Tierra y Libertad (play), 24
time (*see also* anarchism, periods of development; progress; revolution as event; revolution as process; uchronia; valley times), 3, 19–20, 31, 102, 170, 180, 219, 237–40, 270, 296–98, 306, 336, 340, 388–92
Timón: Síntesis de orientación políticosocial (periodical), 299, 302
Tobocman, Seth, 327–38
Tokyo, 37
Tolain, Henri, 46
Toller, Ernst, 261n59, 264–66
Tolstoy, Leo, 35, 37, 48, 50, 52, 73, 156, 289
Torres, José, 349, 364–65, 369, 377
tragedy (*see also* melodrama, victim stories), 43, 246, 251–52, 264–65, 270, 274–76, 288, 329, 365, 374
tramps (*see also* hobos, nomadism), 37, 94, 96, 151, 175, 177–78, 180, 194–95, 237, 247n8, 349

transfer culture, 17, 20
transgender, 56n81, 211n5
transnationality, 22, 38, 189, 289–90, 391
Traven, B. (Ret Marut), 62, 74, 154–55, 168, 181–83, 189, 237–40, 277
Trent, Lucia, 108
Tresca, Carlo, 260n55
Trieux, Jean, 122
trimardeurs (see also nomadism), 96–7, 177
Trotskyism, 112, 121, 285, 367
Trow, George W. S., 346
Tsuboi Shigeji, 111
Tsuji Jun, 252
Tupamaros, 2–3
Twain, Mark, 192
typesetters, 301–2
typography, 302–3, 346
Tzara, Tristan, 135–36

U

uchronia, 222–23
Uemura Tai, 111
Ultraísmo, 68
Umbral (periodical), 302, 347, 349
Umsonst (group), 384
Unabomber: see Kaczynski, Theodore
uncanny, 237–40, 242
union libre (see also free love, marriage), 218
United States (see also Chicago, New York City, San Francisco, St. Louis), 6, 10, 13, 27, 37, 74–6, 81, 86, 91, 97–9, 101n25, 105, 107–9, 112–19, 124–31, 133–35, 137–47, 152, 156, 167, 178, 182n9, 183–88, 196, 198, 205–8, 237–38, 245–47, 252n23, 262n63, 277, 287, 298n31, 302, 309–13, 315, 344, 349, 361–62, 371–78, 381, 384–88, 391–93, 393n31
United States anarchists (see also Abbott, Leonard D.; Beck, Julian; Berkman, Alexander; Bookchin, Murray; Bovshover, Joseph; Browne, Lillian; Cantine, Holley R.; Carruth, Hayden; de Cleyre,

Voltairine; DeDeo, Simon; di Prima, Diane; Duncan, Robert; Edelstadt, David; Everson, William; Ferlinghetti, Lawrence; Glover, Paul; Goodman, Paul; Goldman, Emma; Graeber, David; Graul, Rosa; Mack; Graham, Marcus; Harman, Moses; Holmes, Lizzie; Knabb, Ken; Kornegger, Peggy; Kupferberg, Tuli; Labadie, Joseph; Lamantia, Philip; Lloyd, John William; Malina, Judith; Milstein, Cindy; Nafe, Gertrude; Parsons, Lucy; Patchen, Kenneth; Pimpino, G.; Rainer, Dachine; Reifgraber, Joseph; Reitman, Ben; Reitzel, Robert; Rexroth, Kenneth; Ridge, Lola; Rosemont, Franklin P.; Scarceriaux, Jules; Schwab, Michael; Spies, August; Sacco, Nicola; Slabs, Zeak; Snyder, Gary; Spahr, Juliana; Spivak, Joseph; Tresca, Carlo; Van Valkenburgh, W. S.; Warren, Josiah; Whalen, Philip; Wood, Charles Erskine Scott), ix, 10n23, 13, 17, 23n57, 25, 30–4, 36, 39, 43n46, 47n54, 48–9, 58–60, 63, 75, 79–81, 83–8, 90, 94, 107–8, 112–19, 121–31, 127–29, 133–35, 139, 142, 147, 149, 154n9, 156, 158–60, 163, 167, 168n18, 170–72, 175, 177, 181, 190–92, 196, 205–8, 212, 214, 221, 231, 245–47, 254n29, 262n63, 273–74, 279–80, 287, 292–94, 302, 305, 313, 315–16, 322–24, 327, 336–40, 345, 349, 364, 367, 382, 385–86, 391–93
universités populaires, 60
unmasking (see also masking), 240, 326–27, 369
Urales, Federico, 62, 276
Uruguay, anarchists in (see also Barrett, Rafael; Gatti, Gino; Herrera, Ernesto; Romano, Primina; Sánchez, Florencio), 1–4, 8–10, 51, 165, 243n30, 347
utopia (see also dystopia, heterotopia, uchronia):, 17n43, 18, 70n9, 72, 151–52, 157–60, 192–196,

198–201, 217, 221–30, 234–35,
270, 285, 316, 320–22, 333
utopias, anarchist, 57, 107, 157–60,
167, 180–81, 187–88, 192–94,
198–200, 202–9, 211, 213–14,
221–30, 235, 320–23
utopias, anarchist critiques of, 36,
60n88, 157–60, 229–31
utopias, blueprint, 151–52, 275
utopias, critical, 152

V

Valaoritis, Nanos, 121
Valldeperes, Manuel, 259–60
Vallejo, César, 110
Vallès, Jules, 46, 48, 171, 174, 209–10,
270, 277–78, 307
valley times, 365, 382–83, 387
van Leeuwen, Theo, 337, 340
Van Valkenburgh, W. S., 108
Vaneigem, Raoul, 370–71
Vanguard Group, 118
vanguardism, 111
Vasilyev, Sergei, 361
Vasilyev, Georgi, 361
Vasseur, Armando, 303
vaudeville, 252, 299
Vautrin, Jean, 325
Vecchi, Guglielmo, 94–5
vegetarianism, 291n17, 295n25
veladas, 95, 254, 267
Veramón, Luis, 349
Verfremdungseffekt, 76, 255–56, 374
verisimilitude: see realism
Verismo, 156
Verlag Der Syndikalist, 294
Vernet, Madeleine, 40, 171
Verón, Eliseo, 262
Vertov, Dziga, 358
victim stories, 156, 161–65, 169, 175,
179, 199–203, 210–12, 216, 266,
269–70, 277, 328n25, 373
Vienet, René, 316, 366–67, 369–371
View (periodical), 122
Vigo, Jean, 363
Vila, Vargas, 43, 44–5n47
violence (*see also* anti-militarism,
nonviolence, police, State):, 7, 8,

12, 25, 25, 36n27, 60–1, 70–1,102,
118, 195–96, 216, 263n65, 304,
320, 326, 329, 375, 377, 382, 387
violence, revolutionary (*see also*
attentats, propaganda by the deed),
25, 36n27, 60–1, 263n65, 265–66,
304, 326, 328, 372, 382, 387
violence, sexual, 165, 216, 286, 373
virility: *see* masculinity
vocation, dilemma of, 12–3, 96

W

waka, 73
Warner, Michael, 88
Warren, Josiah, 10n23
Weir, David, 15–6, 29–31, 67, 333,
364
Wells, H. G., 166–67
Whalen, Philip, 113, 129
Whitman, Walt, 49–50, 52, 74–5,
113–14, 128, 133, 136–37, 140,
278, 332
Why? An Anarchist Bulletin
(periodical) (*see also Resistance*),
113, 118, 344
Widmer, Hans: *see* p.m.
Wilde, Oscar, 50–1, 74, 264n67
Williams, Raymond, 5
Wilson, Peter Lamborn (*see also* Bey,
Hakim), 47, 56, 213, 243
*Win: Peace and Freedom Thru Non-
Violent Action* (periodical), 140
*Wingnut Anarchist Collective
Newsletter* (periodical), 40
Winks, Christopher, 315
Wisconsin protests of 2011, 381
Wohlstand für Alle (periodical), 156
women (*see also* feminism, femininity,
sexism), 1, 36n29, 44, 46n49,
102, 111, 147, 159–60, 163n5,
177, 185, 199, 209, 212–18, 264,
265n70, 267–68n77, 270–71,
285–86, 288, 286n8, 286–87, 300,
315–16, 320
women as audience for anarchist
resistance culture, 218, 267, 267–
68n77, 315–16
women as creators of anarchist

resistance culture (*see also* Bevington, Louisa S.; Capetillo, Luisa; Claramunt, Teresa; D'Andrea, Virgilia; de Cleyre, Voltairine; Di Prima, Diane; Goldman, Emma; Graul, Rosa; Holmes, Lizzie; Lacerda de Moura, Maria; Le Guin, Ursula K.; M. R. Martínez, Josefa; Malina, Judith; Michel, Louise; Montseny, Federica; Parsons, Lucy; Rafanelli, Leda; Ridge, Lola; Rouco Buela, Juana; Roussel, Nelly; Sánchez Saornil, Lucía; Takamure, Itsue; Vernet, Madeleine), 44, 57, 50n67, 77, 267–68n77

women in anarchist movements, 22, 25, 35, 40, 43–5, 50n67, 57–8, 61, 68, 73, 118, 251, 260, 262–63n64, 265n71, 298n31

women, anarchist representations of, allegorical, 102, 267, 270–72, 288–89, 329, 331, 372, 376–77

women, anarchist representations of, heroic, 267, 288–89

women, anarchist representations of, as victims (*see also* victim stories), 94, 165, 358, 360

Women's Penny Paper (periodical), 262–63n64

Wood, Charles Erskine Scott, 74–6, 78–9, 109

Woodcock, George, 59–60, 270

word-picture relations, 301–16, 333–34, 340–41n65, 369–70, 375–77

Wordsworth, William, 78

workerism, 84–85n66, 284–85

working class (*see also* proletarian literature, workerism), 6, 10n23, 16, 33–5, 37–8, 46, 49, 51–4, 60, 69, 72, 77, 79, 80, 84–85n66, 85, 89, 91, 93–6, 100, 107–11, 154, 170, 180, 185, 189–90, 200, 216, 225, 248–49, 251–53, 257–58, 260, 263, 284–85, 301, 305, 307–9, 319–20, 336, 344–46, 352–53, 358–59, 362–63, 367–69, 375–76, 381–82, 387, 391

Wu Zhihui, 72

X

Xin Shiji (*La Novaj Tempoj*) (periodical), 291

Xinmin Congbao (periodical), 165–66

Y

Yeats, William Butler, 75n25, 78, 80

Yiddish language, 10–12, 26, 49, 60n88, 75, 84–5, 95, 156

Yom Kippur Balls, 101n25

Yu Seo, 111

yulu, 72–3

Yunque, Álvaro, 110

Yvetot, Georges, 7, 100

Z

Zaïkowska, Sophie, 295n25

Zapatistas, 22–3

Zerzan, John, 16, 233n2

Zévaco, Michel, 215n15

Zimmer, Kenyon, 38

zines, 39, 177, 336, 383–84

Zisly, Henry, 233n2

Žižek, Slavoj, 325

Zoais (Luis García Muñoz), 170, 193–94

Zola, Émile, 34–5, 50–2, 73, 156–57, 261n60

Support **AK Press!**

AK Press is one of the world's largest and most productive anarchist publishing houses. We're entirely worker-run & democratically managed. We operate without a corporate structure—no boss, no managers, no bullshit. We publish close to twenty books every year, and distribute thousands of other titles published by other like-minded independent presses from around the globe.

The Friends of AK program is a way that you can directly contribute to the continued existence of AK Press, and ensure that we're able to keep publishing great books just like this one! Friends pay $25 a month directly into our publishing account ($30 for Canada, $35 for international), and receive a copy of every book AK Press publishes for the duration of their membership! Friends also receive a discount on anything they order from our website or buy at a table: 50% on AK titles, and 20% on everything else. We've also added a new Friends of AK ebook program: $15 a month gets you an electronic copy of every book we publish for the duration of your membership. Combine it with a print subscription, too!

There's great stuff in the works—so sign up now to become a Friend of AK Press, and let the presses roll!

Won't you be our friend? Email friendsofak@akpress.org for more info, or visit the Friends of AK Press website: www.akpress.org/programs/friendsofak